Published by Ockley Books Ltd

First edition published November 2014,
second edition first published April 2017

ISBN 978-1-910906-06-4

Front cover & design by Michael Kinlan

Printed & bound by:
Bell & Bain
Glasgow
www.bell-bain.com

FROM THE BACK PAGE TO THE FRONT ROOM

FOOTBALL'S JOURNEY THROUGH THE ENGLISH MEDIA

ROGER DOMENEGHETTI

OCKLEY BOOKS
.com

SHORTLISTED FOR THE 2015 LORD ABERDARE LITERARY PRIZE FOR SPORTS HISTORY

"Prodigious research and perceptive interpretation of it make this book an unrivalled exposition of the relationship between professional football and the media, a connection that has often been as acrimonious as it is mutually essential, symbiosis with a snarl. It is a lively and compelling story, made richer by the rescuing from obscurity of many characters whose important influence will be a revelation to most readers."

HUGH MCILVANNEY

"In the last twenty years every facet of the football industry has been covered in some way, except the most important of all – the media. Now Roger Domeneghetti has done us all a service by tracing the role of the media in making the game into the national ritual and soap opera and done so in a voice that is scholarly, thorough and pointed."

DAVID GOLDBLATT, AUTHOR *THE GAME OF OUR LIVES*

"An outstandingly readable piece of scholarship, this book addresses every aspect of football's relationship with the media and society and, as one who has lived through the most recent half-century of the game's development, I recognise so much. If I may pick one detail from so many, the portrait of the great James Catton, father of football journalism, was superb."

PADDY BARCLAY

"Roger Domeneghetti's irresistibly enjoyable book offers a fascinating history of football's relationship with the British media, from tabloid headlines and Twitter controversies to fanzines and *Fever Pitch*. Clear, authoritative and clever, with some splendid anecdotes and colourful examples, it is likely to become the definitive word on an often controversial subject."

DOMINIC SANDBROOK, AUTHOR *THE GREAT BRITISH DREAM FACTORY*

"The paradox of sports writing in the UK has always been that cricket was graced by its own 'literature' but not the far more popular, far more intently followed, association football. Domeneghetti examines the culture contrast in an engrossing and comprehensive far wider study of football's media context. Stranger than fiction indeed – football's love–hate relationship with media. Any doubters should read this book."

KEIR RADNEDGE

"... exhaustively well researched ... a breezy conversational style ensures that the dominant perspective here is that of the ordinary fan/reader/viewer. Media-analyst business-speak is thankfully lacking."

WHEN SATURDAY COMES

"Wide-ranging, thoroughly researched and enjoyably opinionated, Roger Domeneghetti's pioneering survey of the symbiotic but often fractious relationship between football and the media is an important contribution to our understanding of modern Britain."

DAVID KYNASTON, AUTHOR *TALES OF A NEW JERUSALEM, 1945–1979*

"Witty, masterful and intelligent ... deserves to be the standard text on the subject."

THE NEW STATESMAN

Entertaining and thoughtful ... a terrific piece of work."

ROY GREENSLADE, THE *GUARDIAN*

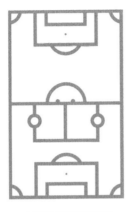

THE AUTHOR

Roger Domeneghetti is a lecturer in journalism at
Northumbria University and the *Morning Star*'s
North East football correspondent. A journalist
for nearly 20 years he has worked for a range of
titles including *sportinglife.com* and the *Daily Star
Sunday*. He lives in Durham with his family and
Bella the cat. This is his first book.

For Amy and Lucy.

You will never know how proud
you make me or how much I love you.

XX Daddy XX

CONTENTS

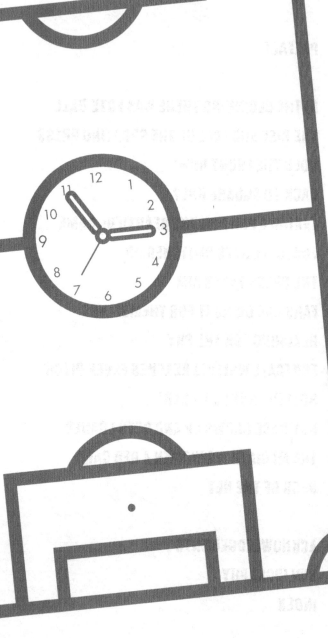

It's Easter Monday, 2012, and there are 17 minutes left of Newcastle United's match with Bolton at St James' Park. What had until that point been a fairly dull, goalless affair sparks into life when the Magpies' young French star Hatem Ben Arfa receives the ball deep in his own half. Fifteen scintillating seconds later he's scored and the home side are on their way to three points. While the Toon Army celebrates one of the goals of the season, a wave of panic washes through the press box as those tasked with writing about the game, myself included, aren't quite sure what they've just seen. Had Ben Arfa received the ball from Tim Krul or Yohan Cabaye? Was he in the centre circle or closer to his own goal when he started his run? How many tackles had he ridden? Which Bolton player could have (perhaps should have) brought him down and taken a yellow for the team? We had to wait for the answers. What had caused this panic? Well, due to a power shortage, the TV monitors in the press box weren't working. Horror of horrors, there were no replays. And there you have it: the media prism through which we experience football has become so omnipotent we almost can't consume football without it – even newspaper football writers are reliant on replays.

The media dominates our lives. Sport dominates the media. Football dominates the sports media. Think about it: if we're not watching football on TV from the comfort of our sofa or with our mates in the pub then we're listening to it on the radio; or we're talking about it on the radio; or we're reading about it in newspapers, comics and magazines; or we're blogging about it; or we're gambling on it; or we're collecting football stickers; or we're tweeting about it; or we're watching people who write about football talk about what other people who write about football have written about football.

By comparison it's rare we actually watch the sport live. Even those who do make their way to a ground every Saturday at 3pm (or 12.45pm, or 5.20pm) will most likely then seek an interpretation of what they've seen from experts in the media. Almost everyone's experiences of the teams they don't support will also be gained vicariously through the media. Such is the power of the media's coverage of football that in 1990 an Italian operatic aria reached number 2 in the UK singles charts simply because it had been used by the BBC as their signature tune for that summer's World Cup. The same tournament provided New Order with their only UK number 1. The 1966 World Cup Final is still the country's most watched TV programme. In the regional newspaper industry, which some feel is in slow, terminal decline, football is one of the few areas of content almost guaranteed to provide a huge hike in sales. The *Liverpool Echo* was up 46 per cent the day after Liverpool lifted the Champions League in 2005, while sales of the city's *Daily Post* doubled. Incidentally on the same day *The Times* sold an extra 70,000 copies. Coincidence? I don't think so.

Without the media our perception of football would be totally different. One of the key moments of the reinvention of the game was Paul Gascoigne's tears in the World Cup semi-final in 1990. Yet it wasn't the tears themselves but the coverage of them, both live on the night and subsequently through endless reproduction, that was the real catalyst. Few in the stadium would have realised he was crying, fewer still would have realised the cathartic affect his emotional implosion would have on English football. It was an image that represented a human-interest story that enabled the game, through the media, to draw in new fans and which subsequently became embedded in the game's cultural heritage. It's easy to forget that Stuart Pearce cried too.

Yet popular histories of the game tend to overlook the huge importance of the media, not just since the 1990s but from its earliest days when it became the sport we could call modern football. There might be a small section here or a chapter there but no sense that the pair have always been inextricably linked. Likewise, popular histories of the media tend to overlook the importance of football despite the fact that the media has always recognised its value as compelling content that could be used to increase its own popularity, as well as providing a consistent spur for technological innovation. Read Andrew Marr's otherwise excellent history of the press, *My Trade,* and you'll find just one mention of sport – when he declares his disinterest in it – and no mention of football at all. He is not alone.

Then there's academia's approach to the subject (or lack thereof). Just before his death in 2012, Nick Trujillo, a professor in sport, culture and the media at California State University, wrote that when he started researching sport in the mid-1980s other academics would ask him why he was studying something so 'frivolous' and when he would be returning to 'serious' work. He would respond sarcastically by asking them what could be more important than sport before pointing out that it is a multi-billion-dollar business which shapes our culture. He would then ask them why they *weren't* studying it.

True, he was talking about sport but which is the biggest sport of the lot? Actually, scratch that, which is the biggest business of the lot? As Sergio Cragnotti, the former Lazio chief, has said: "You tell me another product that is bought off the shelf by three billion consumers. Not even Coca-Cola comes close." Media companies use football to sell their technology – who can forget The Special One rolling around pretending to be James Bond for Samsung? BT are now using live Premier League football as a loss-leader to get people to sign up for their broadband service. ESPN, News Corp, Time Warner, Yahoo and Google have all looked at the English Premier League and considered bidding for the rights to drive customers to their services.

In many ways the history of football media is the history of the media. While the press helped popularise football, football helped make newspapers a mass-market product. Newsreels brought moving footage of the game to the masses and radio brought live coverage into their homes; football was a key selling point of both. Today, if you listen to most regional radio stations on a Saturday or Sunday afternoon you'll still find their schedules dominated by commentary of the local football team's game. The UK has two talk radio stations, one devoted entirely to sport, the other a mix of news and sport. Football dominates both. In the weeks following the 9/11 attacks, Radio Five Live interrupted a breaking news story about a possible plane hijack for live coverage of a press conference with England captain David Beckham ahead of a crucial World Cup qualifier with Greece. Now, you might think that demonstrates slightly skewed news values from whoever was making the editorial decisions on the day (and I might be inclined to agree with you) but ask yourself this: when was the last time a football match was interrupted for a breaking news story?

And what of television? In the 1950s it cemented football's place as the nation's favourite sport while the game boosted TV-set sales. In the early 1990s with football's reputation in the gutter and Rupert Murdoch's News Corporation on the brink of collapse, English football and the media came together once more to support each other in the quest for global domination. Without the money generated through Sky's coverage of the Premier League, it is highly unlikely that Murdoch would have come to dominate the British media in quite the manner that he has. So here's another question for you: would the Leveson Inquiry have happened if the Premier League had stuck with ITV way back in 1992?

Along the way the media has helped turn football events into national events. It has even underpinned our obsession with celebrity and if you want to understand the switch from analogue to digital broadcasting, there is no better example than the football media. Beyond all that, the football media has played a crucial role in shaping key aspects of English culture including notions of patriotism and the stereotyping of other nationalities. It has reinforced class divisions as well as the definition of masculinity and the related marginalisation of women and tacit homophobia. Yet despite all this we don't fully appreciate the importance of the relationship between these two cultural behemoths. Modern football and the modern media are locked together. Born at around the same time, they grew up together, got married young, grew old, renewed their vows and got rich. Sure there have been ups and downs but they're in it for the long haul; there will be no divorce, it would be too complicated, too messy, and besides, I doubt they could live without each other. This is the story of that life-long love affair.

CHAPTER 1

IN THE BEGINNING THERE WAS FOTE-BALL

According to George Bernard Shaw no Englishman can open his mouth without making another Englishman despise him. A bit harsh if you ask me, but if he'd said Sepp Blatter can't open his mouth without making an Englishman despise him, I'd probably say he had a point. It was certainly the case when Blatter took to the stage in Beijing to open the Third China International Football Expo in 2004. Back then the FIFA president said that the sport's world governing body agreed with the Chinese claim that football originated in their country. Cue outrage back in Blighty. I dare say Blatter knew exactly what reaction he'd get, but was he right? Well I hate to break it to you (if you're English that is) but there is significant written evidence in Chinese military manuals and other literature dating back to the Tsin Dynasty from around 255–206 BC referring to a football-like game called *Tsu Chu* (literal translation: kick ball). Designed to train soldiers, the aim of *Tsu Chu* was to kick about a ball made of leather and filled with feathers and score before the other team could dispossess you. There were even people in charge (let's call them referees) whose job it was to stop the players handling the ball. It wasn't modern football – the rules of that emphatically *did* originate in England in 1863 – but all the fundamentals were there and perhaps it's not surprising. One of the reasons that football is so popular is its simplicity; get some mates together, get something that rolls easily and won't break your foot when you kick it and you can play football. It's not exactly rocket science, so is it really a big surprise that there is evidence of kicking ball games all over the world before the FA was formed in 1863?[1]

---

1 *The Mesoamericans had developed a whole range of sophisticated ball games, some of which involved kicking, as early as 1,400 BC.*

The Chinese weren't just ahead of the game on the pitch, they also created the first regular news publication *Jing Bao* (or *Peking Gazette*) in the eighth century BC. There's some debate as to whether this was a newspaper per se as it was a government bulletin produced for the military, but it was certainly a precursor to modern news print, being published almost daily until 1912, and it was one of the first publications to make use of moveable type for printing (from 1638).

In England, the news industry has its roots in the informal exchange of information: gossip and rumour or, to put it simply, people's innate need to be nosey. In fact if there's one aspect of the media, football or any other kind, which remains virtually unchanged, it's this. So closely linked are 'news', 'rumour' and 'gossip', Hans-Joachim Neubauer in his book *The Rumour: A Cultural History* suggests the trio are siblings that all still regularly appear in various forms of media. An alternative version of history steeped in rumour runs beside the established 'facts' in most areas of news, whether it's the assassination of JFK or *The Damned Utd* – David Peace's take on Brian Clough's fateful 44 days as manager at Elland Road. A fiction based on truth – faction perhaps – the original text had to be changed following a legal challenge from ex-Leeds United player Johnny Giles. In short, the desire to pry into and share gossip about the private lives of others is as strong now as it's ever been. Just ask Ryan Giggs or anyone else ensnared in the murky world of super-injunctions and tabloid headlines.

William Caxton introduced the first printing press to England in 1476 and produced mainly religious or literary works that were not widely available. For centuries the elite classes were able to communicate through proclamations, treaties, charters and manuscripts but all the uneducated lower classes had was rumour and gossip and, without the ability to read, for them it was spoken. Like any new technology printing was a double-edged sword. It had huge potential to be a democratising force but this was offset by equally huge potential to be used for repressive purposes. Almost immediately it became a cultural battleground, as would, in centuries to come, newspapers, radio, TV, the internet and social media. It wasn't just a question of ownership of the communication technology but also what was being produced and who had access to it. Like the internet, the printed word was the preserve of those who could afford and understand it, a group that grew over time, but it also increased the quantity and flow of information. Thanks to the printing press, Martin Luther's 95 Theses spread across Germany in a matter of weeks and Europe in a couple of months, bringing the Reformation in its wake and undermining the authority of the Catholic Church. Henry VII, who seized the crown from Richard III in 1485, recognised the power of the printed word and its potential to threaten or support the established order. With this in mind he began to print proclamations and use a network of town criers to spread the official word orally to create authority among the illiterate population. Having read the relevant decree, the criers, or bellmen as they were also known, would then nail it to the door of a local inn giving rise to the saying, "posting a notice" – the forerunner of the postal service.

Such was the revolutionary potential of Caxton's printing press it was initially confined to Westminster Abbey but by 1500 there were five printers in London, a number that had grown to 33 by 1523. The Stationers' Company was established in 1557 in an attempt to allow the growing industry to police itself without the direct involvement of the Crown. News publications in this period were, according to newspaper historian Harold Herd, "mostly a rough blend of fact, conjecture and transparent sensationalism". You could argue that not much has changed. As the years passed, the company's powers grew more draconian, with at least one man, William Carter, a Catholic, being hanged, drawn and quartered for printing "Lewde pamphlettes".

However, the collapse of the Star Chamber and the machinery of censorship in 1640 in the run-up to the Civil War, coupled with new, cheaper printing technology and a relatively high level of literacy (as much as 80 per cent in cities and a minimum of 30 per cent across the country) saw an explosion in the printing of pamphlets. While just 22 were published in 1640, more than 1,000 were printed in each of the following four years and nearly 2,000 in 1642 alone. The British Museum's Thomason collection of publications lists 22,000 new titles over the following two decades. Pamphlets were the new media of the day. Their authors were not journalists passing on news; instead they traded in opinion written in a vernacular style so it could be easily read aloud. They responded to each other's arguments in splenetic fashion through works entitled *A Witty Answer* or *A Vindication to a Foolish Pamphlet*. They were history's first bloggers, producing a cheap product and selling it for next to nothing on street corners or distributing it for free among their friends. They in turn would pass the pamphlets on, creating a complex and organic social network of information exchange – the seventeenth-century version of hitting the Facebook 'Like' button or retweeting on Twitter.

The Reformation saw a return to some sort of regulation of the print industry but the country had caught the media bug. The Crown and the Government realised that suppressing newsprint was not the answer and decided to institutionalise it instead. Roger L'Estrange, a splendidly named former spy, was put in charge and he produced two weekly publications – the *News* and the *Intelligencer* – but when the court of Charles II moved from plague-ridden London to Oxford the *Oxford Gazette* was published, much to his disgust. The first paper to use columns in its design, it was renamed the *London Gazette* in 1666 when the King and his entourage returned to the capital. Although all other papers were banned under the Licensing Act of 1662, it demonstrated that the Government recognised an obligation to supply the population with regular news. The act was abolished in 1694 and England's first regular daily newspaper the *Daily Courant*, which had a circulation of 800, began publication on 11 March 1702.[2] It was founded by Elizabeth Mallet, who set up shop above the White Hart Inn on Fleet Street, the thoroughfare from London's financial district to the city's centre of government. Mallet pretended to be a man so she would be taken seriously in a male-dominated world and was one of the first journalists to claim impartiality, arguing that her readers would have "sense enough to make reflections for themselves".

By the 1720s there were 12 newspapers in London alone and 24 provincial papers. Controls remained but they were more subtle and some were self-imposed under the belief that a moderate press would be dealt with more even-handedly than a radical press. The Stamp Act of 1712 saw pamphlets taxed at two shillings per sheet per edition and newspapers at a penny per full sheet plus a shilling

2   *Rupert Murdoch would be born on the same day 229 years later. Make of that what you will.*

for each advert. Owners responded by upping the cover price but dailies were forced into a long-term hiatus as they became economically unviable. Weekly papers on the other hand survived, although they often relied on political sponsorship for financial security that became increasingly formalised over time. Certain papers would get official subsidies of free post while loyal editors and reporters would gain inside information and favourable pensions. Again, you could argue that not much has changed.

The papers of the eighteenth century were unordered, chaotic affairs dominated by political opinion and rumour. Stories were sorted in a haphazard fashion if they were sorted at all, often being placed in the paper as and when they came into the office. The country's poor communications infrastructure meant it was hard to check facts quickly and there was no professional group equivalent to modern-day sub-editors responsible for doing so, which in turn led to widespread distrust among readers. Daniel Du Foo, better known as Daniel Defoe, author of *Robinson Crusoe*, was one of the few who realised that the industry's future success would be based on an ethical commitment to the truth and he regularly criticised his rivals for their lies, although he also criticised readers for repeatedly buying newspapers they knew to contain errors and lies. Defoe was also one of the first who believed that it was important to go out of the office, witness events himself and report on them. However, the punitively high taxes on paper and advertising in the first half of the nineteenth century ensured newspapers were costly to buy and few people could afford them, meaning the industry did not yet provide rich pickings for the budding entrepreneur.

• • •

Given that they would become such long-term bedfellows, it's perhaps unsurprising that there were so many similarities between pre-modern football and the early media. Both were male-dominated, both were highly localised with similar but markedly different versions developing around the country before they were eventually homogenised, and while the late nineteenth century did mark a point when both became recognisably modern it was far from a sudden shift for either. More than all that, however, both were key areas in the fight for control over the delicately balanced society of the day and were deemed to require strict control and limitation. Until the late 1800s when an increasingly urbanised population became easier to police, the rowdiness associated with football was of constant concern to those in control. This was borne out in early media, which more often than not focused on the dangerous and physical nature of the game whether through matter-of-fact records of death and injury, the many, many legal documents accompanying attempts to suppress the pastime, or more informal yet influential condemnations of the game.

The first record of a ball game in Britain appears in the ninth-century work *Historia Brittonum* and is attributed to the Welsh monk Nennius. It talks of a group of boys "playing at ball" (pilae ludus). Some 200 years later William Fitzstephen wrote a description of twelfth-century London, included as the preface of his biography of his employer Thomas à Becket. There is a more detailed account of an early ball game played as part of Shrove Tuesday celebrations. Fitzstephen wrote that "after dinner all the youth of the City goes out into the fields for the famous game of ball". He noted that the "scholars of each school" and the "workers of each trade" had their own balls and that the "elders, the fathers, and the men of wealth come on horseback to view the contests of their juniors and there seems to be aroused in these elders a stirring of natural heat by viewing so much".

Here then was a sport played by young men in rudimentary teams that aroused the passions of its spectators. Football was an essential part of such religious festivals and it was on days like these that some of the worst incidents took place as part of a violent last hurrah before the austerity measures of Lent took place. Allowing the populace the chance to let off steam in this fashion, on the understanding that the status quo would return the following day, also served the purpose of relieving tension. However, such games weren't merely spontaneous and chaotic outbursts, but were part of England's complex social fabric with diverse rules and customs across the country.

The year 1280 brought the first recorded death from football at Ulgham in Northumberland where Henry, son of William de Elling-ton, was killed after he accidentally ran into an opposing player's dagger. While Henry's demise is obviously tragic, the report was more significant for being the first to refer specifically to a kicking game. This now some 1,400 years after the Chinese first wrote of 'kick ball'. Many other fatalities were recorded and in 1303 one brought another notable 'first' when an Oxford student found the body of his brother who was thought to have been killed by Irish students, while "playing the ball on the High Street" – the first mention of the sport in connection with universities. Numerous less serious injuries were also recorded, such as that of John Hendyman in 1425 who wrote how he "broke his left leg playing with other companions at football". I'm sure whoever tackled him 'wasn't that sort of player'.

The first ban on the game came in 1314 when Edward II prohibited it being played on the streets of London before he headed up North to have a pop at the Scots. Significantly his decree was also the first record of a game called football (albeit in French, the language used by England's upper classes at the time). It didn't work and in 1331 football was banned again and then again in 1365 as it was deemed to be interfering with more 'useful' pursuits such as archery, the same reason given for yet another ban issued in 1388. The decree of 1365 also banned "handball", which suggests that basic rules differentiating games were already evolving. Football was nothing if not resilient and further prohibitions were issued in 1410, 1414, 1477 and 1496, and on into the reign of Henry VIII, one of whose decrees was only repealed in 1845. It was a Royal proclamation from Henry IV in 1409 banning the levying of money on the game that first used the English word "fote-ball". Royal records also provide the first record of football boots, which belonged to execution-happy Henry VIII. An audit of his Great Wardrobe from 1526 makes reference to a pair of ankle-high, strong leather boots designed for football by the Royal shoemaker Cornelius Johnson.

From the sixteenth century condemnation became more common, partly at least because of the increase in availability of print but also because of the emergence of the Puritanical movement. While government was concerned with controlling levels of violence within the game in a bid to prevent civil unrest, the game was also targeted as part of a campaign against any sport or form of recreation from taking place on the Sabbath or other Holy days. Puritans like Sir

Thomas Elliot and the Bishop of Rochester complained about the "beastly furie and exstreme violence" of the "evil game" while in 1583 Phillip Stubbes made a virulent attack on the "devilish pastime" in his pamphlet *The Anatomie of Abuses*. "Any exercise which withdraweth us from godliness," he wrote, "either upon the Saboth or any other day, is wicked and to be forbidden." He went on to decry football's violent nature, complaining that it "encourages envy and hatred, sometimes fighting, murder and a great loss of blood" while also railing at "drunkennesse, whoredome, gluttony, and other filthie sodomiticall exercises". Doing nothing to quell the accusation that Puritans are killjoys, Stubbes even attacked the custom of collecting garlands for Maypoles claiming that of the young women that went into the woods to pick flowers, scarcely a third returned "undefiled".

That wasn't to say that there was no support for the game. Richard Mulcaster, who was headmaster at both Merchant Taylors' and St Paul's Schools, was a strong advocate of the game's positive educational value, suggesting that it provided both social and physical benefits. Differentiating it from "armeball" or "hand ball", he wrote in 1581 of "footeball", a game in which players were members of "parties" (small teams), had "standings" (positions), were coached by a "trayning maister" (manager) and which was overseen by a "judge of the parties" (referee). Mulcaster's positive view of football, which foreshadowed nineteenth-century muscular Christianity, didn't catch on at the time but he wasn't the only author in the period writing about complex, rule-bound versions of the game. Richard Carew's Survey of Cornwall, written in 1603, gives a detailed description of a game involving teams which were evenly matched with each player pairing off against a member of the opposition. They then attempted to block their run towards "goales" created by planting two stakes in the ground "eight or ten foote asunder", with specialist players assigned to guard them. There was also a keen "observation of many lawes", one of which was a rudimentary offside rule: "that he must deal no Fore-ball, viz. he may not throw it to any of his mates, standinge nearer the goale than himselfe".

Another early study of football was provided by Francis Willughby's *Book of Games*, a fascinating insight into mid-seventeenth-century English pastimes. Willughby, who was a member of the Royal Society and considered his book to be a scientific survey, died aged 36 in 1672. His manuscript is unfinished, but his work on football was the first specifically to mention a pitch (of which he provided a diagram). He talks of scoring and elaborates on Mulcaster's suggestion that some players had specific tactical positions, noting that teams leave their "best players to guard the goal". He also repeated Carew's observation that teams were carefully selected: "the players being equally divided according to their strength and nimbleness".

This early football media is crucial to a proper understanding of the game's development. That teams were divided on the basis of ability demonstrates a highly developed concept of play, which, when coupled with the use of albeit rudimentary tactics, rules and a loosely defined pitch, allows us to build a picture of a game far removed from the widely held notion that folk football was a chaotic and spontaneous free-for-all.

Mulcaster might have been ahead of his time but folk football continued to be stigmatised and frowned upon. By the late eighteenth and early nineteenth centuries the rapid industrialisation and urbanisation of society saw huge social upheaval. This precipitated the growth of an immigrant urban working class dislocated from their rural roots and traditions and the recreational activities that went along with them. The tone of the writing on football mirrored this change. As early as 1801 Joseph Strutt, a sports historian, noted that football "seems to have fallen in to disrepute and is but little practised", while in 1842 *The Times* noted that the poor of Liverpool had "been deprived of their games, their amusements and their mirth".

Both overstated the demise of football and failed to appreciate the vibrant nature of working-class life, but football and leisure were changing and by this time religious fears about the game had been overtaken by fears of its impact on another god, Mammon. Moves to regulate the game now had an economic focus; employers wanted a disciplined – and uninjured – workforce and businessmen wanted to protect their commercial property from hordes of young men rampaging through a town. Anti-football laws, such as the 1835 Highways Act which banned the playing of football on public roads, were easier to enforce due to the creation of the police force, and correspondents to newspapers regularly called for the Bobbies to take action against a variety of street games, while councils decreed that football be moved out of town and city centres. However, successive Enclosure Acts meant the geography of the surrounding countryside had changed dramatically in a short period of time and wide-open spaces were no longer available in such large number.

• • •

Industrialisation brought with it the twin processes of commercialisation and commodification, and the gentry and growing middle class began looking for leisure pursuits on which to spend their increasing amounts of spare time and money. Theatre attendance grew, with both low-brow genres such as burlesque, as well as the satirical, comic operas of Gilbert and Sullivan becoming popular. At the same time music hall homogenised a variety of entertainment traditions from semi-rural travelling fairs to the suburban pleasure gardens and saloon bar sing-alongs. Goods such as tobacco, tea, coffee, sugar and chocolate progressed from being luxury items to becoming mass commodities heralding the beginning of a consumer culture. Sport was increasingly commercialised too but it was a slow process. Before it became a commodity which was used to sell other products (such as newspapers or football shirts) or to be sold to the media in its own right it was almost totally ignored in the newspapers due to the cost of the various levies and taxes they had to bear. However its huge popularity couldn't be ignored and a fledgling sporting press developed to reflect that. In the first instance this took the form of monthly journals catering almost solely for genteel interests such as prize fighting, horse racing, athletics and field sports. While they didn't create or manufacture sport, these early publications did reflect its huge social importance, in turn creating a positive cultural feedback loop, which helped popularise and sustain spectator sport even more.

The Jockey Club was established in 1751 and published racing's rules in its own official paper the *Racing Calendar*. Any race that didn't make it into the paper was deemed to be unofficial, allowing the ruling body to exercise strict control over the sport. *The Sporting Magazine*,[3]

3   *Or to give it its full title,* The Sporting Magazine: A Monthly Calendar of the Transactions of The Turf, The Chace and Every Other Diversion Interefting to the Man of Pleasure and Enterprise.

published between 1792 and 1870, was the first sports-specific monthly and under the initial editorship of John Wheble it covered anything that could be considered a sport from pedestrianism (that's walking to you and me), bell ringing, squirrel hunting, dog fighting and duelling, to which it devoted a regular column. The paper also printed the highly literary work of Charles James Apperley under the pseudonym 'Nimrod'. Prize fighting and the gambling that went along with it was the spur for several other titles to be created. *Bell's Life* in London was first printed in 1822 and while it was initially concerned with the gossip surrounding the capital's fashionable set, it's focus began to shift more and more on to sport and in particular news from "the ring". Although it was more populist than *The Sporting Magazine* only gentlemen could write for it, which ensured it gained a reliable reputation, making it an ideal stake-holder for the upper-class 'fancy' (the landed gentry who played and gambled because they had nothing else to do). At its peak as much as £10,000 in wagers on prize fights was passing through *Bell's Life* each year. In 1859 the rival *Penny Bell's Life and Sporting News* was launched, although the original *Bell's Life* successfully sought an injunction over the new paper's name forcing it to become the *Sporting Life*. A raft of similar titles followed and by the early 1880s London was producing four sporting dailies all aimed at the man about town, and celebrating and promoting sport by holding stake money, providing judges, and producing guides, annuals and score sheets. *Bell's Life* couldn't cope and closed in 1886.

While gambling had demonstrated the commercial potential of the sporting press, the growing belief that sport had spiritual and health benefits led to the creation of another range of titles such as the *Shooting Times* and *Horse and Hound* focused on outdoor pursuits such as hunting and shooting. *The Field*,[4] aimed not at the man about town but the family out of it, led the way from its first issue in 1853. It dispatched a correspondent to the Crimean War who expressed the view that the British soldiers' heroics were in no small part due to the field sports they engaged in at home. Eventually the magazine would

---

4   Not *wishing to be outdone by the Georgians, the Victorians could come up with a catchy name when they needed to and this paper was actually called* The Field, The Farm, The Garden, The Country Gentleman's Newspaper, *but we'll stick to* The Field *if that's OK with you.*

incorporate ball sports, and it provided the trophy for the inaugural Wimbledon championships in 1868, as well as having a significant role in the codification of football.

By the early twentieth century there was considerable tension in *The Field*'s offices between its field sports staff who were critical of spectator and professional sports, and the non-field sports staff. Cricket was another sport that was taking on its modern form at this time and several rival specialist publications developed to cover it, including, from 1849, Fred Lillywhite's *The Guide to Cricketers* and John Wisden's *Cricketers' Almanac*, which has now been published every year since 1864. Again, crucially, the publications contained the rules of the game and were updated as and when they changed. Football, still un-codified with disparate variations across the country and no governing body, struggled for representation in this sporting press, but it would be from the pages of the newspapers that the impetus for its modernisation would come.

• • •

By comparison to some other sports, modern football is relatively young and you could be forgiven for thinking that when its birth arrived it was the result of a painless labour – the Cambridge Rules, the meeting at the Freemasons' Tavern, the formation of the FA. Sorted: global domination here we come. However, it was a much longer and far more complex process, starting in the 1840s when rules were first written down at Rugby School and ending only in 1877 when the Football Association finally gained total control over the administration of the kicking form of the game. Two and a half centuries after Mulcaster had been heralding football's benefits, the education system caught up. Well, public schools did anyway. In the late eighteenth and early nineteenth centuries these elite institutions were unruly, rebellious places where middle-class teachers were dominated by their upper-class pupils. In 1797 a riot at Rugby School began with pistol shots in the boarding house and only ended after the headmaster's door had been blown off its hinges and all his books thrown on a bonfire. Twenty-one years later bayonet-wielding soldiers were required to quell an uprising at Winchester School. These were far from isolated incidents with more than 20 erupting in the late eighteenth and early nineteenth centuries.

Over time an uneasy peace broke out in the form of the fagging system that meant teachers had control in the classroom and older boys, or prefects, took brutal control of all extra-curricular activities, of which football was a central part. Remember when you played kick-about with your older brother and his mates, and they stuck you in goal? That was just a modern-day version of fagging where "the small boys, the duffers and the funk-sticks were the goalkeepers twelve or fifteen at each end". Often terrified younger pupils were used as goalposts or to mark out the pitch. Just like their rural cousins these games were violent and bloody affairs with few formal rules, and they varied from school to school. As with the disparate games played by the commoners, industrialisation and a society-wide move away from violent activities meant something had to be done and a new wave of headmasters saw sport and football as a means to exert control over their schools, as well as instilling some much-needed discipline into pupils as one part of a complete moral, physical and spiritual education.

Many believe the famous Dr Thomas Arnold was at the very forefront of the movement; however, that reputation is erroneous. Headmaster at Rugby for 14 years until 1842, Arnold figures heavily in Thomas Hughes' 1857 book *Tom Brown's School Days*. It describes in respectful and glowing terms how Arnold found the school in "a state of monstrous licence and misrule" and was employed in "the unpopular work of setting up order with a strong hand". Hughes' work is, of course, fiction but it would be remiss not to acknowledge Arnold's achievement in successfully transforming the school's fagging system into one which was totally controlled by teachers, leading to greater discipline and less bullying among pupils. Arnold was perhaps able to do this at Rugby as it was less elite than some other schools meaning the social gap between teachers and pupils was easier to bridge, but it set a precedent that others were able to follow. Crucially, Arnold did not make games a formal part of the curriculum nor did he mention physical activity in any of his writings about education theory. In fact it seems he never once espoused the moral value of sport. For him the ideal man had a first-class mind and wanted to broaden it; he had no interest in games.

His erroneous reputation that I mentioned was entirely the product of the media. Arnold courted the press and regularly gained positive headlines on issues of religious, social and political matters. To many Victorians he represented a strong moral ideal but the link with games came not from Arnold himself, but from Hughes, who was a keen cricketer at Rugby and played in the Cambridge University team as well as competing in the Boat Race. In 1875 a 12-year-old French boy called Pierre de Coubertin picked up a translation of the book and became enraptured by the picture it painted. As an adult, de Coubertin would cite Arnold's "formula for the role of athletics in education" as an inspiration for his concept of a modern Olympics. Yet there was no formula, and de Coubertin was really influenced by Hughes' portrayal of Arnold rather than Arnold himself. Nevertheless, from that point on Arnold was held up, wrongly, as the father of the public-school games movement.

In Arnold's era games remained the preserve of the pupils albeit under tighter control. In 1845 they were the first to lay down a set of rules for a version of football. That they did so following the reform of the fagging system and that those rules included a preface focused on prefects' duties suggests there was a link. However it's worth reiterating that this wasn't imposed upon them by the teachers. Two years after the posh nobs at Rugby wrote down those rules for their handling version of football, the even posher nobs at Eton wrote down some rules for their kicking version of the game. These explicitly banned carrying the ball and goals scored over the crossbar, both of which were allowed at Rugby. This wasn't just about football, it was about class. The Etonians, educated in Royal Windsor at a school founded by King Henry VI, weren't about to be told how to play up and play the game by the provincial rugger buggers. Given this rivalry it now seems obvious that we would end up with at least two versions of football but no one was to know that at the time. To complicate matters still further, another set of rules, which would dominate the kicking version of the sport in Yorkshire and the Midlands for two decades, was established in Sheffield in 1857.

Despite these rules there was no compulsion to play sports, and masters who were brutally strict in the classroom were completely indifferent to what pupils did in their free time, leaving them very much to their own devices. Most public schools were in rural settings and had no clearly defined bounds, so pupils spent their free time roaming the countryside hunting, poaching, fishing and trespassing. Pupils at Harrow fought with the navvies building the nearby London and North-Western Railway and stone throwing was another popular pastime. The ground staff never went anywhere without a bag of rocks to enable them to repel attacks from the pupils and anyone who drove a horse and cart near the school was putting their animal at serious risk. At Marlborough College matters came to a head in 1851 when prior to Bonfire Night the headmaster M. Wilkinson warned that any pupil caught in possession of fireworks would be expelled. The pupils responded by advising him that he would have to expel the entire school and at 6pm on 5 November a rocket was launched signalling the beginning of a riot. Property was burned, the gatekeeper severely beaten and several teachers badly injured. Nursing their injuries they retreated, having decided to let the revolt see its course, which it did after four days. Wilkinson was forced to resign and was replaced by a young master from Rugby, a Mr G.E.L. Cotton.

Cotton had appeared in *Tom Brown's School Days* as a teacher preaching the virtue of games for developing men of sound character. When he arrived at Marlborough he made organised physical activity an explicit part of his plan to gain full control of the school, articulating this in a circular to parents in 1853. It was the first time a head teacher had linked games to a school curriculum and was the beginning of the end for pupils' unsupervised free time. Cotton was quite probably influenced by his friend C.J. Vaughan, the headmaster at Harrow. The pair had attended Cambridge together, kept in regular contact and faced similar problems at their schools. Two months before Cotton's circular, the pupils at Harrow created the Philathletic Club to organise school games. The idea likely came from Vaughan, who was very clever in his dealings with pupils and allowed them to take the initiative (or at least to think they were), thus gaining their endorsement.

It's Cotton and Vaughan who should be seen as the creators of the public-school games cult, not Arnold, but of course they didn't get the headlines. There are other reasons why they don't get the credit they deserve. After just seven years Cotton left Marlborough to became Bishop of Calcutta and his relatively short link to the education system ended. A year later, Vaughan mysteriously resigned from Harrow and disappeared from the history books. His penchant for writing love letters to his pupils probably didn't help. For fear that his homosexual activity might be revealed he left instructions that upon his death all his papers be burned and no one should write his biography. As a consequence, much useful information about those initial steps towards the assimilation of games into the wider curriculum is lost to us.

So it is that Uppingham's Reverend Edward Thring is seen as the man who took the baton from Arnold and ran with it. In 1859 Thring opened a gymnasium and employed a gym master and in 1883 the school swimming pool opened. All were unique at the time. He also employed a full-time cricket professional, another national first. This focus on sport was an attempt to improve the moral health of individuals and also reduce divisions between intellectuals and athletes. By and large in the latter aim these initiatives failed and the sportsmen or 'bloods' as they were known were hero worshipped while the more studious students were reviled. Nonetheless the public-school games cult helped spread football into wider society and in particular the universities, and it was from there that the real impetus for the formation of clearly defined rules came.

Initially ex-public-school boys were content to organise games among fellow school alumni – married against single, first half of the alphabet against second half – but the desire to play teams from further afield grew as groups of old boys from various schools met at university and transport networks developed. The question was: whose version to play? Should it be one of the versions played at Eton or Harrow where wide-open playing fields allowed for long, high punts, or the version played at Charterhouse where monastery cloisters restricted players to short passes and dribbling (maybe the seeds for tiki-taka and route one were planted a long time ago). Or should it be the version played at Rugby that became the exception by allowing players to run with the ball after they had caught it? What made the process slightly more complex was the rivalry between the schools concerning whose version of football should come out on top. It's the Reverend Thring's younger brother John Charles, or JC, who gets most of the credit for establishing the unified rules of the kicking code; however, his voice was just one of many being raised in the clamour about how to proceed. Furthermore, that version of history overlooks two things: the part newspapers had to play in the story and the efforts of one journalist in particular: John Dyer Cartwright.

• • •

The debate over the need for national football rules began in earnest in the letter pages of the national newspapers. The first was published in *The Field* on 14 December 1861 in which the correspondent stated: "Unless the public schools will combine and draw up a code of rules we despair of seeing it take the place which it deserves to occupy as a national winter sport." Another letter to the paper asked: "What happens when a game of football is proposed at Christmas among a party of young men assembled from different schools? The Eton man is enamoured of his own rules and turns up his nose at Rugby as not sufficiently aristocratic ; while the Rugbeian retorts that 'bullying' and 'sneaking' are not to his taste, and that he is not afraid of his shins or of a maul or scrimmage." Two weeks later a letter from 'JCT' titled "Football, Simple and Universal" was published calling for a uniform game while making it clear the author was un-enamoured with the Rugby version, which he called "a blot" and a "disgrace". Was this Thring? The initials suggest it was, as does the fact he refers to an unsuccessful attempt to lay down some rules at Cambridge in 1846, something we know Thring did. In 1862, Thring had another crack, producing his famous pamphlet of rules called *The Simplest Game* as "an antidote to the Rugby game".

By late 1863 things were really coming to a head with a flurry of correspondence to that most esteemed of publications, *The Times*. On 5 October, a letter from 'Etonensis' (an Etonian) called for a committee of representatives from the public schools, London clubs and Oxford or Cambridge to agree upon a new set of rules. Replies came the following day from 'Harroviensis' (from Harrow) and 'Carthusians' (from Charterhouse) the former advocating that the rules of the home side were used in each match and the latter agreeing with the call for totally new rules. Three days later Etonensis wrote again reasserting his view that there needed to be "a new game" and 'William of Wykeham' (from Winchester) joined the debate suggesting all the schools' rules be collected before a general meeting was held. Finally 'Rugbaeenis' waded in to the scrum of letters also suggesting the home side's rules were used in any match. An article in the *Eton College Chronicle* entitled "The Football Controversy" proposed a unified set of rules drawn up by committee. However, the author went on to denounce the Rugby game as a "fight" and a "wrestling match" before claiming: "Eton is we believe about the only place in which the game is what its name indicates – real foot-ball." Although the term had been used many times over the preceding centuries, this was the first time it had been used in the modern sense, to explicitly differentiate the sport from a rival, handling version.

There was also another letter to *The Field* from 'JCT' in which the author wrote: "the only plan will be to entirely disregard any existing rules and frame others *de novo*". If this was Thring it suggests he recognised that his attempt to codify the game a year earlier had fallen on deaf ears. However the widespread recognition of the need to find a way forward was clear as using the home side's rules led to one-sided, dull matches and a heightened risk of injury. Yet there was also reluctance by all to relinquish 'their' rules and the shadow of the Eton–Rugby rivalry loomed large over the debate. An impasse had been reached into which stepped Cartwright.

Not a great deal is known about Cartwright's early life. Born in Warwickshire in 1838 to a family of three brothers and two sisters, he was one of the earliest true sports journalists, writing with a detailed knowledge and passion on a range of games from ice skating to quoits and croquet. He turned his attention to the embryonic form of football in a series of ten articles for *The Field* published between 24 October and 26 December 1863, in which his stated aim was to assess "the value of the Game, its present position and the discussion concerning the rules". He even vowed to produce his own compromise rules after first forensically examining the "propositions for amalgamating the existing rules, and making new ones". During the time the series was published the six Freemasons' Tavern meetings at which the FA was formed and its first set of rules agreed upon were held. Given the depth of detail of Cartwright's articles and their availability through the influential *Field* they would almost certainly have had an impact on those discussions.

A few weeks after Cartwright began writing, a series of six similarly in-depth articles written by 'A Lover of Football' also appeared in the *Sporting Gazette*. Some attribute these to Cartwright but that seems unlikely as they have a bias to the handling form of the game and the author had already written a letter stating they did not "concur with Mr Thring that the ball should be kept as much as possible on the ground". Cartwright, on the other hand, seemed to be singing from the same hymn sheet as Thring, believing a new set of compromise laws was the way forward; that students from Oxford or Cambridge should lead the way, as the schools would accept them as an authoritative arbiter, and that the new form of the game should be based on kicking. In his second article he dismissed an unidentified 'Public Schoolman' who presciently had argued for two games "as distinct from each other as cricket is from either – one on the Rugby principle, one on the Harrow", claiming "this would perpetuate, in a very slightly modified form, the evil it is sought to remedy".

In his sixth article, following the publication of the well-received 1863 Cambridge Rules in *The Field,* Cartwright asked whether Rugby might "not have as good a game with rather less violence? Certainly they might. Such a one is now offered them from Cambridge, in the construction of which two of their own players have taken a prominent part. Will they not accept it?" Well, no. At the penultimate meeting at the Freemasons' Tavern the rules were definitively changed to ban carrying the ball and hacking. F.W. Campbell of the Blackheath club walked out arguing that the abolition of hacking would lead to football being "emasculated", adding: "if you do away with it you will do away with all the courage and the pluck of the game, and I will be bound to bring over a lot of Frenchmen who would beat you with a week's practice". You and I know this ultimately ended up with the two codes of football Cartwright warned against, but he didn't. Despite the walkout he was fairly upbeat, abandoning his own plan to create some new rules, and writing: "the necessity for discussion is now, we trust, about to be terminated by a satisfactory settlement, to be brought about in the way we advocated".

Cartwright's contribution to the formation of both football and (indirectly) rugby is perhaps overlooked because ultimately, unlike the younger Thring, he never felt the need to write down his own rules and because he died at the tragically young age of 26. Cartwright drowned in Bristol's Victoria Baths while visiting his sister and brother-in-law in August 1864. It was less than a year after the formation of the FA, which still had some considerable way to go in popularising the kicking form of football and gaining control over the governance of that code. It's not unreasonable to assume that had he lived, Cartwright would almost certainly have continued to frame and shape the debate, analysing it from an outsider's perspective while lending his support to the kicking code. Had he had the chance to do so his voice, not Thring's, might have been the one to resonate longest through history. As it is, Cartwright's last word on the subject, three months before his death, had a pessimistic tone. Writing for *London Society*, a monthly periodical, Cartwright noted that the rugby version is "the most popular of all" while players from different schools still "have no common game and common ground". He then outlined what he considered to be the main sticking points: "Shall the ball be taken up and carried or caught, when kicked in the air? What is off side? And what is on side? Shall there be a cross bar for the ball to be kicked over, as at Rugby or for it to be kicked under, as at other places? Are hacking, charging and tripping legitimate?" The issues would not be fully resolved for over a decade.

The formation in 1871 of the Rugby Football Union and their first rules helped create a clearer divide, but the key event was the amalgamation in 1877 of the Sheffield FA and the London-based FA's rules and the accession of power from the northern body to the southern. Letters to *The Field* were once again the impetus for this latter move. The captain of the Manchester Association Football Club was just one to write in, complaining that: "I think that I may safely say that there is not any district in which the inconvenience of having two different association rules is felt more than here."

It's worth briefly mentioning that a few years before Eton and Rugby were posturing over the length of their rules lists, English ex-pats went through a similar process Down Under where various forms of football, no doubt imported with the settlers and their rabbits, were being played.[5] Again newspapers were influential and it was in 1858 in *Bell's Life in Victoria* that Australian-born Tom Wentworth Wills, who'd been sent to England to attend Rugby School and Cambridge, proposed the idea of organised football in the colony. Wills, who was considered one of the best cricketers of his generation, originally wanted to use the rugby rules before declaring "we shall have a game of our own". In 1859 after also considering the rules of football at Eton, Harrow and Winchester, Wills and his chums laid down the first laws of what would become Australian Rules football.

We'll never know exactly why football became more popular than rugby. Maybe it is because it's simpler. Maybe it was because it was played in more schools and so had more supporters to spread the word. Maybe it was because one of those schools, Eton, was the most influential of all. Maybe it was because the game had a stronghold in Sheffield as well as London or maybe it was because in 1885 the kicking game embraced (albeit grudgingly) professionalism before the handling game. It may have simply been the fact that the kicking game quickly established successful nationwide cup and league competitions, both of which were up and running by 1888. Most likely it was a combination of all those maybes, and as the sport quickly grew in popularity, coverage of it became a central part of the newspaper business.

5   *If you're interested, in America they went through the process in 1873 but that's a whole other book which I haven't written yet.*

CHAPTER 2

THE RISE AND FALL OF THE SPORTING PRESS

The year 1863 is considered to be the definitive Year Zero moment of modern football but as we discussed, albeit briefly, in Chapter 1, it was actually a series of events that occurred over the course of several years that led to the sport's creation. Similarly 1855 and particularly the post-Chartist repeal of the Stamp Act is considered the moment the modern media was born. However the abolition of stamp duty was just one of several factors that helped create what we would recognise as the modern mass-market media. Eleven years earlier in 1844, Professor Samuel Morse sent the first telegraph message "What hath God Wrought!" from the US Supreme Court in Washington, to his colleague Alfred Vail, in Baltimore, revolutionising the communications industry in the process. The telegraph was the internet of the day and within a few years the new technology was being applied to the news industry.

In 1851 Britain's first wire service was established when Paul Julius Reuter founded his eponymous news agency in London. Reuter's initial success had come two years earlier through an investment in the rights to the telegraph line between Aachen, Prussia and Berlin and in a separate investment in the not-so-modern technology of carrier pigeons to provide news from unwired areas of Europe. When Reuter pitched up in England he remodelled his business, making it the sole provider of news to the London Stock Exchange (a service the company still provides today) and one of the few with reliable access to news from abroad. The agency's reputation was cemented in 1865 when it broke the news of Abraham Lincoln's assassination in Europe hours before its rivals, although the news still took two weeks to get from America to England as it came by boat before under-sea telegraph cables were laid. The eruption of Krakatoa in 1883 was the first truly global news event, as it came after the introduction of transoceanic telegraph cables, enabling news of the disaster to spread around the world in hours, yet it wasn't even the most destructive eruption of the nineteenth century. That distinction goes to the little-known Mount Tambora in 1815, still the most powerful volcanic eruption ever recorded. Even at its humble beginnings, the media could still make or break you.

Wire services solved two problems for publishers. Firstly, they provided a regular supply of news, essential to a true daily press. Secondly, they reduced the cost of foreign news to newspapers as they didn't have to invest in expensive technology or foreign correspondents. The wire services commodified news itself and meant that from that point on newspapers would always be produced with an eye on profit, something which was made easier in 1853 when advertising duty was abolished, increasing the commercial revenue available to publishers. The repeal of the Stamp Act, which came after years of campaigning against a so-called "tax on knowledge" by both radicals and conservative reformers, broke down one of the last barriers to a free-market media and in 1861 the journey was complete when the paper duties were also removed.

But still 1855 generally gets the plaudits as it was also the year that gave birth to the first mass-market paper – the *Daily Telegraph and Courier* (now the *Daily Telegraph*) – which launched itself headlong into what the paper itself not unreasonably described as a "new era of journalism". It exploited the lifting of taxes by cutting its daily cover price to a penny and set itself in direct contrast to the elitist nature of *The Times* (which cost seven pence) by copying American techniques such as focusing on crime and human-interest stories, and targeting a more working-class readership. A cover-price war and sensationalism? Modern journalism was here to stay.

It was into this brave new world that James Catton made his first tentative steps. Catton might have cut a diminutive figure in the press box, but he stood like a colossus over the early decades of football journalism. At just four foot ten and a half inches tall he probably didn't need reminding of his height, but his colleagues took pleasure in doing just that, with 'Pigmy' and 'Tom Thumb' being just two of the brickbats thrown in his direction. Catton was unbowed, however, and when he died in 1936 aged 76 he was widely acknowledged by both professional colleagues and sport players and administrators to be a unique talent. Among the eulogies, Trevor Wignall, the *Daily Express'* chief sports correspondent, commented that Catton's reports had been one of the "few things that mattered" for young lads in the early 1900s. However in 1875, when Catton answered an advert for "a well-educated Youth as Apprentice to Newspaper Reporting" and joined the bi-weekly *Preston Herald*, all that was in the future. His father, a university-educated classics and maths tutor with a love of cricket that his son inherited, had in mind a medical career for Catton, but he had no need to worry as the newspaper industry, both sporting and non-sporting, was in a period of explosive growth. There were just 15 provincial dailies in 1856 but by the turn of the century that number had grown to 171 and there were 101 evening papers on top of that. Between 1861 and 1880 the number of towns boasting one daily paper rose from 16 to 47. It was 71 by 1900.

The growing popularity of regularly organised football was also hard to miss and all manner of people sought to cash in. Firms that had previously produced cricket equipment turned their attention to the fast-growing winter sport and began churning out hand-sewn footballs, football boots and nets. As early as 1880 the discerning gentleman could stroll into Manchester department store Lewis's to purchase the latest in designer knickerbockers and coloured football jerseys.[1] Manufacturers of medicines and herbal remedies started targeting their products at football players and even grass seed was being advertised with football in mind. Ever keen to turn a fast shilling the newspapers began to use football as a selling point of their product, in turn cementing the sport, and sport more generally, into England's commercial and leisure sub-cultures.

Having played a crucial role in helping negotiate and establish the early rules of the new sport, newspapers became a means for football's administrators to communicate those still-evolving laws. At the same time the papers defined the new sport's 'seasons' and 'festive' days that would come to usurp the traditional ceremonies of the more-rural

1   *Lewis's was founded by David Lewis but despite its name it was nothing to do with John Lewis, who owned stores in the south. The last Lewis's, in Manchester, closed in 2002.*

past. More than anything newspapers established themselves as the game's information service; advertising and reporting on fixtures, venues and communicating results from around the country that would be pasted in newspaper office windows on the night of games. Despite the boost each provided the other, the relationship between the press and football clubs wasn't always harmonious. In 1894 the *Birmingham Daily Gazette* ended a report on a match between West Brom and Newton Heath with the sentence: "next week Newton Heath have to meet Burnley and if they both play in their ordinary style it will perhaps create an extra run of business for the undertakers". The Manchester club took exception and successfully sued the paper for libel, claiming it had accused them of "brutality".

• • •

Although only an apprentice, or perhaps *because* he was an apprentice, Catton was able to immerse himself in this new urban craze, covering a considerable amount of sport in his eight years in Preston, despite the irregularities of the seasons at the time. With few barriers between press and players he befriended several members of the Preston Grass-hoppers rugby team as well as one Major William Sudell, who was in the process of building Preston North End's famous 'Invincibles'. Catton wasn't around to witness their Double-winning season in 1889 having qualified as a reporter and left the area six years earlier. He was 21, married to Mary, the sister of a fellow reporter, and they already had the first two of their four children. Catton needed a pay rise so in 1883 he left Preston for the *Nottingham Daily Guardian*, answering an advert for a reporter "of gentlemanly appearance". Journalism was still in its infancy; an uncertain career which did not yet have the social standing and respectability, and thus rewards, of other professions.[2] Football, too, was in its infancy and in 1891 Catton reported on the first use of goal nets "in a public match" at a trial game held at Forest's City Ground between teams from the North and South.

During his eight years by the Trent, Catton and sports journalism both established themselves, and before he left the *Daily Guardian*

2   *A contemporary of Catton's on the rival* Nottingham Journal *was J.M. Barrie who was born just a month after Catton in May 1860, but more of Mr Barrie, and Peter Pan, later.*

he had been promoted to the position of "sporting editor", a title that was popping up all over the country as it became clear sport had an increasingly large role to play in the paper business. Something else that was popping up all over the country during the 1880s was the football special. These were hyper-local city or town-specific papers printed on Saturday evenings which became known for the colour of the paper they were printed on, often nicknamed 'The Pink 'Un' or 'The Green 'Un' accordingly. The specials became so ubiquitous that in 1905 an early history of football described how Saturday nights had become "illuminated by innumerable broadsheets in colour like unto the rainbow, devoted solely to the purveying of fact and fancy on the one topic".

The specials were the ultimate consequence of a dramatic change brought to people's leisure time through the twin processes of industrialisation and urbanisation. Leisure in pre-industrial society was like the folk football games which were a constituent part of it; sporadic, relatively unregulated, violent and marked by Saint Monday – the habit of taking both Sunday and the following day off work. In the new world, factory owners wanted a workforce on hand twelve hours a day, six days a week, and they attempted to squash this practice though the use of employment and municipal regulations. However there was also a recognised need for clearly defined leisure time and by 1850 campaigners had won a victory[3] with the Factory Act, which laid out exactly when textile employees would be expected to work, and legislated for a 2pm, half-day finish on Saturdays (with Sundays totally free as had always been the case). The benefit quickly spread to other industries and of all the major cities Liverpool was the last to fall into line, with their non-textile workers eventually getting Saturday afternoons off by the 1870s. Significantly the concessions were in the main granted to industrial not clerical workers and shopkeepers, whose workloads increased as everyone else was enjoying a bit of time to spend their cash. A factory inspector from the era wrote that the benefit of the free Saturday afternoon was that it created a distinction between the workers' time and his masters' and that "the wages can be carried home in ample time for the market and the husband

3   Well, I say 'victory' but the working week actually increased from 58 to 60 hours.

and wife can spend that money together". Nice idea, but it was never going to happen. Instead just as the FA gained control of modern football and the game's expansion began in earnest, so there was an army of working-class men (and it tended to be men) with Saturday afternoons off and a little spare cash to spend – class and gender distinctions which would remain in place until the game's post-Italia '90 gentrification a century later.

The first special to launch, on 30 September 1882 in Birmingham, was the imaginatively titled *Saturday Night*, which offered four pages for half a penny and claimed to be "the very first paper ever established for the special purpose of giving the results of athletic events on the day of their occurrence". This new publication was initially met with some scepticism by others in the industry but by November it was printing two editions – one at 7pm and one an hour later – and by the following January it had a circulation of 15,000. Other publishers dipped their toes in the water, but the scepticism clearly remained as for a couple of years the papers were simply the regular editions with a column of results (and, if you were lucky, a match report) tagged on. Just how great the demand was became apparent in January 1884 when copies of halfpenny papers containing nothing more than the result of the FA Cup fourth round tie between Aston Villa and Queens Park were changing hands for six pence minutes after they hit the streets.[4]

The floodgates had burst and before long every major town or city, certainly those with a professional club, were printing them. By 1889 the *Blackburn Evening Express* was producing four editions of its football special at 5.45pm, 6.30pm, 7.30pm and 7.45pm. To enable them to collect and print as many results as possible at more or less the same time and meet print deadlines, the papers lobbied for a uniform kick-off time, 3pm, across the country – quite an irony given that the 'traditional' kick-off time is now supposedly being undermined by the demands of the media. The specials were sold at a variety of outlets including pubs and their popularity could impact upon those other industries to the extent that in 1908 the Birmingham brewery Mitchells and Butlers held two separate heated board meetings just to decide which football special to supply at its watering holes. The

4   For the record Queens Park won 6-1 and made it all the way to the final where they lost to Blackburn Rovers 2-1.

relationship between the press, football and the brewers was a strong one. Some editions of The Football Pink 'Un – one of the papers at the centre of those heated board meetings – featured as many as 400 adverts for pubs, hotels and restaurants.

The papers were able to meet this huge demand thanks to the latest technological innovations. By the late 1880s the telegraph was increasingly being supplemented by the telephone (and a few decades later the car) although even in the early twentieth century papers were still using homing pigeons to allow their writers to report in the absence of more modern technologies. In these incidences the reporter would take at least two pigeons with him to the ground in a basket along with a pad of thin tissue-like paper. At the end of the first half the reporter would write his report on the paper, attach it to the first pigeon's leg and dispatch it back to the office, repeating the process with another pigeon on the final whistle (or after each goal in important games). Almost every paper had a pigeon loft as well as trained handlers and when the birds arrived back at the office the handlers would ring a bell alerting the sub-editors to their arrival, and a copy boy would be sent to retrieve the hand-written notes. Occasionally the system would fall foul of bad weather, predators or pigeons who weren't very good at the homing part, but as the birds could cover 50 miles in little more than an hour the system was by-and-large a success and popular enough to run in tandem with the telegraph for many years.

The most revolutionary invention was the linotype machine, patented by German Ottmar Mergenthaler in 1886, which meant pages no longer needed to be painstakingly assembled letter by letter. The invention, which Thomas Edison declared "the Eighth Wonder of the World", allowed the print-room compositors to type a series of words into a machine which would then produce a line of type (or lin'-o'-type) in the form of a metal block or 'slug', enabling them to assemble a 12,000-word page in just half an hour. Soon papers were employing clerks who would spend Saturday afternoons writing down in-running match reports phoned in piece by piece by reporters at various grounds. When a line was finished it would be rushed off to the compositors who would input it into a linotype machine, setting the paper throughout the afternoon. If linotype was the icing on the newspaper cake, then the cherry was the new web-fed rotary press, which could produce 6,000 copies of a paper per minute. All this new-fangled technology meant that in 1889 the *Sheffield Evening Telegraph* was able to boast that by special arrangement with the manager of the National Telephone Company it had received the result of Sheffield Wednesday's away game against Wolverhampton Wanderers within four minutes of the final whistle. Its presses were running two minutes later and copies were on the streets of the Steel City less than ten minutes after the end of a match 77 miles away. This rush to be first with results was widely acknowledged to be a driving force behind the developing industry, with a study in 1913 declaring that "incomparably the keenest competition in the newspaper world is developed as the result of rivalry to bring out the earliest news of sporting events". It wasn't without its pitfalls however and mistakes regularly occurred. In the same year as the survey, the *London Star* famously printed the wrong result on Boat Race day.[5]

As the football specials developed so did the need for staff, and while much of the rest of the country was enjoying the day off, journalists, compositors, copy boys and, let's not forget, the pigeon handlers were all being roped in to work on Saturday afternoons, something which increasingly became a contractual obligation while also creating numerous freelance opportunities. There was also an increased need for accurate 'copy' to be 'filed' to newspaper offices as soon as possible after the final whistle, which in turn created a new breed of football journalist who had the ability to take on board what had happened and quickly and calmly describe it in readable, entertaining prose. Wire agencies dedicated to sport or with dedicated sports departments, such as the Exchange Telegraph Company and the Press Association, emerged in the early 1900s as sports results became a commodity in their own right. As well as results, they offered reports from 75 to 2,000 words in length that could be phoned in at a time convenient to the newspaper concerned, or they simply offered their phones for hire.

For those reporters interested in the new sport, football offered an escape, albeit short-lived perhaps, from the drudgery of courts and public meetings; the chance to mix with sporting heroes and for a

5   It wasn't just the sports departments that got things wrong. The previous year several papers, including the Daily Mail, incorrectly reported that no lives had been lost in the Titanic disaster with some even claiming the stricken vessel was being towed to New York.

writer with flair the chance to inject their reports with a colourful turn-of-phrase likely denied in the paper's news section. Yet it was also hard, unglamorous work that should have carried a health warning. At least eight of Catton's colleagues died between 1891 and 1895, one of whom, Tom Sutton, at the tender age of just 41, had suffered prolonged ill-health brought on by the harsh weather conditions football reporters had to endure. Catton himself, in his book *Wickets and Goals: Stories of Play*, gave a detailed insight of how the facilities available for reporters developed over the decades. In the early days they were virtually non-existent and the reporter would be left to his own devices, free to wander around the pitch or even chat to the goalkeepers. Some clubs put out benches or desks but these would be right on the touchline with no cover from the elements or the crowd. The first press boxes made their appearance in the 1890s but varied from ground to ground and sport to sport, with some being very opulent (reporters attending The Oval, for example, had the use of a private toilet). By 1899 a committee had been set up to distribute the 150 seats allocated to the press for the FA Cup Final at Crystal Palace. Catton noted that around that time the telegraph had made its appearance and by the mid-1920s the press had their own entrance to most grounds and access to a telephone on each desk with a direct line to their office.

• • •

In 1891 Catton was on the move again, returning to the North West to join the Manchester-based *Sunday Chronicle,* thus starting a 33-year association with Edward Hulton's group of papers. The group was at the forefront of sports journalism but Catton had to join what was, at the time, their only newspaper to step up the career ladder. Census figures detail the general profession's growth, listing about 2,400 journalists and writers in 1871, about 3,400 ten years later and 5,771 in 1891, yet even in the mid-1890s specialist sports journalism jobs were few and far between. It was at the *Chronicle* that Catton took on the pseudonym Tityrus, in keeping with the industry-wide practice that produced bylines such as 'The Bounder' and the even more intriguing 'Dangle'.

After three years Catton was in charge of the paper's sports coverage before being promoted again in 1900 to the editorship of another of Hulton's titles, the *Athletic News*. Hulton had started his working life as a compositor on the *Manchester Guardian* but he was sacked for producing a racing form sheet and distributing it to pubs and illicit bookies.[6] Undeterred he got the backing of local cotton merchant E.O. Bleackley and in 1871 launched his own one-sheet paper called *The Tissue*. Considered the bible of the racing community it morphed into the *Prophetic Bell* and by April 1873, as it became increasingly popular, Hulton renamed it the *Sporting Chronicle*. Teddy Dawson, a reporter on the paper in the early 1900s, would recount in retirement how they "reported on everything of sporting interest", which ran from sports we'd expect to see reported today to pitching pennies into a pint pot and one-legged races. The profits from this venture enabled Hulton to launch the *Athletic News* in 1875 and move to new premises in Withy Grove. Now the building is called The Printworks and is full of modern bars, restaurants and a multi-screen cinema, but in its heyday under Hulton it was the largest newspaper print centre in the country (his grandson would later claim in the world). It employed some 3,000 people and boasted cutting-edge private telegraph technology. "Just imagine," a promotional brochure proclaimed in 1912, "it can deliver two messages in Manchester while transmitting one to London!"

With the capital a four- or five-hour train journey away, Manchester soon became a gateway to the North, Scotland and Ireland, thus allowing the newspaper market to become truly national.[7] Soon all the major London papers had Manchester offices and printworks, and Hulton and his son, also called Edward, were there to reap the rewards of the booming industry. By 1916 they had bought the *London Evening Standard* and had a portfolio on a par with those of Lords Beaverbrook, Northcliffe and Rothermere, names still synonymous with the newspaper industry today. However, the Hulton dynasty had reached its zenith. Suffering from ill-health, the younger Hulton, who

6   *His dismissal was hardly a great surprise given that the* Guardian *refused to cover racing until the 1960s.*

7   *The* Guardian *was originally the* Manchester Guardian *but completed its move south in 1976. Two years later the Daily Star was launched in Manchester initially as a North-focused daily but it too soon moved south in 1989, the last of the nationals to do so (unless you count the* Daily Sport, *and if you do you're a fool).*

had taken control at the turn of the century, sold up to Beaverbrook for £6m in 1923, two years before his death. Beaverbrook kept the *Evening Standard* as his trophy and sold the rest on to Northcliffe and so, between them, they carved up one of the great early newspaper empires, one that had emphatically been built on sport. The family made enough cash from the deal for the second Hulton's son (also called Edward) to launch *Picture Post* in 1938. It was the pioneer of photo-journalism and become one of the most influential magazines of the twentieth century.

But I digress. In 1887 Hulton cut the *Athletic News*' cover price to half a penny and a year later moved publication from Saturdays to Mondays. Both moves were designed to capitalise on football's growing popularity and both worked a treat. By 1896 it was shifting 180,000 copies a week and had become the country's leading authority on football. The paper was intimately linked with the sport, and Catton's predecessor, J.J. Bentley, who edited the *Athletic News* from 1892 to 1900, was also the Football League's chairman from 1893 to 1910, as well as being vice-chairman of the FA and a director of Manchester United. Charles Alcock, perhaps the most well-known founder member of the FA, along with other key figures such as William Pickford and C.E. Sutcliffe, also all wrote for the paper.

That so many of the game's early administrators were involved with such a key publication demonstrates that they realised that the press was vital in helping them to shape and form public opinion as they navigated the choppy waters between the amateur ideal and an emerging professional sport. The *Athletic News* wasn't just the voice of football but the voice of professional football ownership, articulating and defending the League's and clubs' viewpoints while also reinforcing the sport's hierarchy as the game was structured. Catton had reported on the historic 1885 Freemasons' Tavern meeting that sanctioned professionalism, and his support for the move may well have come from the kinship he felt with footballers themselves. He was an original member of the National Association of Journalists in 1894 and the National Union of Journalists soon after it was founded in 1907. Like footballers, journalists were trying to gain acceptance in a new and uncertain profession that was erratic and required frequent moves from job to job, sometimes to different parts of the country.

Another key change Catton witnessed during his career, and here he was as much an instigator, was the development of reporting style. At the start of Catton's career, reports were long-winded, laborious blow-by-blow accounts weighed down by obscure references to the classics. In one of his early 102-line efforts, the result was buried 12 lines from the end, and while working in Nottingham he opened a report on the local derby in 1890 like this:

> The fierce partisans of each side rubbed their shoulders together, and as I looked round the parallelogram the words of Hecate, in *Macbeth*, were brought vividly to mind:
>
> > *Black spirits and white,*
> > *Red spirits and grey,*
> > *Mingle, mingle, mingle*
> > *You that mingle may!*

Parallelowhat? It's doubtful any modern football writer would attempt an opening paragraph as convoluted as that and it's extremely unlikely it would make it into print if they did. However when Catton started out this was all new; writers like himself were basically making it up as they went along, pioneers in a frontier where no man had gone before. Over the following decades this changed and Catton was one of the driving forces in introducing a chattier style. In the 1920s and 30s some younger reporters still regarded his writing as slightly old school but they also respectfully acknowledged that it was he who bridged the gap between them and what had gone before. Catton's later reports had clearly moved with the times and appeared much lighter, with a more personal style and references to other matches to place the result into the wider context of the sport. A further influence on style was the decrease in both time and space available to the reporter. As the clamour for the football specials increased, editors wanted to pack in more reports without upping the size of the paper, so word counts got shorter and so too did deadlines in an attempt to beat rival publications to the streets and meet the post- match crowds as they came out of the ground. You couldn't quote Shakespeare when you had to file a match report on the 'f' of the final whistle. Yet there was a flip side as the need for speed saw football reporters create a language of their own, incomprehensible to the non-football fan and full of formulaic cliché and stock terminology. In 1959 academics Percy Tannenbaum and James Noah labelled it 'sportuguese', arguing that it had by then become an "integral part of the sports writer's kit-bag, his stock-in-trade", and it's a language still used by many writers today.

If the style of those very early match reports is antiquated, some of the narratives developed at the time are rather more familiar. While the beautiful game had quickly become one watched by the working-class masses, cricket was fast becoming the sport of the upper-middle and upper classes, but like folk football early cricket was a highly violent affair frequently involving death and serious injury to players and spectators. As with football, many of modern cricket's early administrators were also correspondents of the sport so they cultivated an image of a genteel game unsullied by drinking, violence or gambling. What better way was there to do just that than to deflect the blame for any lingering violence on to the shoulders of the 'roughs' who watched soccer? So in 1883 when police had to be deployed at Lancashire's Old Trafford to quell crowd trouble during a cricket match, *The Badminton Magazine* blamed the violence on the "football element".

Football writers had their own concerns, lamenting the impact of that thing English football and English football journalism seems to fear the most: the outsider. Prior to a match between the Scottish and English players of Lincoln City in 1893, the local paper wrote: "Ever since the introduction of professionalism, there has been a big demand in England for Scottish players, but football enthusiasts are now beginning to question the wisdom of going across the border for new blood whilst we have promising young players of English manufacture at hand." To great relief the English players won, leading the paper to contrast the "uncertain foreigners" with the Englishmen who "would try their very hardest to uphold the honour of Lincoln".

And what about those other great outsiders: women? Written by men and aimed at men, newspapers' sports coverage was, well, very masculine and didn't have much room for the ladies. What little there was either focused on body-oriented sports like gymnastics or middle-class sports such as tennis and hockey. When men and women enjoyed the same sport, coverage was skewed towards the former, for example providing reports of male tennis matches but only the results of the ladies'. The prevailing attitude towards women was articulated by Catton (albeit talking about cricket) when he wrote: "Are they not the presiding deities of the tea tent? I am old-fashioned and quaint enough in my prejudices to prefer sport for women as the handmaid of health, and for no other purpose." But what's a bit of sexism and xenophobia when sales are going so well, eh? By 1914 *Mitchell's Press Guide* listed 87 periodicals devoted to various aspects of sport, an increase from 60 in 1894, but just as the sports press was in its pomp it was dealt a blow from which it would not recover.

• • •

In the grand scheme of things that blow and its consequences are rather insignificant but it would be remiss not to discuss the First World War's impact on football and the sports press, as both were now rooted in the wider society. When Britain declared war on Germany in August 1914 most people assumed the conflict would be over by Christmas. It wasn't to be, however, and as with many aspects of life the conflict disrupted the developing football and sporting calendars – the very constituency the sporting press relied on. The Football League and FA Cup both initially offered to suspend their respective competitions; however, both continued after the Government ambiguously told them not to do anything that wasn't called for. Given their contractual obligations, professional footballers were unable to sign up for duty and faced an almost immediate backlash as the County Cricket Championship was suspended. Football's critics also pointed to the large number of amateur rugby players who joined the army. That those same critics chose to overlook the huge numbers of amateur footballers who also joined up showed there was a wider agenda in play that continued after the war when many public schools abandoned football in favour of rugby. World war, it seems, begat class war.

The *Athletic News* under Catton's editorship defended professional football, pointing out that not only was it a business like any other and so entitled to keep running, but it was one which could be used as a vehicle for recruitment and fundraising while keeping people fit and morale high during a time of extreme crisis. Perhaps for the first time, but certainly not the last, the sport became a metaphor for England itself as well as the country's virtues of fair play: "Even Germany has taken up the most popular pastime of the hated English", wrote Catton in 1917. "England is the model, the object lesson, and I hope the example to others. How important it is that we should never lose sight of the fact that Association football is a great English game and that we are copied by other people."

The ongoing opposition to football meant the League was suspended in 1915, decreasing further the quantity and quality of sport the sports press had to report as more of the country's best sportsmen went to the front line. As money became tighter advertising revenue fell so the papers cut their page numbers accordingly. Two weeks after the war broke out the *Athletic News* was down from eight pages to four and while it occasionally managed a six-page edition, by April 1917 it was reduced to just one in its sister title the *Sporting Chronicle*, with a promise "to return when there is a prospect of normal conditions", which it did a month after peace was declared. When football resumed, 'sportuguese' changed slightly as military metaphors all but disappeared. Following a conflict that saw nearly two and a half million young British men killed or wounded it was facile to call the pitch a 'battlefield' or talk of defences being 'bombarded' by centre forwards who were 'top marksmen'. The change was, however, only temporary and such stock-in-trade terms were soon back in the football writer's kit-bag.

As professional football got back to its feet after the war, Catton urged clubs to remodel themselves along Continental lines by developing feeder systems to train young local players in the arts of dribbling and passing with both feet. In 1928 he criticised the inability of First Division players to be able to control the ball and questioned the clubs' reliance on stamina. It was all to no avail; on this score Catton wasn't actually old school but in reality about 90 years ahead of his time. Ill-health forced him to step out of the editor's chair at the *Athletic News*' Withy Grove offices six years after the Armistice and so he headed south to the capital, but it was a busy semi-retirement for the workaholic and although he was divested of his managerial responsibilities he continued to produce reams of copy. No sooner had he settled in his new Wimbledon home than he was writing for the *Observer*, the *London Evening Standard* and *All Sports Illustrated News*. He briefly held the role of guest writer on the *Athletic News* but Fleet Street and the nationals were where the action was at and by now he was the widely acknowledged godfather of the press box. He was an idol to reporters such as Neville Cardus and John Macadam, who would themselves go on to influence subsequent generations of sports journalists.

Catton's 60-year career serves as a potent metaphor for sports journalism itself in that period. He developed from being a wet-behind-the-ears trainee to a qualified writer before occupying newly created and ill-defined roles such as sporting editor on a local daily, and then sub-editor and news editor in the specialist sporting press before finally gracing the nationals. As he climbed up the career ladder the ladder itself was being built in an emerging section of an emerging industry, which was an inevitable consequence of the twin developments of commercial spectator sport and mass-market media.

That the latter stages of Catton's career were spent in London working for various national titles was entirely in keeping with the manner in which the sports section of the newspaper industry had changed. The specialist sporting press was no longer dominant, succumbing to a number of factors following the First World War, and by 1924 the *Sporting Life* had absorbed the *Sportsman* before eventually turning its focus to horse racing and finally ceasing publication in 1998, although it lives on as a website which we'll discuss later. By 1931 the *Sporting Chronicle* had merged with its sister title *Athletic News* and although it staggered on for more than another 50 years, also turning its attention to horse racing in the 1950s, it tipped its last winner in 1983. This speedy demise seems strange indeed when contrasted with the football-led sports press in mainland Europe, which is in rude health. However the popularity of titles like Italy's *La Gazzetta dello Sport*, Spain's *El Mundo* and France's *L'Equipe* is in fact symptomatic of the huge differences between those countries and England.

• • •

L'Equipe was born from the ashes of another paper, *L'Auto*, which was shut down following the liberation of France for sympathising with the Nazis. *L'Auto* had built its pre-war success on the back of the Tour de France, which it first organised in 1903 with the very aim of boosting circulation and overtaking rival paper *Le Vélo*.[8] The race did the job and *L'Auto*'s circulation leapt from 25,000 before that first Tour to 65,000 after it, helping to force the closure of *Le Vélo* in the process. By the 1930s circulation was well over 500,000 and following the war *L'Equipe*, which employed many of *L'Auto*'s staff, took up organisation of the popular race and the Tour's headquarters are still next door to those of the paper. In 1909 the publishers of Italy's *Gazzetta* followed suit and organised the first Giro d'Italia, clearly taking the view that imitation is the sincerest form of flattery. The two competitions are so wedded to the papers that created them that the race leaders' jerseys take their colours from their respective newsprint – the Tour's *maillot jaune* mimicking *L'Equipe*'s yellow paper and the Giro's *il maglia rosa* representing *Gazzetta*'s famous pink paper. Not for the first time the English had led the way, with papers sponsoring and promoting events decades before *L'Equipe* got in on the act. Remember *The Field* provided the trophy for the first Wimbledon tennis championships in 1877 and J.J. Bentley's dual roles with the *Athletic News* and the Football League made the title an authority on the sport. By the time the Tour de France launched, the nationals were already muscling in on sports papers territory, with the *News of the World* sponsoring golf's first PGA matchplay championships. However, no English sports paper managed to link itself to a sport and cement itself into the country's culture in the manner that *L'Equipe* and *Gazzetta* did.[9]

While *L'Equipe* dominates in France, *Gazzetta* is just one of several Italian sports papers in a market defined by the strong and disparate regional identities of a country only finally unified in 1861. England

---

8   *The two papers' rivalry had its roots in the Dreyfus Affair, a complex political scandal which split French society at the turn of the twentieth century. To cut an extremely long story short, Le Vélo was edited by Pierre Giffard, who was a left-wing Dreyfusard, while most of the paper's advertisers, such as tyre manufacturer Édouard Michelin, were right-wingers. They withdrew their support and formed L'Auto.*

9   *Gazzetta's popularity was so great that while he was in prison in the late 1920s, Antonio Gramsci noted that even political prisoners preferred it to the newspaper Il Sole.*

may have a north–south divide but Italy has a north–south chasm and the Tuscan-derived Italian language is still forced to compete with each city's distinctive dialect. *Gazzetta*, based in Milan, takes a fairly general view of football while leaning towards AC and Inter; however, *Il Corriere dello Sport*, based in Rome, focuses intently on Roma and Lazio, and Turin-based *Tuttosport* has little time for any football teams other than Juventus and Torino. Given that sport and the media are two of the most potent weapons in any battle to establish and maintain a cultural or national identity it's no wonder that the sports press in Spain, which has been dominated for years by tension between Madrid and the Catalan capital Barcelona, supports four daily sports papers in those two cities alone (*El Mundo Deportivo* and *Sport* in Barcelona and *Marca* and *AS* in Madrid). Sir John Hall invoked Barcelona when he talked of creating a Geordie Nation around Newcastle's football team in the mid-1990s but it never really rang true. When the people of the North East got to vote on a regional assembly in 2004, less than 50 per cent sent back their ballot papers and of those that did 78 per cent said 'no'. The man who engineered Kevin Keegan's (first) second coming probably wasn't all that surprised. England is a capital-centric country, a characteristic reflected in the modern newspaper market which, unlike in Italy and Spain, and in fact any similar European country, has always been dominated by a national morning press based in the capital city (with, briefly, satellite offices in the North West).

As recently as the mid-1980s it was reported that 90 per cent of all adults were buying at least one morning daily, and these papers were now covering sport in considerable detail. The shift away from a sporting press in England began with the First World War, as the four-year hiatus in organised sport meant the papers' very life-blood was drained away, while the non-sporting press, albeit reduced in size due to paper shortages, could continue to fill their pages with the latest on the conflict and maintain a link with their readers. After the war, as the economic and technological hurdles fell away, the dailies, Sundays and Saturday football specials were able to produce in-depth previews and fast, comprehensive match reports. Already by 1895 the *News of the World* was devoting 14 per cent of its space to sport while the *Daily Mail* had a page of sport from its launch in 1896.

The Times did try its best to ignore football, claiming, for example, that the 1914 FA Cup Final was "of comparatively little interest except to the Lancashire working-classes", but it still employed a cricket correspondent from 1880.

The nationals could couple this coverage with other news that appealed to women, all but ignored both as participants and spectators in the sports press, thus providing a rounded product which, in their minds anyway, appealed to the whole family. The sports press simply couldn't compete. In the long run the football specials also turned out to be far more ephemeral than they appeared and it was their relationship with the thing they loved the most which killed them off. Unlike their European counterparts the papers grew on the back of football's rapidly increasing popularity in the 1890s and they focused almost exclusively on that one sport, paying little more than lip-service to others. The football leagues in Italy, Spain and France were all formed in the late 1920s and early 1930s, by which time their sports press was well established thanks to other sports (such as cycling). Football has come to dominate the European market too, but as it was a late entrant onto the scene it had to state its case for coverage and while it did so successfully the papers never forgot the sports that had served them so well before it came along. This was the undoing of the football specials in England. Once they came under sustained attack from other media and, most damagingly of all, changes to the regular kick-off times that they had insisted on a century previously, they had nothing else to fall back on. A few still survive but they are relics, serving only as reminders of the past.

Catton died in 1936 aged 76, and although his failing health had forced him to dramatically cut his work load, he was still filing free-lance copy for the *Glasgow Herald* and overseeing the records section of the *Wisden Cricketers' Almanac*. The country was hoping against hope it wasn't going to get drawn into another horrific conflict, but as glowing obituaries were being written for Catton, so they might equally have been for the English sporting press.

CHAPTER 3

HOLD THE FRONT ROW!

While there were many boffins trying to create a machine that could capture a moving image at the back end of the nineteenth century, it was Thomas Edison who was the first to project moving pictures in 1891. Made in his tar-paper-covered 'Black Maria' studio in West Orange, New Jersey, Edison's early films included his assistant Fred Ott sneezing, acts from Buffalo Bill's Wild West Show and, in 1884, footage of two cats, complete with tiny boxing gloves, fighting in a small boxing ring. Whatever you might think, it seems our obsession with animals doing stupid things was not born the day YouTube went live.

On 14 June the same year, Edison filmed a bout of six one-minute rounds between Mike Leonard and Jack Cushing,[1] then made it available at a cost of $22.50 per round, demonstrating once again how sport and the media could be brought together to generate profit even at this early stage. However, Edison's Kinetoscope machine was huge and so unwieldy that it couldn't be taken out of the studio. Furthermore, its projections could only be watched by one person at a time. As far as being the father of cinema, Edison was close but the cigar (or cigars) actually went to a pair of French brothers – Auguste and Louis Lumière – who recognised the limitations of Edison's device and overcame them with the Cinématographe, a portable machine which could film a moving image and also process and project it, preceding by more than 100 years the digital camera that lets you play back what you've just recorded. Throughout 1895 the Lumières displayed their films at various photographic societies before their

---

1 *If you're interested, 40 seconds of grainy footage from the fight is on YouTube.*

first public show in France on 28 December 1895. Two months later they repeated the show at the Regent Street Polytechnic in London and in May 1896 they took it to Birmingham's Empire Theatre where it was so popular it was rebooked. Cinema had arrived in Britain.

• • •

In those very early years films were initially shown at fairs, theatres and public halls, although before long buildings were being converted into rudimentary picture houses. These "penny gaffs" or "fleapits" were often shops that had had their windows blacked out and seats installed, but in a demonstration of cinema's growing dominance music halls, theatres and churches were also converted as they saw their own popularity slump. When it became clear the new-fangled invention was here for the long haul, small purpose-built cinemas sprung up in many communities. A commission in 1917 estimated that "half the entire population, men, women and children visit a cinematograph theatre once every week". Two years later the same number was going to the cinema *twice* a week. A shilling (5p) would get you a relatively good (but not the best) seat and half the audience paid even less than that. The cinema had all the benefits of the pub: it was warm, cheap, accessible and on top of that they had a bit of glamour thrown in. However unlike the pub and the music hall, cinemas didn't serve alcohol and this new leisure phenomenon was credited with reducing widespread drunkenness by chief constables and politicians alike, although they were still unrestrained and disorderly places. You might get annoyed when you're at the multiplex and someone's phone goes off or they dip into their nachos noisily, but that's nothing by comparison with the early fleapits where people would eat, sleep, talk and shout at the cinema screen with abandon. The darkness also encouraged "lewd acts" as young courting couples took the opportunity to engage in all sorts of XXX-rated activities, some even getting under the stage and being so vigorous they knocked the screen over.

However cinema was, unlike the pub or football, one of the few activities that husbands and wives attended together, thus breaking down early gender divisions that developed around other forms of leisure. Cinema-going became, like nipping down to the local for a swift one (or ten), a community activity attaining significant local status. Attendance was regular and habitual, quickly dominating working-class leisure and the life of the young. Women in particular flocked to the new picture halls as it presented them with one of the first collective escapes from the day-to-day grind and boredom of work whether at home or the factory. By 1914 there were about 3,000 cinemas around the country, a number that despite the Great War leapt to 4,000 in 1921 with contemporary estimations suggesting another 2,000 were needed to meet demand.

A building boom began and the old penny gaffs, more often than not structurally unsafe, were superseded by a wave of magnificent, lavish and modern new cathedrals to the moving image that were said to provide "acres of seats in a garden of dreams". The Alhambra in Birmingham was decorated like a Moorish courtyard with trailing vines along the walls, a ceiling painted like the sky and a glass-dome light mimicking the moon. "It was," said one patron, "like sitting in the open air at nighttime". Others had exteriors that would not have looked out of place on the Las Vegas Strip. Egyptian pyramids, Chinese pagodas and Jacobean manor houses sprung up all over the country while names like the Roxy, the Rialto and the Trocadero became part of everyday vocabulary, and despite the Depression and mass unemployment, people still flocked to them. Leisure was no longer considered the privilege of the wealthy few; it was seen as a right for everybody.

By the 1930s the talkies arrived (the police were needed to deal with the queues in several towns when they first appeared) and a second wave of cinema building had begun dispensing with the kitsch pyramids and instead utilising cutting-edge, art-deco architecture. Oscar Deutsch led the way by launching his Odeon chain and he soon owned 300 cinemas around the country. These new picture houses didn't just stay in the inner cities; they moved into the suburbs targeting middle-class women, with the knock-on effect of affording cinema widespread social acceptance. Although initially dismissed as "poor man's theatre", in 1932 an educational commission noted that "a fellow of an Oxford college no longer feels an embarrassed explanation to be necessary when he is recognised leaving a cinema".

However, a year later J.B. Priestley was less enamoured, bemoaning the fact that due to cinema's popularity Leicester had only one live theatre show on when he visited the town for his book *English Journey*.

The public desire for leisure was insatiable. By the mid-1930s Bolton, for example, had 47 cinemas within five miles of the town hall[2] and whatever Priestley thought, the picture house was leaving its rivals in its wake. By 1934 annual ticket sales had reached 903 million and by the onset of the Second World War weekly attendance had reached 23 million. The war initially brought a halt to cinemas, along with most other leisure activities, but they quickly reopened and the boom continued, with spending on all forms of leisure increasing by 120 per cent between 1938 and 1944. The record year for the cinema was 1946 when 1.635 *billion* tickets were sold and more than 75 per cent of the population visited the flicks. As astonishing as those figures are they were part of the continuing increase in the consumption of leisure generally. Newspaper circulations continued to rise (hitting their peak in the 1950s) and football attendance hit a record high of 41.25 million in the 1948/49 season. Even the amateur FA Cup was played in front of a sell-out 90,000 Wembley crowd and the fact that the popularity of football reached at an all-time high was in no small part due to the coverage it received in cinema newsreels.

● ● ●

Sport's link with film was always strong as it provided an opportunity to capture the human form in real movement. In the 1880s English photographer Eadweard Muybridge produced a significant body of work at the University of Pennsylvania including a study called *The Human Figure in Motion* that captured models (often naked and never more than partially clothed) engaging in a range of sports including among others football, cricket, boxing and fencing. However, while the machine he invented – the Zoopraxiscope – was the first projection device, he was actually a sequence photographer, capturing sequential still images with many cameras and then running them together to create the appearance of movement.

---

2   *It's little surprise that Leslie Halliwell, author of* Halliwell's Film Guide, *was born in Bolton and took almost daily trips to the pictures with his mother Lily when he was a child.*

The first true English effort, a sports film called *Cricketer Jumping over Garden Gate*, came along in March 1895 and was made by Robert Paul, an early rival to the Lumières. Okay, it's not strictly a sports film (in case you hadn't worked it out it was just some bloke dressed in cricket whites jumping over a gate) but it was a start. The following year Paul went to the Derby and filmed the Princes of Wales' horse Persimmon winning. Having processed the footage overnight, Paul presented the world's first ever sports bulletin the following day to an enthusiastic audience at Leicester Square's Alhambra Theatre of Varieties. In October of the same year Paul recorded the first ever film of a football game in Newcastle upon Tyne, although it no longer exists and there is no record of which teams were playing. The earliest surviving football footage resides in the Lumière collection and is of a practice match in London (possibly involving Woolwich Arsenal) in late 1897. It doesn't show any genuine action, with most of the players being bunched around one goal (which itself is not fully on screen) possibly because the cameraman, Alexandre Promio, wanted to get as many players as he could into the shot.

The difficulties of filming with the earliest cameras can be seen in the minute of footage that survives from the first actual game filmed; Blackburn Rovers' 4-0 home win over West Bromwich Albion in September 1898. The technology wouldn't allow for shots from the stand so cameraman Arthur Cheetham was stationed behind one goal and most of what we can see is of the players off in the distance. Furthermore, given the very high cost of film, cameramen were rationed to filming on a 2:1 basis, that is using 500ft of film to create a 250ft (or one-minute clip), so it was rare in those early days that goals were captured and if they were it was by sheer luck. One of the first regularly to film football was Jasper Redfern, a Sheffield-based optician who turned his hand to filmmaking. He followed his local team Sheffield United around the country and made the first film of an FA Cup Final in 1899 when United beat Derby 4-1. The footage has since been lost but a description of it survives and it shows that already audiences were being presented with more than just film from a static camera, instead getting a rudimentary highlights package with a narrative structure including the beginning and end of the game, a balance between the teams and some crowd footage:

> The Sheffield United players and officials entering the field;
> Mid-field play; Sheffield obtains a corner, showing goal play,
> scrimmage and goal kick; Derby County's only goal, showing
> other goal, enthusiasm of the vast audience, goal keeper busy;
> Players leaving the field.

Having the players entering the field towards the camera was important as it allowed their faces to be seen, heightening the local appeal of the films. Initially at least, it was something the players clearly weren't used to and they had to be directed onto the pitch either by the cameraman's assistant or sometimes just pegs in the ground. The increased presence of filmmakers was noted in an *Athletic News* report from a Merseyside derby in 1902 which stated that the players "filed onto the pitch one after another to please the cinematograph operator". Already at this early stage of their relationship, football was being manipulated by the needs of the camera and the theatre of players entering the pitch in an organised fashion has become a standard feature of football matches as a consequence.

While the major London-based companies began to focus on the big games such as the FA Cup Final, there was also demand from travelling showmen and local entrepreneurs who would commission filmmakers to capture local footage that they could present at fairs. To ensure they enticed the crowds these had a strong emphasis on the local events and there was nothing that appealed to such parochial sensibilities more than football. This growing industry was particularly strong in the North West of England and was dominated by Norden Films run by Saga Mitchell and James Kenyon. The Mitchell and Kenyon Collection, as it has become widely known, spent more than seven decades collecting dust in the cellar of what used to be the pair's shop at 40 Northgate in Blackburn. Then in 1994 workmen renovating the building unearthed the collection, but unless a home could be found for them, the three large metal drums containing 800 rolls of old film were headed for the skip. Thankfully local enthusiast Peter Worden stepped in to take ownership. Worden struggled for the next seven years trying to clean and catalogue the films before realising it was too great a task for a private individual. He gifted the collection to the British Film Institute and it has since been added to UNESCO's

UK Memory of the World Register alongside such documents as the Magna Carta. Mitchell and Kenyon weren't pioneers but the collection is significant because of its size, quality and depth – 28 hours' worth of virtually pristine negatives mostly filmed between 1900 and 1907.

Among the footage of workers leaving their factories, processions, chaotic Lancashire street scenes and people at the seaside, are 55 films of 32 football games. There are also 18 films of 10 matches from rugby's Northern Union that had split from the Rugby Union in 1895 and would become the Rugby League in 1922. The fact there are fewer rugby games and that filming of them appears to have stopped in 1902 provides further evidence of football's inexorable march to dominance. Mitchell and Kenyon's football films suffer from similar technological limitations to others made at the time – rarely were more than two cameras used and these were in fixed positions. Passages of play were short and ill-connected and it would be about 20 years before the camera could follow the ball over any distance. The limited amount of film available to cameramen meant key moments were missed and the focus was on areas of the pitch where most action was likely to take place like the goal, but even then the passage of play that led to a shot was often missed. The film is best used by the modern viewer only as a historical document. The games were significantly rougher than those played today. Goalkeepers rarely caught the ball, as they could still be shoulder-charged by the opposition, so instead they often opted to punch it away. There were few appeals to the referees (dressed to the nines in suit, shirt, tie and cap) and these were polite enquiries as to whether it was a goal kick or a corner, not high-pressure Roy Keane in-your-face moments. Similarly celebrations were also more restrained than they tend to be in the modern game.

Another form of media developing at the time was advertising. The economy was growing on the back of mass-production techniques, increased wages and the subsequent demand for goods and services. What better place to advertise than at a football match where you had a captive audience for 90 minutes? The Collection shows that in the early 1900s clubs had already developed a relatively sophisticated approach to ground advertising. Most adverts were local; for the theatre, local ales or shops in town; and these tended to be on stand roofs suggesting they were permanent or, at least, long term. However, there was advertising of national brands too, like Fry's Chocolate, Bird's Custard or the football fan's favourite, Bovril. These tended to be placed on hoardings around the pitch, suggesting it was recognised they were only temporary or irregular.

While Mitchell and Kenyon's work doesn't provide an accurate record of the games themselves, it does provide an accurate record of how the game was portrayed and packaged to a wider audience. The footage tends to follow a similar narrative structure to Redfern's 1899 FA Cup Final film, with the teams always first shown coming onto the pitch and the crowd being given equal prominence to the players. The majority of fans shown in the films are men between their teens and their fifties from the upper-working or lower-middle class. However, contemporary records show there was not insignificant attendance by both the middle classes and women. In all likelihood they were in the main stands – the one area of the stadia the filmmakers tended not to film. The focus on the crowd broadly and the popular sides in particular had a purely economic motivation. Southern-based Cecil Hepworth was a master of so-called 'factory-gate' films, arguing, "A film showing workers leaving a factory will gain far greater popularity in the town where it was taken than the most exciting picture ever produced. The workers come in hundreds, with all their friends and relations, and the film more than pays for itself the first night." The desire to film football crowds had the same motivation but crucially, by placing fans at the centre of the action, the films generated and reinforced their emotional 'ownership' of the game. This is something that fans have clung on to ever since, despite their lack of more concrete forms of economic and political control asserted by the sport's governing bodies and individual clubs' directors and owners.

The popularity of these 'actualities' or 'topicals' coupled with a network of cinemas across the country and, more importantly, an audience to fill them saw the French company Pathé launch its *Animated Gazette* in 1910. The likes of Mitchell and Kenyon had filmed newsworthy events but these weren't presented with any sense of urgency or on a regular basis. The *Animated Gazette* was born of the cinema but it clearly replicated newspapers in providing a similar news service and, due to the largely low-quality of photo-journalism provided by the papers, the newsreels became a sensation with a public that wanted to see as well as read about their sporting heroes. Released twice a week, the newsreels were about eight minutes long and each had about four to eight items in them. From the very start sport became a key element – the Oxford University Eight's rowing trial was filmed for Pathé's first edition – and football, rugby, racing, boxing and to a lesser extent cricket became staple ingredients of the newsreel diet, providing as much as 40 per cent of the content depending on the company and the time of year (around 20 per cent of surviving newsreel footage covers sport).

Occasionally the menu served up richer fare by providing a sneaky peak at more socially exclusive events such as Wimbledon, Royal Ascot and the Oxford and Cambridge Boat Race. Along with the coverage the events got on the radio, this cemented their position in the country's sporting calendar. That calendar was important for the filmmakers because, like Royal engagements, sport provided a steady stream of scheduled events which tended to be outdoors – important, as the cameras of the day were too bulky to transport quickly to breaking news events and struggled to deal with the lack of light indoors.

• • •

The First World War honed filming techniques and the 1920s cinema boom ensured newsreels would become an even bigger business. While they could provide pictures, they couldn't match newspapers for speed, so instead they played up the drama. As objective journalism was sacrificed for the desire to provide an exciting narrative, football was on hand with highly visual, action-filled, competitive and often dramatic content played out by recognisable characters. In short, the sport was a ready-made soap opera and its storyline was constructed in the cutting room. A significant amount of film was never shown, and, if required, library footage was used or the chronology of a match rearranged. If the newsreels were to be believed there was never a dull game, the drama being heightened by repeating exciting incidents and utilising footage of cheering crowds. Just like their predecessors, the newsreels were not unbiased historical records. They focused on high-profile clubs and matches or games with an amusing storyline that were often pre-selected prior to the event. These included charity matches between professionals and entertainers (ring any bells?) as well as regular coverage of the few annual Shrovetide folk football games continuing around the country. Much as they are today, these were presented as a humorous historical oddity with a puzzling lack of rules, thus hiding the relatively organised nature and cultural importance such games had in the past.

Until the 1950s the cinemas through the newsreels provided the only means of watching football other than attending a live match. This was something which made the Football League very nervous. There was usually some coverage of the build-up to each new season as well as the opening day's games but, fearful that their gate receipts might decrease and clubs might lose money, the League was relatively uncooperative with the newsreel companies although there was no outright ban on filming. As a consequence the majority of football coverage focused on the FA Cup, which provided exactly the right level of spectacle and excitement for the newsreels with its knockout format. It also provided lower-league clubs with a rare chance to be filmed if drawn against more glamorous opposition, although they were stereotyped as "under dogs", "giant killers" or "plucky losers", depending on the result. The regional nature of the competition was played up in an attempt to maintain the interest of all fans all the way to the final even if their team had been knocked out. Often ties were billed as "North v South" clashes and the victory parade of the winning team was always filmed and broadcast. By 1927 *The Times* had labelled the FA Cup Final as the "most important event in British sport", which was some turnaround from its position just 13 years earlier when it dismissed it as being of little importance to all but the fans of the two teams involved. The nature and scale of this heightened early focus on the FA Cup has framed the narratives around the competition in the decades since and ensured it has a special place in the hearts not just of football fans but of the country as a whole, explaining why it has had greater importance than cup competitions in other countries.

Technical limitations also created problems when it came to the coverage of football in Wales, Scotland and Northern Ireland, and the London-centric nature of British culture didn't help. The earlier onset of darkness in Scotland and the distance required to courier film to London restricted coverage to home internationals and the Scottish Cup Final (which benefitted from the popularity of the FA Cup Final). While the other nations of Britain got limited screen time, European football struggled to get any at all, reinforcing English football's insularity. Increasingly the newsreel firms were American-owned so, beyond domestic football, they had a bias towards sports that were popular across the Atlantic such as golf, boxing and tennis, this coming at the expense of coverage of European football and sport from Empire countries. Even cricket struggled because of its complex rules and long, drawn-out, relatively action-free matches.

• • •

As had happened with the newspaper industry a few years earlier, football soon became a commodity in its own right for the film industry. The newsreel companies were no longer using the sport simply as a means of showing off the capabilities of their technology; they were using it to maximise their sales and generate profit. In short they wanted their footage to be exclusive and they were willing to pay for the privilege. The increasing importance and value of moving footage of sport can be seen by the dramatic rise of the cost of filming games at Twickenham. When the Rugby Union sold the photographic rights for matches at the ground in 1929 they accepted £85 for still images and £52 for moving images. Three years later they secured £85 and £90 respectively and in 1931 after the introduction of sound, the still-photo package commanded £90 while the value of the moving-picture package had shot up to £150.

Those prices paled in comparison to the amounts of cash the newsreel companies were throwing at rugby's sexier sibling, football. As early as 1923 the FA had sold the rights for the FA Cup Final – the first at the recently opened Empire Stadium (that's Wembley in new money) – for just under £1,000 to Topical Budget, the Sky Sports of the day. The company had already coughed up for 'exclusive' footage of the 1920 final at Stamford Bridge and advertised its coverage of the 1921 final as "the greatest event in soccer history", demonstrating that hype is not a modern phenomenon. Whether Tottenham's 1-0 win against Wolves lived up to the billing is debatable but Topical certainly upped their game by sending nine cameramen to the match. Not only did they get footage of the goal – from no less than two separate angles – they were also able to film from the stands, creating 'master shots' of the ground and the crowd which *The Bioscope* magazine noted were "very cleverly put together to form a continuous 'story'".

Unfortunately stumping up the cash for exclusive rights didn't actually guarantee exclusive footage and rival companies devised ever more ingenious ways of filming 'pirate' film, which led to the rights holders devising ever more ways to stop them. Initially the French Debrie Sept camera, which allowed the photographer to take still and moving images, was the weapon of choice as it could be easily smuggled into grounds under a jacket or coat. However Topical took to employing heavies to patrol the ground looking for people surreptitiously taking footage. This in turn led to cameramen perching on nearby buildings or even erecting scaffolding so that they could take long-lens footage. Topical countered this by blocking their rivals' views with flags and balloons and using mirrors to reflect sunlight into their lenses. However, thanks to cinema itself Pathé's Jack Cotter would become the most infamous football-film pirate of all.

Born in 1892, Cotter secured his first job as a projectionist at Woolwich's Palace Theatre and, following service in the balloon section of the Royal Flying Corps during the First World War, he returned to the film industry working as a cameraman for Topical. By 1922 he had moved to their rivals Pathé for whom he created his most ingenious scoop. For the 1923 Cup Final between West Ham and Bolton Wanderers, Cotter fashioned a giant hammer from wood, painted it claret and blue with the words "Play Up Hammers" in white, and hid his camera inside. Completing the look with cap, glasses and a false moustache, he strode nonchalantly into Wembley and filmed the match. Adding salt into Topical's wounds he was filmed after the event revealing his cunning ruse, ensuring his place in the history of football media. Cotter's employers added to his footage with aerial shots filmed from the Pathé Autogyro (the Sky Copter *du jour*). In a countermeasure that at least guaranteed some free publicity from the pirated footage, Topical had written its name on the roof of the stadium's stands. The following year the three leading newsreel companies called a truce, making a joint offer for the Cup Final rights to the FA of just £400, an offer that was politely declined. Despite this rebuff, cameramen from all three companies managed to sneak into the ground and film the game anyway. In 1926 Pathé paid £800 for the rights and the price rose progressively over the following ten years until in 1936 the FA turned down £2,000 and decided to film the Final itself, distributing the footage directly to the cinemas and cutting out the middleman.

By the 1930s the newsreels were also attempting to generate publicity for their footage by questioning referees' decisions. They didn't attack the officials with anything like the vigour commentators, pundits and managers do today but it was an excuse to publicise the technology at their disposal – particularly slow motion – and create anticipation before their film was shown at the cinemas. The 1932 FA Cup Final became known as the "over-the-line" final thanks in no small part to the cinema coverage of it. British Movietone News' footage seemed to support Arsenal's claims that the ball had gone out of play before Newcastle's Jack Allen hammered a first-half equaliser at the near post. The film, which mixed voiceover with captions, signposted the incident: "Allen's disputed goal for Newcastle, question being: Did Boyd cross the line before passing?" The incident was then replayed after a second caption: "See it once again from position commanding the goal-line." The goal was then shown a third time with the caption "... and in slow motion" after which a curiously disembodied Geordie voice gave the opinion that "It's a goal why aye, man!" Allen went on to seal Newcastle's victory in the second half, but the newsreel had defined the story of the match. The papers lapped up the controversy and on the Monday after the game the *Daily Herald* ran the headline: "Cup Final goal was not a goal. Film proves it – yet it must stand". The incident also dominated the *Manchester Guardian*'s report that focused as much on the footage (yet to be shown at cinemas) as the goal itself. Their reporter revealed how the film was stopped "by a clever device for several seconds" and even questioned the referee W.P. Harper at his home. The paper also got quotes from Newcastle's manager Andy Cunningham, who deployed a tactic which has been used by the men in the dugout ever since, saying simply: "From my position I could not see whether it had gone out of play or not."

• • •

This commercial imperative meant the film producers were under great pressure to provide what the public wanted, or at least what the cinema owners told them the public wanted. In 1934 the editor of British Paramount News had written "nothing must be included that the average man will not like". It probably goes without saying that this left a fairly short list and items deemed acceptable were chosen because of their inoffensiveness and broad appeal. Cinema's influence was fully appreciated from its earliest days. There were regular debates in Parliament on its possible effects, as well as national and local inquiries, and the National Council on Public Morals (a coalition of religious, educational and political groups) expressed concern that children would replicate the behaviour they saw on screen. The 1909 Cinematograph Act gave local authorities the right to license cinemas and although it was intended to be used to ensure safety[3] it was so loosely worded that it effectively gave them powers of censorship too. With 700 separate authorities to deal with, the film companies were concerned that inconsistency would undermine the profitability of their films. They grouped together to establish the British Board of Film Censors (BBFC) which, while independent, had close links to government and regulated all films by a standard set of criteria. Soon authorities were not censoring films themselves but simply licensing ones that had been passed by the BBFC. On one hand the Board wanted to keep the Government out of the film industry, on the other it wanted to reassure them it was not inflaming or corrupting the public and adopted a very conservative attitude. Films that dealt with issues such as the economic downturn of the 1930s and the resulting unemployment in a humorous or uncontroversial way, like George Formby's 1935 release *Off the Dole*, were passed with no problems. However, an attempt to adapt Walter Greenwood's best-selling novel

3   Early film was made from highly flammable cellulose nitrate which when coupled with the heat of the projectors had led to several fatal fires.

Love on the Dole that dealt with the same issue in much more hard-hitting fashion, was vetoed for several years by the BBFC, which called it "a very sordid story in very sordid surroundings".

Newsreels were no different in this respect to fictional films and what they showed and the narratives they used were selected and shaped by a set of pre-determined policies subject to censorship and profit margins. While they reflected and highlighted popular attitudes, newsreels did so in a way that generated support and consensus for the establishment's ideology by re-emphasising exactly who the social elites were. The image of England and Britain they presented (and more often than not the line between the two was blurred) was one of an orderly society built on consensus, not conflict. If there was a problem the suggestion was everyone should meet it with typical English/British good humour and while the toffs might be in charge they still wanted the best for everyone. Or to put it another way: keep calm and carry on.

Nowhere was this more apparent than in the coverage of football. Following the First World War sporting events became an increasingly regular addition to the list of Royal engagements and football, particularly the FA Cup Final, was top of that list. Attendance at such an important game placed the Royals at the heart of English cultural life, implying they were a 'normal' family enjoying 'normal' events. It also conferred greater legitimacy on football as the country's most important sport. The newsreels lapped it up. Royal and sporting engagements were both hugely important for them and when the two came together it was, well, the match of the day. Images of the crowd celebrating the King's attendance and of the King shaking hands with the teams became a regular part of the Cup Final 'story'. If the King wasn't free or if the game wasn't as important, a minor Royal, mayor or other dignitary would do. It all helped reinforce the country's social hierarchy both nationally and locally.

Once the meet and greet was out of the way it was almost time for the match but first another standard image had to be captured – the two captains tossing the coin and shaking hands with each other and the referee. During the First World War Winston Churchill had compared the conflict to a Test match, calling not just for victory but a victory won in the spirit of fair play. The ethos of 'sportsmanship' or 'fair play' was a crucial component in the construction of "Englishness", enhancing the sense of national superiority while also reminding the working classes that they too should abide by the rules. Of course, the same couldn't be said for Johnny Foreigner. Teams from abroad were afforded the minimum of respect at the best of times, with commentators often making fun of the players' 'strange' names, and the matches were used as an opportunity to re-emphasise the notion of English fair play. Conversely, European teams, it was suggested, regularly resorted to foul play and lost their temper. When Italy, the reigning World Champions, visited England in 1934 *Universal News* framed their coverage of the match in that manner. The match remains notorious for the level of violence on display and the footage focused on the visitors' behaviour. "The Italian temperament is showing", the viewers were told, but the fact that it was England who had set the tone of the game in the second minute when a Ted Drake tackle broke centre-half Luis Monti's foot passed with little mention (I'm sure Drake simply wasn't 'that sort of player'). This was in the days before substitutes and despite their defeat the Italians were heralded as the Lions of Highbury on their return home. The previous year when England travelled to play Italy in Rome the *Universal News* commentator labelled the home fans "excitable" as they celebrated a goal, explaining that "when Italians go wild, there's no half-measures about them". Some 20 years later Pathé was still referring to Italian footballers as "athletes from spaghetti land". Such stereotyping lives on in the pub vocabulary that infuses football commentary today. During the Italy v Germany Euro 2012 semi-final, BBC pundit Martin Keown referred to the Italians as "emotional" (and the Germans, rather predictably, as a "machine") while some English TV pundits would have us believe that Mario Balotelli is the only player in the world with a 'suspect temperament' and that there is something dubious about the fact Ronaldo combs his hair.

There was a surprisingly large amount of time devoted to women's football by the newsreels, with some estimates suggesting as much as 5 per cent of the total football coverage focused on women. At first glance this might seem to run counter to the idea of preserving the status quo, not least following the FA's effective ban on women's football in 1921, and to a certain extent it did. However, it was still viewed through the prism of male dominance, mimicking the way women were portrayed in fictional films. Gracie Fields was the undoubted star of the 1934 hit *Sing as We Go,* playing the working-class heroine who retains her pluck despite being laid off when the factory she works in is closed down. The whole thing ends with the factory reopening (and the Union Jack flying); however, this is not due to Gracie but instead to the efforts of a scientist who I'm sure you can guess was English, male and middle class. So the newsreels' narratives subtly and not-so-subtly continued to remind the viewers that football was really a man's game. Coverage of the women's game was patronising and critical and laced with sexual innuendo, while women players were described in unfeminine terms such as "hefty", "braw lassies" or "fine strapping girls".

Cinema's dominance evaporated when television brought the moving image into the comfort of the viewer's own home and the hire-purchase revolution facilitated mass-ownership of the new product. The newsreels were the real casualties of the battle, limping on into the late 1960s before finally dying out. They leave behind them a rich legacy and not just a fascinating archive of football's past. It's impossible to understand TV's coverage of the sport today without also understanding newsreel coverage of the game. It developed many of the techniques and laid down the templates that have defined the structure and narratives used in TV broadcasts for decades since. More than that, through their focus on the crowd the newsreels made football the people's game, securing its place at the heart of England's cultural landscape.

CHAPTER 4

BACK TO SQUARE ONE?

Football fans in England had to wait a little under 18 months after Armistice Day for the first inter-war FA Cup Final. On 24 April 1920, Aston Villa beat Second Division Huddersfield (who gained promotion in the same season) thanks to a solitary extra-time goal from Billy Kirton.[1] The Villa fans who didn't make the trip down south to Stamford Bridge to see their side lift the trophy for a record sixth time might have found out the result in the hour after the final whistle from a notice posted in the local newspaper office. For a full match report they'd have had to wait until early evening and the publication of one of the many football specials. In 1939 when Portsmouth trounced Wolverhampton 4-1 in the last final before the Second World War, the Pompey supporters who weren't among the 99,370 watching the match at the Empire Stadium in Wembley will almost certainly have been following the action live on a wireless. The transformation brought about in those 19 years by the new medium was huge. England's first radio station was a couple of months away from its first broadcast when Kirton bagged the winner for Villa. When Pompey celebrated victory more than eight million radio licences had been bought and at least 71 per cent of the population had access to a radio set. The spoken word was beginning to reassert its authority over the written word. It all began in slightly less auspicious surroundings – an ex-army hut in Writtle near Essex to be exact. It was from there that Guglielmo Marconi, an Italian-born scientist, launched England's first radio station, 2MT. Often credited with inventing radio, Marconi in

---

1   *The Geordie joined Villa from Leeds United for £500 earlier that season having played just one game for the Lillywhites. Coincidentally he'd also play just one game for England, grabbing their only goal in a 1-1 draw with Northern Ireland in 1922.*

reality brought together the work of many others, including Heinrich Hertz, Michael Faraday and Nikola Tesla, to create the first viable wireless communication system that could produce modulated sound waves, thus allowing for voice and music to be transmitted and not just short, sharp bursts of sound like Morse code. At 7.10pm on 15 June 1920, the few people lucky enough to own or be near a receiver could tune into a pre-recorded concert of operatic music, including a performance from Dame Nellie Melba that ended with the national anthem. It was a short concert; in those very early days Marconi was restricted to broadcasting for just half an hour every week; however, by 1922, 2MT had started daily half-hour bulletins of news and entertainment. The commercial potential of the new medium was becoming apparent and Marconi entered into negotiations with several other interested parties to establish a network of stations across the country under an umbrella organisation called the British Broadcasting Company (BBC). In May 1922, the company launched two new stations in London and Manchester (called 2LO and 2ZY respectively). The company's aim was to cash in by selling wireless sets but they wouldn't shift many units if there was nothing to listen to, so they began the process of filling the airwaves with appealing content designed to make people turn on, tune in and shell out. As with the newspapers and cinema newsreels before, sport was immediately central to the radio companies' drive to maximise sales and generate profit, and once again it reinforced gender divisions. A wireless set was the first piece of domestic electrical equipment many families owned and it would be followed by items like vacuum cleaners, washing machines, fridges and cookers. Marketing for those latter items focused on how they helped enhance the supposedly feminine realm of the kitchen. Adverts for radios focused on how they enhanced the supposedly masculine world of leisure. A 1930 advert for a Pye Portable Radio pictured a man below the words: "Tense with excitement ... thrilled. Almost seeing the game, so clearly does he hear it. Can you wonder what he shouts?" The advert provided the answer too, courtesy of a speech bubble: "Shoot, man! Shoot!"

Sports content was central to the drive to sell radios. On the very first day of its existence 2LO broadcast the first rudimentary running sports commentary with coverage of Ted 'Kid' Lewis' unsuccessful challenge of World and European Light Heavyweight champion George Carpentier at London's Olympia Exhibition Centre. While the owners of the BBC saw the new technology as a blessing, the Newspaper Proprietors' Association (NPA) saw the threat to their monopoly on the dissemination of information at a local and national level as a curse. The NPA's chairman, Lord Riddell, left little doubt about his feelings, labelling radio "modern witchcraft". When he subsequently appeared in front of the Government's Sykes Committee on broadcasting in 1923 he argued that the "broadcasting of racing and football results and similar matter would certainly seriously interfere with the sale of newspapers". Lord Riddell and his newspaper colleagues were particularly worried about the threat to the Saturday football specials. Even after the widespread introduction of the telegraph, telephone and other developments like the linotype machine and web-fed rotary press, the specials were hard pushed to get comprehensive match reports on the streets much before 7pm. On the other hand radio could provide on-the-spot immediacy. This was clearly demonstrated in 1936 when a young Richard Dimbleby reported live on the Crystal Palace fire from a phone box. With the drama happening at 10pm, after the evening papers had been published and some time before the morning editions would hit the streets, it was the BBC's first genuine scoop. With the advent of the car radio and the transistor, listeners weren't tied to their armchairs anymore either. The internet gets the blame for undermining the newspaper industry but the seeds of its decline were sown when radio became the first rival medium able to provide news at a faster pace. Television, the web and Twitter have just followed in its wake.

The BBC didn't get much support from sports governing bodies either. Just like the newspaper owners, those in charge of television were suspicious of radio, believing that live broadcasts would impact negatively on attendances. Similarly the General Post Office, which controlled communication technology in the late nineteenth and early twentieth centuries, cut the BBC no slack as it derived substantial income from press telegrams and was inclined to protect the hand that fed it. Lord Riddell and his chums won the day, and the BBC was subject to very stringent restrictions that effectively thwarted the broadcasting of any live news or sports for the next five years. Even sports bulletins relaying results were not allowed before 7pm. In 1925 the BBC tried and failed to negotiate permission to broadcast coverage of an England v Scotland rugby match, the FA Cup Final, the Derby and the Oxbridge Boat Race. The following year while still effectively banned from providing spoken commentary the BBC was allowed to broadcast "atmospheric" coverage of the Derby from Epsom. It was a disaster. The 1928 *BBC Handbook* described how heavy rain fell all day, meaning that when the race finally got underway "not only were there no sounds from hoofs in the soft going, but even the bookies and tipsters were more occupied in taking shelter under their umbrellas than in speeding home the winner".

In America, by contrast, audiences had been tuning into daily sports reports since 1924 and coast-to-coast coverage of major Gridiron games and boxing bouts was the norm from 1926. The country's newspapers embraced the new technology, with many setting up their own radio stations. In fact in the early 1920s sports fans all over the former colonies were enjoying radio sports coverage. The list included horse racing, cricket and Rugby League Down Under; field hockey in Canada; and rugby in New Zealand and South Africa. In August 1926 the Irish station 2RN covered the All-Ireland Hurling semi-final between Kilkenny and Galway at Dublin's Croke Park. It was the first live commentary on a field game in Europe.

The deadlock between the BBC and the NPA was finally broken in 1926 when the Crawford Committee on broadcasting recommended that on renewal of its licence, the BBC should become a nationalised company but with an independent board of governors free of government control. So the British Broadcasting Company became the British Broadcasting *Corporation* on 1 January 1927 and, significantly, the new company was given permission by the Postmaster-General to provide outside broadcasts. However, this did nothing to soften the stance of the NPA, which included racing and betting news along with birth control in a list of subjects that "would be highly objectionable to a large section of the community" if broadcast. Arguing that their monopoly on information would be destroyed by radio, they continued to fight for, and won, restrictive conditions on the newly formed BBC. The new running commentaries were recorded live but only broadcast after 6pm. Furthermore, as a

sop to the NPA, the BBC warned shopkeepers and pub landlords not
to listen to sports bulletins and commentaries in the earshot of their
customers as this would breach copyright.

• • •

The BBC quickly took advantage of their new-found freedom and on
15 January 1927[2] they broadcast commentary of an England versus
Wales Rugby Union match from Twickenham. A week later came
the first running commentary on a football match when the second
half of Arsenal's League game against Sheffield United at Highbury
was broadcast. An FA Cup tie between Corinthians and Newcastle
followed and the football season ended with the first ever broadcast
of an FA Cup Final. It's significant that it was also the first Cup Final
to include pre-match community singing, which the *Radio Times*
advertised a week earlier as "the largest demonstration this country
has ever beheld". 'Abide with Me' was included at the behest of FA
Secretary Sir Fredrick Wall, who knew it was a favourite of King
George V, and its rich, stirring lyrics created a communal atmosphere
knitting together both teams' fans and the rest of the country.

Creating a sense of national community was central to the public
service ethos of the BBC's first Director General, Lord Reith, who
claimed it would allow listeners to be "present equally at functions
and ceremonials upon which national sentiment is consecrated". He
also recognised sport's capacity to bring the country together through
such "national" events. However, these events had to be established
and it was the BBC that took on the responsibility for doing so by
bringing several of them together in a secular calendar complete
with 'seasons' and 'special days' which were (and still are) repeated
year after year, thus becoming 'traditional'. The Royal Variety Performance, The Lord Mayor's Show, The Last Night of the Proms,
Remembrance Day and Trooping of the Colour became prominent
features of the BBC schedule (and so English culture) and in 1932,

---

2   *It was a pretty big year for firsts. Charles Lindbergh made the first solo transatlantic flight.
Walter S. Gifford of AT&T and Sir Evelyn V. Murray of the General Post Office decided to take
the safer option and just share the first transatlantic telephone call, and to cap it all off* The Jazz
Singer, *starring Al Jolson, introduced cinema audiences to the 'talkies'.*

after nine years of trying, Reith finally managed to persuade King George V to broadcast a Christmas message. The script, written by Rudyard Kipling, declared Christmas to be a "festival of the family" and here was the King, both the head of the country's most important family and the figurative father of the nation, speaking from his home and promoting a sense of national community among the disparate listeners. What has now become a traditional event deeply rooted in England's, indeed Britain's cultural landscape was entirely manufactured by the media.

Sixteen years after George V's momentous broadcast, T.S. Eliot defined culture as a "whole way of life of a people from birth to grave". For the English this way of life included "Derby Day, Henley Regatta, Cowes, the twelfth of August, a cup final, the dog races, the pin table, the dart board, Wensleydale cheese, boiled cabbage cut into sections, beetroot in vinegar, nineteenth century Gothic churches and the music of Elgar". Widespread interest in Gothic churches and Elgar might have diminished a little since Eliot's day but thanks to Wallace and Gromit, Wensleydale cheese is still up there, and thanks to broadcasting so is the importance of sports events like the Derby and the Cup Final.

For most people these sports only gained significance *because* they were broadcast and the decision on which sports were chosen was made by an unashamedly elitist group of middle- and upper-class men at the Beeb. The flipside, of course, was that they were also choosing which sports *not* to broadcast. In the late 1920s the American innovation of circular dog tracks was introduced across England, and the sport became hugely popular. By 1932 some 6.5 million people were attending greyhound meetings in London alone but the sport was all but ignored by the BBC who argued it was not a 'national' sport and encouraged 'un-social' gambling. The same could be said about horse racing but that didn't stop the BBC making that a central part of the new broadcasting calendar. While the broadcaster did play down horse racing's gambling links by ignoring starting prices, betting odds and any mention of bookmakers in their commentaries, just as important was the class composition of the two sports' followers. While the upper classes enjoyed the sport of kings, the working classes were going to the dogs.

As with newsreels, the BBC's concept of 'national identity' was very English. Football commentators were instructed to take a neutral stance on club matches; however, commentary on England games was supposed to build partisanship in the listener while maintaining a veneer of neutrality. When England competed against the other nations of the United Kingdom the required balance was even more delicate and, at times, uneasy, while in commentary on Scotland matches against non-UK teams, the balance between commitment and distance often depended upon how well the Scots were doing. It's a template that, by and large, remains in use today. The BBC's sense of the nation was also very London-centric. While there were some regional early evening programmes like *Midland Sport* and the *London Sports Bulletin*, most broadcasts ignored traditional local sports by focusing on events in, or close to the capital. Thus sports broadcasts fostered a clear idea of which sports and events were deemed to be 'national', thereby making them central to English culture.

Take for example knur-and-spell. Heard of it? Didn't think so. It's a sport which involves hitting a small ball (the knur) as far as possible with a bat (the spell) after it has been released by a spring-loaded cup. It has its origins in the Norse game *nurspel*, and drew huge crowds, particularly in the North of England, well into the 1930s. However, because it was a regional, working-class sport it was marginalised by the BBC. At the same time equally parochial sports with upper- and upper-middle-class associations that took place in London, such as Wimbledon and the Boat Race, became a central part of the company's manufactured sporting calendar and so a key part of the nation's culture. In 1939 Hilda Jennings and Winifred Gill's survey of the impact of broadcasting on the lives of people living in a working-class area of Bristol demonstrated the centrality of radio in creating this calendar. One respondent said about the Boat Race: "Look how that's come to the fore, we never used to hear anything about that, and now there's many wouldn't miss it." By 1930 the race had been labelled an "old favourite" in the *BBC Yearbook* and it was being broadcast annually along with five other events which the Postmaster-General would later make subject to a non-exclusivity arrangement following the creation of ITV in 1955. The agreement was designed to protect the BBC from commercial pressure and from that point no broadcaster could have sole rights to the Boat Race, Test matches, Wimbledon, the FA Cup Final, the Derby or the Grand National. The latter four are still subject to regulation that means they have to be broadcast on free-to-air TV. Yet, like the Christmas message, there is nothing 'natural' or 'obvious' about the supposed importance of these events. Instead that importance was created by a set of converging factors, namely the organisation of sport and its coverage in the media.

· · ·

While Lord Reith was determined for the BBC to become the voice of the nation and to entertain its listeners, he also believed the broadcaster had a duty to enhance its listeners' cultural horizons. He didn't want the audience just to listen to sport; he wanted them to learn about sport too, as long as what was being taught promoted the "right" social attitudes. To this end a series of programmes, such as *Association Football, the Referee and the Spectator* which were broadcast in September 1932 and focused on the need for players to accept the referee's decision as final, were made. However, one thing that was considered not to promote the "right" social attitudes was professional sport. As late as 1948 an internal BBC document stressed the importance of promoting "humble endeavour, good sportsmanship and no transfer fee" in the "reputable sports world" of golf, tennis, rowing and "something called rugger". Football was conspicuous by its absence from the list.

In radio's early years the sport had enjoyed a considerable, albeit intermittent, amount of coverage thanks to good relationships between some BBC staff and administrators at the FA and at several League clubs. By 1931 more than 100 matches had been broadcast but once these broadcasts began, concern was expressed almost immediately, with *All Sports Weekly* magazine reporting in March 1927 that some clubs "had a bitter mind against it". Just over a year later the members of the Third Division (North) called on the League and the FA to ban commentaries, claiming they were keeping fans away from other games, especially those of smaller clubs. In many ways it's an argument that's still being had today – for radio in the early twentieth century read foreign decoders in the early twenty-first century. In 2012 Portsmouth pub landlady Karen Murphy had her conviction for showing Greek coverage of the Premier League quashed. During her six-year battle, then-Sunderland chairman Niall Quinn backed the Premier League's stance, saying he "despised" fans who watched such broadcasts in pubs and claiming they were undermining clubs' attempts to progress. Yet research for the European Commission in 2004 showed that only 6 per cent of fans in England cited TV coverage as the reason they didn't watch games at stadia. The most common reason, given by 39 per cent of respondents, was ticket prices. There's no evidence that coverage of matches on radio affected attendances in the 1920s either. The new medium reinforced the place of football at the heart of English culture, as one commentator from the time wrote: "It would be interesting to know if evening papers ever noted that those coming away from a cup tie or a derby seem just as keen on reading an account of what they have just seen as everyone else."

That lack of evidence didn't stop the split between the FA and the BBC from becoming a chasm and in 1929 the football authorities demanded a fee from the broadcaster to allow them to cover the FA Cup Final. The Beeb, who had covered both the 1927 and 1928 finals, flatly refused but still considered the match to be a key date in their schedule and so assembled a team of eight reporters who all paid for entry. Having watched their allotted part of the match each reporter rushed in turn to a nearby flat the BBC had rented and broadcast for about 10 minutes. Poorly prepared and working without a script, it was almost inevitable mistakes would be made and one of the team wrongly told the listeners Portsmouth had scored when the goal had actually gone to Bolton (who won 2-0). Despite this slip the *BBC Yearbook* claimed the event had been "entirely successful" but the following year the *Radio Times* presented a more sober assessment, suggesting such coverage "cannot be said to compare in the dramatic intensity with the pageant of sound conveyed by the microphone from the crowded stands".

By this stage the FA had gone further, demanding a fee to allow the BBC to cover any FA Cup tie in the 1929/30 season. The battle lines were clear. On one side the FA pointed to the fees they had been receiving from the newsreel companies to allow them to cover the

Cup Final, which had started at £1,000 in 1923 and had been rising since; on the other was the BBC which argued it produced "spoken reports analogous to a newspaper" and pointed to the free access gained by press reporters. In a bid to take the moral high ground and demonstrate the FA's supposed "intransigence" the BBC published all their correspondence on the matter, prompting numerous letters of support castigating the FA as out of touch. Media coverage of football, and particularly radio coverage, had begun to change fans' view of their relationship with the game; it had become something they felt they had a right to experience not just live but also for free. Eventually, in a bid to break the deadlock, the BBC offered to pay £200 to a charity of the FA's choice, but on a matter of principle insisted they pay it directly to the charity. *The Times* supported the BBC's stance in an editorial headlined "Commercial Football", pointing out that the FA Cup Final was sold out and that a broadcast would allow all football fans including "the halt, the maimed and the blind" to listen. The FA replied by demanding a retraction of the accusation of professionalism. Eventually the Bishop of Buckingham stepped in as arbiter and the FA, as much to limit the damage to their reputation as anything else, relented.

The BBC hailed its victory in the *Radio Times* by claiming that "the listening public applauds the generous decision of the Football Association to admit the microphone once again to the Stadium" but it wasn't long before it was kicked out again. From 1931 the League banned live commentary on all its games and the FA banned live commentary on matches apart from the FA Cup Final, Charity Shield, internationals and the Oxbridge varsity match. To deliberately make matters worse for the commentators there was also a ban on players wearing shirt numbers. The BBC, staffed mainly by ex-public-school Oxbridge graduates and with an ethos built on amateur principles, didn't fight too hard to get football back on board. Between 1930 and 1935 they broadcast just 22 football matches compared to 52 Rugby Union games. Professional Rugby League suffered an even worse fate, with just one match broadcast in that time (by comparison, two water polo games were covered). One event the FA did allow to be covered in this period was the FA Cup third-round draw, which came live from the FA Council Chamber for the first time in 1936. That year's

BBC Annual described how a commentator set the scene before "the proceedings were left to speak for themselves". Another key date had been discreetly added to England's media-created sporting calendar. By this time advances in technology and the increasing amount of outside broadcast equipment allowed the BBC to construct radio programmes from a variety of sources. It was at this point in the mid-1930s that Saturday afternoons became synonymous with sport and the BBC schedule was almost entirely devoted to sports coverage as it moved around the country from one sport to another.

The League and the FA Cup were suspended during the Second World War and replaced by the Wartime League and the Football League War Cup. The League relaxed its stance on commentary to help boost morale among the Forces. Following this move the BBC negotiated to be allowed to cover League games on a regular basis after the war, although the League insisted that the studio anchorman was not allowed to say which game was being featured. The listeners only found out when the commentator at the ground began to speak. In 1948 *Sports Report* was launched and it became a central part of the Saturday sporting experience, with a particular focus on the day's football results. As it switched from on-the-spot reporters around the country it made stars of its hosts such as Eamonn Andrews and Des Lynam. Originally starting at 5pm, the hourly round-up moved to the earlier time of 4.42pm as it switched from the BBC's Light to the Third programme in 1964. Subsequent moves followed: to Radio Two in 1970, Radio Five in 1990 and 5 Live in 1994, all the while introduced by its famous theme tune 'Out of the Blue', written by Hubert Bath. When BBC bosses considered ditching the tune in the late 1970s there was an outcry and then-host Lynam compared it to knocking down Tower Bridge. Another national institution had been created.

• • •

Commentary is nothing without commentators and the man behind the microphone for the BBC's first two momentous sports broadcasts in 1927 was Capt. Henry Blythe Thornhill 'Teddy' Wakelam. In his 1938 autobiography *Half Time: The Mike and Me*, Wakelam described how he got the job: "One January afternoon, I was working out some details of a tender, when my telephone rang. An unknown voice at the other end asked me if I was the same Wakelam who had played rugger for the Harlequins, and, upon my saying 'yes', went on to inform me that the owner of it was an official of the BBC, who would much like to see me at once on an urgent matter." The voice belonged to producer Lance Sieveking and within a fortnight Wakelam was on the air and his career in commentary had begun. Those early commentaries were met with praise, *The Times* commending Wakelam's delivery as "notably vivid and impressive" and *The Spectator* suggesting "that type of broadcasting is here to stay". That isn't to say Wakelam didn't suffer the odd mishap; his football debut also provided the first ever on-air gaffe. During half time at Highbury he was heard to say, "What about a beer?" David Coleman would have been proud. On another occasion, while commentating at Wimbledon, Wakelam set fire to his trousers while lighting a cigarette but managed to stamp out the blaze without interrupting his commentary. This consummate professionalism saw him stay at the top of the commentating game for several decades and he would gain another notable first in 1938 when he commentated on the first televised Ashes Test from Lords.

At the Highbury match he was accompanied by a co-commentator, Cecil Arthur Lewis. Lewis, who had been with the BBC from the very start as a writer, producer and director, was a decorated First World War fighter pilot and went on to win an Oscar in 1938 for his screen adaptation of *Pygmalion*. However his role at the Arsenal match was little more than a cameo. Prior to the game the *Radio Times* published a diagram of the pitch divided into numbered squares. Lewis was not only the recipient of Wakelam's half-time drinks request but also acted as 'Number Two' (or 'Dr Watson' as they were sometimes known), calling out the number of the square the ball was in. This practice is often credited as the origin of the phrase "back to square one" but this is by no means certain as it doesn't appear on any surviving recordings. Furthermore, what was 'back' for one team was, obviously, 'forward' for another. The *Manchester Guardian* hailed the experiment as a success, contrasting it with the Twickenham commentary from a week earlier, when Wakelam had been on his own, by saying: "With the chart before one, it was fairly easy to visualise what was actually happening and the cheers and the groans of the spectators help considerably the imagination of the listeners."

Wakelam's momentous broadcast from Highbury in 1927 was followed a week later by coverage of an FA Cup tie between Corinthians and Newcastle, but the commentator for that match was George Allison. Over the next decade Allison went on to establish himself as the voice of football. That voice, described as "rich" and "fruity" in his obituary in *The Times*, was the one that people would have heard when they tuned in for the first ever coverage of the FA Cup Final at the end of the 1927 season. His "number two", the man with the numbers, was Derek McCulloch. McCulloch, another First World War veteran, was known as Uncle Mac and gained fame as the presenter of *Children's Hour* and as the voice of Larry the Lamb. McCulloch was nearly killed in the Battle of the Somme as a 17-year-old after he was caught in a shell explosion. He lay badly injured in no man's land for three days and would ultimately lose an eye. However, in the days before health and safety this presented no barrier to him joining the Flying Corps the following year.

Allison kept up his commentating work even after he became Arsenal manager in 1934. When the Gunners reached the Cup Final two years later he saw fit to swap the commentary box for the dugout. It was the first time the final was broadcast live and the first time two commentators were used, a practice that remains today. Ivan Sharpe and Frederick Creek[3] were the men tasked with sharing the job of replacing the larger-than-life Allison. Along with his phrase "By jove!" the Gunners' boss became synonymous with football commentary. He was praised for his "fairness and impartiality" and his "bright and breezy style" but he wasn't universally popular. A letter to the *Radio Times* in 1929 complained that Allison persistently gave "his personal views on how the game 'should' be played instead of keeping us informed as to how the game 'was' being played". Just two years after the first broadcasts commentators were already splitting opinion.

3 *Both men had been top amateur footballers. Sharpe won the League with Derby County and Olympic Gold with Great Britain in 1912 while Creek played for England once and would manage the Great Britain Olympic team in 1958.*

The letter wasn't just about Allison, nor commentators in general; instead it raised questions about the uneasy equilibrium at the heart of commentary: the balance between expert and popular. Like James Catton and his fellow newspaper football correspondents three decades earlier, the early commentators were pioneers in then-unchartered territory. These days we take commentary and its rhythms and vocabulary for granted but these conventions have developed through a process of trial and error that began with the very first broadcasts. Commentary in those early years mainly consisted of reports at half time and full time, or straight eye-witness accounts given by the "men of the moment", that is top players, in their chosen sport. However, as early as 1925 such efforts were described as "little short of lamentable" by John Stobart,[4] the BBC's Director of Education. These players might have had expert knowledge of their sport but they lacked broadcasting skills and there was an immediate recognition that such skills were crucial and a balance between the two was required.

There was also an immediate recognition that commentary needed a conversational tone and the BBC's first Director of Outside Broadcasts, Gerald Cock, insisted it should be more like a conversation between friends than between a teacher and pupil. Wakelam took this on board, employing "ordinary conversational language" built on "plain, simple everyday phrases" and "natural spontaneous remarks". To help him in this endeavour early in his career, he sometimes sat next to and directed his commentaries at a blind man to ensure both an informal style and that his words wouldn't dry up. However, it wasn't until 1935, when Cock was replaced as Head of Outside Broadcasts by Seymour Joly de Lotbinière, that the loose practices developed over the previous few years became structured. Lobby, as de Lotbinière was known, immediately discontinued the practice of the Number Two calling out where the ball was. Instead he insisted that the commentator paint this image with words and by doing away with this role, room was created for expert co-commentators who could provide insight alongside the description of the game.

In 1939 de Lotbinière wrote in the *BBC Handbook* that "commentary is an art and its successful practice depends on attention to

4   The BBC's motto *"Nation shall speak peace unto nation"* is attributed to Stobart.

a specifiable technique" and he developed that technique himself. It was the pyramid method in which the commentator began with the few most important details – the narrow top of the pyramid – before gradually broadening out with more, less important but still crucial information. Following this advice a football commentator would start by giving the score and the amount of time left. Then they would broaden out by naming the goal-scorers, before setting the scene by describing the weather, the crowd and the ground. Then the commentator would describe any significant periods of play before moving on to what de Lotbinière described as "associative material" such as the teams' league positions, the importance and impact of the possible results and any milestones the game might produce either for the teams or their players. But who was this commentary aimed at? The language that commentators used was dependent on who they thought they were speaking to and de Lotbinière saw the audience for every sport as another pyramid, with a small, highly knowledgeable group at the top, a larger group of general sports fans in the middle and the majority of the listeners with limited knowledge at the bottom. In keeping with the BBC's Reithian values, de Lotbinière wanted to appeal to all listeners, but his template made certain assumptions about the listening audience.

These commentaries might have been intended to bring the nation together but they did so in a very specific way. While women's interest in football actually grew in this period, the commentary was still resolutely aimed at men. On the very rare occasions women were brought in to the commentary box it was to talk about 'female' subjects such as fashion (during Derby coverage for example) as opposed to 'male' subjects like, well, sport. Alongside the country's gender hierarchy its class structure was also reinforced by sports commentary that adopted Received Pronunciation. It's little wonder that the discourses commentators used were so narrow when they themselves were from such a narrow section of society. They were all men, mostly educated at public school and university (probably Oxford or Cambridge) and were also likely to be former amateur players. There was also a strong services influence and at one point alongside Captain Wakelam the BBC also had Colonel R.H. Bland and Lieutenant Commander Thomas Woodroffe in its ranks.

Alongside the perceived conflict within the audience between (male) expertise and (female) ignorance ran a conflict between realism and entertainment within the commentary. On one hand the likes of Wakelam and Allison were tasked with providing the listener with an accurate description of what was happening, while on the other they needed to keep that listener entertained. Once more it was a question of balance, although even implementing de Lotbinière's pyramid method meant the commentator was constructing a narrative around the action and the players involved by determining for the listener what and who was important. Following 1933's introduction of the lip microphone, designed to reduce background noise, microphones were placed around the ground to capture 'natural noises' which were then faded in and out to legitimise the broadcast with a sense of authenticity. This desire for realism remains in radio and television coverage of football, with TV companies introducing 3D coverage. Yet this is merely the pretence of realism, as both radio and TV, and particularly the latter with its slow-motion replays, graphics and multiple cameras, offer a viewing experience significantly different to that of watching a game in a stadium.

• • •

The thing about radio waves is that they travel, and while the BBC didn't have any English-based commercial competition for the best part of 50 years, within a decade it did have a rival. It was inventor-cum-fighter pilot-cum-radio salesman Captain Leonardo F. Plugge[5] (also a Tory MP) who first saw the market for commercial radio. In 1925 he persuaded Selfridges department store to sponsor a 15-minute show on fashion to be broadcast from the Eiffel Tower to England. Not well advertised, it had a single-figure audience but Plugge was undeterred and the following year he formed the International Broadcasting Company (IBC). By 1931 he was buying airtime on European radio stations and broadcasting sponsored, English-language programmes across the channel.

5   Plugge's daughter Gale Anne Benson was murdered by civil rights activist Michael X, real name Michael de Freitas, who stabbed her before burying her alive in Trinidad, an incident referenced in the 2008 film The Bank Job. John Lennon paid for de Freitas' lawyer but to no avail and he was sentenced to death for the murder of Joseph Skerritt, who was murdered with Gale, and hanged in Port of Spain.

Most newspapers, worried about the threat to their advertising revenue, refused to print the stations' listings, a situation which lasted until the 1950s. However *The Sunday Referee* sports paper did carry advertising for the IBC and even launched the International Broadcasting Club, which had 50,000 paying members within three weeks and 250,000 within three months. While a loss of advertising revenue during the Second World War caused the IBC to shut for good, commercial rival Radio Luxembourg fared better.

Launched two years after the IBC the station broadcast from the tiny Duchy and quickly came to dominate the early commercial sector due to its more powerful transmitter that broadcast on the wavelength of 208 metres. Nicknamed Fab 208 the station was taken over by the Nazis and used to broadcast propaganda during the war but this effectively saved the station which resumed normal service after the conflict with its reputation undamaged. The twin evils of commercialisation and gambling which the BBC tried so hard to avoid found the perfect home on the other side of the Channel and from the very beginning the Football Pools companies were the financial force behind the IBC and Radio Luxembourg. By 1935 the seven largest Pools firms were sponsoring around 50 hours of programming a week across the various commercial stations based in northern France. With the BBC concentrating on religious programmes on a Sunday, the two commercial broadcasters commanded as much as 80 per cent of the English radio audience at that time. Listeners as far north as the Midlands could tune in to a music show sponsored by Strang's Pools on Radio Normandy, while on Radio Luxembourg they could find a similar programme sponsored by Vernons, as well as a 30-minute programme devoted to football results sponsored by Littlewoods, who also sponsored a results programme on Saturdays. After the war Radio Luxembourg continued to carry adverts, usually bought in 15-minute blocks, and became synonymous with one for Horace Batchelor's "amazing" Infra-Draw Pools method. The method involved identifying 16 games likely to be draws and then scoring them on a series of criteria to identify the eight games to place on the coupon. Batchelor became famous for asking people to write to him before slowly spelling out the name of the town where he lived "K-E-Y-N-S-H-A-M, near Bristol", in his thick West Country accent,

adding, "I'll repeat that ...", much to the agony of the listeners.[6]
The effectiveness of the Infra-Draw method is open to debate; how-
ever, the adverts did succeed in teaching a whole generation where
Keynsham was located and how to spell it.

Radio Luxembourg held the British monopoly on radio advertising until the pirate station boom of the 1960s and the subsequent
licensing of commercial radio in 1973. The Government banned the
pirates in 1966 and to deal with the threat the BBC created Radio
One and rebranded the Light Programme as Radio Two, the Third
Programme as Radio Three and the BBC Home Service as Radio
Four. The Beeb was also granted permission to launch eight local
stations on an experimental basis. The first, Radio Leicester, was on
the air in November 1967 and BBC research in 1969 showed sports
programmes were, along with breakfast music shows, among the most
popular in the experimental stations. Coverage of football on local
radio has changed markedly in the four decades of its existence. In
the early days it was sparse, featuring little more than brief pre-match
team news and build-up, score flashes and half- and full-time reports.
Initially transmitted by telephone, the quality was poor and the lines
were often one-way, meaning that the studio would be able to hear
what the commentator was saying but not communicate back. The
introduction of the reporter telephone – which had a microphone
attachment – brought improvements in sound quality that continued
with the Commentator Operated Outside Broadcast Equipment
and, more recently, ISDN lines. The content has also changed, often
featuring a much longer build-up, full match coverage and post-match
interviews, and commentators working in teams.

The considerable cost of covering football on local radio, which
could increase dramatically if a team went on a long cup run, meant
that the commercial stations were heavily reliant on sponsorship to
cover the costs. The stations would agree deals guaranteeing the
sponsors a number of mentions or adverts during a broadcast. In
2011 the BBC outlined proposals to cut its local radio budget by 12
per cent (or £15m) a year. While the Saturday-afternoon football
schedule would remain, it was proposed mid-week evening football

---

6   The Bonzo Dog Doo-Dah Band named their album Keynsham *after the advert and referenced*
Batchelor in several of their songs.

broadcasts would be dropped or commentaries shared, a suggestion which caused concern among football governing bodies and radio producers alike. The latter group in particular were fearful that shared commentaries would alienate highly partisan fans. Whatever happens in the future, those highly partisan fans will always have local radio to thank for giving them the first and most enduring platform to air their views: the phone-in.

• • •

In 1963, producers of *Late Night Extra,* a two-hour entertainment show hosted by Don Davis, persuaded the Post Office to allow the transmission of speech through their lines and for the first time hosts could interact live with their listeners. However, these weren't spontaneous calls. Instead listeners wrote in and some were chosen at random and arrangements made for them to be rung before the show. It was more of a phone-out than a phone-in. That subsequent innovation came five years later thanks to the Radio Nottingham show *Where Are They Now?* It would be up the M1 in 1986 that the template was first applied to football by Radio Sheffield's then-sports editor. Robert Jackson's journey to become a radio sports presenter was a long one which took him from National Service in the Navy to a stint as a school teacher and as an inspector for the Potato Marketing Board while he ran his family's fruit and vegetable wholesale business. This latter job also enabled Jackson, who was born and bred in Sheffield, to follow his passion for sport and work for BBC Radio Sheffield on a freelance basis. As supermarkets began to dominate the wholesale scene, he sold up and the move into full-time radio journalism was, as Jackson told me, a "natural progression". By 1986 he was the busiest sports editor in local radio, covering the largest patch which took in both Sheffield clubs – United and Wednesday – as well as Rotherham, Barnsley, Doncaster and Chesterfield. In the summer there was Derbyshire, Yorkshire and Nottinghamshire to cover in cricket's County Championship as well as Sheffield's vibrant boxing scene and the World Snooker Championships. Like most stations, BBC Radio Sheffield ran a sports programme from 2pm and 6pm on a Saturday.

"I had a problem," Jackson said. "We had pretty good listening figures up until five o'clock but once people had discovered whether their team had won or lost and the national results they weren't much bothered. We ran a programme on to 6pm with more in-depth reports and interviews with managers but the listening figures were poor and my boss said: 'we ought to see if we can find something'. I thought, 'I know what we are in Britain; we're a nation of grumblers.' We grumble about everything. If you go to the theatre and a singer misses a note you remember that but you don't remember the rest of the show which was brilliant. Or if you go to a football match and your team win two or three-nil you say 'oh, we should have had six'. We're never satisfied. We worry about the little things that go wrong and don't rejoice about the things that go right. It's a very British characteristic and we tapped into it. We introduced a phone-in from about ten past five and told the listeners they could all have a grumble and we had some amazing calls.

"One chap rang up and said 'I'd like to grumble about my girlfriend.' I asked him why and he said: 'Every Saturday night she wants me to take her out, go for a drink or two, go to a dance, have a right good jolly evening. How can I be cheerful on Saturday night? I support Sheffield United.' That said it all. He just wanted to stay in and be miserable. But after four or five weeks Wednesday won 5-0 and somebody rang in and said: 'I don't want to grumble, I want to praise.' Out of his call the *Grumble Spot* became *Praise or Grumble*. We ran it for about half an hour and at its best I was handling 28 to 30 calls, which in broadcasting terms is very quick so each caller had roughly 30 seconds to make their point. We got quite strict with the time because it packed more callers in and you got a great variety and we got some really funny ones which really made the programme take off."

The on-air grumbles were ratings gold and *Praise or Grumble* quickly became the most listened-to programme on local radio. It consistently out-performed any other programme across the network including breakfast shows, a station's traditional high point, something which continued into the early 1990s and didn't go unnoticed at BBC headquarters. "Once or twice the boss warned me that some suits were coming up from London and they would watch for an hour or two, particularly in this segment of *Praise or Grumble*," said Jackson. "Out of that came all the famous national phone-in programmes. It really was the forerunner." By 1991 *606* was being broadcast on BBC Radio Five with Danny Baker fielding the calls, and in 1995 when Talk Radio UK became the country's third and, to date, final national commercial radio station, the popularity of phone-ins was further acknowledged when they became a significant part of the new station's schedule. In January 2000 Talk Radio became talkSPORT, with phone-ins continuing to form its backbone.

At face value it seemed the phone-in show, whether local or national, was finally giving fans a voice within the game. Yet, was this ever really the case? Professor Ian Hutchby researched non-football phone-ins in the early 1990s and argued that the host always retained control of the situation through such techniques as determining the overall context of the discussion; the use of "the Second Position" (that is speaking after the caller and so being able to challenge and undermine their point of view) and holding the power to end the caller's participation in the conversation. Some hosts gently play devil's advocate, others (who you might say like the sound of their own voice a little too much) come to dominate the programme, while still others, like ex-Manchester United star Paddy Crerand, who would just cut off Manchester City fans who rang his show, take highly partisan positions. Yet in each case, Hutchby argued, the host takes an antagonistic position to engineer confrontation. In those first broadcasts Jackson took a different approach, letting each caller have a brief chance to air their views before quickly moving on to the next person. "I was always conscious of not dominating as the presenter. If you start a two-way conversation it's just your word against theirs. The host of any programme like that, particularly on radio, is terribly important. I think listeners have to have confidence in a presenter."

Yet, even if the host retains control of any one call or programme, Jackson's time on *Praise and Grumble* left him in no doubt not only that phone-ins give fans considerable power but also that football club administrators are acutely aware of this. "Some of the movements which have led to managers being sacked started with one telephone call. Bert McGee, who was Sheffield Wednesday chairman when the show started, said it should come off the air because people were regularly criticising him and the board. Other managers and chairmen as well as players used to say they didn't listen but the moment they were criticised they'd always mention it."

CHAPTER 5

TAKING A PUNT ON THE BEAUTIFUL GAME

People weren't just watching and listening to football; they were gambling on it too and have been ever since The Wanderers beat the Royal Engineers in the very first Football Association Challenge Cup Final way back in 1872. The match, played in front of a crowd of 2,000 at the Kennington Oval, was settled after just 15 minutes when Morton Peto Betts grabbed the only goal of the game with a simple tap-in from Walpole Vidal's[1] cross. Despite the fact that Betts scored the first Cup Final goal and the first Cup Final winner, you'll not find his name on the score sheet. An Old Harrovian, Betts had started the season with the Harrow Chequers and although they had withdrawn prior to their first match in the competition, as it happens against The Wanderers, Betts was technically cup-tied, so he played under the pseudonym A.H. Chequer (A Harrow Chequer). Not only were The Wanderers the first team to lift the trophy but they were also the first to upset the odds-on favourites, as their opponents Royal Engineers, unbeaten all season before the final, had been priced at 4/7 for victory. It was an early victory for the bookies too.

Gambling has a history almost as long as that of football, stretching back at least to medieval times and, like football, gambling has long been seen as socially problematic. In those distant times it was focused on gaming – dice and cards – with 'sport' considered to be activities such as hunting, fishing and archery. Gambling itself was not seen as morally wrong; instead the concern was that it would lead to time wasting among the lower classes. So when Richard II tried to

---

1   Vidal, known as the "prince of dribblers", was just 18 at the time and is still the only winning Cup finalist to still be in school at the time. He went on to feature for Oxford University in the next two Cup Finals.

ban dice in 1388 it was because it stopped men from practising their archery, the reason he also gave for banning football in the same year. However, it seems likely his proclamation was ineffective as it had to be reissued by later monarchs such as Henry IV and Henry VIII.

It wasn't until 1664, when a law voiding all gambling losses totalling more than £100 was introduced, that action was taken against the financial consequences of the pursuit. Despite this, gambling became increasingly popular and widespread until the early part of the nineteenth century. It gave the idle rich, who had ample spare time and cash, something to do, while for the poor, who were far more concerned about the present than the future, it provided the possibility of an immediate windfall coupled with excitement – neither of which would come from making regular savings. People would gamble on sports as diverse as bear baiting, pedestrianism (that's plain old walking, remember) and cricket, the rules of which were, in part at least, established to ensure bets could be settled. Horse racing gained Royal patronage when Charles II laid a course at Newmarket in 1666 and again when Queen Anne laid a course at Ascot in 1710. Truly it was the sport of kings. And queens. And pretty much everyone else, because while the majority of gamblers might not have been able to watch racing, it was the sport they placed wagers on as it grew in popularity alongside the fast-developing gambling industry.

Of course there were some who were not so enamoured by the prospect of a flutter on the gee-gees. In 1802 the Society for the Suppression of Vice set out to stop everything from brothels, pubs and gaming houses to fairs, and over the next half-century opposition to gambling built up a head of steam. Ultimately this led to a Bill in 1853 that banned betting shops by making cash gambling illegal except for at racecourses or in gentlemen's clubs. Effectively the ban only covered the working classes, those who couldn't afford to attend a racecourse or obtain credit. It was a double standard that would continue for over a century (and it explains why James Bond is always in a high-class casino and never in a high-street bookies). Despite the new law, gambling continued to thrive and was simply pushed onto the street where, if anything, it became more overt. Numerous social histories talk of street bookies who would operate standing on a chair behind a locked back-yard gate taking in betting slips and handing down winnings as appropriate. Their "dogger-out" would wait at the end of the road watching for the police and often allowing themselves to be arrested so the bookie could escape. Failing this, bookies would simply bribe the police, so there were relatively few prosecutions. If they weren't taking bets themselves, bookies had agents in all manner of places from pubs, barbers and local shops to factories, warehouses and labour exchanges. By 1895 the *Westminster Review* claimed "betting mania is all prevalent".

This cottage industry was facilitated by the press. Not only did they print detailed information about runners and riders, thus allowing punters to make (supposedly) informed decisions on which horses to back, but the introduction of the telegraph system meant they could also print starting prices and results. These were the bedrock of off-course betting. Robert Roberts in his book *The Classic Slum*, an autobiographical history of Salford in the early twentieth century, claimed gambling helped many "on the road to literacy". While men would avoid books as they considered them effeminate, they learned to read by checking form in the newspapers. "Many a child, too," wrote Roberts, "would spell out the list of 'Today's starters and jockeys' for unlettered elders, make out their betting slips and so improve in handwriting and in vocabulary."

• • •

Given the widespread popularity of gambling it was inevitable that when football appeared on the scene as an organised, codified sport it would prove attractive to bookies and punters alike. For the former, it kept business going in the winter months when the flat-racing season had come to an end; for the latter, it was a chance to have a small flutter on a game they could actually watch. While the sport was in its infancy, gambling on it mainly took place at grounds before and during games (and you thought in-play betting was all thanks to the internet) and the first tipping sheet *The Incomparable Football Forecasting System* was printed in 1879. But it was with the creation of the Football League in 1888 that gambling on the game really took off. Prior to this, odds could only be offered on single matches, with just three possible outcomes. Once the game became more structured, bets could be taken on several matches at once; this increased the number of possible outcomes and thus the available odds. The League's first season coincided with the launch of Alfred Harmsworth's newspaper *Answers*. The first issue sold 12,000 copies but Harmsworth, who pioneered populist journalism aimed at the working class, then introduced a guessing competition with the prize of £1-a-week for life and sales rocketed to 352,000 within 24 months. The newspaper 'promo' had been invented and the value of fixed-odds pre-match betting was soon recognised by sports papers. They began to print coupons with a series of games that could be combined by the punter, in turn popularising this form of betting. It was an innovation developed by the Lancashire-based press, with Edward Hulton's Manchester sports papers at its heart. By the 1890s, Bolton's *Football Field*; the *Lantern*, based in St Helens; and Hulton's own *Athletic News* were all issuing coupons with prizes as great as £5. Very soon the coupon market was flooded by a whole host of publishers who decided to dispense with the boring newspaper bit and just print the coupons and tipping sheets.

The anti-betting lobby was horrified by the popularity of such competitions and in 1895 they tried unsuccessfully to prosecute Ava Stoddart, who published *Sporting Luck*. Five years later they tried again and were successful, Stoddart's downfall, the second time around, being precipitated by the *Sporting Luck* having offered a free coupon that was viewed by the court as an incitement to gamble. Buoyed by their victory the anti-betting campaigners targeted several other newspaper proprietors, and even *Answers'* guessing competition fell foul of the law (although by that time it had done its job). To keep the competitions legal, papers included the coupons in the cover price, and to avoid accusations that they were a lottery, the papers played up the level of skill involved. They also introduced other skill-based games such as the snappily titled "Where Should the Ball Be?"

Bookies, on the other hand, simply moved abroad (if they hadn't done so already to enable them to accept cash bets on horse racing) and employed a series of agents to conduct their business. While most betting serviced only local markets, football-coupon betting had a wider reach due to its connection with newspapers and also the weekly nature of football which allowed enough time for coupons to be distributed, collected and checked. By 1907 a survey for the anti-betting lobby estimated that 250,000 coupons were being distributed each week in Liverpool alone. The explosion in coupon betting linked the competitions that newspapers ran in the early years of football to the development of the Football Pools, which would come to dominate the gambling market after the war. It demonstrated the popularity of football betting and also that small wagers on something which couldn't be rigged, at least not on a large scale, were just harmless fun. As Nicholas Fishwick wrote in *English Football and Society, 1910–1950*, it allowed the Pools to move from the backstreet to the high street, "to be sold more like cigarettes than cannabis".

Efforts to thwart gambling did continue and the 1920 Ready Money Football Betting Act meant anyone who knowingly wrote, printed, published or circulated coupons for cash football betting could be fined or even sent to prison. To get round the problem, the bookies simply started credit betting, by taking the stake a week in arrears. It was the final important step which enabled the Pools to take off. It's hardly surprising that firms from the North West, namely Littlewoods and Vernons, would dominate given the popularity of football coupons in the area; however, the idea originated in Birmingham. The Pools are based on the *pari-mutuel* system of betting,[2] which differs from fixed-odds gambling as the punter is not betting against the house but against the other players. Under the system, all the stake money is combined in a pool. Then taxes and the organiser's commission are deducted and the remainder of the pool is shared equally among those players who have made a winning bet. It was already being used in horse racing with the Totalisator – or Tote – when enterprising bookmaker John Jervis Bernard introduced the system for football betting. He began to distribute coupons with no odds, instead saying that winnings would be distributed proportionately to successful punters' stakes, after he had deducted 10 per cent commission. Business was slow to start and Bernard soon sold out to David Cope Ltd, but one man was watching with interest: John Moores.

---

2   *The* pari-mutuel *system was invented in the 1860s by Joseph Oller, a Catalan impresario during the Belle Époque. He was subsequently jailed by the French authorities for 18 days for illegal betting before the practice became accepted and widespread. His fingers burned at the racecourse, Oller went on to open the Moulin Rouge in 1889.*

At the time Moores and his friends Colin Askham and Bill Hughes worked as telegraphists with the Commercial Cable Company (CCC). Prior to the First World War, the trio had worked together as Post Office messengers in Manchester before joining CCC and being sent to its cable station in Waterville in County Kerry, a key part of the company's inter-continental network. After serving during the war (Moores as a wireless operator in the Navy) the trio met again at the CCC's Liverpool office. It was where they were working when Moores persuaded his two friends that they should each invest £50 in their own version of Bernard's Football Pools competition ahead of the 1923/24 season. To maintain their anonymity while they kept up their day jobs, the three new business partners decided to use Askham's surname at birth (he had been raised by his aunt and taken her name). So, Littlewoods Pools was born.

The friends had 4,000 copies of their first coupon printed but the company they had engaged to distribute them was run by a strict Methodist, who cancelled the contract once he saw what he was distributing. The trio had to distribute the coupons themselves outside Manchester United's ground, Old Trafford. Of the first 4,000 given out, only 35 were returned and things got worse before they got better. Another 10,000 coupons were given out at a match in Hull, with only one being returned, and by the end of the season Littlewoods had incurred losses of £600. A crisis meeting followed and Askham and Hughes decided to cut their losses, selling out to Moores, who kept the firm running with the help of his wife, sister and brother. By the following season the company had brought in £257 and by 1927 income had risen to £2,000. Five years later, aged 35, Moores was a millionaire and he was able to diversify into the mail order business. By 1937 he had opened his first department store in Blackpool. The firm even made parachutes, ammunition and parts for the Wellington bomber during the war and the family's name would become synonymous with Liverpool. Moores was chairman of Everton from 1960 to 1973 and his nephew David Moores was chairman of Liverpool from 1991 to 2007.

The key benefit for Littlewoods was that as they took a commission before distributing winnings, they could not be financially ruined by a big win for one punter. Any whiff of profit brings rivals to the field and in 1925 brothers Edmund and Vernon Sangster, also from Liverpool, founded Vernons, with their headquarters opposite Aintree. To help increase the size of the market the Pools companies expanded the number of games on offer, with shortened lists for smaller prizes being offered under names such as "easy six" or "family four". By the 1930s gambling was second only to cinema as a leisure pursuit. Boosted by people's reduced working hours (and so increased leisure time) and an increase in disposable income, spending on gambling grew from £63m per year to £22m between 1920 and 1938 (and that was just the over-the-counter stuff we know about). The Pools success within the betting market was based on the fact that while casual punters could chance their arm, serious punters could test themselves by reading the form and employing their knowledge. They pored over the coupons and the form guides to the extent that the Pools were considered the working-class equivalent of *The Times* crossword. A 1938 survey by The Pilgrim Trust noted that a man "who has been lucky enough to win money on the pool acquires thereby a definitive social standing, and his views on very different matters are heard with respect".

As we've seen, the Pools firms sponsored music and football results programmes on commercial radio stations such as Radio Luxembourg and they also placed adverts in the press and produced their own papers. Vernons printed one called *The Bulletin*, which discussed what punters could spend their winnings on (still a staple question on game shows today) while their rivals produced the *Littlewoods Sports Log* complete with tips from the "Little 'ol man o' the Woods", a tipping gnome. During the inter-war years, around seven million people were entering the Pools regularly and their popularity even extended to other countries. In the early 1930s some 200,000 people were entering from Sweden until their Government set up a state-run pool (Switzerland and Finland soon followed suit). In Britain the number of players increased to between 10 and 14 million in the 1940s and about a third of the adult population returned a coupon at some point. To put that into context, around 16½ times as many people were entering the Pools at their peak than were actually watching football.

In 1976 some 37 per cent of adults were still regularly entering the Pools, with the majority doing so weekly. Various studies of the

Pools found that while the majority of those who entered were, like the majority who watched football, working-class men, there were significant numbers from a broader cross-section of society. The very poor, who might not be able to afford a ticket for a match, could have a small bet on the game, while the middle and upper classes found the Pools an interesting pastime. During the 1960s Nigel Lawson, then editor of *The Spectator* magazine, did the Pools religiously. When a colleague told the Chancellor-to-be to "think of the odds" Lawson replied: "think of the winnings". It wasn't just men who were thinking of the winnings. The Pools crossed gender as well as class lines with between 15 per cent and 20 per cent of winners being women, thus weaving football into the social and cultural fabric of English society and confirming its place as the country's national sport.

Alongside this was the ongoing moral battle over gambling. Anti-gamblers painted punters as "ignorant dupes" who were "feckless" and "weak-willed", while they, by contrast, were branded as "cranks" who couldn't stand to see other people enjoy themselves. No matter which side of the fence you sit, I'm sure you'll be pleased to see that the debate was conducted in an adult manner. Regular commissions on the subject could find little evidence of a relationship between gambling and poverty or crime. On the contrary, the overwhelming majority bet well within their means and the evidence given to the Royal Commission on Gambling in 1932 was that most gambled for amusement with "no severe strain on their resources". Stake amounts on the Pools in particular were relatively low – ranging from six pence to a couple of shillings. So while the number of people who bet on the Pools was high, the amounts of money involved were less than in both horse racing and greyhound racing.

Despite this the FA told a Royal Commission on Gambling in 1932 that betting made football susceptible to bribes from bookies as well as potential hostility from crowds should the result be going the wrong way, but they had very little evidence to support their claims. The Commission was however moved by the argument that betting on football might attract new, younger gamblers and so recommended a ban that would include the Pools. In response the major Pools firms joined forces to create the Football Pools

Promoters Association and, with support from the press and public, lobbied the Government, who ultimately ignored the Commission's recommendations.

The game's authorities remained ardently opposed to the Football Pools both on moral grounds and because the Pools profited from football but gave nothing back. So the Football League, led by its vice president Charles Sutcliffe, a Methodist, decided to take matters into their own hands. In October 1935 they banned clubs from advertising the Pools. It was the opening salvo in the so-called 'Pools War'. A meeting of clubs on 20 February 1936 voted to allow the League's management committee "to take such steps as it deems expedient to bring about the suppression of betting". Sutcliffe's plan was to alter the original fixture list and withhold new fixtures for long enough each week to prevent the Pools firms from printing and distributing coupons. The plan was ratified by 64 of the 85 member clubs and the League scrapped the fixture list for Saturday, 29 February, secretly issuing new fixtures to the clubs just 24 hours ahead of kick-off. There was public uproar, with British Paramount News suggesting it was a bid to stop a "gigantic £20m a year flutter".

George Orwell, writing in *The Road to Wigan Pier*, provided a sense of the widespread outrage that the League's move provoked. Orwell was in Sheffield at the time and noted that Adolf Hitler's reoccupation of the Rhineland, which happened in the same week, and the subsequent possibility of war "aroused hardly a flicker of interest" but the Football League's decision to stop publishing their fixtures flung the whole of Yorkshire into "a storm of fury".[3] The move also caused unexpected anger among the clubs, some of whom found their attendances well down while five, whose new opponents were in the FA Cup, found themselves with no game at all. Leeds United, Manchester City, Sunderland and Derby County called a rebel meeting at Leeds Town Hall on Monday 2 March claiming Sutcliffe's plan was in breach of three rules. Despite the fact it fell on the same day as a management committee meeting in London, 36 of the 44 full League members attended and they voted 26-0 (with ten

3   Orwell also wrote that the Pools were so important that they were one of the things that had helped avert revolution in Britain. The others were fish-and-chips, art-silk stockings, tinned salmon, cut-price chocolate, the movies, the radio and strong tea.

abstentions) to fight the move. The clubs wanted a return to the status quo and the Leeds resolution was passed at another League meeting a week later. After two weekends of confusion the original fixture list was reinstated. Twenty-three years later the Football League gained copyright over its own fixture list in a court judgement and entered a 10-year deal allowing the Pools firms to use them. The FA soon followed suit with Cup fixtures.

The quick end to the Pools War was a decisive victory for the Pools firms but the Second World War broke out three years later, putting the brakes on their growth. Encouraged by the Government, they came together to form the Unity Pools during the conflict, concentrating their businesses in the Liverpool offices of Vernons and Littlewoods – a massive boost for the two already-huge firms. When peace was declared there was a move among MPs to nationalise the Pools and thus benefit from the companies' financial and personnel resources. However, with their energies focused on developing a welfare state and the National Health Service, the Labour Government stopped short of such action, instead imposing a 10 per cent tax levy on the Pools firms in 1947. It was a pragmatic move by politicians who had realised they could do little to abate the widespread popularity of gambling.

By 1949 the Pools levy had been increased to 30 per cent and the Government had taken a significant step along the path towards the re-legalisation of betting shops. Shermans responded by introducing Pools on Australian football matches in the summer months during the English closed season. They were soon the third-biggest Pools company but even they were swallowed up by Littlewoods in 1962. The smaller firms simply couldn't cope with the triple whammy of the concentration of business in Liverpool, the increasing tax levy and the introduction of the new treble chance game that offered punters three different stake options. Players gravitated towards the bigger firms with bigger prize pools, which in turn increased their prize pools further and created a downward spiral for the smaller firms. There were still 251 Pools firms in February 1948 but that number had fallen to just 42 by the end of 1950. By 1974 there were just five firms left and when the Lottery came along in 1994 to poop the Pools party, just three remained: Vernons, Littlewoods and Zetters, which was founded in 1933. But we're getting ahead of ourselves.

Pools firms had already tapped into the world of celebrity to boost publicity by getting stars such as Laurel and Hardy to present cheques to the winners but the advent of the age of TV, in which anyone could have 15 minutes of fame, heralded an obsession with Pools winners who won big. In 1961, 25-year-old Viv Nicholson, a housewife from Castleford, vowed to "Spend! Spend! Spend!" when she picked up her cheque for £152,321 (and eight pence) from a youthful Bruce Forsyth. Spend she did and within a decade she was declared bankrupt. Nicholson's rags-to-riches-to-rags life story was subsequently made into a musical starring Barbara Dickson that ran on the West End for two years from 1998. She even graced the cover of The Smiths' single 'Heaven Knows I'm Miserable Now' in 1984. The season after Nicholson hit the jackpot the Pools themselves gained TV celebrity as the weather played havoc with the fixture list. It was the coldest winter since 1740. Snow lay on the ground in the south of England for 62 consecutive days (the most since then was 10 in 1987) and rivers, lakes and in some places even the sea froze over. The first few postponements came on Saturday 22 December but the following week, after snow had swept south from Scotland, 35 of 45 games were called off. Just three FA Cup third-round games took place on 5 January and it would be another 66 days and 261 more postponements before the round was complete. So it would continue until the end of February. While Arctic snowfall might have been enough to bring football to its knees, the Football Pools were made of sterner stuff and on 26 January 1963 the Pools Panel came into existence.

The Panel was introduced to the world on the BBC's *Saturday Sport*, a precursor to *Match of the Day*, with the camera panning down the line-up of ex-players Ted Drake, Tom Finney, Tommy Lawton, ex-ref Arthur Ellis and the chairman Sir Gerald Nabarro, a Tory backbench MP (whose secretary was a young Christine Hamilton). The members of the Panel got £100 each for their troubles but their initial selection of 7 draws, 8 away wins and 23 home wins from 38 games met with some anger. The *News of the World* reported that "people were calling it a farce" and ran a cartoon that showed two people comparing their entries and saying, "We were right about our suggestions – it was the Pools Panel that got it wrong." Despite the early criticism, the Panel became so important that in its heyday its decisions were broadcast live on *Grandstand* from the imposing Grand Connaught Rooms in Central London[4] where it convened. Even when the members didn't meet, the numbers of key games for the Pools – score draws and no-score draws – would be read out at the end of *Final Score*.[5]

The Pools Panel now comprises just three men – Roger Hunt, Gordon Banks and Tony Green – all of whom have been members since the 1970s during which time their work has actually increased. In the past the Panel only used to meet when 25 or more matches were called off; now they meet if only one Saturday game is postponed – and that includes games moved for the benefit of TV.

The Football Pools' dominance of the long-odds betting market continued for several more decades and in 1990 it was announced that the Pools firms would help fund the transformation of English football stadia to the tune of £100m over five years through the Football Trust. Four years later Littlewoods became the first sponsors of the FA Cup, an irony no doubt not lost on those who could remember the football authorities' animosity towards the Pools in their early years. The deal was worth £114m over four seasons but it was a last hurrah. By the end of the year the UK finally got round to introducing a state lottery, which began the Pools' speedy decline.

The Government had dipped its toes into the gambling market in 1956 with the introduction of Premium Bonds but these were essentially loans to the Government with the interest paid in prize money so, apart from Albania, the UK was the last country in Europe to have a state-sanctioned lottery. One of the key reasons for the delay was that, in effect, the Pools were a lottery. It gave punters a shot at a high-value prize in a long-odds competition in which they chose several numbers from a list and hoped they came up (and that no one else had picked the same ones). Just like a lottery, the

---

4 *The Connaught Rooms are built on the site of the Freemasons' Tavern where the FA was founded in 1863 and they were the venue for the meeting at which the Premier League was created in September 1991. Oh, and they have been the HQ of the Freemasons since the 1700s.*

5 *Since the inception of* Final Score *as part of* Grandstand *in 1958 only four people have read the classified football results: Len Martin until his death in 1995, Tim Gudgin until 2011 and Mike West since then. Mark E. Smith of* The Fall *has also read them as a one-off.*

overwhelming majority of players – as many as 80 per cent – chose the same numbers week after week with no consideration of which games those numbers corresponded to. Furthermore, while lotteries proved financially appealing to governments as a source of revenue (many sprung up around the world in the 1970s and 1980s during the oil price-led economic slowdown) the Exchequer was already raking in £300m a year from the Pools firms.

Successive governments knew that creating a lottery, whatever its benefits, would mean losing revenue from the Pools firms, who in turn lobbied hard against the idea of a lottery that might destroy their business. Ultimately the introduction of the Lottery was based on the assumption that it would generate more income for the Government. The Pools were mainly played by older men while evidence from abroad suggested the Lottery would be more attractive to younger people and women. The Lottery's rules were simpler and its game wasn't seasonal (there was no break in the summer when you had to pretend to know what was going on in Australian football). The introduction of Lottery terminals meant smaller long-term running costs and so a bigger potential prize fund than the Pools which would make the new game more attractive, in turn increasing demand and revenue for the Government.

Here the Pools companies only had themselves to blame. Although they had semi-automated their checking process, in 1990 they were still employing 96,000 coupon collectors. Not only was this costly; it was a highly antiquated way for consumers to enter, requiring them to post their entry form or be around when the coupon collector came to call. The Lottery, on the other hand, could be entered while you popped to the corner shop or supermarket. In its first 12 months more than four times as much was gambled on the Lottery than on the Pools the previous year. The Exchequer drew 13 per cent of the Lottery pool, some £510m, while good causes took 28 per cent of the pot.[6] The following year, the Exchequer scooped a £626m jackpot. In effect the Government had ditched their Pools coupon for a Lottery ticket and all six numbers came up. As a concession, the Pools firms

---

6   *In the first year, these good causes included the deprived pupils of the £10,000-a-term Eton School, which was awarded £4.5m for a new sports centre to complement its gym, two swimming pools, 30 cricket squares and 24 football, rugby and hockey pitches.*

were allowed to advertise on TV in 1997, the first time gambling advertising had been allowed other than for the Lottery. Eleven years later the three remaining Pools firms – Littlewoods, Vernons and Zetters – were bought by Sportech Plc and effectively merged under the name The Football Pools. They still have about 60,000 regular players but their heyday is long since past.

• • •

The launch of the National Lottery in 1994 might have been a bitter blow for the Pools companies but it was the year in which football began to show its muscle in the traditional betting market. For the first time the World Cup became a bigger betting event than the Grand National. Four years after Pavarotti and Gazza's tears, the football love-in continued unabated and, despite England's absence, about £60m was gambled on the tournament. Two years later when football came home, just slightly less was bet on the European Championships, although as there were fewer matches the amount staked per game was greater. Further confirmation of the trend came when Michael Hills rode Shaamit to victory in the Derby, which coincided with the opening day of Euro '96. Betting on Epsom's showcase race was down from the previous year, prompting Ladbrokes spokesman Mike Dillon to say matter-of-factly: "Punters are now more interested in football betting."

It had been a long hard battle for the bookies to reach that point. The Betting Act of 1853 had forced them on to the street and the Ready Money Betting Act of 1920 forced them into credit betting which favoured the Pools companies. Their success prompted book-makers to begin to offer fixed-odds coupon betting on football. This differed from Pools betting as the bookies offered set odds on certain outcomes (say 25/1 on three draws) instead of divvying up the stake pool among the winners. This meant they had greater liabilities than the Pools firms (they were unquantifiable before the games had been played and theoretically unlimited). To compound matters they couldn't hedge their bets as they could on, say, a horse race where odds would be changed on each runner in relation to the amount staked across the rest of the field to 'balance the book'.

While fixed-odds coupon betting wasn't new, William Hill led
the way in the aftermath of the Second World War. Hill had started
taking bets aged 19 while working in a factory in Birmingham in
1922 but when he lost everything he moved to London and started
again at White City greyhound track. By 1934 he'd opened a credit
office in Jermyn Street; five years later William Hill was a limited
company that actually managed to expand its trade during the war
years. As the conflict drew to a close, Hill set up a separate company,
William Hill (Football) Ltd, to focus on fixed-odds football betting.
Between 1955 and 1959 the turnover on this form of gambling was
less than half of that on the Pools, but at £45m it was still a huge
success and William Hill's rivals Ladbrokes decided they wanted a
piece of the action. At the start of the 1960/61 football season they
launched their own fixed-odds coupons and William Hill sought a
court injunction to stop them. When that failed, the firm launched
a copyright claim that eventually ended in the High Court, where
William Hill won. Ladbrokes altered their coupon and battle was
rejoined, with the odds on offer getting more and more competitive.
Eventually odds of up to 75/1 were available for any three draws as
opposed to the average payout of 5/1 for the same set of results on
the Pools, and a considerable number of punters switched from the
Pools to fixed-odds coupons. By 1964 William Hill's annual turnover
was £50m, a third of which was thanks to the coupons.

It wasn't to last. That year a 25 per cent tax on the fixed-odds
coupons was introduced by Tory Chancellor Reginald Maudling. The
Pools companies had lobbied the Government hard for the different
tax regulations between their coupons and those of their fixed-odds
rivals to be brought in line, something that the move duly accom-
plished. The Prime Minister, Harold MacMillan, had been quietly
concerned about the political implications of the tax and wrote to
his Chancellor saying that the administration had "reached the nadir
of our popularity" and that it was "no good making fresh enemies".
Nonetheless Maudling went ahead and introduced a betting levy in
his 1963 budget. As a consequence, turnover on fixed-odds betting
fell from approximately £65m in 1963 to £15m in 1965, and then to
just £5m in 1968. By comparison the Pools firms were still taking in
the region of £126m. By the end of 1964 the Tories had been turfed

out of office and Charles Layfield, a senior executive at William Hill, was in no doubt as to why, claiming Maudling had "antagonised millions and killed an industry in three months". Despite the slump, fixed-odds betting limped on until 1972 when Chancellor Denis Healey increased the tax on the coupons to 42 per cent effectively killing them off for good.

Two years later, thanks to the unlikely figure of John MacFarlane, fixed-odds betting on football was reborn in a different guise. A radical left-wing political activist, MacFarlane was a member of CND as well as the Scottish National Party and was still attending SNP conferences in 2005 aged 93, the year before his death. In a career that took in jobs as varied as organic farmer and social worker, MacFarlane worked for William Hill before becoming the managing director of Queens Bookmakers, which was owned by Greek Cypriot restaurateur Sir Reo Stakis. It was while he was in that role that, ahead of the 1974/75 football season, MacFarlane came up with the idea for bypassing the heavy tax levy on football coupons. His plan, which became known as 'champion fixed odds', was simply to price each game separately, with different odds for the home win, the away win and the draw. Although a fear of match fixing among bookies meant punters could still only bet on a minimum of three games – a 'treble' – crucially under this system all trebles were no longer priced the same but depended on the games chosen by respective punters. MacFarlane argued this made his system 'individual odds' betting and thus only subject to the standard betting duty of 7 per cent. Customs and Excise made Queens' coupons a test case and in a one-day hearing Scotland's Court of Session found unanimously in favour of the bookmaker.

The move was another, albeit grudging, step towards gambling's acceptability. When the 1960 Betting and Gaming Act legalised off-course betting for the first time in 107 years it created the conditions for bookmakers to introduce corporate structure to their businesses. From 1 May the following year the street bookies would finally be able to come out of their back-yards and open betting shops, and they did so *en masse*. In the first six months 10,000 had opened and the number grew to 14,388 by 1963. The fact that just under 12,000 bookmaking permits had been issued suggests most of them were small, independent firms. The big bookmakers had initially been disinterested in the changes, considering them to be simply street betting in a different form (as well as being slightly wary that the change would undermine their credit business). However, the temptation of the new legal cash betting market was too strong for them to resist and they began to buy out existing smaller bookmakers. The market began to consolidate and by the late 1980s three firms – William Hill, Ladbrokes and Coral – dominated the market, owning just over 40 per cent of the betting shops, which accounted for more than 60 per cent of turnover.

Despite the move to allow betting shops, there was still an underlying concern about the potential effects of gambling and so no visual enticement was allowed and the shops' windows had to be blacked out or shuttered. They were little more appealing inside. There were no chairs, no radio or television, and all that was allowed were betting slips; a counter where the bookie sat, protected by wire mesh; the 'boardman', who had to chalk up prices before a race and results after them; and 'the blower' – a verbal wire service provided by Extel. So dull were the new establishments that in his diary Rab Butler, the Tory Home Secretary who introduced the reform, likened them to an undertaker's premises. Some older punters claimed the new shops lacked something without the frisson of a possible raid by the police but racing pundit John McCririck, who was only 20 at the time, made the trip to a small first-floor bookies off Piccadilly in London on that first day and found the "tiny emporium was glorious bedlam". In 1986 the laws were relaxed further and punters were able to sit down and enjoy a hot drink (well, an insipid, warm drink) from a vending machine as they watched live racing coverage on TV thanks to the SIS channel. However, within a decade they would be able to do more than that – they would able to bet from the comfort of their own homes.

• • •

When Teddy Sheringham completed his hat-trick in Tottenham's 5-1 win over Hereford United in the FA Cup third-round replay on 17 January 1996, he had no reason to consider the match to be a historic one. Chris Armstrong also grabbed a brace in what was a routine victory for the North London club, allowing them to quickly forget the slight embarrassment of being held to a 1-1 draw by their Third Division opponents at Edgar Street 11 days earlier. However, the seemingly innocuous Wednesday-night match was a momentous occasion because of the actions of one man: Jukka Honkavaara. The Finn staked $50 on Spurs to win and when they did, he scooped a princely $2 and a place in the history books. He'd just won the world's first online sports bet. That the Scandinavian did so on an English game with a German bookmaker based in Antigua just about sums up the transnational nature of the internet, something that created the environment in which anti-gambling laws could be bypassed.

That said, it was a piece of legislation that kick-started the online betting boom. In 1994, two years before Honkavaara decided Tottenham were a sure thing to beat Hereford, the Government of Antigua and Barbuda passed the Free Trade and Processing Zone Act. What that did was create an area where company profits would be tax-free; however, to receive this benefit firms – including gambling companies – had to apply for a licence. The income derived from issuing these licences is how Antigua and Barbuda benefits. The twin-island nation is still one of the online gambling industry's most popular, albeit rigorous, licensing jurisdictions, with many online casinos and sports betting websites operating under licences granted by its Directorate of Offshore Gaming. This nascent regulatory framework was the crucial final piece of a three-part online gambling jigsaw.

The first was computer software. This had initially been used in gaming in the early 1960s when Edward O. Thorp, a professor at Massachusetts Institute of Technology, wrote a computer programme on his IBM 704 to analyse Blackjack decks. He went on to write the best-selling book *Beat the Dealer* on the basis of his research prompting a number of casinos to briefly change their rules.[7] By the early 1970s casinos were beginning to replace mechanical slot machines with electronic versions and by the end of the decade they had introduced video poker with IGT's Draw Poker machine leading the way. The game was a hit, becoming a casino mainstay, and over the following 15 years, improvements in software and graphics led to the proliferation of similar games. Second, in the 1990s the internet and encryption software that allowed for secure online financial transactions arrived on the scene, creating a virtual environment in which casinos could let players who weren't actually in their buildings play these games. Finally this was complemented by the real-world legal environment created by Antigua and Barbuda's free-trade law.

The Gaming Club was the first to take advantage when it opened its online casino in October 1995 but initially punters could only play for fun. Next on the scene was Intercasino, the first online casino where players could win (and lose) real money. They would also launch Intertops, the firm that took Honkavaara's bet in January 1996. In the same year, driven in part by Euro '96, other firms started launching websites displaying their available odds. By the end of that year, there were about 15 online gambling sites worldwide. Twelve months later there were more than 200 and the internet had begun to dramatically change the landscape of sports gambling across the world.

Governments and sports governing bodies struggled to keep pace. In England in September 2001 betting shops started accepting single bets on football and the following month tax on bets, which had reached a peak of 10 per cent, was abolished completely (it was replaced by a levy on bookies' gross profits). The 2005 Gambling Act effectively made online gambling a legitimate industry by 'white listing' places like Antigua and Barbuda, allowing their licensees, several of which were UK companies, to operate on the UK mainland. Finally, in September 2007 bookies and gambling websites were allowed to advertise on television and radio. It's easy to forget that the ubiquitous nature of online gambling is, just like the ubiquitous nature of televised football, a relatively recent phenomenon. Despite this, the numbers are astonishing and demonstrate how fast this section of the industry is growing. In 2013 online gambling expenditure broke the £2.5bn barrier for the first time.[7] Of that, sports betting accounted for £1.138bn – a 79 per cent increase in just four years. And, thanks to what the UK Gambling Commission called the "access anytime, anywhere" nature of smartphones and tablets, football is leading the

---

7   *This figure accounts for the combined online expenditure on poker, casino, bingo and sports betting.*

way, with online revenue for the sport 169 per cent greater than for horse racing, the traditional market leader.

• • •

Football wasn't just a driving force for growth; it was also the driving force for innovation that transformed sports betting. In 1998, while he was working on a secret project at GCHQ, Andrew Black developed the idea for an online betting exchange which allowed two gamblers to bet directly against each other by setting their own odds and cutting out the middleman; the bookmaker. That site was Betfair. "I was building websites for other people at the time and my background just happened to lead me to have the right thoughts," Black told me. "I'd worked in the London Stock Exchange, I'd worked as a hedge fund trader in New York and I'd spent a year as a professional gambler. So I had the three important pieces: the internet piece, the exchange piece and the sports betting piece, and I knew them all very well and I was in a very good position to build the website." Right from its launch in mid-2000, football was important for the site. "Euro 2000 was effectively our launch event," said Black. "Our very first event was the Oaks and the Derby but we focused on football because the exchange does work extremely well on football and also it was a good event to launch into. It was something solid with two games a day that everybody would be focusing on. If we had had too much going on – too much noise – nothing would really get going. After that we moved on to other things."

Just 10 months after launch the amount bet on the site each week had reached £1m. A year and a half after launch weekly turnover had reached £10m. This huge growth demonstrated that there was an eneormous amount of untapped demand and the internet was the way to access it. "When we launched, horse racing was the number one betting sport by a long way, but it was reasonably clear that a shift was already happening and it was clear it was going to continue," said Black, who went on to have a stint as owner of Swindon Town and now co-owns stables with Michael Owen. "The only thing that had stopped football being bigger before was that bookmakers were so inefficient at pricing up football matches because they didn't have computer technology. At the beginning of each week they would print off a great big sheet and it would apply to all Saturday's football. Having printed it on the Monday, if something happened on the Tuesday they weren't able to react. The shift from racing to football really occurred when everything moved online and suddenly the possibility of amending the prices on a real-time basis became reality. So the bookmakers were no longer shackled by the fact they had to maintain this great big sheet of prices during the week. Once that was broken things started to move to where the demand was."

By the end of Betfair's first full season in operation the site had launched its first in-play market on the UEFA Cup Final in which Liverpool beat Alaves 5-4. "It was absolutely amazing, that market. It did an unbelievable amount, or what we thought at the time was unbelievable," said Black. "When we launched in-play none of the bookmakers was doing it. We invented in-play if you like. For the first year and a half the big guys ignored us, then they started really panicking they would lose customers and so they began to search for ways to compete, which opened doors to a new generation of betting, in particular around in-play. One of the reasons no one was doing it was that nobody knew how to do it. Once they realized they could lift our prices that's pretty much what everyone did, although no one would admit it for a long time. So we created this in-play revolution that so many others followed."

David Williams, Director of Media at Ladbrokes, also acknowledges the dramatic impact the in-play markets have had on football betting: "If you look at the marketing strategies of all the major bookmakers in 2014, an awful lot of marketing and promotional spend was funnelled purely into the 2014 World Cup, and if you look back at what was being promoted, it was all about in-play. Football is the biggest in-play sport of the lot. To put it into context, 20 years ago it was just another sport and was a long way behind horse racing and even greyhound racing. You either bet on the football coupons in the betting shops or you didn't bet on football at all. Now football is enormously important across all of the platforms. There is a huge appetite for in-play betting, probably higher than we anticipated when it started a few years ago."

Williams said that "north of 60 per cent" of turnover on football is on in-play betting, while as recently as 2010 it would have been less than 10 per cent. But it's in danger of being eclipsed by a new kid on the block: cash out. "It's a game-changer regarding what is available to punters and football fans," said Williams, before telling me about a punter who had recently scooped £116,000 on a tenfold accumulator with a £5.05 stake. "He let his accumulator run for its duration, so had it gone wrong he would have been left with nothing. What was absolutely fascinating was that when we did a press release on the story, social media lit up with people saying that had they been in that position they would have cashed out. So whenever we are talking about a big winner, the added part of that conversation now is should that punter have cashed out; would you have cashed out in the same position? Everyone is talking about it. Cash out in digital was probably the most significant thing in 2015."

Williams told me that what he called "the inexorable rise of football betting" showed little sign of slowing, not least because, when we spoke, the 2016 European Championships, for which three of the four Home Nations and Ireland had qualified, was just around the corner. "That will ensure that football continues to be marketed very aggressively," said Williams. This growth appears, superficially at least, to be driven not by football per se but by televised football. "There is absolutely no doubt that the combination of football and television is a very happy marriage as far as bookies are concerned. A televised football match creates a huge surge in activity. If people can watch it, they'll bet on it," said Williams. However, he went further and identified the convergence between television and digital media as the real driving force behind the massive increase in football betting. "People no longer sit down and watch a match with a pint in one hand and a newspaper in the other. Increasingly they're sitting down with a phone in one hand and a tablet in the other. One will have their betting app while on the other they may be checking Twitter. The concept of multi-screening is proving more prevalent than it was a few years ago. Punters who are betting in-play or pre-match want more information. They want more statistics than they did a couple of years ago and they get that by multi-screening."

This demand for statistics has created more discerning customers who want more from the bookmakers' online services. Williams explained: "We can't just stick up the odds and say: 'over to you, Mr Customer' because if we do the customer will say: 'if you want me to have a bet you're going to have to give me a bit of data, a bit of information; the kind of data that traditional customers would expect to find in a betting shop on the wall with horse racing."

Talking of betting shops, digital media is also blurring the lines between betting online and in the high street. "There is a big drive towards what is rather clumsily called multi-channel," said Williams. "You're still getting 18- to 35-year-olds going into a betting shop on a Saturday morning and placing their coupon or their football accumulator. However they may not want to go back to that shop at the end of the day if they're a winner. But you can now scan that coupon into your phone or your tablet and get your winnings into your account. Or you can have a bet on your mobile and go into your local shop to get the cash out if it's a winner, and to some people that's very appealing; they like being given cash in their hand by the bookmaker. It's an interesting concept, bookmakers using their retail estate to promote digital betting, and a shop on the high street where digital customers can literally go and collect their cash.

"No longer is that betting shop simply a place for old-fashioned retail bets. Some of our younger customers prefer to use a self-service betting terminal with no interaction with the staff. Is that a retail bet or a digital bet? You're on the high street so it's a retail bet but it's using a digital product within a traditional betting shop." And what's the biggest sport on those terminals? You guessed it: football.

The ubiquity of the Pools helped cement the sport into the fabric of our society during the twentieth century by ensuring millions of fans and non-fans alike checked Saturday's results as part of their weekly routine. Now, through the convergence of televised football and the internet, football is repaying the favour by underpinning the massive growth in online gambling, which shows no sign of diminishing any time soon.

CHAPTER 6

FOOTBALL GETS SWITCHED ON

"John Logie Baird" is probably the most likely answer to the pub-quiz question: "who invented television?" The reality's a little more complex; just like the early broadcasts, the early history of television is a bit fuzzy. As with the Lumière brothers and cinema and Guglielmo Marconi and radio, Baird utilised the work of others as a basis for his own designs, key among them being the now little-known Australian inventor Henry Sutton. As far as inventing things goes, it's a travesty that Sutton's name is not up there with the very best. Alexander Graham Bell popped over to Australia to take a look at his telephone system and among many other things Sutton also invented a prototype helicopter, the world's first portable radio, the world's first colour printing press, the first car in Australia, the world's first front-wheel-drive car, the world's first four-wheel-drive car and the "electric light globe" (that's a light bulb to you and me). However, Sutton was geographically isolated from the world's scientific community and had no desire to gain material wealth, so, like many of his Australian contemporaries, he rarely sought patents, instead sharing his work in various journals for "the national good", meaning his work was inevitably 'borrowed' by other, less altruistic people (for example, he invented the vacuum pump, which the Swan-Edison company 'borrowed' for their own light-bulb design). So it was that in 1887, Sutton laid the foundations for Baird to 'invent' television by devising what he called the telephane system.

Not for the last time sport provided the impetus for advancement and innovation in media technology, as Sutton wanted to transmit moving pictures of the Melbourne Gold Cup the 70 miles to his home town of Ballarat.[1] Considered by many to be his *magnus opus,* the telephane system combined the work of others, namely the Kerr effect, the Nipkow disc and the selenium photocell (I could pretend that I understand what those things do, but I won't) into the first feasible television design. However, there was a weak link in the system. Radio had yet to be invented so Sutton had to use telegraph lines that didn't have the required bandwidth to transmit good-quality moving images. Given the lack of comprehensive records, there is debate as to whether he actually managed to broadcast pictures of the race at all. Some suggest that contemporaries said it worked "quite well" and that he later demonstrated his invention in England and France. Others suggest that, due to the technological limitations, the idea never made it off the drawing board. Given that Sutton worked in relative obscurity, we may never know for sure.

Perhaps we'd have a better idea had he lived in England and tried to transmit pictures of the Cheltenham Gold Cup the 84 miles to London – not just the capital of the country but of the whole Empire. Where there is agreement is that it was the available technology that was the problem, not Sutton's concept. He didn't seek a patent for his telephane but did share his work in the influential *Telegraphic Journal and Electric Register* on 7 November 1890, in an article which was subsequently republished in the equally high-profile *Scientific American* in 1905 and that described pretty much the same system that Baird used four decades later. By then the technology had caught up with Sutton's genius and the race was very much on to transmit moving pictures by radio.

A host of inventors were having a go with, depending who you believe, varying degrees of success. In June 1925 American Charles Francis Jenkins transmitted pictures of a slow turning windmill from a naval radio station to his lab seven miles away in Washington DC. However, Jenkins could only transmit silhouettes whereas Baird was the first person to develop a television system that had tones and shadows, and he demonstrated this to 40 members of the Royal Institution on 26 January 1926. He quickly enlisted the department store Selfridges to allow him to demonstrate his product to the public

---

1   For the record, the race was won by Dunlop in a then-record time of 3 minutes 28 seconds, apparently much to the delight of the bookmakers.

and by 1928 the store was selling his Televisor for between £20 and £150 (a reasonable £900 to £6,800 in today's money) with the promise that it would be delivered when a television service became available. That it's Baird's name which lives on in the popular conscience, while his rivals are consigned to the late-night slots on the History Channel, demonstrates once again that if you don't grab the headlines, you don't get the credit.

• • •

Sport continued to play a key part in the early development of television. On 10 May 1928 Bell Telephone Laboratories set up a camera on their roof and filmed some men playing tennis – the first television footage filmed outdoors – and a little over three years later Baird conducted the first outside broadcast of the 1931 Derby. America and Britain led the way in TV and both created systems that were built upon, and therefore very similar to, their radio networks. In the US a series of commercial, privately owned stations that derived revenue from advertising were created, while in Britain the BBC public service model was employed. The Beeb launched an experimental TV service in 1932 using Baird's 30-line system; however, at this stage television was dismissed as nothing more than a very expensive toy. By 1934 a Government Television Advisory Committee entrusted the corporation with developing a high-definition service (I say "high-definition" but it's all relative) and on 2 November 1936 the service launched from Alexandra Palace to around 2,000 expectant viewers in a 40-mile radius.

Initially the Beeb alternated between Baird's improved 240-line system and the 405-line system of his rivals Marconi-EMI, but after three months the government committee settled on the latter and Baird was effectively out of the television business. It should be pointed out that the Nazis beat the BBC to launching a TV service by a couple of months, just in time for the Berlin Olympics in July and August. It was the world's first sports broadcast, with pictures beamed to about 25 'viewing parlours' around Berlin as well as the Olympic Village. It was clear that Adolf Hitler and his Minister of Propaganda, Joseph Goebbels, recognised the cultural importance of televised sport and the power it has for promoting national interests. Back at the BBC it was all a little more benign and with Gerald Cock at the helm as the first Director of Television and many of his colleagues from BBC Radio joining him, it's little surprise that the early TV outside broadcasts mirrored the events that formed the backbone of the BBC's radio coverage. This served to reinforce the cultural importance of certain events while continuing to marginalise others. Just as on radio, greyhound racing suffered despite its popularity. By 1951, 210 licensed dog tracks were being visited by 200,000 punters a week. Notwithstanding the efforts of Head of Outside Broadcasts Seymour Joly de Lotbinière, who was keen to avoid damaging relations with the owners of Harringay, Wembley and White City stadia, all of which hosted other events, the sport would not be televised until 1953. Even then race results were banned from news broadcasts.

BBC TV focused on the events already framed as having national importance by radio. With Royalty at the top of the list, George VI's Coronation procession in 1937 provided the subject matter for the corporation's first outside broadcast. The BBC also had a hierarchy of sports events; the 'musts', 'shoulds' and 'mights', which were built on the upper-middle-class, Oxbridge, amateur ethos of the BBC staff. The musts were: The Derby and Grand National, the Boat Race, Test matches, Wimbledon, Rugby Union internationals, major boxing bouts and the FA Cup Final. As the BBC used these events to further weave itself into the country's cultural fabric, so in turn the events themselves became more important for the nation. The 1937 Wimbledon Championships were broadcast soon after the Royal procession, with the BBC using three vans – one for the camera, one for the transmitter and the third for the generator – to cover the event. Viewers couldn't see the ball, and, not for the last time, the on-court action was overshadowed by the star appeal of the Royal Box as the camera was turned to film Queen Mary, the Queen Mother, taking her seat. These minor issues aside, TV sport had arrived in England and coverage of that other parochial, upper-class event, the Oxbridge Boat Race, followed in April 1938.

Not only did Cock use live events to strengthen and secure the BBC's position as the nation's cultural ambassador but he also used them to determine what the BBC's TV service, and in many respects television itself, should represent. While cinema newsreels could provide the thrill of the moving image, it was often days or even weeks after the event, and while radio provided the immediacy of live coverage in the intimacy of the listener's own home it lacked pictures. Television blew the pair out of the water by providing both, and this made the football authorities fearful of the consequences the new medium might have for the attendance figures of games being played at the same time as broadcasts – a fear that would dominate their thinking for decades to come.

Football had been the focus of several test transmissions in 1937, with Arsenal, whose manager George Allison was also a BBC radio commentator, providing the venue and the teams, but the sport would have to wait a little longer before it got its screening on the public service. Cock started negotiations with the FA in December 1937 and three months later, following a period of intransigence, was moved to write to FA Secretary Stanley Rous saying: "Here is the beginning of a great industry, the progress of which depends to a great extent on the co-operation of institutions such as the FA." With a bit of persuasion from Rous, the Council finally gave permission for the broadcasting of a Home International between England and Scotland on 9 April and the FA Cup Final between Huddersfield Town and Preston North End a few weeks later. A sense of how laborious it was to organise coverage of these events was provided by a new *Radio Times* column devoted to television called *The Scanner*. A couple of nights before the Home International the BBC broadcast coverage of the British Cruiserweight Championship bout between Len Harvey and Jack McAvoy at Harringay Stadium, about six miles from Wembley, and *The Scanner* reported that: "Far from being ample, the twenty-nine hours' interval is giving something of a rush job."

Rush job or not, the coverage was a hit and from the very start the appeal of live football was recognised as something that could sell both televisions and television services, with *The Times* claiming: "To see these events as they take place is something different in kind from a news-reel after the event; it has a particular thrill and would alone make the possession of a set worth while." The BBC even developed a marketing slogan: "Television is Here – You Can't Shut Your Eyes To It". Only it wasn't here for very long. At noon on 1 September

1939 the screens went blank – right in the middle of a Mickey Mouse cartoon – and two days later war was declared. By that time 23,000 combined television and radio licences had been sold to a totally London-based audience that was able to watch around two-hours of programming per day. The demand was such that it was estimated there would have been 80,000 licence holders by Christmas of that year. The BBC claimed the shutdown was to prevent the Luftwaffe from using signals from Alexandra Palace for navigation (in fact the transmitter would be covertly used to jam German radio signals) while many technicians were seconded to the war effort. The Football League was suspended too; however, in contrast to the damaging effect that the First World War had on the sports press, televised football coverage would re-emerge soon after VE Day.

• • •

Despite Nazi resistance starting to crumble on mainland Europe, in September 1944 the resumption of television was still some distance in the future. However, that didn't stop a significant number of Britain's sports governing bodies, including both the FA and Football League, from launching a pre-emptive strike against the BBC's TV service. They joined forces to establish the Association for the Protection of Copyright in Sport (APCS) in an attempt to protect their products, and the issue wouldn't be fully resolved for nearly a decade. The BBC began broadcasting again a little bit sooner. On 7 June 1946, announcer Jasmine Bligh employed typically British understatement to welcome viewers back "after the short interruption". As well as *Mickey's Gala Premiere*, the cartoon that had been interrupted by the conflict, the transmission included Margot Fonteyn dancing and a variety show.

The next day the Beeb was in familiar territory; an outside broadcast of a key national event. They covered the military parade from the London Victory Celebrations, thus quickly reconfirming their place as the nation's cultural ambassador. The television service was still playing second fiddle to the more-established radio service and was also restricted by the austerity of a country which had won the war but was in the process of losing the peace. Gerald Cock had retired due to ill-health and his successor Maurice Gorham would later write in his book *Sound and Fury*: "I was running television in a country that could hardly afford it, for I do not think anybody would maintain that if we had not had television before the war we should have started it in 1946. Our equipment was hopelessly old fashion in design, the actual gear we used was mostly ten years old, and it was inadequately served."

A national fuel shortage forced the BBC off the air for a month in February 1947 but by then they'd managed to start broadcasting football again, with Barnet and Wealdstone's Athenian League match on 20 October 1946 at Underhill providing the occasion. Barnet were the leading amateur side of the time and their League match against Tooting and Mitcham was due to be filmed before it was rescheduled due to the Bees' FA Cup commitments. Viewers were treated to interviews with the two captains, Wealdstone's C.A.P. Edmonds and Barnet's Dennis Kelleher, who the *Barnet Press & News* described as "smiling but fidgety [and] nervous". In 1944 Kelleher had escaped from a P.O.W. camp and spent 22 days on the run across Europe before walking into his home and casually saying: "Hello, folks. How's the war?" Three days after his return he helped Barnet to a 2-1 victory over Grays Athletic. That he was visibly nervous in front of the camera demonstrates the effect that the latter can have on even the most heroic of people. Other than the interview with the captain, viewers also got to see part of the first half and the whole of the second half of the match, although as the *Radio Times* noted just over a week later, they didn't get to see much of the ball: "Bad light towards the end of the afternoon made it appear that the players [...] were kicking an invisible ball. Next time it is hoped to have the ball specially whitened." On the plus side as the *Press & News* reported: "The two bald-headed Wealdstone players were easily picked out." The writer was sceptical about the likely success of such broadcasts, arguing, "many Amateur Cups will be lost and won before television deters fans from clicking the turnstiles each Saturday". His conclusion was hardly surprising given that the broadcast from Underhill saw a record crowd of 5,000 turn up, in no small part due to the novelty of the television cameras.

With the League restarting after the war it was a bumper time for football that saw attendances peaking in 1949. The BBC sought to exploit this to promote its new service and was on hand to film Chris Duffy score an extra-time winner as Charlton beat Burnley in the 1947

Cup Final. A fuel crisis had been averted but there was still significant rationing. Despite this, the Labour Government gave permission for the match to be broadcast during a period of the day when domestic electricity use was otherwise prohibited. There were complaints, not least about the fact that Easter Sunday services had not been offered the same dispensation. The next key sporting event the BBC covered was the London Olympics in 1948; the original Austerity Games. The city had been awarded the 1944 Olympics but they were cancelled due to the war and the crushing financial burden of the conflict meant Britain almost forewent the chance to hold the Games in 1948. They went ahead thanks to the support of George VI, who insisted that they could revive the country economically (ring any bells?).

Whether it had the effect desired by the King is debatable but the BBC made huge advances in their outside broadcasting capabilities, outstripping anything achieved by the Nazis' coverage of the previous Games 12 years before. The facilities were state-of-the-art with 15 commentary boxes and 16 open positions in the Empire Stadium and another 16 commentary points at the swimming pool. Staff were seconded from the regions and as well as offering a daily programme, *Olympic Sports-Reel 4,* the BBC broke into other programmes for key events (establishing a practice which annoys non-sports fans to this day). On average there was five hours of live coverage a day, with one day having 7 hours and 35 minutes. This achievement received praise in the *Daily Express* from John Macadam, who wrote: "Such Olympic successes have set the key for the months ahead. Whatever the failings of television as a medium for other entertainment, it really does serve sport brilliantly." The 1948 Olympics was long considered to be the greatest achievement in the BBC's history but sadly only 43 seconds of the 68 hours and 29 minutes of footage captured in the fortnight still exists, as tele-recording was in its infancy. At the time, however, it provided a huge boost to the BBC television service, with the number of sets in London leaping from 14,500 in 1946 to 66,000 by the end of 1948.

By 1950 about 350,000 TV licences had been issued and the FA Cup Final between Liverpool and Arsenal (which the Gunners won 2-0) had been watched by approximately one million people, with a noticeable drop in League attendance on the same day. The Beeb argued this was the case across the country and not just in areas that had TV (at that stage, just London and Birmingham) and so must have been because of the weather, not the Cup Final broadcast. Unconvinced, the Government set up a Sports Television Advisory Committee to monitor attendance figures. They noted another drop in attendances during the 1951 Cup Final broadcast despite the fact that the BBC had agreed to only broadcast the second half after a plan to delay the final by a week to avoid any clashes with League games was rejected. Fortunately (or unfortunately for Blackpool fans) Jackie Milburn obliged the viewers by grabbing a brace in the second half as Newcastle ran out 2-0 winners.

The Assistant Postmaster-General Sir David Gammans argued that a longer-term study was required while also noting that the Cup Final led to "reduced attendances at other sporting events held on the same day, and that this effect is more marked at minor sporting events". The APCS was still militating for a form of copyright control, with some sports governing bodies jealously eyeing the fees American TV companies were paying, while others were concerned that people might watch "re-diffused" coverage of games at cinemas or through shop windows instead of going to grounds and paying. The BBC responded in kind, suggesting they would focus on sports "willing to co-operate with mutually advantageous broadcasts" while the "obstructionists" would receive no coverage. The die was cast, for 1952 at least, and the FA, under some pressure from the Football League, said the BBC could film the Cup Final but only broadcast it a week later, an offer that the BBC politely declined, making that year's Cup Final the last not to have been broadcast on TV. Just as during the radio-rights dispute following the 1929 Cup Final, a third party had to step in and settle the disagreement, although this time it wasn't the Bishop of Buckingham but the Government in the form of the Copyright Committee. Their October 1952 report suggested that the copyright should be given to the broadcaster, who could more easily control re-diffusion and reimburse the sports organisers accordingly. So it was that the BBC agreed to pay the FA £1,000 to broadcast the 1953 Cup Final, a broadcast which would set the template for TV football coverage to this day.

• • •

Eight grim years after the end of the Second World War Britain was entering a bright, modern era. The political parties had reached a Butskellian consensus and there was a widespread sense of optimism and aspiration that manifested itself in two things. First was the Coronation of a young Queen, which ushered in a New Elizabethan era, and second was a sense of technological process of which TV was the most visible form. The pair came together in the broadcast of Queen Elizabeth II's Coronation. Initially the Cabinet decreed that only "a cinematograph film of the event" should be made and broadcast to the plebs later in the day; however, the Queen herself stepped in and asked her Government to reconsider, which they duly did. There was massive anticipation for the Coronation and the TV coverage of it which when coupled with increasing wages and falling costs of sets saw a huge rise in sales of televisions.

Viewing figures for the event were huge and it was the first time that the number of people tuning in on TV outnumbered those listening on radio. Some 7.8 million people watched in their own homes, 10.4 million in other people's homes and 1.5 million in pubs, music halls and cinemas (a further million viewers were able to pick up the signal in France). It was a golden summer for the country. On the day of the Coronation, *The Times* revealed that Edmund Hillary had conquered Everest (with a bit of help from some bloke called Tenzing Norgay). Four days later Gordon Richards, Champion Jockey 26 times and recently awarded a knighthood in the Coronation honours list, won the Derby at last on Pinza, in his 28th and final attempt. By mid-August England's cricketers regained the Ashes after 20 years of hurt. Even tea was no longer rationed. What more could you want? Well, how about one of the best FA Cup Finals of all time, live in your living room as you enjoyed a cuppa? A little over four weeks before the Coronation, 10 million viewers enjoyed just that.

If the match had happened in any previous season I doubt I'd be writing about it now and I doubt you would have heard of it. When you think about the history of English football – the sport's key moments – more often than not you're actually thinking about the history of *televised* football. What came before is forgotten, or overlooked, because it's harder to see. This has reached its apogee with the Premier League's Year Zero approach to the record books but it can be traced back to 1953. Take for example the 1935 final just 17 years before; what do you know about that game? It was a six-goal thriller which saw West Brom fall behind to Sheffield Wednesday as early as the second minute before pulling the game back to 2-2 with 20 minutes to play. However the Owls ran out winners thanks to a brace in the last five minutes of normal time from Ellis Rimmer, who had scored in every round.[2] I doubt few but the oldest or most ardent fans from the blue-and-white half of the Steel City can tell you much about the Rimmer Final (as I have just named it). Instead it's just one of many footnotes from the FA Cup's pre-television history.

The 1953 Cup Final was, however, an altogether different affair, with one of England's best-known footballers, 38-year-old Stanley Matthews, taking centre stage. Even the televising of the match has been falsely mythologised, with many wrongly claiming it was the first Cup Final to be broadcast on television. While that's not true, it was the first Cup Final to be seen by what could be considered a mass audience. New transmitters had been built in the West Midlands, the Pennines, Scotland and Wales, meaning that, while there were still gaps in coverage, television was at last a genuinely national service. That service wasn't totally responsible for creating the mythology of the 1953 final; however, it facilitated the distillation of several key cultural narratives into an event the nation could watch as a unified community.

In many ways the Cup Final was a dry run for the Coronation. The Queen was in attendance – the first reigning queen to watch a Cup Final – and the event provided an opportunity to reinforce the sense of consensus and social unity that the dawning of the New Elizabethan era supposedly represented. It was also the first time TV coverage of a football match had a 'story' constructed around it, focusing the viewers' attentions on the actions of one individual to the exclusion of all else (something to which we're now accustomed). A process that started with cigarette cards, with their focus on individual players, and spilled over into newspaper match coverage had now found its way on to the television screen.

2   *Rimmer joined Wednesday in February 1928 when they were seven points adrift at the bottom of the First Division. They survived and went on to lift the title in the following two seasons. In his ten years at Wednesday, Rimmer, who was a left-winger not a striker, scored 140 goals – more than twice as many as Stanley Matthews managed in his whole 27-year playing career. Just saying.*

Like Richards and the Derby, many considered the match to be Matthews' last chance to ensure his career wouldn't end trophy-less. He'd already been on the losing side in two FA Cup Finals, the most recent one being just two years previously in the half-broadcast match won by Newcastle. In his preview of that game, Geoffrey Green of *The Times* christened the match 'The Matthews Final' but instead Jackie Milburn stole the show. So, two years later when Matthews got another shot at Wembley glory and was successful, the story had already been written. Green triumphantly dusted off his moniker, ending his match report: "Nothing like that had ever happened before. I doubt it will ever happen again. That was the 'Matthews Final'". In a sense he was right: nothing like that had happened before. Without the all-important broadcast the final would probably have little more significance today than the Rimmer Final just 17 years earlier. Yet it shouldn't be forgotten that while Matthews finally got his winner's medal it was in large part thanks to three goals from Stan Mortensen, but why let the first and, as I type, only FA Cup Final hat-trick at Wembley get in the way of a pre-determined narrative?

While he didn't pick up any more team honours, Matthews did become the inaugural recipient of the Ballon D'Or in 1956. Nine years later he became the first footballer to be knighted and in April of 1965 his testimonial was transmitted live across Europe from Stoke's Victoria Park thanks to the Eurovision TV network. An estimated 112 million people tuned in to watch an International XI featuring Lev Yashin, Alfredo di Stefano, Ferenc Puskás and Eusebio defeat a Matthews XI that featured, among others, England stars Jimmy Greaves and Bobby Charlton. It was the final proof that while Matthews wasn't the first football celebrity he was the first football celebrity of the TV age. And what of the FA Cup Final? By 1954 only a handful of Third Division matches were scheduled to take place on the same day and they kicked off at 6.30pm. By 1956 the FA Cup Final was the only game to take place that day. The journey that had started with newsreels and continued with radio coverage was complete. Coronation year saw the FA Cup Final ascend the football throne and become the most important match of the season.

• • •

While the English were doing what they do best and patting themselves on the back in a gigantic garden party, the rest of the world had been quietly moving on without them. Just a few months after TV delivered the high of the Matthews Final it also delivered the low of England's 6-3 evisceration by Hungary at Wembley. Due to the row between the FA and the BBC, England games, like the FA Cup, had been absent from TV screens since October 1951 but they returned in late 1953 in time for the FA's 90th anniversary celebrations. The Hungary defeat was probably not what they had in mind but the result should not have been as big a shock as it was. Three years earlier in 1950 the FA deigned to enter the World Cup for the first time, and in their second game of the tournament (in what was only their second-ever game against non-European opposition) England were humiliated in a 1-0 defeat at the hands of the part-timers from America. However, the English press played down the significance of the defeat and, in the absence of TV coverage, a result which should have set alarm bells ringing barely registered on the English public's collective consciousness; like the Rimmer Final it went unseen and so could be easily airbrushed from history. Following that game, Yugoslavia, France and Austria all visited England in 1950 and 1951 and all drew 2-2. The hat-trick of draws, all of which were broadcast live from half time onwards, suggested that a home defeat was in the offing for Walter Winterbottom's side and it finally came at the hands of the Mighty Magyars at Wembley in November 1953.

As Hungary's captain Ferenc Puskás began juggling the ball with his feet as the teams waited to kick off, the BBC's young commentator Kenneth Wolstenholme appeared to sense what was about to happen. "Well, there's an exhibition of ball control ..." he began, almost fearfully. "Just look at that from the inside-left Puskás. If we see a great deal of that I think we're going to have an awful lot of trouble holding these unbeaten Hungarians." And an awful lot of trouble was exactly what England had as Puskás and Nándor Hidegkuti tore the home defence apart. The second half was broadcast live, with the game being re-shown in full later in the evening, and the coverage meant that the reality that English football was being surpassed on the pitch was unavoidable. The return fixture in Budapest in May 1954 was seen as an opportunity to quickly restore the balance of power, with the *Daily Mail* declaring: "England chance of revenge: Hungary worried." If the Hungarians were worried their nerves settled quickly. They opened the scoring in the tenth minute and ten minutes later they were 3-0 ahead, eventually running out 7-1 winners. To date, it is still England's heaviest-ever defeat, yet the game, like the defeat at the hands of the USA, wasn't shown on TV and so it's the trauma of the 6-3 result which is seared into English football's psyche.

The next full international to hit the small screen was England's thrilling eight-goal, extra-time draw against Belgium in Basel in June 1954. It was their opening game in the World Cup in Switzerland – the first such tournament to be broadcast live as technological limitations meant there had been no coverage of the 1950 World Cup in Brazil. The Eurovision TV network, launched by members of the European Broadcasting Union 10 days before the tournament kicked off, transmitted 9 of the 26 games to 5 countries across Europe. However, Eurovision could only transmit one match at a time, so when England played their next game, a 2-0 victory over Switzerland, Eurovision was instead broadcasting Hungary's 8-3 demolition of the West Germans. With Switzerland being the host nation, Swiss television was able to broadcast the England game live within their own country but England fans had to wait three days for the BBC to broadcast 10 minutes of highlights. Eurovision did transmit England's 4-2 quarter-final defeat against the reigning World Champions, Uruguay, but the BBC chose to show only the second-half. This was common practice for friendlies that took place on the same day as League fixtures but a strange decision for such an important match being played in the close season.

Nonetheless Eurovision, which would become more famous for its eponymous singing competition and the knockabout *Jeux Sans Frontière*, had recognised that improvements in air travel and TV technology were making football a pan-European game – a game without frontiers if you will – a position cemented by a third techno- logical innovation: floodlights. There had been various experiments with floodlights dating back to 1878 when Sheffield United rigged up some lamps powered by steam engines around Bramall Lane, but it wasn't until the 1930s that the technology allowed for regular night games to be given serious consideration. Arsenal's innovative boss Herbert Chapman had floodlights built into Highbury's West Stand, only for the FA to promptly ban their use.

The ban was only lifted in the early 1950s and then initially just for friendlies; it wasn't until 1956 that the first League game, between Portsmouth and Newcastle, took place under floodlights. It was an opportunity the BBC was quick to seize on. Until that point, the FA Cup and internationals aside, the Beeb had been limited to broadcasting games from the Amateur Cup and the Senior London Cup along with fixtures involving teams from the Armed Forces. Now, English clubs started playing mid-week friendlies against foreign opposition and, crucially, these games were not covered by the League's ban on TV so the BBC was able to get access to high-profile teams and matches, giving them the chance to boost their coverage.

One team and one game in particular became synonymous with these 'floodlit friendlies': Wolverhampton Wanderers' match against Honved in December 1954. At the time, Wolves were reigning English champions, skippered by England's captain Billy Wright, while the Honved side was led by Hungary's captain Puskás, and included the 1954 World Cup's top scorer Sándor Kocsis, as well as three other members of the Hungary team that had humiliated England home and away the previous season. The game was seen as a quick chance to get revenge (of sorts) over the Hungarians. Wolves were a metaphor for England, Honved a metaphor for Hungary and arguably the rest of the world.

Over the years the match has become highly mythologised as innovative and pioneering yet it was not the only match of this sort to be played at the time. Such friendlies were commonplace. Wolves themselves hosted a range of teams including the South African national side, Racing Club of Buenos Aires, Spartak Moscow and Moscow Dynamo before the Honved game. A couple of months earlier West Bromwich Albion, Wolves' local rivals who they had pipped to the 1954 title, played the Hungarians in Le Soir Festival of Football, a mini-European tournament in Brussels also involving Austria Vienna and KNC Anderlecht. The papers dubbed the West Brom–Honved game the "match of the century" yet there was no live TV coverage (and WBA lost 5-3) so it has since faded from memory. While Baggies fans are no doubt sick of hearing it, not only was the Wolves–Honved game televised but the hosts, sporting special satin shirts which supposedly showed up better under the floodlights, won. Their manager Stan Cullis noted how the Magyars had looked less than mighty on a muddy pitch in Bern's Wankdorf stadium in the World Cup Final against West Germany a few months earlier so he had the Molineux pitch heavily watered. Ron Atkinson, then an apprentice at the club, recalled decades later how they were instructed to make the pitch "nice and heavy". Roy Peskett of the *Daily Mail* reported that the playing surface looked "like a cattle ground at the end of a four-day show in the rain". Despite being 2-0 down after just 14 minutes, Wolves eventually ran out 3-2 against the tiring Hungarians.

The sense of the awe the match created among TV viewers is palpable from the memories of George Best, who as an enthralled youngster watched the game "through the magic of television". It was, he wrote in his 2001 autobiography *Blessed*, "love at first sight". Sat in front of the tiny black-and-white set of his neighbour Mr Harrison the eight-year-old George "was mesmerised" as the floodlights "turned football into theatre". When Wolves "played sides like Moscow Spartak and Moscow Dynamo, it was as though they were playing against aliens". As a boy Best "dreamed of wearing the famous gold shirt" but he had to settle for the red of Manchester United with whom he won the European Cup in 1968, a tournament also inspired by Wolves' famous victory. Following that win over Honved the *Daily Express* claimed that "Wolverhampton Wanderers became club champions of Europe" while the *Daily Mail* went one step further: "Hail Wolves, Champions of the World." One French journalist in particular, Gabriel Hanot, took exception to England's arrogant response to the win, arguing, "we'd better wait until the Wolves travel to Moscow and Budapest to proclaim their invincibility; but if the English are so sure about their hegemony in football, then this is the time to create a European tournament".

Hanot wasn't the only one calling for an organised European tournament. On the morning of the Honved game Desmond Hackett of the *Daily Express* asked: "How long will these glamour teams continue to draw the crowds for non-title matches? How much more sensible and absorbing in this jet plane age to organise a European Cup series under the lights that may not always be so golden. Let the league champions of each nation go into the hat for a quick knockout competition. It should be a soccer best seller: Wolves, Celtic, Honved, Dynamo, FC Austria, Milan, Kaiserslautern, Racing Club de Paris and so excitedly on and on." However, it was Hanot who had the will to get the competition up and running. Faced with intransigence from FIFA and the relatively young UEFA, Hanot decided *L'Equipe*, the paper he worked for, would organise the competition on an invitation basis. Faced with a threat to their powerbase, UEFA quickly decided to take control of the tournament, which began in the 1955/56 season. Not all the initial entrants were national champions and the English declined to send a team; however, very quickly the competition created a new front in the TV rights war in England.

• • •

As English football kidded itself that a narrow victory on a quagmire of a pitch in the Black Country had reasserted the country's rightful place at the top of the football world's pecking order, the BBC's pre-eminent place as the country's main broadcaster was under threat. A new commercial TV service was considered a key way of expanding Britain's television service although there were dire warnings from both the left, which argued commercial television would lead to a dumbing down of working-class culture, and the right, which argued it would lead to an Americanisation of society. Some might argue history has proved them both correct but despite the controversy ITV became a reality with the Television Act of 1954.[3] The new network was to be regulated by the Independent Television Authority, which awarded franchises on a fixed-term basis. Initially the network was divided between Associated Rediffusion, which covered London on weekdays; Associated Television (ATV), which covered London at weekends and the Midlands during the week; Associated Broadcasting Company (ABC), which covered the

3   *A clause was inserted into the Act banning commercials during Royal broadcasts. This was prompted by the fact that US television had interrupted their coverage of the Coronation with adverts, one of which featured a chimp called J. Fred Muggs.*

Midlands and the North at weekends; and Granada, which covered the North during the week. "The Big Four" companies launched between September 1955 and May 1956, and between 1957 and 1962 they were joined by a host of other franchises such as Anglia and Tyne Tees.

It's been argued that the BBC didn't take the birth of a rival seriously but the facts suggest otherwise. On 22 September 1955, the night before ITV's launch, BBC radio broadcast the most dramatic episode of *The Archers* to date in which Grace Archer was killed in a stable fire while trying to rescue her horse, Midnight. Eight million people tuned in to listen to the tragedy, which made the front pages the following day and led to thousands of distraught listeners calling the BBC. It overshadowed the launch of ITV, which was exactly what the head of the Light Programme, H. Rooney Pelletier, had intended. Some months before, Pelletier had outlined his plan in a top-secret memo, saying: "The more I think about it, the more I believe that a death of a violent kind in *The Archers*, timed, if possible, to diminish interest in the opening of commercial television in London, is a good idea."

The Outside Broadcast Unit also wheeled out the big guns and sport was one of the key weapons used against the new TV network. In 1954 in the run-up to the birth of ITV the BBC's head of Outside Broadcasting Peter Dimmock launched a mid-week sports magazine programme called *Sportsview*. A topical mix of outside broadcasts, films and studio segments with the top sports stars of the day, *Sportsview* enshrined Wednesday night as a slot for sport and its editorial style even influenced *Panorama*. When ITV launched, Dimmock scheduled a special two-hour *Sportsview* labelled as "probably the greatest sporting night of the year" up against it. Four years later he oversaw the launch of *Grandstand* on Saturday afternoons, a timeslot already earmarked for sport by BBC Radio.[4] Given this onslaught, ITV simply couldn't compete for the coverage of most sports.

---

4   It took Dimmock several months after Grandstand's *launch to persuade the powers-that-be to allow the show to finish at 5pm instead of 4.45pm. The extra 15 minutes meant* Grandstand *could provide a proper football results service, the downside being that* Children's Hour *was shortened to just 45 minutes.*

The BBC had had years of unrivalled dominance to build on. They had the top sports and the top sports broadcasters tied up in long-term contracts and they had the contacts, the equipment and the expertise to produce sports coverage well; sports authorities trusted them. Furthermore, the fractured and regional structure of the ITV network meant each franchise had its own set of priorities and, initially at least, none really had the cash needed to mount a sustained challenge to the BBC for national sports rights. Had the franchises been organised around programme type, or had the franchises formed a jointly owned sports company (as they did with news by forming ITN), then things might have been different. Instead, in its early days, ITV's sports coverage was "sparse, random and sometimes amateurish" according to Bernard Sendall in the weighty, six-volume history *Independent Television in Britain.*

However, football – and the Football League in particular – was one sport the new TV companies targeted. The game enabled them to overcome the key problems they faced – in that it was regional in nature and it was a market the BBC had yet to tie up. There was a benefit for football too. A new buyer in the market meant that for the first time they had leverage to extract a value for the rights they considered reasonable (their hand would be strengthened still further with the advent of pay-TV in the late 1980s, but more of that later). While the League Management Committee's key concerns were financial – how could they ensure clubs were adequately compensated for any loss of revenue at the turnstiles? – they were also fearful of the unknown and so put up considerable resistance to any coverage of live League football. That resistance was personified by one man – Burnley's chairman Bob Lord.

Labelled "the Khruschev of Turf Moor" by Arthur Hopcraft, Lord was chairman of the club for 26 years between 1955 and 1981, overseeing its most successful period. Nine consecutive top-10 finishes were crowned by the League title in 1960, and in 1962 the team were runners-up in both the League and FA Cup. These achievements have faded from memory, in part, ironically, because of Lord's suspicion of television. He banned cameras totally from Turf Moor between 1964 and 1969. By 1966 most clubs had reluctantly given in and were at least allowing edited highlights of their games, but two – Everton and Burnley – held out. In January of that year Lord refused to let a BBC TV crew into Turf Moor ahead of an FA Cup replay with Bournemouth, ripping up their letter of accreditation. He went on to threaten to sue both the BBC and the FA saying: "I don't care if Harold Wilson has given permission, this match must not be televised." His anti-TV stance continued for many years but took an unwelcome turn in 1974 when he told a Variety Club function that "We have to stand up against a move to get soccer on the cheap by the Jews who run television." Leeds' Jewish chairman Manny Cussins took exception to Lord's anti-Semitism, leading to a tit-for-tat boycott of the Elland Road directors' box by the Burnley board members.

It's easy to portray Lord as an intransigent dinosaur, not least because of his dubious attitude to race relations and his truculent manner, but reading his autobiography (the modestly titled *My Fight for Football*) Burnley's butcher's-boy-made-good comes across as a man ahead of his time on many issues. He argued that the increasing monopolisation of England internationals by Wembley[5] was starving "the great cities and centres of football which 'made' the game [allowing] London to cash in". Lord called for the men in the middle to become full-time professionals assessed by a panel of former referees and he argued that they should clamp down firmly on the "ball-or-ankle" tackle. In a less physical game, Lord suggested, "the flair player, the individualist, would get a better chance", adding: "heavy-footed clodhoppers are no use against the Continentals". He also argued that English football "lags against the Continentals" because the top teams played too many games, especially towards the end of a season. This, Lord claimed, was the reason Burnley ended the 1961 season empty-handed.

In mid-March of that year the Clarets were still in the European, FA and League Cups. However, despite having won the first leg of their European Cup quarter-final against Hamburg they crashed out 5-4 on aggregate before losing in both the domestic cup semi-finals. Furthermore, Lord's attitude towards television was the prevailing one until the late 1980s and was motivated by a desire to keep a semblance of parity in football. The argument was simple: TV coverage would lead to a fall in attendances that the big clubs could deal

---

5   *Until England's match with Argentina at Wembley in 1951, only games against Scotland were played at the stadium, other internationals being held at grounds around the country.*

with but a club like Burnley, hailing from a town with a population
of little more than 80,000, could not. Ultimately it wasn't a drop in
attendances that destroyed the parity in English football; it was a
monopolisation of TV cash by the big few. However Lord was right
about the consequences; could Burnley win the League today?

• • •

If the football authorities were unclear as to exactly how their relationship with television should develop, neither the BBC nor their new
rivals had any such doubts. In 1954 before ITV had even launched,
Dimmock, aware of the threat the new service posed, offered the
Football League £250,000 to cover League matches. It was a staggering
sum for the time and so the offer was almost immediately withdrawn
as the Beeb simply couldn't pay it, but the offer gave the Football
League's negotiator, assistant secretary Alan Hardaker,[6] an idea of
the riches that might now be on offer. In March of the following
year both the BBC and the ITA put separate bids to the League for
the rights to show excerpts of some League games, with the caveat
that they wouldn't reveal in advance which games would be shown.
In May ITV's two weekend companies – ATV and ABC – started
approaching the big clubs in their regions, such as Arsenal, Aston
Villa and Manchester United, and offering £1,000 a match for live
broadcast rights. At a time when a full house would generate in the
region of £3,000 in gate receipts it was a huge offer.

The BBC countered by offering £1,500 a game for just 10 games
a season. "Viewers do not want the airwaves awash with too much
football," they claimed in an attempt to allay the growing fears of
the small clubs. The FA's chairman Arthur Drewry[7] argued that clubs
should be allowed to negotiate individually but the smaller clubs led
by Burnley voted overwhelmingly against the proposal. Instead they
threw their lot in with the BBC, who paid for a one-season deal to
record 75 matches with no recording lasting longer than five minutes

---

6   *Hardaker would become Football League Secretary in 1957.*

7   *Drewry was also a director of Grimsby and President of FIFA at the time, and although Walter
Winterbottom was the manager, Drewry actually picked the England team which lost to the USA
in the 1950 World Cup.*

(unless only one game was available in which case ten minutes was allowed) and no recording being broadcast before 10pm. It was a deal they would be able to renew relatively cheaply three times until 1961. Once again the BBC used it as a weapon in the war against ITV, announcing the deal on the eve of their rival's launch and at the same time launching a Saturday-night show *Sports Special* – a sister programme to *Sportsview* – on the back of the deal.

How did the big clubs respond? Well, they threatened to form a breakaway league, with Newcastle United leading the way. In October 1953, the club had faced Falkirk, then managed by Bob Shankly (Bill's older brother), in what was the first televised game in Scotland. The *Newcastle Journal*'s correspondent, Ken McKenzie, was unimpressed, writing: "Falkirk FC and their supporters held high revel", after the Bairns gave Newcastle a "sound beating". "What Newcastle got out of the historic game", he continued, "will not take much adding up. Not much in cash, maybe less in prestige." Although McKenzie didn't know it at the time this was the first in a series of games between clubs on either side of the border that became known as the Anglo-Scottish League.[8] By 1955 Newcastle's vice-chairman Stan Seymour, who had also played for and managed the club, was claiming that ITV was willing to broadcast a ten-team, mid-week, floodlit league with each team playing each other four times. The proposed league was not designed to replace the Football League, but the latter banned its teams from taking part. Crucially, however, the FA *had* given Seymour's plan its blessing (something which would also be key to the creation of the Premier League) so the teams could have gone ahead had they wanted to.

That they didn't was down to Manchester United's entry into the European Cup. While the reigning English champions Chelsea, under pressure from the FA, declined to enter the inaugural season of the competition, Scottish club Hibernian (who had actually finished fifth in the Scottish First Division the year before) did enter. They reached the semi-finals, playing six games in total and pocketing

8   *It wasn't the first time the formation of a Scottish-North East league had been considered. In September 1904 representatives of Hearts, Hibernian, Dundee, Newcastle, Sunderland and Middlesbrough met at the Imperial Hotel in Edinburgh to discuss such a plan, although it ultimately came to nothing.*

a tidy £25,000 in increased gate money and TV revenue along the way. Seymour's mid-week League was tempting to Matt Busby and the United board but the European Cup was even more so. Home games in the competition were guaranteed to sell out, as United would be representing England abroad, and away games would get high audience figures as travel was difficult for fans. Furthermore Granada, which was based in Manchester and covered the North during the week, was fast becoming the most financially powerful ITV franchise. The mid-week games were exactly what they wanted to draw in viewers and there was no Bob Lord to stand in their way. The first televised game was Manchester United's 2-2 semi-final draw against Real Madrid at Old Trafford in April 1957. United were knocked out having lost the first leg 3-1, but the game drew in 6.5 million viewers – a record for any ITV programme at the time. The age of the armchair supporter had begun and so had the age of the super-club. United received £2,500 per home game from Granada which, when combined with their takings at the turnstiles, boosted their revenue by £60,000 for that season, while at the same time massively increasing their exposure. At the club's annual general meeting Busby declared United to be "a household name throughout the Universe".

The European Cup was also a godsend for ITV. After the League had rebuffed their advances they'd been left with just shared coverage of the FA Cup, which was mainly mid-week replays, or competitions they organised themselves, such as five-a-side Sunday league with famous ex-players, run by ABC. The first live football on ITV came on 3 January 1956 when Rediffusion broadcast the second half of the Southern Junior Floodlit Cup Final between West Ham and Chelsea, with Danny Blanchflower commentating. Less than a fortnight later came the network's disastrous first coverage of a live FA Cup game. Arsenal travelled to Bedford Town for a third-round replay and thousands took time off work to watch the game, played on a Thursday afternoon as Bedford had no floodlights. The viewers were left disappointed as the cameras broke during half time, ending the coverage.[9]

9   *The Gunners ran out 2-1 winners after extra time.*

Undeterred, in the summer of 1956 ATV came up with a bumper offer so good that Hardaker said: "It almost made one believe in fairies at the bottom of the garden." The contract offered £50,000 in return for the right to televise the second half of around 35 League matches per season. To avoid a clash with other games, it was proposed the kick-off would be delayed until 6.15pm with ATV covering travelling and accommodation costs for away teams. On top of all that they offered a pot of £60,000 to compensate any clubs that could show that attendances had fallen due to the coverage. And as a final sweetener they offered to pay for a special film to advertise the League across the network.

It was the first serious deal to televise live League football and so it was referred to a special committee two months later and ultimately rejected by the smaller clubs, once again led by Bob Lord. The League's stance actually hardened as they leant on the FA to get coverage of several Cup games that were due to be played on the same day as League matches banned. These included the sell-out tie between West Brom and Birmingham that was due to be broadcast on the first night of the ABC's new Midlands service – the last of the Big Four regions to launch.

ITV came back with another deal, offering £1,500 to both featured clubs for each half-game shown plus £5,500 for each game to be split between all 92 clubs, a move that established for the first time the concept of at least some of the TV money being shared between all the League's teams. It was on this basis that a breakthrough seemed to have been made when in 1960 ABC offered £142,000 (£92,000 for exclusive rights and £50,000 to advertise the game) for the rights to show the second half of 26 games from all four divisions. This was to be paid into a pot and distributed between all the 92 clubs. The League Management Committee finally voted in favour of the deal only for the big clubs, with the belief that all the money should go to them, to threaten legal action over who controlled the rights to the games. Despite this, on 10 September 1960 the momentous occasion came when League football finally hit English TV screens as ABC broadcast the second half of Bolton's 1-0 win away at Blackpool. It was set to be the first in a series of games (or half-games) broadcast under the title *The Big Match*. The box-office star Stanley Matthews missed the match through injury and matters were made worse by the fact it was a fairly drab affair with the only goal coming in the 79th minute courtesy of Bolton's Freddie Hill. While the kick-off time had been delayed until 6.50pm to avoid clashing with other games, the 17,166 crowd at Bloomfield Road was lower than normal. Blackpool secretary Richard Stead suggested it might have been because the visiting Bolton fans "didn't want to get caught up in Illumination traffic" but it was enough to reinvigorate the League's fears and, coupled with the threat of legal action, the series was immediately cancelled.

The restrictions saw several innovative attempts to screen games via closed-circuit TV. It's little surprise that Coventry City, with the forward-thinking Jimmy Hill at the helm, were at the forefront of these experiments. Two away matches were shown on big screens back at Highfield Road, the first being against Cardiff on 6 October 1965. Fans paid a slightly increased entry fee, but the match was a success, with the *Daily Mail* reporting that the crowd of 10,295 was "as animated as if they had been at Cardiff". Before the Football League met to consider a new TV deal from the BBC in 1967, a firm called Viewsport arranged to broadcast a League match between Arsenal and Manchester United at Highbury back to Old Trafford and an FA Cup tie between Everton and Liverpool at Goodison Park back to Anfield. The broadcasts were huge successes attracting attendances of 28,000 and 40,149 respectively, persuading Viewsport to make an offer to the League of £36,000 to broadcast 12 such games per season. Once again the bid was rejected, along with the Beeb's offer.

The option was left open for individual clubs to broadcast away matches under special circumstances, particularly European games. Both legs of Leeds' Inter-Cities Fairs Cup quarter-final with Rangers were shown on big screens, with 43,177 turning up at Ibrox. While this brief period has its legacy in the Fan Zones created for major tournaments and European cup finals, such broadcasts failed to take off as the novelty value of standing on a cold, wet terrace to watch TV wore off. There were technical difficulties too – the equipment was bulky and difficult to use and on several occasions in bad weather screens tore. Some games were subsequently shown at cinemas, such as England's match with West Germany in 1975, which also saw a screen erected in the ground for replays, much to the disgust of *The Times*' Geoffrey Green who wrote "this may be alright for dog or stock-car racing but scarcely fit for a game already prostituted in too many ways". Newcastle United showed several European ties at the Telewest Arena in the late 1990s as well as some League games at the local Odeon cinema in the days before St James' Park's 1998 expansion when the club had a waiting list of 20,000 for season tickets.

Despite the lack of coverage, fans found the game creeping onto their screens in other ways. The BBC produced a soap opera called *United* that was focused on life at a fictional Second Division team called Brentwich. Filmed at Stoke's Victoria Ground, the 30-minute, twice-weekly show ran between 1965 and 1967 gaining audiences of up to six million people. *United* ended after 147 episodes, all of which were wiped along with 100 of the first 253 episodes of *Dr Who*; the overwhelming majority of Patrick Moore's live coverage of the moon landings; Kenneth Tynan's infamous first televised use of the word 'fuck' and a host of other iconic programmes. All episodes of *Monty Python's Flying Circus* were scheduled to be deleted but one of the team, Terry Jones, stepped in and bought the copies from the BBC in 1975. Some early episodes of *The Likely Lads* were also wiped, but not the 1973 episode in which Bob and Terry spend the best part of a day trying to avoid finding out the score of England's match with Bulgaria so they can win a bet. They succeed, only to learn the match had been rained off. The sitcom *Till Death Us Do Part* used football more insidiously to get laughs. with Anthony Clavane arguing in his book *Does Your Rabbi Know You're Here?* that the show was responsible for the anti-Semitic racism directed at Spurs fans to this day. The programme's central character Alf Garnett frequently ranted against "those Spurs Yids", even going as far as to suggest the Blitz was an attempt to destroy Spurs' ground White Hart Lane.

• • •

Following the ill-fated broadcast from Bloomfield Road in 1960, it would be 23 years before another live League game was shown on TV. The haggling over rights in the late 1950s and early 1960s established the basic politics of televised football. Within the TV companies, ITV focused on the live coverage of big, evening, floodlit games while the BBC focused on highlights of League matches, the FA Cup and internationals. The clubs split between the few big clubs who considered themselves the draw and so wanted all the cash and the small clubs who wanted the money split evenly in a bid to maintain financial parity. It was a pattern that wouldn't really change until the late-1970s when ITV had the financial muscle to begin to outbid the BBC but it's still the foundation of how rights are divided now. The nature of the coverage also stayed fairly static in that period. The BBC and ITV continued to simultaneously cover the FA Cup Final, and in 1968, in a response to the popularity of the 1966 World Cup Finals, the ITV networks launched a series of regional, Sunday-afternoon highlights programmes, such as Tyne Tees' *Shoot*, Anglia's *Match of the Week* and the most famous: London Weekend Television's (LWT) *The Big Match*, which would eventually give its name to the network-wide football coverage. These ran alongside *Match of the Day*, which went out on Saturday nights, and the BBC and ITV negotiated together with the League, ensuring that the cost of the deal was kept to a minimum.

It was all very different in America where the National Professional Soccer League launched in 1967 with a $1m deal (in the region of $35,000 per club) with CBS for live coverage of the 'Game of the Week'. The League lasted just one season before merging with the United Soccer Association to form the North American Soccer League. However, the deal demonstrated the riches that were on offer from US TV firms even to football, which was supposedly a poor relation to gridiron, baseball and basketball. Although the bumper TV deals may not have crossed the Pond, a range of American production and presentation techniques did. The use of replays was introduced in sports broadcasting by Canadian TV director George Retzlaff in 1955 during the programme *Hockey Night in Canada*. At the time it was an expensive and slow business that kept the viewers waiting several minutes after the incident, but it was a start.

Eight years later when Jack Ruby shot Lee Harvey Oswald as he left Dallas police station the replay hit the big time. The increasing use of magnetic film meant the American TV news companies could easily and incessantly replay the incident. A young CBS sports director called Tony Verna was watching and he modified a normal videotape machine, which then enabled him to introduce instant replays into the coverage of an Army and Navy gridiron game less than two weeks later. The effect was considered so amazing at the time that the commentator Lindsey Nelson was moved to say: "This is not live, ladies and gentlemen, Army did not just score again." Verna titled his autobiography *Instant Replay: The Day That Changed Sports Forever.* It was a bold claim but not one without some justification. Until that point, watching sport on TV had merely been a substitute for attending a game in person. The instant replay and its slightly younger sibling the slow-motion replay altered the structure of coverage. The fluidity of televised games was broken and the replay dominated both the build-up to and immediate aftermath of matches, facilitating the talking-heads panel format.

If watching football over and over again in slow motion hadn't blown your mind then what about watching football from the other side of the planet, live and in colour? The Eurovision TV network had linked most of Western Europe, allowing English fans to see the World Cups of 1954 and 1958 in Switzerland and Sweden, but coverage of the 1962 World Cup in Chile was limited to radio and two-day-old highlights gained from film flown over from South America. Probably because of the logistical problems, ITV left coverage to the BBC, who sent a grand total of two commentators – Kenneth Wolstenholme and David Coleman. The launch of satellites like Telstar, Relay 1 and Syncom III meant the 1964 Tokyo Olympics could be broadcast live to America and Europe, and the World Cup in England in 1966 was the first such tournament to be broadcast via satellite, allowing viewers around the world to see Bobby Moore lift the Jules Rimet trophy.

Back at home around 32.3 million people tuned in to watch the famous 4-2 victory, but as hard as this is to imagine now, it was not a TV 'event'. The BBC kicked off their coverage at midday while ITV started theirs an hour later, but clearly neither were anticipating extra time for the game, which kicked off at 3pm. The Beeb had scheduled a Laurel and Hardy short film to start at 5.20pm while on the other side an episode of *Robin Hood* had been due to start five minutes earlier. The tournament came too early for colour TV in England, which was launched on BBC2 the following year. The Beeb didn't waste any time taking advantage of the new technique and the 1968 FA Cup Final between West Brom and Everton was the first to be broadcast with the new innovation. However as BBC2 used the more advanced 625-line UHF system, which not everyone could view, the BBC, who shared coverage with ITV, also showed the final on BBC1, meaning all three English TV channels showed the game live – heaven for football fans, hell for everyone else.

Colour and satellite transmission finally came together on English screens for the 1970 World Cup. The *TV Times*' science editor Peter Fairly marvelled breathlessly in the run-up to the tournament that "Pictures of World Cup soccer in Mexico will have travelled at least 50,000 miles and possibly further in one third of a second! They will come via landline and satellite, boosted into space by one giant 'dish' and caught by another, coded by one computer and de-coded by another, converted from one standard and reconverted into another. As one ITV engineer put it: 'The soccer stars think *they* have a headache – they should start talking to *us*.'" European TV companies insisted that kick-off times were moved forward to coincide with the peak viewing times back home, meaning many matches kicked off in sweltering midday heat. The players weren't the only ones sweating their way through the tournament though. The BBC came under serious pressure from ITV, who for the first (and to date only) time bested them in a World Cup ratings war – something Jimmy Hill described as "a TV sporting miracle". Both stations gave blanket coverage to the tournament, and both had pundits, with the BBC's including Brian Clough, Ian St John and Bob Wilson, all of whom would go on to make names for themselves in the media.

For three weeks, however, the Beeb were overshadowed by what Hill described in his autobiography as a "cunningly conceived battle plan: a fully representative, qualified and opinionated panel". Along with John Bromley, Hill assembled a team of pundits including Malcolm Allison, Derek Dougan, Pat Crerand and Bob McNab – an "accidental" inclusion after the Arsenal player was left out of the England squad by Sir Alf Ramsey. Innovatively, Bromley and Hill then decided to use their pundits as a panel so they could bounce off each other. Bromley also took the decision to hole the quartet up in the Hendon Hall Hotel and sign off their sizeable bar bill without question. The result was ground-breaking and incendiary and set the template for football coverage for years to come. José Mourinho might have had *that* coat but The Panel got there first. They were four "handsome, athletic young men dressed flamboyantly in carefree, colourful fashion", to cite Hill again.

It was in this period that Allison morphed into the erudite but controversial and opinionated "Big Mal". When England lost in the quarter-final, the four men removed their Union Jack ties and threw them on the floor in a choreographed show of disgust. Later Alan Mullery, blamed by Allison for that defeat, came into the studio for his right of reply and threw one of his England caps at his tormentor. The Panel weren't beyond criticism themselves, especially after Allison asked then answered his own question: "Why are we technically better in Europe? Because we play against peasants, teams who play in primitive ways!" The ITV switchboard was jammed with people complaining about the comment but this was dwarfed by fan mail and 'The Panel' were regularly mobbed by autograph hunters. The seal on their new-found fame came when they were joined for dinner one night by Michael Caine, who just wanted to "have a drink with the lads". Hill concluded: "The war wasn't won during the 90-minute- or-so games but in the five minutes before, the ten minutes at half time and the ultimate collective verdict at the end. It wasn't accidental. It was calculated coldly and clinically and it worked." Sadly, today's PR-conscious football panels are a watered-down imitation. Oh to see Wayne Rooney chuck one of his England caps in Mark Lawrenson's face after a bit of criticism. It's just never going to happen, is it?

During the games, the increasing use and power of computers allowed for the introduction of a range of techniques, such as captions that helped supply more information more quickly and split screens that allowed the viewer to see different angles of the same incident or two separate incidents at the same time. Different broadcasters were also able to cherry-pick images, enabling them to create different coverage and different narratives around the same event to serve their own purposes. In turn these narratives were supported and enhanced by the pundits. While football broadcasting was said merely to present reality to the viewers, these technological developments and their use were in fact making it a less 'truthful' experience which was no longer a mere substitute for attending matches in the flesh. Like the cinema newsreels decades before, what the TV companies were starting to do was construct an 'ideal' version of the match, a version where the key parts (chosen by the TV companies) were replayed in close-up or in slow motion and then analysed in controversial terms by the stars of the day. TV coverage was no longer just documenting what took place on the pitch; it was turning it into entertainment.

CHAPTER 7

THE PRESS TAKES AIM

Looking back now, from a world saturated by instantaneous digital media, it seems inevitable that the immediacy and intimacy of first radio and then television would kick-start the long, slow decline in newspaper sales. However, surveying the scene in the 1950s when few people had televisions and the *News of the World* could shift more than eight million copies each Sunday, that would have seemed a fanciful prediction. Other than going to a game, newspapers were emphatically still the place for fans to get their football fix, something demonstrated by the fact that there were 11 press men on Manchester United's fateful flight from Belgrade in February 1958. That might not sound many by today's standards but there was no one from TV or radio on board and the journalists accounted for a quarter of the 44 passengers and crew when the plane crashed in Munich.

Writing about his time working at the *Manchester Evening Chronicle* in the 1950s, Keith Dewhurst paints a picture of a world unrecognisable today. Northern reporters barely read the London papers, saw few reports of matches between southern teams, and as for foreign teams? Forget it. But Manchester, you may remember, was the Other Fleet Street, the national press' gateway to the North of England, Scotland and Ireland. With the League champions on their doorstep it was inevitable that the journalists based in the city would be eager to travel with the team as it aimed to better its exit in the European Cup semi-finals the previous season. Travel was a lot more difficult then; the only reason the plane was in Munich was because few aircraft could make the flight from Belgrade to Manchester without a refuelling stop. The BEA Elizabethan aircraft was not one of them. So, if you were a journalist you either travelled with the team or you didn't travel at all.

Just as Manchester United lost eight players in the crash, so the Manchester press corps lost eight journalists. They were Alf Clarke of the *Manchester Evening Chronicle*, H.D. Davies of the *Manchester Guardian*, George Follows of the *Daily Herald*, Tom Jackson of the *Manchester Evening News*, Archie Ledbrooke of the *Daily Mirror*, Henry Rose of the *Daily Express*, Eric Thompson of the *Daily Mail* and Frank Swift of the *News of the World*. The three surviving newspaper men were Ted Ellyard and Peter Howard, the *Daily Mail's* telegraphist and photographer respectively, and Frank Taylor, who was severely injured but eventually went back to work at the *News Chronicle*. In his book *The Day a Team Died*, Taylor recalled how before take-off he turned to the other writers to tell them there were plenty of seats at the front where he was sitting but, already settled, they stayed at the back where most of the fatalities occurred.

The Busby Babes had achieved much before they were decimated and it's likely they would have achieved considerably more; their best years were still ahead of them. The journalists who died were cut down in their prime, giants of a competitive but ultimately close-knit profession with decades of experience between them. Contemporaries talk of H.D. Davies in the same breath as the legendary cricket writer Neville Cardus, who like Davies wrote for the *Manchester Guardian*. But the doyen was Henry Rose, the most-read football writer the *Daily Express* ever had. When he went to report on a game the paper would put up placards around the ground saying: "Harry Rose is here today" to advertise the fact. It meant it was the biggest match of the day and in Manchester the crowd would chant those words and greet Rose's arrival in the press box with cheers. Liverpool fans had other ideas and The Kop would ritually greet Rose at Anfield with a chorus of boos to which he would, cigar in one hand, salute them by raising his brown trilby with the other.

After the crash, Manchester came together to grieve, yet it was not one of the players' funerals that drew the most mourners but Rose's. Four thousand people attended and Manchester's 1,000-strong force of taxis, none of their meters running, drove them along the six-mile procession route from the *Daily Express* building on Great Ancoats Street to Manchester's Southern Cemetery. Crowds ten deep lined the way to watch the cortege pass.

The aftermath also had an impact on the general approach to reporting football. At the time of the crash United were looking to win their third straight League title and also had the League, FA Cup and European Cup treble very much in their sights. Thanks to the exposure that Granada's coverage of their European exploits had brought, United had become a household name and so the tragedy occupied front pages for days, becoming the first story to persuade news editors that sport could have genuine news value. There was still stubborn resistance in some quarters though. The day after the tragedy, readers of *The Times* would have found no mention of it until they reached page eight and then the article was relatively emotionless and played up the safety record of the nationally owned airline involved. The disaster also indirectly led to quotes becoming a key part of match reports. The crash happened on a Thursday and just two days later the papers had League games to cover, so news reporters like Derek Meek, the *Manchester Evening News'* political leader writer, were switched to sport. They treated matches like they would any other event and began to ask 'experts', such as the managers, for quotes to add to their pieces. This innovation stuck and was accelerated, first by the need to keep pace with the broadcast of post-match interviews on the BBC's new highlight show *Match of the Day* and then by the tabloid revolution that swept through Fleet Street at the end of the 1960s.

• • •

Eight years before the Munich tragedy, Archie Ledbrooke, one of the reporters who died, co-wrote *Soccer From the Press Box* with Edgar Turner. Despite its title it's not so much about football writing as the journalists' view of a range of topics connected to the game. However, in one chapter they do focus on their own profession, making a plea in mitigation to their readers asking them to remember that the writers often do their job against the pressure of time while exposed to the elements. There's a brief mention of the tools of the trade; no laptops or Wi-Fi for the reporters back then, just typewriters and maybe their own phone to ring through a report. Yet for all the differences it's the similarities that are the most striking.

Ledbrooke and Turner outlined what they considered to be the four types of match report for a normal Saturday game. There was the report for the Saturday football special; the report for the Sunday-morning paper filed an hour and a half after the game at the latest; the Monday-morning paper report, written with more reflection and filed on Sunday; and "the running commentary put out over the radio either as sound alone or with a TV camera to show the actual scene". The pair made those observations in 1950, but has much really changed in the intervening six decades or so? Well, you can't guarantee that a game's going to be on a Saturday anymore and now most people take their running commentary with pictures from the scene. As we discussed in Chapter 2, the Saturday specials are essentially a thing of the past, so let's replace them with the online, in-running match report. Other than that, it's pretty much the same.

Where you do find a difference is in the tone of the reporting, particularly that surrounding the England team. *Soccer From the Press Box* was first published in the year that the part-timers from America beat England in a World Cup match in Belo Horizonte's Estádio Independência. It was the equivalent of England losing to San Marino today, yet the headlines were nothing like those that would now greet such a defeat. The only goal of the game was scored by Joe Gaetjens,[1] a Haitian accounting student and part-time dish-washer, and it's fair to say the result was a fluke. Gaetjens' winner was less a header and more a fortuitous deflection; England hit the woodwork on several occasions, missed a hatful of chances, saw a string of other attempts saved by Frank Borghi and were denied a clear-cut penalty. But the score sheet doesn't lie, although one apocryphal story suggests that a sub-editor back in London thought that it did and simply changed it to read England 10-1 USA. Another such story claims that English papers were edged in black the day after the game. Neither tale appears to be true. Most newspapers at the time were still subject to post-war paper rations and so had few pages, with only one devoted to sport.

1   *Gaetjens went on to play for Paris Racing Club before returning to Haiti in 1954. Gaetjens himself had no interest in politics but his family were ardent opponents of Haitian dictator François Duvalier. In 1964 Gaetjens suffered the consequences and was arrested by the country's militia and never seen again.*

On the day of the USA debacle the sports story that took precedence was the West Indies' 326-run defeat of England at Lord's. It was the first time the Caribbean team – part-timers like the Americans – had won a Test on English soil; that they did so by such a margin and at the home of cricket only rubbed salt in the wound.[2] By comparison the football team's woes were viewed as merely an aberration; after all, England could still have qualified for the final group had they beaten Spain in their next game. They didn't. Following the team's elimination the *Daily Herald* did print a small 'obituary' of English football, mimicking the one that had been printed in *The Times* after the England cricket team lost to Australia in 1882, but that was pretty much it. Even Ledbrooke and Turner's brief discussion of the result in the revised second edition of *Soccer From the Press Box* focuses less on the damage to England's reputation and more on what America might have achieved if their players took up the sport full time. The muted reaction was due to the fact that football had still not gained the total dominance it has over other sports today and given that the World Cup wasn't considered to be that important, why should a result from it be seen that way? Furthermore the match was not broadcast on TV; it was one of those games that was out of sight and so out of mind. As such it has become a footnote to and not a key part of a narrative of ongoing national decline.

That narrative was up and running by 1953 when, as we noted earlier, the Hungarians turned up at Wembley and destroyed England 6-3. After the match the *News Chronicle* ran a picture of the visitors' goalkeeper, Gyula Grosics, walking on his hands, with the headline "NOW THE WORLD IS REALLY UPSIDE DOWN", while the *Daily Mirror* declared the defeat to be the "Twilight of the (soccer) gods". These headlines weren't just down to the fact that the match was broadcast on television. Professor Stephen Wagg, who first wrote about the relationship between football and the media in *The Football World* in 1984, thinks the changing attitude among football writers is also important in explaining the contrasting reactions to the America and Hungary defeats. "What happened between 1950 and

2   *Following the victory, which set up a 3-1 series win for the visitors, West Indian immigrants who had watched from the stands ran onto the pitch in joy. Police moved in to arrest them but were stopped from doing so by an MCC official, who allowed the celebrations to continue.*

1953 was that, one way or another, the Popular Press in particular came up with a way of rendering the England football team," Wagg said. "England was suddenly redefined as the country that gave football to the world and every defeat had obvious implications. It was an affront to the nation and the people running the team had to be put in the dock. They were 'muddlers' and 'meddlers'. I feel that some rather intuitively clever football writers in the 1950s sensed an on-coming mood of national decline."

This mood was created by a double anxiety about Britain's declining position in the world. The winds of change were blowing across the Empire bringing decolonisation in their wake and as the Cold War began, so the fear of the Communist threat from the East grew. In America this anxiety manifested itself indirectly through science fiction films where blobs or pods that took over people's minds (the Soviet Army) would land from space (the East) before being defeated by scientists and/or soldiers (the US Government), thus reassuring the viewers that the Red Menace could be repelled. Back in Blighty that anxiety manifested itself indirectly through football. Let's not forget that a young George Best, glued to his neighbour's TV set, found teams like Moscow Spartak to be other-worldly, later describing them as 'aliens'. Even Sir Bobby Robson, watching England's defeat by Hungary from the Wembley stands, was later moved to say that the visitors "were men from Mars as far as we were concerned".

It was through this developing ideological prism that the match was viewed. In 1946 pressure from the West forced the Soviet Union to allow Hungary to hold a free election. Ferenc Nagy, the leader of the Independent Smallholders' Party, swept to power with 57 per cent of the vote. The Communists gained just 17 per cent but their leader Mátyás Rákosi soon took control after Nagy was forced to resign and flee the country after his son was kidnapped. Anglo-Hungarian relations soured in November 1949 when Edgar Saunders, a British businessman working in Budapest, was arrested for spying. He confessed to the charges and was subsequently jailed for 13 years in what the West branded a show trial. Although it now seems pretty clear that Saunders did in fact have links to the British intelligence services, when he was released after serving just four years (most of it spent in solitary confinement) the English press took the opportunity to remind its readers what dastardly cads the Hungarians were. The timing, just a few months before the Wembley game, set the tone for the match.

Like the English press, the Hungarians also saw what happened on the football pitch as a metaphor for the country as a whole, portraying their victory as a symbolic confirmation of the merits of the collective nature of Communism over the individualism of capitalism. Whether or not that's true, it was a direct contrast to the way the build-up of the match had been portrayed in the English press. "If you knew your football history you would have known that Hungary had a very rich football tradition going back to the 1900s," said Wagg as we sat in his office at gorgeous Carnegie campus in Leeds. "The football writers either wilfully ignored that or were ignorant of it. If you read the press the day before the 1953 game it was the working-class lads of the free world, who learnt to play the game kicking a bundle of rags round the cobbled streets of the North of England, versus some Communist robots, who were going to be programmed but weren't going to stand a chance against the spontaneity of the English. If you see film of the game then that was an absurd proposition because the virtuosity is pretty much all on the Hungarian team. They ran rings round solid but fairly predictable players like Billy Wright. Good players, but that day they looked like mugs."

One reason for the shock of the 6-3 defeat to Hungary was the insularity of both English football and the English football press that Wagg hinted at. It was insularity which Willy Meisl, an Austrian football writer living and working in England in the 1950s, acknowledged in his book *Soccer Revolution*. While the FA had refused to send a team to the first three World Cups and also wanted English club sides to stay out of the European Cup, the press were equally uninterested in what was happening beyond the country's shores. Meisl, whose brother Horst was a pioneer of Austrian football, pointed out that following England's elimination from the 1950 World Cup all but one of the press pack headed home. "Could you imagine Britain's leading film critics leaving Cannes International Film Festival after the showing of the British films?" he asked in consternation.

The English football journalists' departure from the tournament meant they were blithely unaware of exactly how far down the global football pecking order the country had fallen. So, as a consequence, England's fans were oblivious to the true significance of the defeats to Spain and in particular America because, Meisl argued, the "sports press doesn't tell them what is happening elsewhere – for the very good reason that the sporting journalists themselves are hardly aware of it". This was just one of a list of criticisms he levelled at the English press, key among them being the need to find "a story" and the continuing use of "overstatement". According to Meisl, the former meant that football writers, all the while writing "down to the lowest denominator", were not as concerned with describing the details of games as they were with finding a sensational angle. The latter meant that the more superlatives the writers used, the more of them the readers were used to reading, thus creating an ever-increasing spiral.

More often than not the two tactics came together, an approach well illustrated by a story Wagg told me. "I interviewed Walter Winterbottom once when I was quite young," he said, "and towards the end he mentioned a match he had watched at the 1954 World Cup. He was high up in the stand and he happened to be chatting to the legendary Desmond Hackett and they briefly became aware of some altercation down by the players' tunnel. Hackett turned to Walter and said: 'What was that?' Walter replied: 'Well I didn't see very much, but I think there was a bit of a bust-up between a couple of the players', and Hackett said: 'that sounds good'. Before Walter knew it Hackett had rolled a fresh sheet of paper into his typewriter and began typing. Walter leaned over his shoulders and read the first line, which was: 'I have been thrown over a fence' and Hackett turned to Walter and said: 'I'm going to get a new coat out of this.'"

The match was the infamous World Cup quarter-final between Hungary and Brazil, and Hackett's creative account of the 'Battle of Berne' in which he detailed how his jacket was ripped and his shirt torn while he rescued referee Arthur Ellis' wife and children from the melee made the front of the *Express*. Not only did he get a new jacket but he got a new watch too after he detailed how his was 'smashed' and subsequently filed for a new one on expenses. Lord Beaverbrook, the *Express'* owner, was so impressed by his reporter's bravery that he gave him a gold replacement to cover his loss. FIFA investigated the incident but could find nothing concrete to support Hackett's version of events. "Well, if you see it happen it detracts from the story," Hackett would say of the incident in later years.

"It was a dream fracas," said Wagg, "swarthy South Americans versus Communists, and even though he didn't see it, Hackett was soon imagining it for the British suburbs. I think the moral of that story is that guys like him who were not sophisticated in many ways, certainly not sophisticated about politics or cultural trends, could sense a mood in their readership. They had to, to write the stuff that they did, and that's my feeling; that somehow, maybe by being in their own saloon bar around 1953 and 1954 and hearing people who read the *Daily Express* talk, they picked up this mood and began to write it through football." Wagg's comments echo those of Frank Taylor, one of the Munich crash survivors, about Henry Rose. Taylor said that Rose acknowledged that he wasn't the best sports writer but "he knew what the man in the four-ale bar was angry about and that's what he gave them". Like Hackett, Rose picked up a mood and wrote it through football.

This was all part of the tabloid revolution which began in the mid-1930s, a revolution kick-started by the development of radio and the creation of the Audit Bureau of Circulation. Radio broke the newspapers' monopoly on delivering the news, while, from 1931, the Bureau provided advertisers with accurate circulation figures and newspaper publishers with a clear idea of who was buying their product. To maintain their readerships in the face of radio's challenge, newspapers turned to product differentiation and the Bureau's figures helped them do this. For the first time journalism was more about the audience than the content and increasingly this audience was constructed as a composite of an idealised reader. At the same time, more news was available due to improvements in technology but there was less room for it as advertising became more sophisticated and took up greater space within the papers. Up until that point newspapers had, like the BBC, imagined the audience to be the nation as a whole and focused on national events to reinforce the sense of community and thus the status quo. Now papers were crafting stories for their readers, who they projected as normal and sensible, setting them against 'abnormal' or 'mad' others. Britishness and in particular Englishness was increasingly defined through this 'us' and 'them' dichotomy.

The first editor to understand the new way of working was Arthur Christiansen on the *Daily Express,* who wanted his paper to appeal to people in the "backstreets of Derby" or "the Rhyl Promenade". In 1934 Harry Guy Bartholomew took Christiansen's template and used it to relaunch the *Daily Mirror,* at the time struggling with an ageing readership of 700,000 of which about 100,000 were literally dying each year. Bartholomew felt there was room for a left-of-centre paper with broad populist appeal to the working class, running counter to the individualist conservatism of the *Daily Mail* and *Daily Express.* Bartholomew was convinced that readers wanted to look at, rather than read, papers and while he believed they were politically aware, he felt they wanted a more entertaining product. So he cut the length of stories and the amount of social and economic news and instead provided a mix of entertainment, humour and stories relevant to the lives of the working and lower-middle class.

By the end of the Second World War the *Daily Mirror* had adopted the slogan "Forward With the People" and it played a key part in the 1945 Khaki Election that turfed Churchill out of office and swept the Labour Party to victory. You could say it was the *Mirror* Wot Won It. All this was provided in a tabloid format that could be folded and kept in a worker's overalls and read in bite-size chunks during the day. By the late 1940s the paper was selling about 4.5 million copies a day prompting historian A.J.P. Taylor to claim that through the *Daily Mirror* "the English people at last found their voice". However, a contemporary journalist working for the left-wing *Daily Herald* (which would ironically become the *Sun*) took a dimmer view, writing that the *Mirror* "demanded a new race of journalists with none of the inhibitions ruling in other newspapers, a frenzied gusto in dredging the news for sensational stories of sex and crime and a complete lack of reticence in dealing with them".

It was during this time that papers began to have an imaginary conversation with their readers using a tone and language they understood, and this led to the increased use of the individual voice, which in turn made columnists household names. At the front there were *Daily Mirror* writers like Godfrey Winn and William Connor, who wrote under the pen name Cassandra. At the back there was Henry Rose, the *Daily Express* reporter who was cheered into the press box, Reg Drury of the *News of the World,* or the *Sunday Express'* Alan Hoby, "The Man Who Knows" (or, as some uncharitably called him, "The Man Who Knows Fuck All"). Yet what the football writers knew and what they reported were two different things. This was a time when the link between players and reporters was still a close one. They shared similar backgrounds and earned similar salaries; if anything the hacks were slightly better off as they had expense accounts, but there was no desire to expose players' private lives – in fact the press wanted to present a respectable image of the country. When a famous international footballer was involved in a car crash in London in the late 1950s, the name and occupation of his passenger – a prostitute – was kept out of the papers.

Scandal had to have specific news value to hit the headlines; it was not enough for one of the people involved to be famous. Take, for example, the Profumo affair in 1963. The story was not, as it would be today, that a Tory MP (John Profumo) had been cheating on his actress wife (Valerie Hobson) with a topless dancer (Christine Keeler). No, the story was that the Government's War Minister was sharing a mistress with a Soviet naval attaché and suspected spy (Yevgeny Ivanov). This was a security risk; this was a news story although, even then, it took months before the papers printed what they knew. The fact that it involved a mix of sex and espionage, the same ingredients that had helped the first James Bond film, *Dr No,* woo cinemagoers the previous year, was a happy accident. By the end of the 1960s the rise in popularity of television and the beginnings of modern celebrity culture led to a change in that approach. By that time, some believed that the *Daily Mirror* had become too highbrow for its readers and that there was room in the marketplace for an updated version of what the paper had represented in the 1930s. One of those people was a young Australian called Rupert Murdoch.

• • •

"Are you keen on sport?" Murdoch asked. "I have to be, the customers are," came the reply from Albert 'Larry' Lamb, the Northern Editor

of the *Daily Mail*. It was a Saturday night in early autumn of 1969 and
the pair were enjoying a lobster dinner at Rules[3] on Covent Garden's
Maiden Lane. As the conversation and the Pouilly-Fumé flowed,
Murdoch, who had bought the *News of the World* at the beginning
of the year, interviewed Lamb for the editor's job of another paper
he had just acquired, this one a daily. Over the course of the night,
which ended with whisky in Murdoch's office, they had effectively
planned the editorial policy of the paper for several years to come.
However, Murdoch informed his guest that he had a short-list of
several other candidates to interview. He'd be in touch in a week or
two. At 2am Lamb, tempted to take the job if it was offered, had just
retired to his hotel when the phone rang; it was Murdoch. "Bugger
the shortlist," he said. Lamb was the new editor of the *Sun*.

The question about sport was, of course, not the only one Murdoch
asked, but it was crucial. Murdoch had no great interest in sports
when he was a child, but when he started working in the newspaper
industry he quickly realised that sport sold papers. When he bought
a paper he focused much of his early attention on its sports department as well as the amount of sport it covered. Sport was what he
later called a 'battering ram' and one he would use time and again
to break his way into various sections of the media marketplace in
different countries. Lamb was equally aware of its importance for
the "sex, sport and contests" philosophy required of a populist,
predominantly working-class paper like the *Sun*.

While Lamb was willing to dispense with almost all of the 27
specialist correspondents that the old *Sun* had employed, sport was
one specialism that could not be done without (the other was politics).
He took the view that big sports events like the FA Cup Final were all
the readers would be talking about on the day in question. So unless
a really big news story broke at the same time, the *Sun* would have
the Cup Final on the front and back pages as well as in a four-page
pullout inside. When the tabloid relaunched on 17 November 1969
the front-page splash concerned a horse-doping scandal but it was the
other popular working-class sport, football, that was the real key. Its
importance was made clear in the last edition of the old version of

---

3   Rules is the oldest restaurant in London, having opened in 1798.

the paper when Murdoch wrote a leader asking readers to "REACH FOR THE NEW SUN". Along with the serialisation of Jacqueline Susann's racy novel *The Love Machine*[4] and the chance to win cars and colour TVs, he promised readers "inside soccer stories by the top names – a million pounds' worth of soccer talent". It was the only sport Murdoch mentioned.

Lamb didn't have to look far to find the man to assemble these top names. The majority of the staff for the relaunched paper necessarily had to come from the journalists recently made redundant by IPC's sale of the paper to Murdoch, so it was made known that applications would be accepted from all of them. One read simply: "I am Sports Editor of the *Sun*, 46 and still ambitious. Yours sincerely, Frank Nicklin." He was hired and would become a key figure in shaping not just the *Sun*'s football coverage, but football coverage throughout Fleet Street over the following decade.

A Derby County fan and keen cricketer, Nicklin began his career on the *Derby Evening Telegraph* before joining the Royal Air Force. Twice shot down over enemy territory during the Second World War, twice he escaped and after the conflict he returned to Derby where he was able to cover his beloved Rams' FA Cup triumph in 1946. Then, like most of his contemporaries, he undertook a tour of duty in Manchester working on both the *Daily Herald* and the *Manchester Evening News* where he was credited with crowning the tragic young United team of the 1950s 'the Busby Babes'. From there he followed the well-trodden path to London to work on the *People* before moving to the newly created *Sun*.

On the day of the launch, Nicklin re-emphasised Murdoch's pledge to readers, promising that the paper's sports pages would have "four rows of teeth" and also that "its bite will be as big as its bark". They would, he said, "HAMMER the establishment. EXPOSE the fiddlers and ponces. DESTROY the cheats, the rogues, the villains." But before all this hammering, exposing and destroying could get underway Nicklin had some very tricky logistical problems to deal with. Murdoch had bought the *Sun* to utilise spare capacity on the

4   Susann had first found success three years earlier with the novel Valley of the Dolls, *and while* The Love Machine *is not at all racy by today's standards, it shouldn't be forgotten it was released less than 10 years after Penguin Books was tried for obscenity for publishing* Lady Chatterley's Lover.

London printing presses he acquired when he bought the *News of the World* a few months earlier. They could produce five million copies a night but lay idle during the week; the *Sun* solved that problem although it created another one. The decision to print only in London and distribute the paper via the country's rail network meant that once the timings had been worked out the deadline for the *Sun*'s first edition was set at 8.15pm. The *News of the World* could cope with that as Saturday football matches were done and dusted by 4.45pm leaving enough time to include reports before the paper had to be printed. But the early deadline effectively meant the *Sun* could not report on mid-week, night-time games in the North as most of the sports pages for the editions bound for Leeds, Liverpool, Manchester and Newcastle had to be ready before such games had even kicked off.

To compensate, Nicklin filled his pages with features, columns, readers' letters, nostalgic articles about the past, in short the 'story' of which Willy Mesil had been so disparaging. When the *Sun*'s distribution network improved and they were able to include match reports from northern games in the relevant editions, the readers complained that they were missing their 'fix' of football gossip. Nicklin had guessed that as the punters could now get the scores and headlines from radio and the growing TV network, a comprehensive and regionalised results service – long considered essential to the success of a newspaper – was no longer so important.

TV had made footballers more famous than ever and the abolition of the maximum wage meant they were no longer just key figures within their sport but also working-class lads made good; exactly the kind of people advertisers wanted to embrace. It was the beginning of the footballer as a modern celebrity and the punters wanted to know what these celebrities had to say, especially the original modern celebrity footballer: George Best. In the week of its launch the *Sun* printed an interview with the Manchester United star and he was soon writing a column for the paper. I say writing; Best was actually putting his name to a column that was being written for him. When he told *Sun* reporter Frank Clough to get lost one time too many for Lamb's liking, the editor decided the *Sun* could do without the errant Manchester United star. Brian Clough, then with Nicklin's beloved Derby and arguably the first modern celebrity manager, took a different approach, calling Nicklin and saying: "If you're going to give soccer a big shout like that, I'll write for you myself."[5]

The paper's erratic distribution also meant they couldn't guarantee which editions were going to which parts of the country. So Nicklin insisted that the Monday edition included coverage of every League game from the previous Saturday. Again, the punters loved it and the *Daily Mirror* was quick to follow suit, convinced that it was all part of the *Sun*'s master plan. In fact, Lamb, Nicklin and their colleagues were extremely envious of the *Daily Mirror*'s ability to regionalise their editions effectively. Nicklin also encouraged his writers to use short, punchy language; to give provocative and personal opinions and not to take any issue or anyone too seriously. If they strayed to the wrong side of the line, the sub-editors were ordered to add in the required hyperbole. Nicklin wrapped it all up in an innovative approach to design, using bold headlines and big pictures. Like Rose and Hackett in the 1950s, Nicklin had an intuitive grasp of what the readers, or "folks" as he called them, were thinking and how to articulate that mood through football. Lamb described him as a "pie-and-pint man" and Nicklin agreed. "He was right," he said before his death in 2002. "I'd be down the pub talking sport like our readers."

• • •

Another man who had a clear idea of who his readers were and what they wanted was Lamb's successor, Kelvin MacKenzie.[6] MacKenzie first joined the *Sun* as a sub-editor in 1973 after working his way up through the local and regional press. Loud and aggressive but exceptionally good at his job, he soon came to Murdoch's attention and was made managing editor of the *New York Post* before returning to England and ultimately, in 1981, the editor's chair of the *Sun*. By this time the paper had moved to the right of the political spectrum. When Murdoch bought the *Sun* it was left-wing and it gave its backing to

5   Later on, in 1979, Nicklin also gave Jimmy Greaves the chance to break into the media with a weekly column. After his well-publicised battle with alcoholism, it was an offer that gave Greaves renewed self-confidence and purpose and for which he said he was immensely grateful when others were closing doors on him.

6   Lamb was initially succeeded by Bernard Shrimsley in 1972 before reclaiming the editor's chair in 1975, after which MacKenzie took charge.

Harold Wilson in the 1970 General Election. Wilson lost but the *Sun* supported him again in February 1974, an election which resulted in a hung parliament. Another election was called for October 1974 and the *Sun* took an equivocal stance towards Wilson and Tory leader Edward Heath, running the headline: "WE'RE SICK OF THE TED AND HAROLD SHOW!" Five years later the paper 'voted' Conservative for the first time, printing a 1,700-word leader imploring its readers to do the same. Lamb claimed that he and Murdoch, both of whom had socialist leanings in their youth, did not reach the decision without pain, but the pair felt Margaret Thatcher's economic policies would be hugely beneficial to the newspaper industry and furthermore she was determined to curb the trades unions who had been a constant thorn in the industry's side. Another crucial factor that pushed the *Sun* to the right was the launch of the *Daily Star* in 1978. At the time the *Sun* had only just overtaken the *Daily Mirror*, which was explicitly supporting the Labour Party. Had the *Sun* remained non-committal or backed Labour again it would have opened the way for the *Daily Star* to become the only right-wing, working-class daily paper. Initially at least, the *Sun*'s shift to the right was more of a business decision than an ideological one.

If it was a decision that had caused Lamb and Murdoch problems, it was not one MacKenzie had any qualms about. He was an ardent supporter of Margaret Thatcher and on the rare occasions he disagreed with her, MacKenzie would still declare "she's wrong but she's strong". Maggie (as the *Sun* called her) had won the 1979 election thanks to a 9 per cent swing to the Conservatives among skilled manual labourers, nearly double the national swing to the party of 5.1 per cent. It was from this socio-economic group that the *Sun* drew most of its readers. MacKenzie characterised them as, "the bloke you see in the pub – a right old fascist, wants to send the wogs back, buy his poxy council house, he's afraid of the unions, afraid of the Russians, hates the queers and weirdoes and drug dealers".

With MacKenzie at the helm the tone and content of the paper's vernacular veered even further to the right as its imagined conversations with the idealised reader were attuned to the sentiments of this 'right old fascist'. Every hot summer day was a "SCORCHER!" and every Page 3 girl was a "STUNNER" greeted with a chorus of

"COR!" or "PHWOAR!" Of course, no one defines you more than the people you don't like and for the 'right old fascist' those were clearly identified as "PLONKERS" or, worse, "SCUM". Political issues were reduced to the simplest terms. "HOP OFF YOU FROGS" was the *Sun*'s response to a campaign by French farmers to block imports of British lamb in 1984.

MacKenzie was able to give full vent to his Thatcherite jingoism during the Falklands War in 1982 as the paper thumped its tub and spat bile like an English lager lout marching into a bar in Ibiza. Readers were urged to boycott corned beef while a series of "Argie-Bargie" reader jokes were run, with £5 and a can of Fray Bentos "non-Argentinian" beef for each one published. The paper then launched "undie-cover" warfare, revealing that "thousands of women" were wearing specially made knickers embroidered with the name of the ship their husband or boyfriend was serving on. The *Daily Mirror* was attacked from the off, as was the "whining namby-pamby ultra-Left, who always run scared at the first sign of crisis", and the *Sun*'s attitude to a negotiated peace was summed up simply with the first of its infamous headlines from the period: "STICK IT UP YOUR JUNTA". After peace talks broke down, the paper reworked the headline: "STICK THIS UP YOUR JUNTA" over a story explaining how "the first missile to hit Galtieri's gauchos will come with love from the *Sun*". It would, readers were told, have "Up Yours, Galtieri" painted on the side. The strongest reaction to that story came from troops in the task force, who thought it was a sick stunt and wrote letters of complaint and even burned copies of the paper. It speaks volumes about the *Sun*'s coverage that when *Private Eye* ran a spoof page with the headline "Kill an Argie, Win a Metro" the troops in the Falklands thought it was real while MacKenzie's response was: "Fucking brilliant, why didn't we think of that?" On 4 May the sinking of the *Belgrano* was greeted with the infamous headline "GOTCHA", a gut reaction to the news from features editor Wendy Henry.[7] After weeks of the *Sun*'s nationalist rhetoric, it was no doubt what right old fascists across the country were saying as they raised their pints in celebration.

---

7   *Despite its infamy, the headline only made the few first editions of the paper, which were seen in the North. When it became clear there had been massive loss of life even MacKenzie got cold feet and changed it to "Did 1,200 Argies drown?"*

The jingoism continued unabated after the conflict, with the *Sun*'s reaction to Argentina's defeat by Belgium in the World Cup later that year. "ARGIES SMASHED" screamed the paper. "They strutted, they cheated and afterwards they bleated. That was the arrogant Argentines last night. They swaggered on as world champions, and crawled off, humiliated by little Belgium ...

Nicklin had gone by this time, one of several senior staff from the Lamb days who did not fit in with the ethos of the new editor. The pair had had frequent rows when MacKenzie was a sub and Nicklin feared the worst when his nemesis was given the top job. Absent from the office for a year following a battle with bowel cancer, which included an operation he expected he wouldn't survive, Nicklin returned to work two weeks after MacKenzie took charge. He was paid off within days but soon resurfaced at the Hayter's Sports Agency, which he ran well into his 70s. MacKenzie wanted his reporters to "monster their victims" and "piss all over them", and it was in keeping with this ethos that David Balmforth, who was running the *Sun*'s sports desk by the end of the 1980s, declared it now had "eight rows of teeth".

• • •

In 2007 the journalist Hunter Davies went to visit Paul Gascoigne in the Notting Hill hotel where he was staying at the time. As they chatted away Gazza asked: "Where are all the players?", pointing out that the men in the dugout were now dominating the back pages. Davies was intrigued and after he bid his friend farewell he did a bit of research, working out that over the previous month Arsene Wenger, Sir Alex Ferguson and José Mourinho had had more written about them than all the players in the Premier League combined. It was a phenomenon that Stephen Wagg had spotted when he wrote *The Football World* in the mid-1980s: "The gist of that book is that sometime in the 1960s and 1970s football at the highest level became a television show," he said. "People knew about football and knew football people and the game itself primarily through the media, they perceived it as a media activity. The best illustration I can find for that is the football manager about whom there is a huge global preoccupation just the same as there is with football itself. Most people in the 1960s, probably the majority of the population, had heard of Don Revie, Brian Clough, Alf Ramsey, Bill Nicholson, Matt Busby, Bill Shankly, but how many of them could name the managers who managed those respective clubs beforehand? Nobody except the local aficionados would be able to answer that question, which shows how football became a cross-media event."

I wonder how many England fans know that Walter Winterbottom, with his gloriously inter-war name, was Sir Alf's predecessor. Maybe more than I think but Ramsey was the first England manager of this cross-media age. Winterbottom was, to an extent, at the mercy of the FA's international selection committee. In 1950 that committee decided that Stanley Matthews should take part in a goodwill tour of Canada, forcing him to miss England's first match in that summer's World Cup. Even though he was free for the following game against America they didn't pick him because they didn't want to change a winning team. Following the infamous 6-3 defeat at Wembley in 1953, it was the committee, not Winterbottom, who were identified as "the guilty men" by Desmond Hackett in the *Daily Express*.

It was after this defeat that a concerted campaign began to appoint a manager who was a former professional with sole powers of selection. Ramsey was the papers' and the fans' choice and the FA did as they were told and gave him the job in 1963. Not for the last time, the appointment of the England manager was heavily influenced by the press. When Ramsey's wingless-wonders won the World Cup the manager was knighted in 1967. Of the players (the guys who'd actually broken a sweat) only captain Bobby Moore was honoured the same year with an OBE. Hat-trick hero Geoff Hurst had to wait until 1975 for his MBE while five of the team received no recognition from Her Majesty until 2000.

Sir Alf's ennoblement, with its implicit suggestion that success was principally down to him, meant the manager myth was completely sown into the fertile football-media culture, from which point it grew. However, there was a downside for the man in the dugout. While Sir Alf single-handedly won the World Cup, seven years later he single-handedly failed to qualify for the 1974 tournament. Success hinged on the final qualifier against Poland at Wembley in October 1973. Needing a win, England could only manage a draw, with Jan

Tomaszewski, Poland's 'clown' of a goalkeeper (as Brian Clough labelled him), keeping them at bay.[8] For the country which had been so dismissive of the World Cup just a quarter of a century earlier, non-qualification was a disaster and for the first time the manager was in the firing line. The *Sun*'s Frank Clough penned a report headlined "THE END OF THE WORLD!" and what he wrote is worth quoting at length: "I can't find it in my heart to be critical of this England performance, disastrous though the result was. Most of them gave everything for England […] So the question this morning is what does the future hold for Sir Alf Ramsey? Nobody likes to hit a man when he is in the depths of disappointment, but his entire future must be in the melting pot." The message was clear: the players did all they could, so blame must lie with the manager. It was pretty tame by what would follow and there was a six-month stay of execution, but after goalless draws against Italy and Portugal, Ramsey was sacked in April 1974. The dam had been breached.

Fast-forward seven years to September 1981 and Maggie Thatcher's boys took one hell of a beating in Oslo (well, they lost 2-1 to Norway), putting qualification for the 1982 World Cup into serious doubt. By this time the rhetoric in the press had been ratcheted up several notches and just the prospect of missing out on the tournament was enough to spark outright calls for the manager's dismissal. Under the headline "FOR GOD'S SAKE, GO, RON" David Shapland, who had replaced Frank Nicklin as the *Sun*'s sports editor, wrote: "England were humiliated by the no hopers of Norway last night […] it was a defeat that must spell the end of Ron Greenwood's career as England manager." As it turned out England qualified for España '82 after Romania lost their last three qualification games and Greenwood quit after the tournament. He escaped at just the right time.

This was the first year of Kelvin MacKenzie's *Sun*, which was only just starting to "monster" and "piss all over" its victims, so what Greenwood suffered was light compared to his immediate successors, Sir Bobby Robson and Graham Taylor, who happened to be thrust

---

8   Again, the English media's insularity meant they were unaware of Poland's real ability. Far from being clowns, they finished third in the subsequent World Cup, with Tomaszewski being voted the tournament's best keeper. Two years later he was part of the Polish team that won silver at the Olympics.

into a brutally aggressive three-way tabloid battle. The situation was not lost on Robson, who noted in his book *So Near and Yet So Far*, published in 1986, that it was his "misfortune to be caught in the middle of a newspaper circulation war". In the same book he wrote about how in the early months of his tenure he was spat on when he went to St James' Park after he had dropped Kevin Keegan. For sure these were the actions of a very small minority and I don't mean to tar all Newcastle fans with the same brush through mentioning it, but it demonstrates how the increasingly abusive treatment of the England manager in the press was leading to increasingly abusive treatment from some fans.

Robson endured that abuse until the 1990 World Cup, in which England reached the semi-finals. To date, it's the country's best performance since winning the 1966 World Cup and it enabled the press to recast Sir Bobby as a giant of the game following his death in 2009. The eight years of ordure they had heaped on him were conveniently forgotten.

It is unlikely that will be the case with his successor, Graham Taylor, who will probably always be connected to one particular headline. Success with Lincoln, Watford and Aston Villa meant Taylor was a clearly outstanding candidate to take over from Robson, but the optimism generated by England's glorious defeat in Turin meant that the reaction to perceived failure would be even more intense. Infamously after defeat by Sweden in a group match that saw England knocked out of Euro '92, the *Sun* ran the headline "Swedes 2 Turnips 1" and superimposed Taylor's head onto a picture of the latter root vegetable. Things went from bad to worse and Taylor's family were also on the receiving end. After England lost 2-0 to the USA in America the following summer, Taylor's wife, Rita, was confronted by a mob of reporters in her front garden. Asked for a comment, she declined, saying she didn't give interviews, to which a tabloid reporter replied: "About fucking time you started, then." England failed to qualify for the 1994 World Cup and Taylor resigned in November 1993, a move the *Sun* greeted by reprinting the turnip photo on its front page along with the triumphal headline "THAT'S YER ALLOTMENT". Years after leaving the job Taylor still had people shouting "there's the fucking turnip" when they saw him, while others spat at or poured drinks over him. When he later met MacKenzie, the erstwhile *Sun* editor dismissed Taylor's complaints as oversensitivity, saying it had all been a bit of fun.

Terry Venables was appointed Taylor's successor in January the following year, the month MacKenzie left the *Sun* to become managing director at Sky. Other than the first 15 months of his editorship when Ron Greenwood was in charge of the national team, Robson and Taylor were the two England managers whose reigns coincided with MacKenzie's time at the *Sun*. They were the main victims of the ethos he brought to the paper as it was manifested on the sports desk. True they were also monstered by the *Daily Mirror* and the *Star* but in the race to the gutter it was the *Sun,* a rabid, drooling pit bull with its eight rows of teeth bared, that led the way. The managers that followed Robson and Taylor still had to face the press pack, but while each will bear scars, none was mauled as viciously as Robson and Taylor. Fourteen years after the latter oversaw failure to qualify for the 1994 World Cup, England failed to qualify for Euro 2008 following a 3-2 defeat to Croatia at Wembley. It was raining and the England manager, Steve McClaren, made the bizarre decision to use an umbrella, allowing the *Daily Mail* to brand him "A WALLY WITH A BROLLY". In comparison with what had gone before it was like being nipped by a playful terrier.

• • •

While Taylor had the misfortune of taking over an England team on a high, the opposite was the case for his successor Terry Venables, and given that England was hosting Euro '96, there was no danger of non-qualification. Furthermore, in the 19 matches between Venables taking charge and the opening game of the tournament, England lost just once, to Brazil. For once the heat was off the manager, and instead the tabloid agenda was focused on England's European neighbours. MacKenzie may have left Fleet Street but his shadow loomed large as his protégé Piers Morgan led the tub-thumping; something he did in the pages of the *Daily Mirror*. Morgan had been editor of the *Sun*'s "Bizarre" column under MacKenzie and when he graduated to the editorship of the *News of the World* in 1993

Morgan acknowledged his mentor, saying: "I owe it all to Kelvin. He's always been there for me."

Two years later, aged just 30, Morgan took the helm at the *Daily Mirror*. Tasked with closing the sizeable gap in sales of about 1.5 million readers he said he planned to make the *Daily Mirror* a more aspirational version of the *Sun*. So he dropped the word "Daily" from the masthead, dusted off his old boss' tactics sheets and went to work. An ardent Tory at odds with the *Mirror*'s traditional left-wing stance, Morgan did away with political content and employed *Sun*-style headlines. Daily stories on the recently launched National Lottery were twinned with celebrity and Royal 'exclusives', and on one occasion Morgan printed a picture of Princess Di in floods of tears after she'd been chased down the street by paparazzi. The *Sun* had refused to buy it, considering it to be too intrusive.

Unlike MacKenzie, Morgan never had a war to sink his teeth into, but a football tournament on his doorstep was the next best thing. Euro '96 took place a little more than six years after Tory Agriculture Minister John Selwyn Gummer shoved a beef burger down his infant daughter's throat to demonstrate that mad cow disease was nothing to be scared of. However, two months before the tournament began, Selwyn Gummer's colleague, the Health Secretary Stephen Dorrell, admitted to the House of Commons that in actual fact it might be. The *Mirror* greeted Dorrell's admission that ten new cases of Creutzfeldt-Jakob disease were possibly linked to bovine spongiform encephalopathy by screaming "MAD COW CAN KILL YOU", while the *Daily Mail* asked hysterically "COULD IT BE WORSE THAN AIDS?" Within days the EU had imposed a worldwide ban on the export of British beef and related products and the tabloid press suddenly forgot the potentially fatal health implications and focused instead on the damage the dastardly Europeans' actions might do to the British economy. It was "THE CATTLE OF BRITAIN" according to the *Sun*, which declared: "SCARE'S A LOAD OF BULL".[9] Once again the tabloids had reduced politics to a simple 'us' against

9   *While BSE could kill you, the danger it posed wasn't worse than AIDS. It's worth pointing out that the EU's ban, which was finally lifted in 2006, was in many ways as nationalistic as the British press' coverage of it. There was no attempt to identify the source or draw distinctions between farmers, breeds of cattle or even organic and non-organic beef. The whole of Britain was treated as a homogeneous unit.*

'them' dichotomy. This was the backdrop to press coverage of Euro '96. This was Morgan's Falklands.

It wasn't just the *Mirror* editor who saw the tournament through this prism; the link between politics and football was made explicit in the *Sun* when Jimmy Greaves was quoted as saying: "our football team finally gets the chance to do what our politicians are too scared to try, and stuff it right up Europe". As Venables' team progressed, so the patriotic fervour grew. In the run-up to England's quarter-final with Spain, the *Mirror* printed a list of "10 NASTIES SPAIN'S GIVEN EUROPE", which included syphilis, Spanish flu and the Inquisition. Alongside these were printed a series of racist jokes, but this was just a warm-up act. Victory in that match meant England would face Germany in the semi-finals and Morgan distilled the "Two-World-Wars-and-one-World-Cup" mentality of the terraces into a declaration of football war. A cut-out-poster front page with the headline: "ACHTUNG! SURRENDER! FOR YOU FRITZ ZE EURO CHAMPIONSHIP IS OVER" was illustrated with pictures of Stuart Pearce and Gazza wearing Second World War Tommy helmets. The paper also sent a tank to the German team's hotel, although it was stopped on the M25 by police. Morgan later revealed that he seriously considered sending another tank to 'invade' the Berlin offices of Germany's leading tabloid *Bild* and hiring a Spitfire to fly over the German training camp.

In the age of New Labour and Brit Pop and with the Tory Government limping towards emphatic defeat in the following year's General Election it was a huge misstep. The Press Complaints Commission received 67 complaints – the most since the *Sun*'s coverage of Hillsborough in 1989 – and Morgan was forced into an apology. Stuart Higgins, his counterpart at the *Sun,* tried to take the moral high ground, pointing out that their "LET'S BLITZ FRITZ" headline was relegated to page four (after a Page 3 girl, predictably getting her "FRITZ OUT FOR THE LADS!"), and to be fair by comparison their coverage, which called for fans to be peaceful, was muted. Germany won the game on penalties and, in the aftermath, there were disturbances across the country, which, concluded the National Heritage Select Committee, the press "may well have had its effect in stimulating". That conclusion is hard to prove with any certainty but it's fair to point out that while on one hand the tabloids are quick to condemn violence among football fans, on the other they have no problem in cultivating the xenophobic sentiments those violent fans tend to express. It must have all been terribly confusing for the right old fascists in the pub, used to seeing this kind of content in the *Sun*, not the "whining namby-pamby ultra-Left" *Mirror*.

• • •

Euro '96 was also notable for being the first football tournament to come after the broadsheets started taking a real interest in the sport. While football writers were always essential to the tabloid product, broadsheet editors were less convinced of the merits of the sports desk, which was more often than not dismissed as the "Toy Department". That all changed in the 1990s thanks to the vision and perseverance of one man in particular, David Welch, the sports editor of the *Daily Telegraph*. Born in 1948, Welch, the son of a lorry driver, was a talented athlete in his youth and studied physical education, English and history at the Loughborough Colleges. Unsure of where his future lay, Welch answered an advert for the position of racing correspondent on the *Leicester Mercury*. A keen student of the turf he made the job his own and quickly became one of the youngest sports editors in the country. Fleet Street beckoned and in 1984 Welch joined the *Telegraph* with a fulsome reference from his bosses at the *Mercury*, who he believed were keen to get rid of him due to his constant demands for more resources.

Two years later Max Hastings became the *Telegraph*'s editor and although a self-confessed "sports illiterate" he recognised that there was an opportunity to dominate the market in that area. Welch was the man to lead the charge and by 1989 he had become the paper's sports editor. He was convinced that instead of being a section hidden away at the back, sport could be used to drive sales of the paper as a whole and so in 1990 Welch launched a sports supplement. Now something we take for granted as a standard part of all newspapers, at the time it was a revolutionary idea. Initially printed on Mondays the supplement was so successful it was soon also produced on Saturdays before eventually appearing every day of the week. The huge success meant that while Hastings was sometimes tough on the budgets of his other departments, he tried, within reason, to give Welch everything he asked for and the number of sports staff grew from 38 in 1987 to 67 by 1995.

One of the many young newcomers Welch recruited, along with Sue Mott, Giles Smith and Paul Hayward, was Henry Winter, who joined the paper from the *Independent* in 1994. Around that time the *Telegraph* was printing about 1,000 words a day on football but that soon increased fivefold. Despite not being an avid football fan himself, Welch understood the massive impact Sky's coverage of football would have in promoting the game and the players and so poured resources into covering the sport. Equally he recognised the glamour of the Champions League and so sent Winter to all-Italian games. Initially the young reporter was the only member of the English press in attendance but others soon followed. This expansion of football writing is one of the biggest changes Winter has seen while working as a football writer. "The tabloids have always been strong, the broadsheets have expanded, the Sundays have got bigger," he told me. "One of the great helps for newspapers, and a wave I've been lucky to ride, is that Sky has scattered matches across the week, which has given papers the opportunity to expand. There's also the rolling news service, which you have to respond to, so tiny little things suddenly become a huge state occasion. It's gone from being a small planet to a huge universe. Take the World Cup Final in 1966: some papers only had one writer there. If England had reached the World Cup Final in Rio the broadsheets would have had a minimum of eight staff each, excluding photographers, and that's the other side of the world as opposed to an eight-mile yomp from Fleet Street as it was in '66."

The *Telegraph*'s supplement captured the middle-class football zeitgeist that had emerged from the fanzine movement and the success of Nick Hornby's *Fever Pitch*. Its success, along with the increased exposure of football through Sky and England's hosting of Euro '96, helped persuade other broadsheet editors that football could help drive sales. In the months before the tournament, Murdoch visited the offices of *The Times* and promised increased recourses to expand the paper's sports coverage in the run-up. The *Observer* dispatched the Booker Prize-winning novelist A.S. Byatt to England's Euro '96 semi-final with Germany. She described the England players in their grey strip as being "like floating shadows on the bright emerald-gold grass, the colour of Monet's shades" while England's keeper David Seaman "was resplendent. A striding, scarlet lord entirely comfortable in his beauty. A bullfighter". The *Independent* sent Germaine Greer, who "bathed in testosterone" and described Gazza as having "the unflagging enthusiasm of a puppy".

In 1965 Brian Glanville wrote an article in *Encounter* arguing that British sports journalism was "still looking for an idiom" that could bridge the divide that he suggested existed between the writers in the popular and quality press. The former, he argued, had a large readership but were forced into using a highly stylised style of writing while the latter could write as they pleased but would only ever reach a small audience. The tabloidisation of the market certainly appears to have brought the two sections of the market closer together and Winter believes it's becoming easier for writers to move between them. "Whether I'd have the discipline to write for a tabloid I don't know," he said, "but you get someone like Oliver Holt who used to be my counterpart on *The Times* – a brilliant football correspondent – and he's now a fantastic red-top columnist and writer. There's Matt Dickinson, who's now chief sports correspondent of *The Times*; he was a really, really good old-school news-reporting football hack on the Manchester beat on the *Daily Express*. So there is that fluidity. If I think up a line, I'll occasionally give it to one of my mates on the tabloids. Here's an example: Chelsea were playing Basel in the Europa League under Rafa Benítez and obviously the fans sing about him being "the Spanish waiter", so I said to my mate on the *Sun*: "it makes a change, the Spanish waiter getting one over Basel". I think that made their back page; you wouldn't get that in a broadsheet but it's vaguely amusing so those things do get passed around because we spend all of our time together. We do television together, we do radio together, so all those edges that distinguish one end of Fleet Street from another have been flattened down."

• • •

The introduction of the *Telegraph*'s supplement and the increasing interest in football among the broadsheet, or quality, press was part of the ongoing tabloidisation of the newspaper market. The most obvious manifestation of this was the papers' change in form. Murdoch relaunched the *Sun* as a tabloid in 1969. The *Daily Mail* followed suit in 1971; the *Daily Express* in 1977; the *News of the World* in 1984 and the *Sunday Express* in 1992. Then in 2004 the *Independent* and *The Times* followed suit, leaving the *Telegraph* as the only daily broadsheet, while the *Guardian* is published in the hybrid Berliner style. Alongside this literal tabloidisation the 'quality' press also took on the style and news values of the tabloids. All papers increasingly focus their content on entertainment and lifestyle features at the expense of politics, public affairs and international news.

This was all accelerated by the launch, of first, *Hello!* and then *OK!* magazines, with their focus on celebrity. Following the *Mirror*'s "ACHTUNG SURRENDER" front page, the *Guardian* called for "an escape from the tabloid agenda". It was too late. Already the *Sunday Times* had referred to England's victory over Scotland as "the routing of the clans" while the *Sunday Telegraph* met quarter-final success with the headline "Spain still can't beat an English Seaman", a course the *Observer* also sailed declaring "Seaman Sinks Armada". Some criticise this process, but such complaints tend to be a repetition of those levelled at the popular press down the years. Remember the *Daily Herald* journalist decrying the "frenzied gusto" of the 1930s version of the *Daily Mirror*? When you think about it that sounds pretty similar to the outrage aimed at the *News of the World* in its final days in 2011. Each generation tends to bemoan the shorter articles, bolder headlines and more sensational tone and content of stories they are presented with; these changes become the norm for the following generation, which has similar complaints of its own, while everyone looks to the distant past and agrees the papers back then were, well, boring.

This shift also led to an increase in the amount of reporting of football at both ends of the newspaper market. If it hadn't been the dominant sport before, by 1998 football was unequivocally the driving force behind the increase in newspaper sports coverage.

"Forget news, forget celebrity gossip, forget hard-hitting investigative reporting", wrote the newspaper trade magazine *Press Gazette*. "If you want to sell more copies of your newspaper, what you want is more of the f word: football." Sports editors and their bosses were listening and now about half of broadsheet sports coverage is devoted to the sport while in the tabloid press the amount is closer to three-quarters. Yet you can't help feeling that despite all these extra words not a whole lot more is being said. A significant proportion of football 'news' comes from the same place: press conferences or agencies such as the Press Association. Most of the time football reporters have access to the same information and so are essentially writing different versions of the same story. More often than not what gets discussed at a press conference will be determined by the reporter with the loudest voice. Typically the manager will repeat the answers they've just given in a different interview on TV. As Frank Nicklin identified back in 1969, the readers are getting the actual information from other media, so the press are left with comment; the search for the all-important 'story' and the use of 'overstatement'.

Take for example the reaction to Rafa Benítez' comments after Chelsea's FA Cup match with Middlesbrough in February 2013. The windowless press room at the Riverside is not huge, about twice the size of the average living room, and it's right under the seating so it has an awkward pitched roof on one side which I've seen more than one person bang their head on. It's dark and cramped at the best of times and on the night in question it was packed, making it even more so. Before Benítez came in, there was already some indication from Twitter that he had criticised Chelsea fans in a post-match TV interview. The Spaniard repeated the criticisms in his press conference and the following day the papers variously described it as a "rant", a "meltdown" or Benítez "losing it spectacularly". This is odd, because what I saw was a man totally in control of himself delivering a calm and measured critique of the behaviour of a small section of the club's fans, the short-term, chaotic nature of the club's administration and the attitude of some of his players. This was not a wild-eyed, finger-pointing Kevin Keegan disintegration. He didn't liberally pepper his comments with expletives as did Joe

Kinnear when he first met the North East press pack in 2008,[10] nor did Benítez tell anyone to "fuck off" like Harry Redknapp did when Sky's Rob Palmerby had the audacity to call him a "wheeler-dealer". In fact Benítez didn't even raise his voice. Watching the conference on TV later, it appeared to be a long-winded ramble. It wasn't; the questions had simply been edited out so it looked like he was repeating himself, when in fact he was brief and to the point. The repetition came from the journalists who asked the same thing several times in slightly different ways. Of course, the papers were unable to report what the Chelsea boss had said straight, as that had been done by TV and to a lesser extent by social media, so they turned to comment and analysis, but there was little mileage in suggesting that Benítez might have been right. No, portraying him as a man on the edge of a nervous breakdown was a far better story.

It's not just the search for the 'story' that has changed the way football is reported. The media's interest has propelled footballers into the realms of national, and in some cases global, celebrity. While they might have been able to rely on journalists turning a blind eye to their indiscretions in the 1950s, this is no longer the case, so they're now guarded by a phalanx of advisers protecting their 'brand'. The balance of power has shifted and news is freely given, but what kind of news is it? Julie Welch began reporting on football for the *Observer* in the 1970s and noticed a change about 20 years later. "When I started it was brilliant because the players were there for you and the managers were there for you. Now you have to go through lots of PRs and bodyguards and there's always someone sitting in on interviews," she told me. "About the second interview I did was with Norman Hunter, the Leeds United winger. I just rang up Elland Road and said: 'Can I speak to Norman Hunter?' and they fetched him out of the dressing room to speak to me. I went up to Elland Road and we just sat in the reception and I interviewed him. It was just fantastic, it was so different. You'd go to parties and you'd be talking to the great Bobby Charlton. So when you've been in that world the present world seems, in a way, untrue. You're not getting the real person,

10   *Kinnear opened the conference by asking, "Which one of you is Simon Bird?" When Bird, who writes for the* Daily Mirror, *identified himself, Kinnear sneered "You're a cunt" before rattling off another 51 swear words in little more than five fun-packed minutes.*

you're just getting a sanitised series of quotes. To interview a player in the 1970s and the 1980s you could find out what made them tick, you could ask questions that they hadn't been asked before and they would give you sometimes quite revealing detail about themselves."

Paul Gascoigne was the first football celebrity of the Premier League era, but at the same time he was a throwback; an un-media-managed star who existed in a world that was increasingly media-managed. In October 1992 while he was training with the England squad at Bisham Abbey ahead of a crucial World Cup qualifier against Norway, Gazza was approached by a camera crew from the Scandinavian country's NRK network. "Do you have a message for Norway?" journalist Thor Eggen asked. "Yes. Fuck off, Norway," came the reply. Unlike David Beckham, who has managed his celebrity so successfully he is arguably the most famous footballer ever, Gazza had no concept of himself as a brand. He was, in effect, still a lad in a pub in Gateshead and so he said the first thing that came into his head. But the incident also highlighted the difference in the media environment that the pair operated in. When Gazza told Norway to jog on, the Premier League was less than six months old; Sky Sports News was just a twinkle in Rupert Murdoch's eye; only Sir Tim Berners-Lee and a few of his chums had access to the WorldWideWeb; and Twitter was not around for us all to share our *faux* outrage. The furore was brief. This was a far cry from 12 years later when the *News of the World* published claims by Rebecca Loos that she'd had a four-month fling with Beckham following his move to Real Madrid. At the time Roy Greenslade, the former editor of the *Daily Mirror*, was moved to say the Beckham–Loos revelations were the biggest story since the serialisation of Andrew Morton's book about Princess Diana in 1992. Maybe they were, but you can't help but think there's something amiss when the suggestion that the England skipper has had an affair is given yards and yards of column space while allegations about transfer bungs in the Premier League or corruption in FIFA are routinely ignored.

One journalist who has doggedly investigated the latter is Andrew Jennings and he believes that it wasn't always this way. "If you wind the clock back to the 1970s the *People*, which was then a very dynamic Sunday newspaper, investigated corruption in football, and in the *Sunday Times* sport department you had the most wonderful group of writers including Keith Botsford. Motor racing was his thing but he also wrote about football corruption and João Havelenge the former FIFA president, which is how I came to know him. He's the sort of writer who takes your breath away; someone who wrote about sport, as opposed to someone who did sports writing. They had a wonderful sports editor in John Lovesy, who commissioned the likes of Keith and Brian Glanville."

Jennings has won numerous awards for exposing corruption in both football's world governing body, FIFA, and the International Olympic Committee, and speaking to him it's clear he's scathing about the lack of investigative reporting that comes from the sports desks of the press in the modern age. "There's a number of very, very good investigative reporters on the sports front in Brazil because corruption breeds good journalism everywhere but in what we used to call Fleet Street. They are a cabal of uselessness apart from one or two exceptions like David Conn and Nick Harris. The culture of news doesn't penetrate the sports desks. They don't do research, they never do what any real journalist does, which is ask, 'Where are the documents?'"

His criticisms have brought a strong defence of their trade from many football writers, who not unreasonably argue that exposés like the *Sunday Times'* investigation into FIFA corruption are just as valid as Jennings' own work on the subject. At the same time they claim that pressure from rolling TV news and the instantaneous nature of the internet and social media create ever-greater time pressures. When these are coupled with budget cuts that inevitably impact on staff numbers, there is simply neither the time nor resources to spend months, even years, on one story. Furthermore, they argue, football is a small world and reporting it requires access that creates a tricky balancing act. Just one story that a club doesn't like can get a reporter banned from the press box or press conferences, making it all but impossible to do the job in the longer term.

Jennings did acknowledge that it is editors, not reporters, who should bear the responsibility for the situation: "You have to blame the bosses, at the end of the day an editor should be saying: 'Go and get the story or don't come back.' If executives aren't hiring people who can get stories and keeping them bloody well at it then you're not going to get the stories. They assume that because the sports editor got the result of Spurs versus Chelsea everything's alright. They never say 'we're breaking stories and you're not'." However, at the same time he dismissed the other pleas in mitigation. "Papers are strapped for cash, so it's easy for them to say 'we can't spend time investigating', but they can if they want to, you can do anything if you want to. Journalists should get stories, not embrace the press release culture. We should find out what people don't want published. This is the crucial thing: it's so easy to report in the interests of the people they cover. It demeans our sports culture if we're not getting good information. I repeatedly hear 'but we might lose access' and I reply 'what, you mean access to be lied to?' The funny thing is I'm the only journalist in the world who's banned from FIFA press conferences but it doesn't stop me getting the stories."

One of those stories was broadcast in November 2010 on the eve of the secret FIFA vote to decide which countries would host the 2018 and 2022 World Cups. England had made a bid to host the former tournament but were eliminated in the first round with just two votes. After the process Andy Anson, the bid's chief executive, declared that FIFA executive committee members had told him that the English media had killed the bid, which conveniently ignored the substance of Jennings' documentary that suggested the bid was never going to win. Even Ian Wright got in on the act, preaching from his pulpit in the *Sun* that he "would love to see some proper investigations into FIFA rather than this Jennings bloke shouting at people". Clearly Wright, never one to get shouty, was unaware of Jennings' 400-page book *Foul! The Secret World of FIFA: Bribes, Vote Rigging and Ticket Scandals,* which was first published in 2005, or his *Panorama* documentary *FIFA and Coe,* broadcast in 2007. Or perhaps he just doesn't consider them 'proper investigations'.

Despite the criticism, Jennings argues he is giving fans the stories they actually want. "We got attacked and attacked and attacked. Everyone was briefing against us from the FA to the Government. Jeremy Hunt, the Culture Secretary, was putting pressure on the BBC to transmit the programme later. They didn't know what was in it, they just knew it was 'allegedly damaging'. What was fascinating to me was that the following summer I was the keynote speaker at the Football Supporters

Federation Annual Parliament. I have no expertise in football or the football world – I joke that I shouldn't be sent to a football match because I might get the score-line wrong. The fans don't need me to interpret what's happening in the game of football; however, they know that FIFA's corrupt and they wanted me to tell them more."

CHAPTER 8

FANS ARE DOING IT FOR THEMSELVES

On 12 September 2012 David Cameron took to the floor of the House of Commons and in a statement lasting a little more than 12 minutes apologised to the bereaved and the survivors of the Hillsborough disaster on behalf of the Government and the country for the "double injustice" they had suffered. That morning, following months of diligent analysis, the Hillsborough Independent Panel had released its findings and they were unequivocal. In response the Prime Minister was, he said, "profoundly sorry" for "the failure of the state to protect their loved ones" and also "the denigration of the deceased". Cameron acknowledged that the trauma suffered on Merseyside had been compounded by an attempt to blame the victims with a narrative focused on hooliganism. The report he said was black and white: there was simply no evidence to support that narrative. The media responded too. The truth was out, they proclaimed; the blame lay at the feet of Sheffield Wednesday Football club, Sheffield City Council, the FA and most of all South Yorkshire Police who created that narrative through a huge cover-up. There was, however, no acknowledgement from the media that their way of working, coupled with their portrayal of football fans, created fertile ground in which the police lies could take root and grow.

News is a product; journalists don't just report it, they create it by prioritising some aspects of a story over others. They tend to seek simplistic explanations which focus on one cause, thus overlooking the context and true complexity of the issue at hand. Furthermore, journalists tend to rely on certain 'trusted' contacts who are expected to be detached and accurate. So, as is often the case, in the search for the causes of Hillsborough precedence was given to official statements, particularly from the police, but also from politicians and FA officials. The bereaved and survivors were relegated to providing the 'emotional' side of coverage through human-interest stories. This allowed the police to detract attention from their own failings by apportioning blame to the supporters, the most infamous example being the *Sun*'s front page just four days after the disaster in which, under the headline "THE TRUTH", they falsely claimed that Liverpool fans stole from the dead and beat up and urinated on policemen administering first aid. The headline and the man who wrote it – Kelvin MacKenzie, who else? – have been repeatedly held up as an example not just of the worst excesses of Hillsborough coverage but also of tabloid journalism more generally, but it is rarely acknowledged that the rest of the coverage was little better. The false allegations printed in the *Sun* were first printed in the *Sheffield Star* the day before, and featured on both the ITV and BBC news bulletins that night. On the same day as the *Sun* splash, the allegations also made the front pages of the *Daily Star*, the *Daily Mail, The Times*, the *Telegraph,* the *Daily Express* and the now-defunct *Today.*

Yet is it any wonder that the media took this path? The alternative route raised some serious questions about Margaret Thatcher's aggressive brand of capitalism. Nearly 700 people were killed in a series of disasters that beset Britain in the late 1980s. Names such as Zeebrugge, Piper Alpha, King's Cross and East Midlands Airport became synonymous with tragedy. They were bookended by the fire at Bradford's Valley Parade stadium that claimed 57 lives in May 1985 and Hillsborough, which claimed 96 lives a little less than four years later. In the aftermath of Hillsborough the Socialist Workers Party produced a poster with a photo of an emotional Liverpool fan sitting alone among Hillsborough's mangled fencing and the words: "Thatcherism: Ten Years of Disasters". It might have seemed like cheap political point scoring to some, but it captured the anti-Thatcher mood at the time and the fundamental link wasn't lost to others either.

Writing in the days after Hillsborough, Edward Greenspon, the European Business Correspondent of Toronto's *Globe and Mail*, pointed to common themes identified in the inquiries into the other recent tragedies. There was, he wrote, a "rampant disregard for safety in private and public services; poor communications once disasters occur; inadequately trained and overworked staff; and, especially, dilapidated public services". That was never going to be the focus of the Hillsborough story for the English media. Just as Lord Justice Taylor had found that while hooliganism played no part in the tragedy the "fear of hooliganism" had "strongly influenced the strategy of police", so the narrative of hooliganism strongly influenced the coverage of the disaster. Liverpool fans *could* be easily demonised because at the time, due to the actions of a minority, *all* football fans were labelled as hooligans.

• • •

In the 1980s football violence was considered to be a relatively recent phenomenon – a dark path that the game had taken in the 1960s leaving behind a much more peaceful past. However, that wasn't the case. In his autobiographical history of the Salford slums, Robert Roberts wrote about the groups of youths that congregated menacingly on street corners dressed in bell-bottom trousers, heavy leather belts and thick iron-shod clogs. They "sought escape from tedium in bloody battles with belt and clog – street against street" and earned the condemnation of respectable citizens, police and magistrates. Swap the bell-bottomed trousers and iron-shod clogs for Lois jeans and adidas Samba (and let's face it you'd probably want to) and you're talking about late 1980s Casuals. But don't go thinking it was just the commoners who were revolting. The authorised biography of soldier, journalist and politician Bill Deedes, written by Stephen Robinson, reveals that before the Second World War it was considered "rather off-side" if the annual cricket match at Lord's between Harrow (which Deedes attended) and Eton didn't end with a mass brawl between rival pupils in front of the pavilion. Ted Croker had a more-than-valid point when he told Margaret Thatcher to get *her* hooligans out of *his* game.

And that was the point: there had always been violence at football matches; it's just that the quantity and sensational nature of the coverage of it hit an upward curve in the 1960s. The emergence of this media-driven 'hooligan' narrative is traced in the book *The Roots of Football Hooliganism* by Eric Dunning, Patrick Murphy and John

Williams. The authors argued that the media constituted "an active ingredient in the phenomenon" of football violence, adding that press coverage in particular seemed to play "a part in both de-escalating the problem of football hooliganism in the inter-war years and in escalating it from the 1960s onwards". This, they argued, distorted the perceptions of football violence, and as a consequence football fandom generally, that non-football fans and politicians had, many of whom had themselves never been to a game. In turn, more often than not discussion of the subject was "emotionally and politically loaded, based on superficial knowledge and often simply wrong".

As early as the late 1880s, with organised football in its infancy, there was a range of violent incidents at games. With few travelling fans these tended to be pitch invasions or attacks on visiting players and referees who were regularly "baited" and "mobbed" or punched and stoned. Between 1895 when FA records began and the outbreak of war in 1914, 238 major incidents of violence were reported to the authorities by referees. The actual number is likely to be much higher as the figure didn't include incidents the men in the middle didn't consider worth reporting or incidents outside grounds. However, the FA only took action 26 times and press reporting of the trouble was relatively matter-of-fact, descriptive, not sensationalist.

In 1889, the *Birmingham Daily Mail* reported that a Wolves player was hit by an object thrown from the crowd. Witnesses saw "a red-headed youth shying stones into the field and heard a gang of men urge him on". A match in December of that year between Worksop and Stavely Olympic led to the referee receiving "a nasty blow under the jaw". He then had to be spirited out of town by the police as the "natives were waiting for him". A match between Burnley and Blackburn in February 1890 ended with the referee hiding first under the grandstand, then in a nearby house, before being driven away in a cab chased by a stone-throwing mob. The only hint of condemnation this drew from the press was the use of the term "a disgraceful scene". The past is, of course, a foreign country and it must be noted that there was a higher tolerance to violence in the late nineteenth century and that police tended not to make arrests, so these incidents were not seen as *news*worthy and descriptions of them tended to be buried in general match reports.

It's not clear whether the level of violence in the inter-war period increased – reported incidents went up but so too did the number of games and the number of people watching them, so creating a complex picture. What is clear though is that the violence didn't go away, nor was it sensationalised by the press. In November 1922 the *Daily Express* ran a story headlined: "Mob breaks loose at Brighton: Policeman stunned by a spectator". The referee was chased and a policeman injured when a corner flag was thrown onto the pitch as thousands of "hotheads" stormed out of the stands. In 1934 a report in the *Leicester Mercury* reported on damage caused to a football special train by a "hooligan element". However, it was a matter-of-fact report that quickly went on to describe the "gay scenes" in the city centre following the match. Police were not mentioned at all.

This violence is somewhat at odds with the picture painted of the period, a picture that usually depicts a policeman on a white horse at the first Wembley FA Cup Final in 1923. At the time the ground had a capacity of about 127,000 and the FA in their wisdom decided to let a significant number of fans pay on the day. This led to huge overcrowding, with *The Times* reporting that as many as 300,000 gained entry. Mercifully unrestrained by perimeter fences, spectators poured onto the pitch, delaying kick-off. Looking back they're perceived as an orderly crowd cleared by PC George Scorey on his horse, Billie. However, take off your rose-tinted spectacles and look at the photos of the day closely and you'll see a line of horses, all but one of which was black. At a glance the black horses merged into the dark-clothed crowd but Billie, a grey, appeared white and so stood out. Likewise, newsreel footage shows black horses encroaching onto the pitch during the game as they held back the crowd. Following the match Billie and PC Scorey became minor celebrities, reinforcing the sense that the pair dealt with the crowd alone, a myth that perpetuates today through things like the White Horse Bridge at Wembley station. The overcrowding was in part caused by fans of both clubs – West Ham and Bolton – forcing their way into the ground after the turnstiles were closed, and after the game some spectators invaded the Royal Box ransacking it for souvenirs. Yet modern histories downplay these issues (if they're mentioned at all) because they don't fit the mythical narrative of a game followed by peaceful fans in an idyllic past.

That narrative also informs popular understanding of the game in the immediate post-war years but again the reality was different: violence was still an issue. Assaults, pitch invasions and missile throwing continued and in one incident at a match between Preston North End and Burnley on Boxing Day 1947 a linesman was shot in the chest by an air rifle. If that happened today football would collapse under the weight of screaming front-page headlines, strongly worded editorials, rolling TV news coverage and thousands of tweets per second, yet at the time these incidents passed with little comment.

By the late 1950s the tone of coverage was changing. Papers began to focus on incidents of football violence, such as fans smashing up "excursion trains" and "louts" attacking players on the pitch, as *news* stories distinct from match reports. However, the coverage was still not yet sensationalist in tone. In 1959 the *Leicester Mercury* claimed: "Admittedly there has been a minor outbreak of acts of hooliganism this season on the part of individuals here and there, but for the most part English soccer crowds are good-natured and well behaved, comparing favourably with any in the world." While football violence was being recognised as a problem, it was seen as a minor one that did not require a draconian solution. The introduction of fences at Everton's Goodison Park in 1963 was not hailed by the press as a positive or even necessary measure. In fact several papers called for their removal and as late as February 1964 the *Daily Mail* argued that "hooliganism rather than indifference" was preferable at football matches.

However, society was changing fast. A growing youth culture was emboldened by rising wages and an end to National Service that created a literal break from the past. Anxiety about the behaviour of young men was heightened by an increasingly sensationalist press. A few weeks after the *Daily Mail* article, Mods and Rockers fought each other *en masse* in Clacton over the Easter weekend, leading to 97 arrests. It was the start of the first mass-media scare about youth behaviour, fuelling speculation there would be a repeat over the Whitsun holiday a few weeks later, and the prophecy fulfilled itself as hundreds of Mods fought with their leather-clad rivals. Two people were hospitalised and 64 arrests were made after running battles between the police and about 400 people at Margate; 56

arrests were made at Bournemouth and 76 were made at Brighton after violence that was later immortalised by *The Who*'s rock opera *Quadrophenia*. The press used emotionally charged terminology such as "orgy of destruction", "battle", "attack", "siege", "riot" and "screaming mob" – exactly the sort of language that had been absent from the reporting of football violence but that would from then on become a central part of it.

The increased press focus on youth disorder in general meant football matches began to be seen, along with beachfronts, bank holidays, music halls and pubs, as a time and place where violence could be found. In turn, football officials became concerned that outbreaks of fighting during televised games would lead to violence at other matches and frighten away other fans. With national confidence already faltering following the Second World War and the debacle of the Suez Crisis, these fears intensified in the run-up to the 1966 World Cup, which would be the first beamed live around across the planet via satellite. What could be worse than the rest of the world seeing how badly behaved England fans were? It was from this point that the media played an active part in escalating the problem.

Certain matches were determined as being likely flashpoints in advance, thus heightening the likelihood that that was exactly what they would become. "The press started to take an interest in it," said Dougie Brimson, who has written about the history of hooliganism and the media's role in it. "I equate it to dog attacks. They happen every day, but it's only when you get a really bad one that it suddenly becomes big news and then all of a sudden you have loads of them; all of a sudden it becomes a massive news story. That's what the media are like: they set the tone."

In 1974 the *Daily Mirror* printed a 'League of Violence' charting the number of arrests per club. Manchester United were at the bottom with the most. Then one week the table was flipped. United, still with the most arrests, were at the top. Overnight the perception was that they had gone from being the country's 'worst' hooligans to being the 'best'. A gauntlet had been thrown. The club met Cardiff in September 1974 and the press coverage in the build-up focused more on the likely trouble than on the match itself – the first time this had happened. As it turned out there was less violence than expected.

However, serious trouble did flare up when United faced West Ham at Upton Park the following month but the tone of the coverage was ambiguous with the *Sun* reporting how the travelling fans were for once "on the receiving end of a mass punch up". This ambiguity continued two years later when United fans fought with St Etienne supporters in France and were predictably condemned as a disgrace. Why? Because, according to the *London Evening Standard,* they'd been "humiliated into surrender by a Dad's Army of peace-loving French fans".

The media brought further publicity for football violence the following season when *Panorama* took its cameras to The Den to film Millwall's three hooligan gangs. The *Halfway Line* were the youngest; they could graduate to *Treatment*, who wore surgical headgear, or *F Troop* – the "real nutters, self-confessed loonies like Harry the Dog". Reporter David Taylor's posh voiceover, and the warning about "language you don't normally hear on television", seem almost comical now, but the documentary had a massive impact. Here for the first time were organised 'firms' with names and a uniform; in short an identity. "Hooliganism really took off after the *Panorama* documentary," said Brimson. "It caught the public's imagination because it was a shock. Then you started to see hooliganism become organised, you had all the named mobs springing up." From that point onwards violence spiralled but the gangs weren't just looking for a fight, they were looking to boost their notoriety that was fuelled by the media. Brimson continued: "In the 1980s you had so much going on all the time. I remember a story about Chelsea fans stealing a pram with a baby in it that a woman had left outside a shop. It was massive news but that's what it was all about back then. It was like the Mods and the Rockers – you wanted to be in the paper, everyone had a scrapbook."

The escalation reached its peak in 1985. BBC viewers tuning in for the FA Cup quarter-final between Millwall and Luton at Kenilworth Road in March instead saw fans fight running battles with each other and police. Seats were ripped out and used as weapons. The game was stopped twice and the fighting resumed at the final whistle. A few weeks later Ian Hambridge, just 15 and at his first football match, was killed when a wall collapsed during rioting at the Birmingham–Leeds match at St Andrews. The following month TV viewers were left shocked again when rioting led to the deaths of 39 people at Heysel before the European Cup Final between Liverpool and Juventus. This tragic period was also blighted by the fire at Valley Parade, which although nothing to do with football violence only added to the horror. In just 21 years hooliganism had gone from being considered preferable to indifference to perceived as a disease. *The Times* printed an editorial headlined "Putting The Boot In", saying that football was "a slum sport played in slum stadiums and increasingly watched by slum people" and Thatcher called for action. It was in that climate that Liverpool and Nottingham Forest fans arrived at Hillsborough on 15 April 1989 to be confronted by a police force and ultimately a media which viewed them all as hooligans. Yet supporters themselves had already had enough. They started to express their disenchantment with the game's establishment and through both the Football Supporters Association (FSA) and the spread of fanzines they were using the media to do so.

• • •

The editorial of the first post-Hillsborough edition of *When Saturday Comes* stated that all football fans were "deemed to be passive accomplices to the sociopathic minority. The police see us as a mass entity, fuelled by drink and a single-minded resolve to wreak havoc by destroying property and attacking one another with murderous intent. The implication is that 'normal' people need to be protected from the football fan. But we are normal people." It went on to cite the rise of the FSA and fanzines as a signal that fans might get to wield some influence on the administration of the game. Just as 1985 was the year in which the term 'football fan' became synonymous with the term 'football hooligan' in the wider consciousness, so it was the year that fans began to take control of their own identity.

In the aftermath of Heysel, a group of Liverpool fans met in a pub and decided to form the FSA. Its chair Rogan Taylor sent letters to several newspapers appealing for members and around 120 people turned up to the first London meeting, many of them fanzine editors. It was a forum for them to make contacts and exchange copies of their publications, providing impetus for the growing movement. The FSA also began to actively use the media to project a positive image of fans. Anthony Vickers, now chief sports writer for the *Evening Gazette* in Middlesbrough, was a founder member of the Teesside branch. "When the FSA was set up football supporters were the enemy within. While fans were demonised on the front pages, they were more or less ignored on the back pages, and at the time that was true in the local press too. So we set about educating sports reporters first. All over the country FSA branches were set up and they started trying to get local papers on board by putting out press releases and giving them good news stories. In Teesside for instance we had monthly meetings and we'd invite along a match-day police commander or a referee and every time we did we made sure the local paper was notified. They came along because they were getting a story out of it and what they saw was a lot of articulate fans discussing the game on a very well-informed level. We also made a point of always giving out our telephone numbers to the press so we were always accessible whenever there was a story so they could get a fans' perspective instead of just accepting the police's version of events."

The Hillsborough tragedy and the Liverpool fans' treatment in the aftermath reinforced the FSA's determination and they set up fans' embassies during Italia '90. "At that point any England fan who went abroad was pretty much a target for the local police to smash their head in, no questions asked," said Vickers. "We suspected there'd be a lot of trouble in Italy and there were two or three big campsites where the England fans were directed. We had lawyers, journalists, medical staff and local interpreters on hand to make sure that if there were any areas of potential friction we were there straight away and also to make sure that our story got out. As it happened that was really useful because at Rimini there was a mass-deportation when the police rounded up loads of completely random English people, including a couple of people who just happened to be there on holiday with their families. They chartered a plane with 247 seats and they arrested 247 people, but before the plane landed in England we were able to ring our contacts in the national press. So the next day rather than the story being 'England fans deported after rampage' it was actually about the fact it had been a fishing expedition by the local police. Over the next couple of years with the start of the Premier League we were already embedded and most journalists had a couple of fan contacts they would ring regularly for stories."

While the FSA and the fanzine movement developed separately from each other, Vickers acknowledges it was a mutually beneficial relationship. "Fanzine people in most clubs were left-wing types who spoke out against things like racism and sexism, so I think it was a good fit with what we were doing. We were a national organisation and they were locally focused but there was still a lot of overlap and we gave each other a boost."

When Saturday Comes (WSC) along with *The End*, a Liverpool-based fanzine, was at the vanguard of this growing movement which saw hundreds of fanzines spring up around the country in the 1980s. They offered fans a voice, an outlet for their grievances but also the opportunity to express themselves creatively. It was in effect a third way distinct from mainstream football coverage and club programmes. Football fans were relatively late entrants to the world of self-published media. In the very early days fan comment on the game was restricted to the pub; a cathartic outlet to dissect results and criticise players and officials. An early fan movement led to the creation of the National Federation of Football Supporters Clubs in 1927, which printed its own monthly newsletter, imaginatively titled *The Supporter,* for two years. As education and literacy improved, some clubs also allowed supporters groups a column in their programmes. However, no criticism of the club was allowed, so the only place fans could really vent their spleen to a wide audience was in the letters pages of the local paper.

It wasn't until the 1970s and the growth of the underground press and titles like the *Liverpool Free Press* and *Oz* that the first fan-produced football magazine was born and it was in no small part thanks to *Private Eye*. You might think it odd to call the country's best-selling current affairs magazine a 'fanzine' (albeit one focused on news) but it had all the requisite hallmarks in its early days. Launched in 1961 it was initially written by non-professional journalists; a group of friends who had worked together on the Shrewsbury School magazine *The Salopian* and gone on to Oxford University together. It was also produced on cheap print technology, namely a typewriter and Letraset, and it defined itself against professional media with content that often bordered on libellous. Following its initial success *Private Eye* gained funding from Peter Cook and others through a company called Pressdram and became a professionally produced publication. While *Private Eye*'s interest in football has mostly been limited to coverage of the fictional FC Neasden and more recently the regular *Premiersh*ts* cartoon, it has had an influence on the football fanzine genre.

The magazine's first decade of success wasn't lost on a couple of Cambridge undergraduates who applied a similar format to football and launched *Foul!* in 1972. Steve Tongue and Alan Stewart proudly declared their new venture "the alternative football magazine". Tongue went on to become chief football writer on the *Independent on Sunday* and several other contributors also went on to become mainstream football writers including Harry Harris, Eamon Dunphy and Stan Hey, who created the TV series *The Manageress*. Hey told me: "It was slightly outside the mainstream at a time when everything was pretty glum and most people were toeing the line and there was only one line to toe. There were seven or eight dailies, your local paper and not much exposure for the game on television. The mood then was fairly bleak. After the optimism of 1966 and the glorious failure of a 3-2 defeat to Germany in 1970, Alf Ramsey had gone back to a sterile style of football. There was a key game in the 1972 European Championships in Berlin which people of my generation remember. Ramsey played Norman Hunter and Peter Storey in front of the defence and we got a nil-nil draw. Then there was the Ibrox stadium disaster in 1971, which we wrote about. There was a lot of material that the mainstream press didn't really touch. It was a collective really; if you felt pissed off with football you could send something in. We didn't have phone-ins like 606 or talkSPORT but it wasn't just a grumblers' charter; there were people with a lot of valid points to make."

Initially produced in the offices of the university newspaper at night, the magazine, whose name parodied titles like *Goal!* and *Shoot!*, eventually moved to a small room above a butcher's shop in Paddington after it received financial backing from Sunderland fan Sir Tim Rice. "It's the only thing he's lost money on, by the way," said Hey. *Foul!* also received support from Pressdram, enabling it to improve the quality of its production and distribution and achieve a peak circulation of about 10,000. The *Observer* called it "the *Private Eye* of the terraces" and flicking through back issues the similarities are clear. Both had photos with bubble captions on their front covers and as *Private Eye* critiqued and lampooned news writers and the political establishment, so *Foul!* critiqued and lampooned sports writers and the football establishment.

Imitation worked both ways and *Foul!* was the first to publish Colemanballs-style cuttings of mistakes from newspapers. However, like *Private Eye*, *Foul!* wasn't just an arena for sixth-form humour; it also undertook serious journalism, in particular focusing on footballers' fights to get more contract freedom and often lambasting the Professional Footballers Association for not being radical enough. "Mainstream writers didn't like it," Hey adds. "They thought it was childish, which it was, but a lot of stuff we put in it, like the jokes and cartoons, was borrowed later on. We weren't welcome. We were wet behind the ears and a bit dim like all young blokes are. We'd had various complaints and legal threats but then one journalist took exception to something we'd written in our book so he sent us a writ. We were going to fight it but our lawyers said: 'Grow up. You're students, you've got no money. They'll take everything you earn for the next 20 years.' So we cut the offending paragraph out of the book and ended up putting in an apology." In total 34 issues of *Foul!* were produced over four years before, Hey said, they "gradually ran out of money and the mood changed – people fell out of love with football when we didn't qualify for the two World Cups in the 1970s". Stewart, *Foul!*'s co-creator, briefly worked for *The Leveller*, another similar title, but it was a much more short-lived publication.

It wasn't just the team behind *Foul!* that was influenced by *Private Eye*. "I used to love it," Peter Hooton, founder of *The End* told me. "Apart from the obvious public-school-boy humour, I wanted to have that equivalent for the masses in Liverpool. We just used to attack sacred cows. Our main targets were Liverpool personalities like Cilla Black and Jimmy Tarbuck, the list goes on. We were bored of hearing how great the Sixties were." However, it was the rise of punk, which coincided with *Foul!*'s demise, that was the real impetus for Hooton and the new wave of football fanzine editors. In the spring of 1974 Malcolm McLaren and Vivienne Westwood opened their clothes shop SEX on London's King's Road, signalling punk's arrival in England and the end of the post-war consensus. It had been on the cards since those Bank Holiday riots in the mid-1960s but at least after a weekend fighting, the Mods and Rockers could go back to their day jobs. It was hard to even get a day job if you were sporting a huge, green Mohican and had a couple of safety pins through your nose.

Fanzines became a central part of the punk scene, with Mark P's *Sniffin' Glue*[1] – its title taken from a Ramones album – leading the way. Produced on a photocopier in his girlfriend's dad's office, it unashamedly declared itself "FOR PUNKS". When the music press started covering punk, *Sniffin' Glue* stopped; it had done its job. The fanzine also spawned a host of imitators and in 1976 *Melody Maker* journalist Carolyn Coon wrote that a "do it yourself" mentality was central to the punk ethos and fanzines were a clear manifestation of that. The use of ransom-note-style lettering (i.e. letters cut from newspapers) as used on the *Sex Pistols'* album covers subverted the tabloid and music press as well as traditional notions of producer and consumer. This set punk in opposition to the capitalist establishment, but also gave a voice to a movement that was being demonised by that establishment. In his 1991 book *England's Dreaming*, which charted the rise of punk, Jon Savage quoted one of his diary entries from 1976: "Fanzines are the perfect expression – cheaper and more instant than records. Maybe THE medium. A democratisation too – if the most committed 'new wave' is about social change then the best fanzines express this. Perhaps most importantly outside saturated London, they provide a vital function as a base/co-ordination point of the local scene." It was exactly what football fans needed – a cheap, instant, local forum in which to rail against the commonly held misconception that the game was only able to appeal to the lowest common denominator.

It was this ethos that led Hooton to launch *The End* in 1981. "I went into Probe Records in Liverpool and I came across an anarchist fanzine which had a picture of Charles and Diana on the front and then

---

1   *Its full title was* Sniffin' Glue...and other Rock 'n' Roll Habits for Bleedin' Idiots! *and Mark P's full surname was Perry.*

there was eight pages of really nasty, vicious attacks on the absurdity of a Royal wedding in a country crippled by unemployment. It was very funny as well but I thought not many people are going to read this, maybe just a few punks or anarchists. At the same time I was going to football matches and concerts and I'd keep bumping into the same people but there wasn't really a magazine which reflected that. I thought it would be a crossover between football and music but I also wanted the type of thing that was reflected in the anarchist magazine. Our whole emphasis was very punk orientated. We had no heroes, no one who was looked up to as an icon. There was a healthy distrust, or mistrust, of the authorities."

Hooton joined forces with his friend Phil Jones, who had already produced a mod fanzine called *Time for Action,* and in the October after Charles and Di got hitched they produced the first issue of *The End,* which claimed to be a "brand new magazine with an accent on music". Initially sales were slow to non-existent but within a few issues they'd built up a strong following and were selling 5,000 copies per issue. In 1984 Hooton and Jones along with writers Mick Potter, Tony McClelland and Paul Need got national exposure. They squeezed on to the sofa at the *Oxford Road Show* studios to be interviewed by John Peel, who said *The End* was about "music, beer and football, the very stuff of life itself" and declared it his favourite fanzine. "*The End*'s been regarded as a football fanzine but it wasn't really," said Hooton. "It had champions like Paul Du Noyer at *NME* and Janice Long who said it was about football so people took it for granted, although we did deliberately target people who went to the match because there was a fashion element to it."

In many ways *The End* was more concerned about football fans than football itself and over its short life-span it reflected and rein-forced the importance of constantly changing terrace fashions among various groups of opposing fans, each trying to outdo the other in the style stakes. Arguably the manner in which this Casual aesthetic spilled off the terraces and into mainstream youth culture was *The End*'s most enduring legacy but the link with hooliganism, perhaps inevitably, led to accusations that Hooton denies. "People used to say we glorified football hooliganism but we were doing the opposite; we took the piss out of it – humour is the best way to combat violence like that. One of the biggest compliments we got was from one of the right-wingers in the city who could hardly shift his paper. He knew we sold 5,000 an issue and called us a 'lefty pink pop mag indoctrinating the youth of the city'."

By the second issue Hooton and Jones had labelled their lefty pink pop mag "The north's finest music paper". Yet looking through old copies, there's a clear shift in content over the 20 issues. Initially interviews with people ranging from The Clash and Billy Bragg to Alan Bleasdale and Derek Hatton sat alongside reviews, and humorous pieces about "Billy Bullshitter", the much-copied *Ins and Outs* column and poems and letters from readers. By the final edition there is no music content but a considerable amount focused on football including the cover and several articles. Significantly there was a typically sarcastic piece about "football fanzines cropping up everywhere". *The End* ceased publication in May 1988 as Hooton's band The Farm began to have commercial success, their album *Spartacus* topping the charts in 1991. "One thing about *The End* is that it inspired a lot of people to think: 'Well if they can do it then so can we'," said Hooton. "Terry Farley would write to us and say he wanted to start a fanzine and eventually he did with *Boy's Own*."

Farley, who along with co-editor Andy Weatherall would become an influential DJ-producer in the growing club scene, printed the first issue of his magazine in 1986. *Boy's Own* took the opposite journey to *The End*, starting off with a strong focus on football and terrace fashion before becoming dominated by music. *Boy's Own* printed the first article on acid house in 1988 written by another DJ, Paul Oakenfold. When interviewed for a *Boy's Own* anthology in 2010, Farley made the point that that genre of music grew out of the football Casual culture. This football/pop crossover was cemented when New Order bagged their first and only number one with 'World in Motion', England's official 1990 World Cup song, for which Weatherall did several remixes.[2] By then *The End*'s inspiration had spread to all corners of the country. There's a clear lineage from the magazine's characters like Billy Bullshitter to Sid the Sexist in *Viz*. Chris and Simon Donald, the Geordie brothers behind the comic, had written

---

2   *The song was originally called 'E for England' but the FA decided against using that title for some reason.*

to Hooton and his colleagues asking for advice on how to improve their circulation and by the late 1980s they had become a mainstream publication selling more than a hundred thousand copies per issue.

There was also some crossover with *WSC,* and a letter from one of its founding editors, Mike Tischer, appeared in the final issue of *The End.* "There was loads of good stuff in that one," Tischer wrote of the previous issue, "but I can't stick all this stuff about fashion." Here at the start of the fanzine revolution in the mid-1980s was the first manifestations of the two different approaches to football in the magazine market: one focused on football for football's sake, the other on a lifestyle of which football was a key part. "They sent us an early copy," said Hooton, "and we sent them one back and they replied: 'This isn't a football fanzine, it's nothing to do with football; you're more obsessed with terrace fashions' and they were right. But shortly after that their stencilled copies became an exact replica of *The End* in terms of design – three columns of text and photos. I think the layout of our magazine may have influenced them but the content was very different."

While *The End* fused football, music, fashion, politics and drugs, *WSC* was always focused on the game. Tischer and his friend Andy Lyons, who still edits the latter magazine, had a mutual love of music but while they toiled away the hours working at the Soho branch of Our Price they spent most of their time talking about football. So they decided to produce a one-off football fanzine to give away with their music fanzine, *Snipe.* In the first issue they said they wanted to provide an alternative to "clichéd, hackneyed, lazy journalism" and for a name they took the title of a song by Irish punk band The Undertones. "It was mainly the notion of being able to do things for yourselves that influenced us," Lyons said. "Most music and football fanzines were sold through the post or at concerts or matches. It was a way of personal expression through your own means, without going to a larger company."

The pair sent a copy of the first issue to the *Guardian*'s Phil Shaw who wrote the paper's 'Soccer Diary' on a Saturday. "We got loads of letters the following week, something like 200, but we'd only done a few photocopied issues so we had to do a second print run of the first issue. It developed very slowly after that; it took the best part of a year to produce five issues and it wasn't on sale in shops for another 18 months; we were relying on word of mouth and a few independent bookshops." The success of *WSC*'s first issue coincided with the launch of the FSA at that first meeting in London. "The fans' protest movement ran in parallel with the fanzine movement; they had similar roots," said Lyons. At the time the game had a very bad image in the media and people who weren't interested in it felt it was a law-and-order problem, so there was a defensive reaction from football fans who wanted to show that they weren't all hooligans. These things grow out of adversity."

Lyons and Ticher soon got support from a magazine company called Brass Tacks based in Charing Cross Road that allowed them to use their facilities after hours. What had initially been an irregular publication became bi-monthly, then every six weeks, then monthly. By issue five *WSC* was properly typeset and had increased its print run to 1,500. By issue 14 it featured spot colour, had moved to its own offices in Clerkenwell and gained a distribution deal. By March 1988 it was selling 4,000 copies per issue. The following season was key for the quickly developing fanzine movement. In March 1989 *WSC* organised a trip to see England play in Albania. It was designed to show that fans could organise themselves and have fun responsibly, as well as to get publicity for the magazine. Although the coach broke down in Kent and again in Yugoslavia, requiring an extra £1,000 to be spent hiring a second coach, it was a success. Several of the people who paid to come on the trip were journalists and the resulting publicity saw *WSC*'s circulation double to 20,000. The number of fanzines around the country had also risen to about 200 and the movement was gaining widespread attention. In May of that year, *NME*'s Richard North wrote: "If fanzines' eruption is old news, then the scope and intensity of its continuation is a surprise." He included a guide on how to produce one, generating further impetus.

Lyons remembers: "There were a lot of people around the country who were starting their own fanzines so we started to list the ones we knew about and each month there'd be new titles. Eventually by the end of the Eighties and the beginning of the Nineties we had a big double-page list with about 300 or so." The list had grown from 22 in January 1988 and at one stage had to be split into three sections printed over three consecutive issues. In all, more than 600 titles were listed in at least one issue of *WSC*. By printing the names and addresses of these fanzines *WSC* played a crucial role in the development of the new and growing market by becoming a central point of contact between the fanzines and their readers.

The fanzines were mainly one-club focused but some focused on specific issues or events such as club ownership or a move to a new ground. There were two fanzines focused on women's football – *Born Kicking*[3] and *Sunday Kicks* – and a gay and lesbian fanzine *The Football Pink*.[4] Prior to Italia '90 three World Cup-focused fanzines were produced, one English and one Scottish; they were celebratory in tone, while the third called for hooliganism. It had a significantly lower circulation than the others and was less well produced, with some suspecting it was a spoof but, true to form, it was the one that gained mainstream media attention, with the *Sun* branding it 'This Evil Mag' in May 1990.

WSC's sales peaked at 40,000 during the following World Cup and by then they had inspired many people to produce their own fanzines, one of whom was Rob Nichols, who took over the reins of Middlesbrough fanzine *Fly Me to the Moon* in 1990 and is still printing an issue for every home League match. "It was quite an exciting time. *When Saturday Comes* had a list of all the other fanzines and you were definitely aware you were part of some sort of movement all over the country and that's why fanzines were so well received," says Nichols. "Our first issue, in 1988, was four pages long with no staples but it sold out and within a year we were selling 2,000 copies, which from a crowd of about 8,000 was incredible. It showed fans were very dissatisfied with what they were getting from the media and how they were getting pigeon-holed almost as the enemy within. They wanted to express themselves, they wanted to read what other fans had to say, they wanted to look at cartoons, they wanted a laugh and they wanted something that represented them. It went cheek by jowl with the growth of the FSA. It was a real reaction to what was

3   Born Kicking *was edited by Jane Purdon who now works for the Premier League as Director of Governance.*

4   *The fanzine was produced in Manchester by the Gay Football Supporters Network, which the* Gay Times *claimed was the biggest special interest gay group in the country in the early 1990s.*

going on – the shock of what had happened at Bradford and Hillsborough, the proposed ID card scheme. It was a depressing time but there was also optimism because fans felt they could have a voice and they might be able to do something about it. When Hillsborough happened Rogan Taylor from the FSA was on TV all the time. People were listening to what fans said."

Whether there was a conscious effort to 'rebel' is debatable, but what Hey, Hooton, Lyons and Nichols all separately told me is that their aim was to give people a voice; somewhere to have their say. "In those days you couldn't really get your thoughts across to anyone, so writing letters was a form of expression," said Hooton. "We were inundated with them from all around the country; people used to think we made them up but we didn't have to. Fanzines gave people an outlet which they didn't have at the time. Now everyone has a voice on Twitter."

That easy access to the internet and social media has dealt a blow to the fanzine movement but its importance is widely acknowledged; Sky Sports News reported the fact that Wolverhampton Wanderers' fanzine *A Load of Bull* ceased publication in 2012[5] but the movement's legacy lives on. "Back then you felt as if all the journalists were middle-aged or middle-class, there were no radical journalists," Hooton added. "Now you have Tony Evans at *The Times* who was in The Farm and read *The End* and Tony Barrett – they're more a reflection of what fans think on the street." Fanzines had a huge impact on the growth in football literature (more on that later) and Lyons recalls how he was contacted by the BBC as football basked in the post-Italia '90 glow. "Janet Street-Porter was head of youth programmes and she'd received various football-magazine-show proposals which had mentioned *WSC*," he said. "So they asked us what we thought of the ideas; our involvement didn't go much further than that but it led on to shows like *Standing Room Only* and *Fantasy Football League*." Later still, Nick Hancock, the host of *They Think It's All Over,* said the show was "a natural progression from the humour of fanzines". Most have long since disappeared completely and those that still print have passed their circulation peak but its clear that fanzines, which

5   A Load of Bull *was founded in 1989 and printed 158 issues. Editor Charles Ross said he stopped because the fanzine's voice had "gradually become drowned out".*

were initially on the outside of the mainstream football journalism, have changed its landscape forever.

CHAPTER 9

REACHING FOR THE SKY

"Welcome to *Match of the Day*, the first of a weekly series on BBC Two. This afternoon we are in Beatleville." With that sentence Kenneth Wolstenholme introduced highlights of Liverpool's home game against Arsenal on 22 August 1964, and heralded the beginning of regular League football on English TV. It was an inauspicious start, with only 20,000 people – less than half of those who watched the game live – tuning in, but the show was launched just in time to catch the wave of football's post-war popularity. *Match of the Day* was moved to BBC1 after England's success in the 1966 World Cup and on the opening day of the 1967/68 season five million people tuned in for the first show of the season to see Everton run out 3-1 winners against champions Manchester United, thanks in part to two goals from a young Alan Ball. The programme cost £80,000 an hour to make, which was considerably more expensive than most sports broadcasting at the time, but as John Motson wrote in his history of *Match of the Day,* thanks to cutting-edge technology such as electronic cameras and action replay machines "by the late '60s two matches which had finished just a few hours earlier could be shown in colour, sensitively edited, even before the cocoa had cooled".

At its peak the highlights show had an audience of 10–12 million – considerably more than paid their hard-earned cash each week to stand on the terraces – and it made household names of Motson himself as well as the likes of Jimmy Hill and Des Lynam. *Match of the Day*'s success prompted the ITV regions to launch their own highlights shows. Despite the two companies bidding for rights in unison (and thus keeping the price down) the BBC insisted on keeping the Saturday-night slot to itself. Over the next few years ITV asked the BBC to alternate the slots on several occasions but the Beeb refused, so the ITV regions were limited to Sunday-afternoon coverage. Although the two TV companies divvied up the games in an equitable manner, the Sunday-afternoon slot never got the same ratings. It just wasn't part of the match-day routine.

The request wasn't purely football related. BBC had Saturday nights sewn up with a schedule that included shows like *Dr Who*, *The Generation Game* with Bruce Forsyth, Michael Parkinson's eponymous chat show *Parkinson* and, of course, *Match of the Day*. Swap *Strictly Come Dancing* for *The Generation Game* and Graham Norton for Parky and it's remarkable how little that line-up has changed. ITV, and particularly London Weekend Television (LWT), which ran for just two and a half days over the weekend, wanted to break the BBC's stranglehold on the lucrative Saturday-night schedule. Led by its new Director of Programmes Michael Grade, LWT had by 1978 managed to prise Forsyth away from the BBC for the new, ill-fated show *Bruce Forsyth's Big Night*[1] and the rights to the football highlights were next on his shopping list.

"The audience from football was very, very valuable to advertisers and it was very valuable to us because of the demographics and also the ratings," said Grade; "they were much higher in those days because there were only three channels back then and it seemed to me that we should have a crack at getting them." By November that year and unbeknown to the BBC, Grade had struck a deal with the League's negotiator Jack Dunnett, the chairman of Notts County and a Labour MP. "I knew Jack very well and he suggested to me the idea that we might want to bid; that was how it all started. We discussed it internally and decided this would have to be done quietly. We bypassed the sports negotiating team but I did not bypass the managing directors of the other ITV companies." Over brandy at the House of Commons and then in secret meetings at Dunnett's flat, Grade offered £5m over three years for the exclusive rights to football highlights. Effectively the cost of the rights had increased from £420,000 a season to £1.6m. The story was broken by Norman

---

1   *The show lasted for just 13 episodes, in one of which Brucie spent 10 minutes having a pop at media criticism of the programme. It would not be until 1981 and the broadcast of* Game for a Laugh *that ITV started to make up ground in the Saturday-night ratings battle.*

Giller in *The Evening News*[2] and the paper's sports editor Peter Watson labelled the exclusive "SNATCH OF THE DAY". The term stuck, demonstrating that the best headlines are often the simplest.

"Once the deal was announced the BBC was obviously very upset; they went bananas. They started legal proceedings under breach of contract, Treaty of Rome, OFT, you name it they threw the book at us but it never got that far," Grade recalled with a chuckle. It was, according to the *Daily Express* at the time, "TV WAR!" and the paper quoted Cliff Morgan, the Beeb's Head of Outside Broadcasting, saying: "This wasn't defeat, it was deceit. But we will fight back and we've got just the buggers here to do it I'll tell you." However, for the ITV companies the audacious move wasn't just about football. "The thing that we all wanted was the alternation with the BBC of big sporting events," said Grade. "We were both covering the Olympics, we were both covering the World Cup, we were both covering the Cup Final. It was ridiculous, it wasn't fair to viewers. But the BBC had an advantage because they didn't have advertisements and they were very reluctant to agree to alternate coverage. We said if we got *Match of the Day* we could use it as a tool maybe to get an agreement on alternation, that was the strategy. We would either end up with *Match of the Day* ourselves or we would trade it for an agreement on alternation and that's exactly what happened. There was an agreement that Brian Tesler my managing director negotiated with Robin Scott of the BBC."

Under the new four-year deal they would at last get the opportunity to alternate the Saturday and Sunday slots with the BBC. "We were in the business of selling airtime at premium rates and from that point of view it was a success, the advertisers loved it because there was very little football on television at that time," said Grade. However, not everyone was happy with the new arrangements. Just as *Match of the Day*'s launch had coincided with a boom in football's popularity, conversely this deal was sealed just before a period of decline. Furthermore, the chopping and changing of the Saturday and

---

2   *Launched in 1881, the* Evening News *was London's best-selling paper for many years. However it was eventually overtaken by the* London Evening Standard *with which it merged in 1980. The* Evening Standard's *masthead included the words "incorporating* The Evening News" *until its redesign in 2009.*

Sunday schedules was not ideal for either the TV companies or the viewers and as a consequence by January 1983 the combined viewing figures for the Saturday and Sunday shows had fallen by eight million. Gary Newbon, the Head of Sport for Central Television, was moved to say, "We don't want Saturday-night football ever again on ITV. Soccer on Sunday fits in better with the way we do programmes and television viewing."

His words would come back to haunt ITV when they launched *The Premiership* in 2001 and decided to broadcast it at 7pm on a Saturday, a key primetime slot. They poached not only the rights but also host Des Lynam, who opened the first show by looking at his watch, then the camera, and saying: "Better for you, better for all of us." How wrong he was. The first show got four million viewers and, perhaps because it contained just 28 minutes of actual football, the second slumped to 3.2 million, helping ITV to its worst Saturday night for five years. By November Des and *The Premiership* had been dispatched to the 10.30pm slot.

That was for the future, however. In 1978 The Snatch of the Day episode demonstrated two things very clearly. The declining viewing figures proved to the TV companies that live coverage was preferable to highlights. For the football clubs Grade's audacious move had shown that the revenue on offer to the clubs could be increased significantly if genuine competition was injected into the rights market. While all this was going on, an event that was equally important for the future of televised English football – although no one knew it at the time – was also taking place. A small pan-European satellite TV channel owned by the merchant bank Guinness Mahon and the UK entertainment company Trident began to make test transmissions from the Orbital Test Satellite. The channel's offices were in London's Grafton Street but its signal was aimed at cable networks in Finland, Norway and Malta, although anyone in Britain with a large enough dish could pick up the signal. By 'large enough' I mean about 10ft across. Few private individuals had one. By 'few' I mean about 50 and all they could watch were cheap American imports and repeats of British shows. Despite the lack of fanfare Sky TV had been launched.

• • •

In 1983 the BBC and ITV made what amounted to a joint bid worth £5.2m to allow them to alternate live coverage either on a Sunday afternoon or a Saturday evening. Not only were the BBC and ITV in particular determined to secure live coverage of football, they were also fully aware of how sport was packaged and broadcast abroad. The other big European Leagues – Italy, Spain, Germany and France – had insisted that their TV companies paid for the privilege of showing live matches and, led by America's example, the 1970s saw the amount of televised football across Europe increase fourfold. However, the English League had been hamstrung by its own intransigence. During the 1978 negotiations, Grade made a failed attempt to persuade the League's secretary Alan Hardaker to allow some live coverage. "They were convinced – which they were wrong about – that live football on television would kill the game. I said 'if you're not on television live you're not a sport these days'. They didn't buy that argument at all. They thought it would just kill the game, they didn't realize what it would do for football, which has since been proved. It was old thinking; they were frightened of television, for the same reason that movie producers wouldn't sell movie rights to television in the early days; they thought it would kill cinema. It was just nonsense." There was another problem. In 1979 Liverpool had signed a deal with Hitachi and become the first club to wear a sponsored shirt in a League match.[3] Since then many clubs had followed suit but the TV companies – the BBC in particular – refused to let sponsors' names appear on TV. This reticence had commercial implications for the clubs, who rejected the joint rights bid and turned their attentions to a rival offer made the following month by a firm called Telejector Video Communication Systems Ltd.

Owned by the London and Liverpool Trust, Telejector was offering £8m for the rights to broadcast coverage of games to 5,000 specially installed screens in pubs, clubs, hospitals and schools. According to a report in the *Guardian* at the time the League welcomed the proposal not just because of the money on offer and the fact that Telejector

---

3   Kettering Town of the Southern League were the first team to have shirt sponsors when they penned a "four-figure" deal with Kettering Tyres in 1976. The Football League threatened them with a hefty fine and the offending words were removed but Bolton and Derby County backed Kettering's appeal against the Football League's ban and it was lifted in 1977. Derby then signed a deal with Saab but only wore the shirts once – for a team photo.

had no problem with shirt sponsorship, but also because it would reduce the TV audience to about a million and thus (supposedly) increase attendances. The League tacitly accepted Telejector's bid and although the firm ultimately pulled out of negotiations, they proved useful in gaining a concession from the TV companies. Although the next joint bid from ITV and the BBC offered no more money they were now prepared to allow shirt sponsorship as long as the logos were reduced in size by 50 per cent. On 15 July 1983, a little over six weeks before the start of the season, the deal was done.

So, on 2 October, 17th-placed Spurs took to the pitch against 10th-placed Nottingham Forest[4] in the first live televised League game since the Blackpool v Bolton game in September 1960. There were fears that viewers, used to highlights that focused on the selected 'best' bits of a match, wouldn't take to sitting through coverage of a whole game including the 'boring' bits. Some papers greeted the new innovation by running two match reports – one of the game and one of the coverage. Irving Scholar, by then the main shareholder at Spurs, was, like many of his counterparts, wary that the coverage might have a detrimental impact on the gate receipts at White Hart Lane. He need not have worried as the crowd that day – 30,596 – was the biggest in the First Division that weekend. Entertained by Chas 'n' Dave before the match, the Tottenham faithful saw their side come back from a goal down to grab all three points thanks to a Steve Archibald winner in the 85th minute.

After the final whistle ITV's host Jim Rosenthal and pundit Jimmy Greaves, clipboards perched on knees, interviewed Spurs' chairman Douglas Alexiou in a cramped box that seemed barely big enough for the three of them. It's interesting and significant how much of their conversation focused on the success of the match as an 'event' in light of the fact it was televised. There was little discussion of the game itself as Rosenthal suggested that as "an advertisement for live football both teams have done us proud" while Greaves played up the unpredictable nature of football. "You never know what happens out there and that's what this game is all about", he said. "As far

---

4   Forest went on to finish the season in third place while Spurs finished eighth. Forest also reached the semi-final of the UEFA Cup but lost to Anderlecht, who were retrospectively banned from European competition for bribing the referee. The Belgian side went on to lose the final on penalties; to Spurs.

as you're concerned, can football and television live quite happily together this season?" Rosenthal asked Alexiou. "I think we got on quite well today," came the reply.

ITV in particular agreed. The success of the coverage confirmed what the advertiser-funded network had thought for some time – that Sunday afternoons, long considered a 'dead' slot, could draw as many as 10 million viewers, most of which were young men with high disposable incomes. Before the two-year 'experimental' contract was halfway through they were looking for an extension, with the number of games increased from 10 to 16 plus the option to show other games on a regional basis. Not everyone was happy however. The bigger clubs had been disappointed both by the size of the deal and, perhaps more importantly, the size of their share of the deal. Once £300,000 a season was put into a pot to compensate clubs should their attendances be down, each team got an equal share of the rest: £25,000 a year. This compared with the £2,500 *per game* Manchester United received from Granada during their European Cup exploits more than 25 years earlier in 1956. Clubs in the Fourth Division would pocket the same as the clubs that actually appeared on TV – the ones that drew the audiences. The League had already made a major change to its structure by allowing clubs to keep 100 per cent of their home gate receipts, a move that greatly enhanced the revenue of the clubs with larger attendances, but those clubs still felt they were entitled to a bigger share of the TV pie. In their own minds they were the box-office draw.

The 1983 TV deal highlighted the two battles underpinning rights negotiations at the time. On the one hand was the League against the TV companies (acting in unison) and on the other hand were the few big clubs against the many small clubs. As with five years earlier those involved learned two clear lessons. Firstly, Telejector's brief involvement demonstrated that concessions could be wrung out of the main terrestrial broadcasters when the marketplace became even a little bit competitive. Secondly, it reinforced for the bigger clubs the fact that they were never going to get access to the share of the TV revenue they felt was rightfully theirs under the current set-up. At the same time the young Sky TV was struggling. Despite its European scope the channel had a budget little bigger than the smaller ITV companies and no way to make money due to a lack of encryption technology coupled with rudimentary delivery technology. All the players lining up in the European satellite TV market were waiting for just that: a high-powered satellite via which to transmit their services, and the means to charge for those services. Sky's owners decided the wait was too costly and called it a day, selling up for a nominal £1 plus debts. The buyer: Rupert Murdoch.

• • •

While the TV firms were keen on televised football, they were also keen to try and keep the cost as low as possible and so in February 1985, again effectively bidding as a team, they offered the Football League a four-year deal worth £3.8m in the first year, rising incrementally each season over the course of the deal. In return they wanted the rights to show 19 live games; 16 League matches plus two League Cup semi-finals and the League Cup Final, plus an option to show regional matches. The League now had a media man on the inside. Robert Maxwell had bought Oxford United in 1982 and was the owner of the Mirror newspapers and the main shareholder in MTV Europe. His opinion held sway among other club owners. At a League meeting at the Great Western Hotel in Paddington on 14 February 1985, Maxwell called the deal "mad, bad and sad", claiming that football was worth as much as £10m a season to the TV firms and pointing out that the only way to extract its true value would be by splitting up the BBC–ITV partnership. Swayed by Maxwell, the League rejected the offer and the two TV companies immediately called their bluff. Their offer remained on the table but there would be no compromise.

The League formed a television subcommittee including Maxwell, Scholar, Chelsea's Ken Bates (whom Scholar nicknamed "the Bearded Barbarian") and Norwich chairman Arthur South, who were mandated to go back to the TV firms on the understanding that the maximum number of games to be screened per season would be 10. On this basis they offered the TV companies two packages running over two years: the first was for 10 live matches plus the rights to show highlights over 21 weekends; the second was for the League Cup Final and two semi-finals plus the rights to highlights over 31 weekends. The League also offered the TV companies the option to buy all or part of the two packages; in other words exclusivity. ITV and the BBC refused to budge. Jonathan Martin, the BBC's Head of Sport, said that he would simply show snooker instead; it was cheaper and more popular. He had a point; only a few weeks earlier 18.5 million people had stayed up until well past midnight to watch as Dennis Taylor potted the final ball of the final frame to take the World Snooker Championship from reigning champion Steve Davis.

Furthermore a catalogue of hooliganism and disaster was weakening the League's negotiating position almost by the week. The nation had watched in horror as a fire claimed 56 lives at Bradford's Valley Parade. It was the same day that teenager Ian Hambridge was crushed to death by a collapsed wall as Birmingham and Leeds fans fought at St Andrews. The season ended with the Heysel tragedy in which 39 fans were killed before the European Cup Final between Juventus and Liverpool. English clubs were banned from Europe indefinitely which in turn meant that for the foreseeable future many end-of- season games were rendered meaningless as the League now offered no route to Europe via the UEFA Cup, lowering the game's value to the TV companies even further. "We don't depend on football and if it loses its slot there is no knowing if it will ever get it back," Martin said at the time.

In response the League accused the TV companies of lacking the will to come to an agreement and even approached the Office of Fair Trading. It was to no avail and as the 1985/86 season kicked off in the August sunshine, League football – including highlights – was absent for the first time since Kenneth Wolstenholme introduced *Match of the Day* from Beatlesville in 1964. In contrast to what the chairmen had feared all along, the lack of TV coverage did not prompt a rise in match attendance; it coincided with a huge fall. The start of the season saw the biggest-ever drop in gates. In December the League agreed a £1.5m deal for the remainder of the season and the following July they signed a two-year deal for £3.1m. Both were on less favourable terms than the deal turned down in February 1985 and while the TV firms gained free access to any match for highlights they gave no guarantee that highlights would be broadcast regularly. The League's capitulation appeared complete.

As the League as a whole conceded ground to the TV companies so the smaller clubs also conceded ground to those in the First Division. The protracted rights negotiations in 1985 had been the catalyst for a significant change within the League as in-fighting broke out, a breakaway was threatened and power began to swing decisively in the favour of the bigger clubs. Unhappy with the way the League was structured, the so-called Big Five clubs had been meeting informally since 1981. There was talk, led by Manchester United and Everton, of a breakaway the following year but it was the arrival on the scene of men like Irving Scholar, who became the main shareholder at Tottenham in 1982, and David Dein, who became the vice-chairman at Arsenal in 1983, that proved crucial.

The pair were self-made millionaires and their influence brought a significantly more commercial ethos to both the Big Five and the League. Keenly aware that the value of football was not being realised they looked to the way sport was marketed and televised in America for inspiration. Dein in particular was taken with the way the NFL was marketed. A regular visitor to Florida where his wife Barbara's family lived he had seen how both Gridiron and baseball were packaged, as well as the American approach to merchandising, and was moved to say that they were "light years ahead" of English football. Furthermore, both Dein and Scholar, along with several other chairmen, felt that the bigger clubs should have greater power to control their own affairs, plus a larger share of the money on offer.

After the League rejected the TV deal on offer in February 1985, Scholar approached advertising agency Saatchi and Saatchi for advice on what exactly the rights were worth. Their report was produced by executive Alex Fynn who had first met Scholar when he produced a TV ad for Spurs featuring the team, comedian Peter Cook and Tottenham fan and grandmother, Mrs Ridlington. "Come and join the 35,000" they implored and the ad worked a treat as Tottenham recorded their highest attendance of the season at the next match. Fynn's report, *Football and Television: Its Influence on Programme Costs and Advertisement,* was in many respects simple maths. The advertising revenue gained during football broadcasts in the 1983/84 season was compared with the advertising revenue during the same slot without football. The difference – around £6m – was the value of football. For the BBC, who didn't have advertising, the best way of looking at it was to compare the cost of programming that would generate similar viewing figures. A recent Hollywood blockbuster, for example, would cost about £500,000 to buy, so a 16-game deal was worth at least £8m a season. Either figure was considerably higher than the £3.8m the TV companies had just offered.

But Fynn, who the *Sunday Times* would later christen "the spiritual godfather of the Premier League", didn't just have a clear idea of what he considered to be the true value of football; he also had some radical ideas about how the game should be restructured. "The basis of my strategy was that football is an event – both a live event and a television event," said Fynn. "But in terms of being a live event, English football is both a national event and a local event. When the Premier League was created, remember you had 22 clubs in it and founder members were Oldham and Coventry: when they played each other, that was a non-event; the national event was when Manchester United played Arsenal or whenever the big clubs played each other. Similarly in the Third and Fourth Divisions, if you make Carlisle play Exeter, nobody's interested in the game unless there are issues of promotion and relegation at stake. It's far better to make Exeter play Torquay or Hereford or even, if they're good enough, Tiverton.

"So at the top you have national events and at the bottom you have local events and the League should be structured so everyone has their place in the system. If it's done like that and meritocracy is the criterion then you can rise from the local third division – because I advocated three local, regional divisions – all the way through the system to the top." But surely Oldham and Coventry could still meet in the top division of such a structure? "Then they would deserve to be there," Fynn said. "The only way they were in that position was because there were 22 teams there. Again, what I advocated was that you must have a competitive division. If you had a maximum of 20 clubs in a division there would be fewer meaningless games, a better standard of football and lower costs but the football administrators have no vision in restructuring. Their attitude is 'play more games, have more money'."

With Fynn's document in their hands, the Big Five met in Birmingham on Sunday 29 September 1985 along with representatives of Newcastle, Manchester City and Southampton to discuss a way forward. The clubs felt that their best option was to break away; why split the cash on offer from TV between 92 clubs when they could split it between 10 or 20? Two days later the story hit the press with the *Daily Mail* breaking the story. Under the headline "SUPERLEAGUE REBELLION" Jeff Powell detailed the clubs' plans to resign from the League and form their own. Two weeks later the chairmen of all the First and Second Division clubs met in London but couldn't agree a way forward. Reflecting what Fynn said, the two factions were fundamentally at odds over the issue of a reduction in the size of the League.

The smaller clubs, led by Ron Noades of Crystal Palace, didn't want fewer games as that would lead to lower gate receipts. Conversely, the bigger clubs felt that a decreased number of games would reduce supply to the TV companies, thus increasing their value; as Scholar wrote: "to generate the sort of income we needed required partnership with television and the promotion of what Alex Fynn called an 'event'". Following this meeting, Scholar, Edwards and Carter explored the possibility of a British League and British Cup. They went to Scotland to meet representatives of Rangers and Celtic, who said that along with four other clubs they would be willing to leave the Scottish League. However the following month the breakaway was averted at a meeting in Heathrow when the rest of the English League agreed to the First Division clubs' demands for a change in the voting structure, a reduction in the size of the top tier, plus 50 per cent of all TV and sponsorship money going to the top division. The introduction of the play-offs was part of the deal, designed to appease the smaller clubs. It was an uneasy peace that wouldn't last for long and there was still a lack of competition in the TV rights market, which led to the League's humiliating climb-down over the rights in December 1985.

A significant development in the television marketplace occurred the following year when the Independent Broadcasting Authority awarded five 'direct broadcast to satellite' (DBS) licences to British Satellite Broadcasting (BSB), a conglomerate that included names like Granada, Virgin, the magazine firm Reed International (which had owned the *Daily Mirror*), and the French media company Chargeurs.

This meant that for the first time there was a viable third bidder in the marketplace for the football rights. The American experience showed that there were three driving forces in the success of pay-TV: porn, the latest movies and exclusive sports rights. Due to UK regulations porn wasn't an option, so BSB turned their attentions to the other two and in May 1988 they made their move with a snazzy presentation at the Royal Lancaster Hotel offering the Football League a ten-year deal with a guaranteed payment of £9m a year, building to more than £25m a year. The League issued a press release triumphantly proclaiming that "FOOTBALL PROPOSES NEW TV DEAL FOR NINETIES" that would "net football a minimum of £200m over the next ten years". With pound signs spinning round in front of their eyes the League chairmen were overjoyed and almost unanimously applauded the offer.

The Big Five were pleased there was competition in the marketplace but they had concerns about the viability of BSB, which had yet to even launch its own satellite at that point and wouldn't do so for more than a year. They were also wary that the new service would have a relatively small audience. The two factions were split again. While the smaller clubs were thinking in simple cash terms – which deal would generate the most income – the bigger clubs were thinking in terms of cash *and* exposure. BSB might have been offering a considerable sum up front but the risk was that football would become a fringe sport on an as yet untested network. There was a further concern about what would happen if BSB went bankrupt. This point of view proved prophetic. When BSB merged with Sky the deal they had done with the FA for England internationals and the FA Cup game simply transferred. Had the League done a similar deal there would have been no contract negotiations in 1992 or 1996, which would have severely reduced their income over the period they covered.

Greg Dyke, ITV's new Chairman of Sport, was watching with interest. At the time Dyke, who went on to become Director General of the BBC and Chairman of the FA, was best known for saving TV-AM with the help of Roland Rat and ditching wrestling from the ITV schedules. Wrestling was a hugely popular TV sport with an estimated 21 million tuning in to watch Big Daddy's grudge match with Giant Haystacks at Wembley in June 1981 (the bout itself lasted a disappointingly short two minutes and fifty seconds). However, its popularity was on the wane and Dyke wanted to refocus ITV's attentions onto sports that could deliver the audience so craved by advertisers: young, free-spending men. He recognised that the BSB bid, if successful, could deliver a hammer blow to that strategy. He also knew that just as football had driven the sale of TV sets in the 1950s, so it could drive sales of satellite dishes in the 1990s. If he could prise the rights out of BSB's hands he could undermine the new rival before they'd even started broadcasting. He was introduced to David Dein by Trevor East, the Deputy Head of Sport at Thames Television at Suntory, a Japanese restaurant in the West End. "Having talked to David, I worked out that the way in was through the big clubs," Dyke recalled some 25 years after the event. "If I got the home rights to those five clubs, that would have done; BSB could have had the rest. And that's what we did."

Dyke and a delegation from ITV met representatives from the Big Five teams at the Belfry restaurant in Knightsbridge. He was asked whether ITV and BBC had effectively operated a cartel in the past and he admitted they had, immediately earning him the trust of the football men present. "If there are seminal moments that change everything," wrote Scholar, "then this was one of them." Dyke then revealed the terms of a deal he wanted to make for the exclusive rights to broadcast football. The offer was £750,000 each to the Big Five plus another £2m split between another five clubs, which would ultimately be Aston Villa, Newcastle, Nottingham Forest, Sheffield Wednesday and West Ham; a neat geographical coverage of the ITV regions. By targeting just 10 clubs ITV could offer them more than under the terms of the BSB deal but pay less, as they were dealing with fewer clubs.

Once the details of the ITV 10 breakaway plan were made public the Football League took out an injunction to stop them in their tracks. At a meeting between all the First Division clubs at Villa Park, Dyke extended the offer to all of them on the understanding that the division would be reduced to 18 teams. Threatened with a mass walkout the League capitulated, agreeing to alter the terms of the Heathrow agreement so that the First Division clubs' share of the TV revenue increased from 50 per cent to 75 per cent. Dyke's final offer was £11m for 18 League games, two League Cup semi-finals and the League Cup Final, but before it and the BSB deal could be put to the League for a vote, BSB withdrew their offer. "I got flak inside ITV for paying too much," Dyke told me. "That's funny now." The ITV deal included the rights for highlights but they were never used. *Match of the Day* was placed in mothballs. The BBC threw in their lot with BSB who turned their attentions to securing the rights for the FA Cup and England internationals. They also won the right to televise foreign football.

Rows followed over the broadcasting of matches at ITV's pre-ferred time of 5pm on a Sunday. On one occasion Dyke refused to reschedule a match between Arsenal and Liverpool that fell just days before an England game. The wounds would not heal for some time. Furthermore, although it wasn't widely known at the time, Dyke had agreed with the Big Five chairmen that those teams would feature more often, therefore guaranteeing them greater match fees, more exposure, advertising and sponsorship revenue. Effectively the BBC–ITV cartel had been replaced by an ITV–Big Five cartel and while it suited them it left a bitter taste in the mouths of the BBC and many of the smaller clubs. Almost immediately they reasserted their authority. The reduction plans were reversed and the First Division was re-enlarged to 22 teams. Philip Carter was kicked out of his role as League president and David Dein was booted off the management committee. The cracks were still there though, and they would only get bigger.

• • •

On 11 December 1988, a few months after Dyke and ITV had prised the League rights away from BSB, the *Ariane 44* rocket blasted off from a launch pad in Kourou, French Guiana. On board was the Société Européenne de Satellite's (SES) *Astra 1A* satellite. Rupert Murdoch had leased four of the available 16 transponders, in effect the ability to broadcast four channels, as well as the option to buy another two when SES's *Astra B* launched. The new station was supposedly pan-European and so it wasn't subject to British regulation but it was very much targeted at Britain; in other words it was a modern equivalent of Radio Luxembourg. By 5 February 1989 it was broadcasting. By the middle of the year it was losing £2m a week. Sky had predicted a million dish sales by the end of the year but after five months they'd managed to shift just 10,000. Andrew Neil, who Murdoch brought in as founding Chairman on Sky, later wrote that BSB and Sky had recreated the VHS/Betamax dilemma consumers faced when video first launched – people simply weren't buying Sky dishes in case BSB's 'squarial' turned out to be better.

While the two rival services weren't yet signing up the number of customers they had hoped for, they were trying to entice them with movies. All the research and experience from home and abroad demonstrated that movies would be a key front in the satellite war. So they fought a hugely expensive battle for rights, committing around $1.2bn between them over the next five years, half of which had to be paid whether the films were shown or not. In many respects it was a nonsensical strategy. The UK had an extremely high level of video ownership and people thought nothing of nipping to the video store to rent a movie. The two companies weren't just battling each other, they were battling the country's rental culture. That culture was so ingrained that at the start of 2013 Blockbuster still had 500 stores across the UK.

CNN's then owner Ted Turner, watching from the other side of the Atlantic, said the companies were "haemorrhaging red ink", and they were. BSB had spent in the region of £800m before it had really seen the light of day and by November 1990 it was costing £8m a week just to keep going – an outlay that was threatening not just its own survival but that of the blue-chip media firms involved in the consortium that owned it. For Sky the situation was only marginally better, with start-up costs in the region of £122m and a first-year loss of £95m. Something had to give so, in July 1990, Murdoch and Peter Davis, the head of the BSB consortium, were brought together for dinner at Claridge's Hotel by US investment banker John Veronis. The pair could not agree a way forward, not least because Murdoch had a distaste for working in consortia and he felt Sky could win if only they could hold on long enough to see BSB collapse.

By late September that seemed a forlorn hope as Murdoch's own financial problems were looking increasingly terminal. In the 21 years since he'd met Larry Lamb in Rules to discuss the editorship of the

Sun, Murdoch had built the small family business left to him by his father into a global media behemoth with interests in Australia, Britain, Hong Kong and America. It was a business built on a mountain of debt somewhere in the region of AUS$10.5bn owed to 146 banks across the world. By October 1990 it looked like the mountain would collapse under its own weight, so with his company's profits and share price falling, Murdoch called in Citibank, to help restructure his firm's massive debts. By January the following year they had made a debt-restructuring deal with all his creditors. To alleviate some of the pressure, Murdoch called Davis back and told him he was willing to talk. Over the following month under the codename Operation Eagle and with the two companies labelled 'Box' and 'Sox', secret negotiations were conducted on Murdoch's ranch near Adelaide and then at the discreet Luckman Park Hotel in Wiltshire. On 2 November BSB and Sky merged to form BSkyB. I say merged; it was a takeover in all but name. Sky had swallowed its rival. While the terms of the deal split equity in the company down the middle, other crucial aspects favoured Sky. Their *Astra* satellite would be the new firm's broadcast platform, rendering the infamous squarials redundant and effectively destroying BSB's physical presence. That move was compounded by the fact that the new company would be called BSkyB and trade under the name Sky. Most significantly Sky effectively gained operational and editorial control of the newly formed company by being allowed to appoint the new chief executive.

That man was Sam Chisholm, who Murdoch had brought in to run Sky just months before the merger. The son of wealthy New Zealand farmers, Chisholm had cut his teeth on Australia's Channel Nine where he started selling airtime in 1967 before eventually becoming managing director, overseeing its rise to become the country's most popular TV station. In the process he gained a fearsome reputation, acquiring the name in Antipodean circles of the Most Feared Man in Television, something which preceded him to England. There the head of Eurosport, Dave Hill, told his English colleagues that he had to psych himself up for meetings with Chisholm by playing 'The Ride of the Valkyries' for ten minutes beforehand. Those colleagues were aghast as they already regarded Hill as the quintessential, no-holds- barred, aggressive Australian.

Between them Sky and BSB had spent £1.5bn before they dragged themselves to the altar and they'd committed to spend around another $1.5bn (£670m) over the next five years for movie rights. Furthermore the combined company was losing in the region of £14m a week. Chisholm's first job was to cut costs. Following the merger, he spent 84 days holed up in the Four Seasons hotel in Los Angeles renegotiating those prohibitive deals with representatives from Disney, Warner and the other Hollywood studios, eventually reducing them by about 40 per cent. Virtually all 580 of BSB's staff were made redundant or left of their own volition. Staff on short-term contracts did not have them renewed and even some of Sky's staff were let go to reduce the wage bill by about 50 per cent. In 1991, Murdoch's film subsidiary 20th Century Fox hit pay dirt with the film *Home Alone,* which grossed $500m, giving him some much-needed financial breathing space. By the following year, a semblance of stability had arrived at Sky with losses at a manageable £1.5m a week. However debts were still at £2bn and interest payments were rising. Sky had won the satellite war but renegotiated movie deals and judicious cost cutting were not enough. Murdoch and Chisholm both recognised that if they were to also win the peace they needed to find programming that would embed their service into English culture and so they made it their mission to secure the rights to the new Premier League.

If the pair needed any persuading, it was provided by cricket. In early 1990 Sky scooped up the rights to the England cricket team's tour of the West Indies. BSB had passed on the deal due to the uncertainty of their launch date, which when it finally arrived was nine months late. The BBC had also passed and it was not a surprising decision given that the West Indies had won the last three series between the two teams by an aggregate of 14 Tests to zero. On top of that they'd lost just once in 30 home Tests during the 1980s while by contrast England had won just once in 25 Tests in the previous three years. Ian Botham and David Gower had been left behind. It seemed a dead rubber. England were 20-1 outsiders for the opening match of the series at Sabina Park; however, remarkably they won it by nine wickets. It set up a gripping series that England ultimately lost 2-1 but during that winter a Sky dish was the hot ticket.

Football was a hotter ticket though. "It's always been the thing that will sell a sports channel of any sort," said Jeff Stelling, who was at BSB in the early days and who now presents football on Sky. "In a way that's why football was the main draw for TV and radio sports coverage in the early days. From a TV point of view it was of huge significance, as it is now, and that's why when the bidding war came round Sky literally put all of its apples in that particular basket. It was absolutely essential they had football rights and not just any football rights but football that a mass audience would watch.

"Over the years the eye for continental football has become more finely tuned so we do watch Spanish, Italian and German football but with all due respect to other divisions, in terms of viewing figures it has to be top-level English football." In the early 1990s Chisholm also felt there was considerable room to offer a better product than ITV was serving up at the time. After Leeds United secured the title in 1992, host Elton Welsby asked Howard Wilkinson (the club's manager) how he was feeling, only to interrupt him mid-answer to enable the channel to cut to commercials before *Bullseye*.

• • •

It's easy to cast Murdoch and Sky as the villains of the piece and to accuse them of stealing football from free-to-air TV but the reality is that it was sold to them. The birth of the Premier League was characterised by the self-interest of a number of parties, not least those in charge of the FA at the time, who took the opportunity to assert their authority over the Football League once and for all. In the aftermath of the Hillsborough disaster the future of the uneasy working relationship between the FA and the Football League was in the spotlight, and in October 1990, the League put forward a plan called *One Game, One Team, One Voice*. What they proposed was for the two bodies to enter into a power-sharing arrangement with equal representation on a joint board controlling the English game. It was a plan that Fynn believes had considerable merit. "You only have to look at the system in Germany. They had a system where the DFB was really the sole body that controlled all football, although there was an element that controlled the clubs and others that controlled the national team, the coaching and grassroots. Although they've separated now after a review in 2000 there's still a much closer liaison than operates in England. The Bundesliga and the national team have a relationship where there is compromise and mutual self-interest. There's no compromise in England."

Two months after the League unveiled their plans, the FA revealed their own *Blueprint for the Future of Football*. Graham Kelly, who had in 1988 swapped Lytham St Anne's, where he was the League's secretary, for Soho, where he became the FA's chief executive, said there was "concern" about the 50–50 split in the League's plans, which he described as "a hastily hatched curate's egg". However, to give his plan credibility he needed a way of excluding the Football League, and the Big Five clubs were about to give it to him. In November 1990 they met for dinner at LWT's plush 18th-floor dining room with Greg Dyke, ostensibly to discuss the renewal of the League's TV contract. Dyke's message was clear: he couldn't guarantee more money so the big clubs had a choice: take a smaller share of the pot or take radical action.

"I said to them: 'Look you're not going to get this deal again. The amount of money will stay the same but you're not going to get the carve-up that ensures your million pounds a year, so what are you going to do?' and they left the dinner and went to see the FA." The clubs had been angered by the treatment of David Dein and Philip Carter after the last TV deal and so decided to set up a breakaway league that would give them control of their own affairs, including the sale of the TV rights. Liverpool Chairman Noel White was an FA councillor and was aware of the opposition to the League's power-sharing plan. He felt a deal could be reached and so along with Dein he approached Kelly and the FA chairman Bert Millichip. In March 1991 the First Division clubs met at Goodison Park and agreed to break away; the following month the FA council gave their approval. By June the clubs had resigned and the Premier League would be a reality from August the following year.

Fynn was brought in to work on the FA's blueprint and would later say that to their shame the FA let the Premier League run away. "Let's put it this way," he said. "Success has many fathers and because the Premier League is regarded as a phenomenal success, many people will claim that they were really influential. I would have to say that the people who were involved in it, like David Dein, like Rick Parry, like Greg Dyke, were all pragmatists. Greg Dyke supported it largely for television reasons, he was primarily interested in the big clubs. David Dein believed that what was in Arsenal's best interest was in English football's best interest and to a large extent that was true. Rick Parry was fundamental in getting the clubs out of the Football League and into the Premier League. This may sound like an arrogant statement, but I got the feeling the only person who was thinking about the clubs, the country and the fans was myself, not even the FA. I soon became a nuisance to the FA because I was insisting on certain things which they felt not particularly important. They had broken the power of the Football League; they now thought they had a system that they thought would help the national team. But how could it help the national team when you are playing games at the behest of Sky and you are playing 42 games in the top division? There was no vision there, just short-termism among the breakaway clubs and the administrators and the FA."

Once the breakaway was in motion the newly formed league had to ensure they secured a lucrative deal for their TV rights. Looking back now it's easy to think that came down to a straight fight between ITV and Sky, and ultimately that's what it would become, but initially there were other players in the game. As the jockeying for position began, the Swiss Bank Corporation approached Dein with the idea of a subscription service broadcast through the *Astra* satellite, similar to that offered by Sky, but owned and run by the Premier League itself. Neil Duncanson, then head of sport at Chrysalis Television, was asked to draw up a proposed schedule for the channel, which was rather unimaginatively code-named Project Premier. Under these proposals there would have been a live game every night except Thursday, the equivalent of 32 games per month, with estimated profits of £50m in the first season alone. However, the estimated £20m start-up costs were considered too prohibitive.

There was another player in the market, Full Time Communications (FTC) set up by, among others, Gerald O'Connell, one of the brains behind the Club Call phone lines. Their idea was to show every game in the Premier and Football Leagues in full but not live and their research showed that there were around one million households that would be willing to pay £10 a month for the privilege of being able to watch them. This would bring in about £100m in the first year alone but significantly also leave room for the Premier League to negotiate a separate deal for live rights. FTC had two problems however. Firstly there were concerns about the validity of the company's financial backing (it would have ultimately come from the Saudi Arabian royal family but it was not in place in time) and secondly the Premier League and the FA were not willing to be part of a deal that included the Football League. The FA's head of external affairs, Glen Kirton, made it clear that as the League had done so much to stop the runaways, they were now going to "teach them a lesson". Neither the FTC nor the Project Premier offers were put to the Premier League chairmen; however, the Premier League was able to use them as bargaining chips to push up the value of the rights.

Dyke later admitted he was complacent, believing that the support of the Big Five clubs would be enough to deliver the rights of the new League to ITV and so neglecting to woo the smaller clubs. Another strategic mistake was to overlook the significance of Irving Scholar's sale of Tottenham to Alan Sugar, the man who owned Amstrad, the company that produced the dishes for Sky. If anyone had a reason to see Sky bid successfully it was Sugar and he played a crucial role when the Premier League chairmen met at the Royal Lancaster Hotel on 18 May to consider ITV's and Sky's bids. Dyke's associate Trevor East presented each club representative with a sealed envelope with their offer – £262m over five years, more than had been speculated. When Sugar saw ITV's offer he rushed to the lobby of the hotel, where Trevor East saw him engaged in an agitated phone call. "You don't seem to understand what I'm talking about," he shouted. "These are the figures. Take them down. You better get something done. You better get somebody down here quickly. Blow them out of the water."

It's a great story, which is why it's been told so often, but sitting quietly in an ante-room the Premier League's chief executive Rick Parry had already phoned Chisholm with the details of the ITV offer, enabling the Sky chief to fax through a revised, increased offer of £304m over five years. It did indeed blow ITV out of the water, although Chisholm later revealed that Murdoch had been prepared to pay double what he actually did. Sky won by 14 votes to 6, with two clubs bizarrely abstaining. Dyke immediately sought an injunction on the basis that their bid had been leaked but in the absence of a confidentiality agreement it got nowhere.

It could have all been very different. Once they decided to mount a bid, Murdoch asked Chisholm to explore the possibility of a joint offer with ITV, so the Sky chief arranged to meet Dyke for lunch at Langan's Brasserie. There the New Zealander offered the ITV boss a deal which he said had Murdoch's blessing: "Why don't we get together to fuck these football clubs?" Dyke declined: "First I thought we'd win; secondly I had a degree of loyalty to the clubs that had supported us three years earlier and I didn't think it would be right to fuck them; thirdly there was an in-built anti-Murdoch thing," he said. "It was a mistake really for ITV; we should have done the deal but of course it was deeply illegal and anti-competitive. I thought we would win anyway because we had the big clubs on our side. Rick Parry told us we'd be fine, and of course he got wooed by Murdoch."

Rebuffed by Dyke, Chisholm turned his attention to the BBC and in the final week of negotiations it was announced the terrestrial company would bid for Premier League highlights but only on the condition ITV didn't get the live rights. Effectively the Beeb had joined forces with Sky, enabling the satellite broadcaster to claim that there would still be some free-to-air coverage of the League. As they were bidding alone, it also meant ITV had to find £20m more than Sky – the amount the BBC had bid for the highlights. Jayne Thynne, the *Daily Telegraph*'s media correspondent, broached the subject at a BBC press conference in April 1992. Thynne asked the BBC's chairman Marmaduke Hussey, who had been a board member of Murdoch's Times Newspapers, if he had worked together with his former boss on the football rights deal and if so what had been the terms of their deal. Hussey, flushed with anger, banged his walking stick on the table and stormed out but Dyke is in no doubt as to what happened: "Murdoch nobbled Hussey. If you are the chairman of the BBC you are not involved in sports rights negotiations but he was. Murdoch got him." Sky's bid had been a success, in part, thanks to licence-fee payers' cash.

Success is perhaps an understatement. Once Sky had secured the rights to the Premier League they encrypted their sports service, enabling them to charge for two subscription channels – movies and sport. By the time their coverage kicked off with Nottingham Forest against Liverpool on 23 August, they had already signed up one million customers willing to pay £5.99 a month to watch the sparkly new Premier League (or the rebranded First Division). By the time Sky renewed the contract in 1996 the number of people with one of Sky's dishes slapped on the side of their house had risen to six million – a 200 per cent increase on the pre-Premier League figure. In the same period losses of £188m a year had been turned into an annual profit of £257m while debt had been reduced from £1.8bn to £518m. It's easy to overstate the importance of the Premier League rights to Sky's success, and while Fynn told me they were "absolutely vital" for Murdoch's company he did so with a caveat. "People may think that football saved Sky; it didn't. Sky were already finding their way to success through a proliferation of channels and particularly films. Football underwrote their sports service, accelerated their take-up and cemented their success. It was an additional attribute along with movies and the youth channels; it was the package that was enhanced by football."

Chisholm was in no doubt: for him football had been the turning point. It was also a turning point for English football as money flooded into the game. With the new league yet to celebrate its fifth birthday Newcastle signed Alan Shearer for a then-world record £15m. In the same closed season their North East rivals Middlesbrough plucked Fabrizio Ravanelli from Juventus just weeks after he'd scored the winning goal in the European Cup Final. In a few short seasons the 'slum' sport had made quite a turnaround from its late 1980s nadir. Since then player salaries have rocketed. By 2011/12 two-thirds of the Premier League's £2.4bn income disappeared on wages alone.

Club owners have also cashed in. Martin Edwards – one of the Big Five – almost sold Manchester United to Michael Knighton for £10m in 1989; following the launch of the Premier League he sold off shares at opportune moments, netting at least £65m. While owners and players fed at the trough, the cost was passed on to the fans, and not just through the subscription they had to pay to watch on Sky. In 1991 the cheapest seat at Old Trafford cost £5.75; now it will set you back £36 – a 626 per cent increase. In the final season of the old First Division, kids could stand for 90p; now they can get in for a bargain £22 – an increase of 2,240 per cent. They're the sort of figures to make a payday lender blush. Maybe.

There wasn't just a cost to the fans but also to the English national team and in a sense this has come full circle for Dyke, who became Chairman of the FA in July 2013. "All those guys who set up the Premier League were great believers; they all say that it was a great success. Which it is," he said. "It's been a massive success except it's owned by foreigners, managed by foreigners and played by foreigners, which has great disadvantages for English football, particularly the England team. As I'm just finding out, the biggest fuck-up in the world was that the FA didn't ask for anything," he continued. "It was ridiculous. The Premier League would not have happened if the FA had said 'No'. What they should have done is ask for a set of things. But the trouble was that Bert Millichip and Graham Kelly were not the brightest blokes off the block and they so hated the Football League that actually they saw it as a way of putting the knife in instead of saying: 'Hang on, if this works it would be a massive opportunity for the England team.' If they'd said: 'You can only have 16 sides; you've got to release players at certain times so they can join up with the England team; we want a percentage of your television income' they'd have got it all. But they asked for nothing. It was a terrible mistake for the FA and everybody knows it."

Fynn agrees that the success of the Premier League has not helped the English game as a whole. "If you're the supporter of a Premier League club it's been golden years; if you're a supporter of the national team then you're set for perpetual disappointment. If you're the supporter of a small club you're always striving very hard but the system's against you. It's obviously been very important to the members of that very select group, i.e. the Premier League, but there are only 20 members at any one time. For the rest of football the Premier League has been a disadvantage. Professional football is more important than 20 clubs alone and when 20 clubs have all of the hype and all of the money it has really set the English game back in terms of the development of the national team.

"We don't have an English League anymore, we have an international League that happens to be played in England and as a result of that we have fewer English players coming through the system. The Premier League clubs dominate everything, they are cosmopolitan and I would therefore be astonished if the English national team repeats even the feats of 1990 because the system is against them. While other countries have recognised there is a place for both clubs and country, the bottom line in England is that the clubs in the Premier League dominate and are the paramount force"

• • •

The success of Sky Sports' coverage was built on a foundation laid by BSB. The former broadcaster assembled a team including several people who would dominated Sky's coverage for the next 20 years. Richard Keys was prised off the TV-AM sofa to become the host. Andy Gray was tempted away from his job as assistant manager at Aston Villa to become the main analyst; Martin Tyler was poached from ITV where he was the second-choice commentator behind Brian Moore, and Jeff Stelling was brought in as a sports newsreader. Stelling was also at TV-AM, where the sports coverage was, he said, "virtually non-existent" and he leapt at the chance to join the new venture. "I'll be honest; I absolutely detested working at TV-AM so for me it was an escape. I knew the risks involved, but equally having not had any real TV exposure it was a great place to go and start to learn.[5] I thought things couldn't get any worse so I might as well give it a go."

"When the takeover happened those of us working for the old BSB were told it was an amalgamation – it was never an amalgamation, it was a takeover," said Stelling. "But they did take a few of the important people across; that happens in any takeover in any line of business – you take the cream and spit out the rest and that's what happened there. So they did have a base, there's no doubt about that." Stelling, who described himself as being "a complete no-name" at the time, was one of those to be spat out but after brief spells at

5   Stelling wasn't the only person who started to learn at BSB. The network also provided the platform upon which many of the biggest names of British comedy in the 1990s built their careers. These included Alistair McGowan, Stewart Lee, Jo Brand, Mark Thomas, Steve Coogan, Chris Morris and Armando Iannucci. Jools Holland hosted a music show and Chris Evans fronted a breakfast show. Virtually no recordings of any of these early performances still exist.

Tyne Tees, Channel 4 and Eurosport he eventually found his way back to Sky, where he became one of the hosts of *Sports Saturday*, the forerunner to *Soccer Saturday*.

"It was a sports show with no sport," said Stelling. "In those days we had virtually nothing in the way of rights, so rather like *Final Score* did for years, we had a vidiprinter from 4.30pm but we had to fill until then from 12 or 1pm without any rights and we had all sorts of bizarre things. We had a synchronised swimming team running through their routine in the studio but of course without any water. Come Christmas I remember the bizarre scenario of Allan Lamb the England cricketer throwing balls at me that I had to catch with a Velcro hat as we demonstrated that season's must-have toys. On World Cup Final day in 1994 I was with my co-presenter Suzanne Dando and we had to stage our own Subbuteo version of the World Cup Final. That was our offering. Needless to say I couldn't take it seriously and I got a severe rollocking for that." The acquisition of the Premier League rights meant that over time the programme became more football focused (as it were). The panel would discuss the previous week's action then switch to some Rugby Union or horse racing before returning to the panel to discuss the day's results.

In 1996 the decision was taken to make it a football-only pro-gramme and *Soccer Saturday* was born. But why is it such a success when it is essentially a group of blokes sitting round watching and talking about football the viewer can't see? "Principally it's because it filled a gap in the market," said Stelling. "Five Live or Radio Two covered football but they had a live game so if you were the supporter of a small local team you had no idea what was going on with your team. Or you could listen to local radio but then you weren't really getting a national picture. So the other alternative was to watch Ceefax as the pages turned round at an interminably slow rate. We filled a gap in that we provided a service from which you could find out what the Arsenals, the Manchester Uniteds and the Liverpools of this world were doing but at the same time you could find out what the Hartlepools, the Rochdales and the Accrington Stanleys were doing. That was the first and most important thing about it. It provided a scores and information service that gave more of a sense of involvement. I think the other thing, hopefully, was that over the years the panel has become increasingly important in providing thought-provoking opinion, debate, humour, to put a bit of packaging around it. The irony is we'd wonder if we could fill the darn thing, now we haven't got enough time to talk about the things we want to talk about."

While the 1980s had been marked by the TV companies' almost total disinterest in football, *Soccer Saturday* was symptomatic of the proliferation of football-related content aimed at every possible section of the market that began to fill television schedules after the Premier League was born. *Soccer AM* started at 7am on a Saturday morning and targeted children, while *Fantasy Football League* inhabited the post-pub slot on a Friday night and targeted grown-up kids who'd long since forgotten what 7am on a Saturday morning looked like. From 1992 onwards the TV companies were clambering over each other to get their hands on any football rights they could. Games from a variety of different leagues were scheduled in direct competition, with each broadcaster declaring success, often using different and fairly dubious measuring tools. It was not a great time for ITV. The Premier League rights defeat meant that almost overnight they had gone from being the leading broadcaster of English football to being third in a three-horse race. Not only had Sky and the BBC tied up the rights to the Premier League but they'd also got the rights to the FA Cup and England home games through Sky's merger with BSB. ITV still had the rights to the League Cup, which could guarantee the odd big-name tie, and they did a deal with the Football League. It was just like the early days of commercial television as there was no network-wide strategy and the ITV regions decided individually how to cover the sport. Some, like Central, which had several of the new First Division's top teams like Leicester City in their region, broadcast a match more or less every Sunday but not all followed suit.

Even Channel 4 also got in on the action. Chrysalis, which had advised on the mooted Full Time Communications bid for the Premier League rights, had been working on a documentary chronicling Paul Gascoigne's rehabilitation from an injury that he received in the 1991 FA Cup Final. His comment to producer Neil Duncanson that it was a shame no one would be able to watch him after he moved to Lazio prompted an idea that the company should bid for the rights before

selling them on, something they duly did to Channel 4 along with a
Saturday magazine-style programme called *Gazetta Football Italia*
for £1.6m. The initial idea was for Gascoigne to front the coverage but
the job eventually fell to James Richardson, who had been working
behind the scenes. It was a huge success, sometimes topping 2 million
viewers at a time when some Premier League matches on Sky were
being watched by as few as 400,000 people.

The next big scramble came in 1996 when the Premier League
rights came up for renewal. It was imperative for Sky that they were
successful again, and while they had the right to match any rival bid
the prospect of a greatly increased outlay was not one they welcomed.
There were some other big players in the marketplace, namely United
News & Media owned by Lord Hollick and a consortium involving
Carlton and the Mirror Group, now fronted by Murdoch's erstwhile
lieutenant Kelvin MacKenzie. The link between the *Mirror* and the
TV station L!ve TV was crucial as the paper would be the propaganda tool for the football service, just as the *Sun* had been for Sky
Sports. The three parties put their proposals to the Premier League
chairmen in June 1996 at the Coombe Abbey Hotel near Coventry.
The United News & Media deal was £1.5bn for ten years. However,
despite the eye- watering sum on offer the clubs were wary of committing to one relationship for such a long time. The Mirror–Carlton
presentation was professional and offered £650m over five years. Alan
Sugar's role was again crucial as he slated the Mirror–Carlton bid for
favouring the Eutelsat satellite provider to broadcast which he said
would provide an inferior-quality picture to the *Astra* satellite used
by Sky. His message was clear: stick with who and what you know.

Eventually, and as always, it was money that did the talking. Sky
offered £670m for four years – around £10m per club per season. It
was £20m more than the Carlton–Mirror bid and double what the
league had received in 1992. Only Arsenal's David Dein voted against
the deal. In the same year Sky scooped up rights for the League and
the League Cup and did a joint deal with ITV for the FA Cup and
England games, although Sky got first pick, meaning that between
1997 and 2001 Murdoch's company dominated the football TV
marketplace. There were a few crumbs left and in May 1997 Channel
5 managed to pick up the rights for England's World Cup qualifier

in Poland. Once again the sport demonstrated its pulling power by delivering the infant channel's biggest audience to date.

Four years later the three main rights deals all came up for renewal at the same time and Sky again secured the Premier League rights, breaking the £1bn barrier for the first time. The BBC won the rights to show the FA Cup and England matches and in the biggest surprise ONdigital scooped up the Football League rights in a three-year deal worth £315m. Hosted by Gabby Logan, rebranded as ITV Digital and kicking off with Manchester City against Watford on 11 August 2001, the service was doomed from the start. While people with cable could subscribe to Sky Sports, satellite customers could not subscribe to ITV Sport. As well as this inconvenience, ITV Sport were forced to fit around the more glamorous fare served up on Sky, often scheduling games at 6.15pm on a Sunday.

It was a nightmare for travelling fans and the matches had to compete with the dramas and soaps offered by the terrestrial channels. Furthermore, ITV Digital could not offer any matches between big-name clubs – the national events that Fynn argued were fundamental to success. The season was not even two months old when Bradford's 1-0 defeat away at Nottingham Forest provided an ominous portent of what was to follow. Both clubs had graced the Premier League in the previous three seasons yet barely 1,000 viewers tuned into their Thursday-night clash.

With less than a season gone and with £178m still to be paid, ITV Digital looked at the numbers and went into administration, asking the Football League to renegotiate the deal down to £50m. The League refused and also rebuffed a second offer of £74m, forcing the channel to cease broadcasting. Most clubs had factored the ITV Digital money into their budgets for forthcoming seasons and some had spent it already. While it would be wrong to suggest that the channel's collapse was wholly responsible for the financial woes that beset many of them at the time, it certainly pushed some of them over the brink and into administration themselves. The League sued Carlton and Granada, the main ITV companies behind ITV Digital, but the High Court ruled they had no obligation to pay. A settlement of £6m was agreed and the League sold the rights to Sky for four years at a knockdown £95m. League chiefs David Burns and Keith Harris were forced to resign.

The seeds for this financial disaster had been sown in 1996 when the Premier League offered the Football League a deal that would have given the 72 Football League clubs between 20 per cent and 25 per cent of any combined future TV deal. It was essentially bringing the Premier and Football Leagues back together or as David Sheepshanks, then chairman of Ipswich, later described it, reconnecting the Football League "to the rocketship". All but one chairman, Leyton Orient's Barry Hearn, voted in favour of the deal. However just ten days later the Football League board did a deal with Sky for £25m. It was a huge increase from the £7m they had been getting from ITV until that point but it was also a huge mistake. Had they taken the Premier League offer, 20 per cent of the next TV deal would have earned them £42m – almost double their money immediately. In 2011 the Football League signed a deal with Sky for £195m; had they thrown in their lot with the Premier League their share would have been closer to £600m. "They should have taken that deal," Fynn said, "but it was really in a sense that 'you can come on board with us but you'll be second-class citizens, but at least you'll be rich second-class citizens'. They disapproved of the patronage that would be necessary but it was a bad commercial decision not to go ahead."

By this time Murdoch had repeated the trick in America for his Fox Network by shelling out $1.58bn (about £1bn) for the rights to the NFL for the next four years. By gaining control of the Sunday games from CBS, Fox went from being a bit-part player in the US TV market to one of the four star names. Local stations switched affiliation, boosting audience figures, and advertisers followed suit, boosting revenue. Fox was also able to advertise its other shows during match-day coverage, creating a ripple effect across the schedule. Murdoch then shored up his position by signing a $575m deal with Major League Baseball and $155m for National League Hockey. He next switched tactics slightly, hoovering up the Los Angeles Dodgers baseball team for $350m.[6] In 1998 he attempted to do the same with Manchester United, offering in the region of £623m for the club.

6   *Murdoch's touch is not always golden. In 2004, he sold the Dodgers to Frank McCourt for $430m but when McCourt offloaded the team in 2012 he cashed in to the tune of $2bn – a record price for a sports team. More to the point, it's expected that the LA Dodgers will be able to charge $3.5bn for the rights to televise its games over the next 20 years. The likely buyer of those rights? Rupert Murdoch.*

Greg Dyke, by now a board member at United, was against the deal and he wasn't the only one, with fans, other clubs, and even the Premier League's chief executive speaking out against the proposal. The implications were clear throughout the media. *Mirror* editor Piers Morgan wrote in his diary: "The consequences are obvious and awful. The *Sun* would get all the access they need to Britain's biggest club and we'd get squeezed out." Furthermore, if Sky owned United they'd have the inside track on Premier League rights deals. For their part Sky argued that United would still only have one vote in 20 and even offered to withdraw from any TV negotiations.

Other clubs and media companies started courting each other. Arsenal spoke to Carlton, Liverpool spoke to Granada and Newcastle announced its intention to sell up to NTL should the Sky deal be given the green light by the Monopolies and Mergers Commission. To widespread surprise and jubilation it was comprehensively thrown out after hundreds of people and organisations submitted evidence against it. The *Sun* and *The Times* condemned the ruling. It was a short-lived victory. Following the collapse of ITV Digital, both Setanta and US sports giants ESPN have tried to take on Sky and failed. Now it's the turn of BT. In 2012 they scooped 38 Premier League games for £246m per season, helping increase the clubs' haul by 70 per cent.

If that amounted to BT parking their tanks at the end of Sky's drive, the following year they parked them squarely on their rival broadcaster's lawn by securing a three-year deal for the rights to all the Champions League and Europa League matches for £897m – double what Sky and ITV had paid previously. The deal had a significant impact on the TV rights market in a number of ways. Firstly it saw Sky lose a core part of its mid-week football content, thereby decreasing the quality of their offer to customers and reducing the company's ability to increase the cost of its sports package. Secondly, it put them on the back foot when it came to bid for the Premier League rights again in 2015. "Having won the Champions League, BT were less exposed to the Premier League auction, whereas it meant Sky were more exposed," Sarah Simon, a senior analyst at Berenberg Bank, told me. "Once Sky lost the Champions League it meant they absolutely had to win the bulk and the best of the Premier League and they paid through the nose to do that. BT had more options going into the EPL auction because they'd got the Champions League already."

And so it proved. Sky, who simply could not afford to lose the Premier League rights, submitted mammoth bids which amounted to £4.2bn over three years for the rights to show 126 Premier League games a season from the start of 2016/17. For their part, BT agreed to £960m for 42 games a season. The deal meant the total package increased by 70 per cent again. Between them the two companies will be paying on average £10.2m per game or £113,000 for each minute of football broadcast.[7] "Am I surprised?" said Richard Scudamore, the Premier League's chief executive, at the time of the deal. "Of course, the little old Premier League, doing quite well here." And the reason the League is doing so well is because of Sky's reliance on having the rights. "Sky will tell you – and this is what they told everybody before the auction – they weren't that reliant on the Premier League," said Simon. "So it was not a 'must have at any price' and yet they increased their outlay by 83 per cent. Is it sustainable at 83 per cent? No. I think what they say and what they pay tell you a different story."

Football rights are a key component in the "quad-play" battle. The Holy Grail for companies like Sky and BT is to get customers signed up for TV, Broadband, landline and mobile in a bundle, thereby promoting loyalty (or, to take the cynical view, making it harder for customers to disentangle themselves and switch allegiance to a variety of providers). This is why BT entered the football rights market in 2012 – in part to stop Sky poaching its broadband customers – and three years later shelled out an eye-popping £12.5bn for mobile phone company EE. That deal prompted Sky to open up talks to buy O2 from Spanish company Telefónica but they were beaten to the punch by Hong Kong-based Hutchison Whampoa. Coming at it from the other direction, Vodafone, the other big player in the UK mobile market, launched its own TV service in 2016. "BT's strategy is not to say: 'you now need to disconnect your Sky'," said Simon. "I think they'd acknowledge they're not going to dislodge Sky but it needs to

---

7   To put this into context, Sky will be paying the same for six and a half minutes of football as they were for ninety minutes in the very first deal in 1992. Top drama, like the BBC's Sherlock, costs about £2m per episode.

be enough for the consumer to say: 'I won't take Sky broadband, I'll take BT broadband.' It's more about driving the BT broadband product than driving the BT TV product. In the same way that Sky's broadband product when they entered the market was more about TV – 'if you take our TV product, you can have broadband for free' – so this is BT saying: 'if you take our broadband product, you can have Champions League'.

As the lines begin to blur between TV and digital, a picture starts to emerge of what football broadcasting might look like in the future, although it's a future we've already had a glimpse of. Back in 2009 Setanta bought the rights to broadcast England's World Cup qualifier against Ukraine at the Dnipro Arena but went bust before the game was played. The rights holders Kentaro tried to sell them on to another TV company but as England had already qualified there were no takers at the asking price of around £5m. So the Swiss-based company made the radical move of appointing digital sport specialist Perform to stream the match live on the internet – a first for an England international. Punters could sign up for £4.99, or £11.99 nearer kick-off, and some 250,000 did (with actual viewers said to be around the 500,000 mark). At the time the move was criticised by MPs and fan groups alike. It's easy to forget but back then not everyone had the internet; more often than not broadband was neither super nor fast and few TVs were smart. For this reason the game wasn't shown in pubs, although the Odeon chain did screen it live in 11 cinemas across the country. The situation was described as "disastrous" and "an outrage"; however, Kentaro's chief executive Philipp Grothe predicted it was the future and it's beginning to look like he was right.

Technology has advanced significantly since then, and continues to do so apace. Streaming quality has improved as has our viewing experience as we move from TVs and laptops to tablets and mobiles with better graphics cards and processing speeds. More significantly, what we watch and the way we watch it has also changed dramatically. Increasing numbers of people (so-called 'cord-cutters') are ditching subscriptions with traditional broadcasters for streaming services. The NFL in America has begun exploring ways in which to exploit this. In October 2015 the Buffalo Bills' game against the Jacksonville Jaguars at Wembley was streamed exclusively live on Yahoo! It pulled in an average of 2.36m viewers, lower than usual TV viewing figures but not bad given the time difference with America and the fact that neither team had made the play-offs in the best part of a decade. More to the point, Yahoo! proved that it was possible to broadcast a live match in high quality via streaming technology and pull in advertisers (including the likes of American Express, Toyota and Microsoft). Following this qualified success, in early 2016 the NFL announced that it was in discussion with "prospective digital partners" to stream a simulcast of their Thursday-night games alongside broadcasters CBC and NBC which won shared rights to televise the games from the start of the 2016/17 season. From the NFL's point of view, this is an experiment. Aware that fans' viewing habits are changing, they are testing different types of media and distribution models, so that when their biggest broadcast rights deals expire in 2021 they are able fully to exploit the available technology to maximise their revenue.

The names of several digital companies were bandied about as "prospective partners", including Amazon, Apple, YouTube, Yahoo!, Verizon, AT&T and even Facebook, but ultimately the NFL plumped for Twitter in a $10m deal. None of these companies are under the illusion that they will replace the traditional broadcasters in the immediate future. However, as our viewing habits change, what better way to accelerate the growing trend and persuade more people to cut the cord, not to mention buy more set-top boxes, Firesticks and iPads, than to be streaming popular live sport like the NFL? It's Rupert Murdoch's 'battering ram' strategy repurposed for a digital age. For the league it's a chance to appeal to the cord-cutters via a platform whose success is built on its immediacy, with the league's commissioner, Roger Goodell, acknowledging: "Twitter is where live events unfold." If the experiment works it won't be long before the likes of Twitter and Amazon and the Premier League, which will surpass the NFL in terms of revenue generated by rights deals in 2017, start making come-hither eyes at each other.

CHAPTER 10

FOOTBALL WRITING
REACHES FEVER PITCH

The nineteenth century was a period of tumultuous change for England, nowhere more so than Nottingham. An important settlement since the Roman era, by the early 1800s the town was the centre of the lace industry for the whole British Empire. This brought huge wealth to the area but also an exponential and chaotic growth in population that meant the town had some of the worst slums in Europe. Residents of those slums torched Nottingham Castle in the 1831 Reform Act riots and the following year 330 people died during an outbreak of cholera in the town's Narrow Marsh and Broad Marsh areas. Half a century later Nottingham had become a city and some of the most famous names in British industry had been established there. John Player had started selling tobacco ready weighed, packed and labelled; Zebedee Jessop was running his first department store; the Boot family had made their chemist shop a limited company, and just off Raleigh Street Frank Bowden was building bicycles. It was to this more settled Nottingham that the diminutive young reporter James Catton we met in Chapter 2 had moved from Preston with his wife Mary and their two children in 1883. As he toiled away in the Foreman Street offices of the *Nottingham Daily Guardian*, little more than 200 metres away on Pelham Street, J.M. Barrie was taking the first tentative steps on his long literary career in the offices of the rival *Nottingham Journal*.

The man who would become most well known as the author of Peter Pan[1] was employed for three guineas a week to write the *Journal*'s

1   *There is some speculation that Nottingham's Arboretum Park was the inspiration for Barrie's descriptions of Neverland. Barrie lived on Birkland Avenue near the Arboretum, which would have provided a scenic walk to work.*

leaders and a column on Mondays under the byline Hippomenes, as well as essays every Thursday under the title 'A Modern Peripatetic'. Although not a sports writer, several of Barrie's articles focused on cricket. The first appeared in July 1883 and featured an account of a match between two fictitious village teams, Slowcum Podger and Mudcombe. It's a whimsical tale punctuated by some delightful turns of phrase which hint at the quality of writing Barrie would later produce.

Barrie's stay in Nottingham was a brief one. By October 1884 the owners of the *Journal* were looking at ways to cut costs, and after deciding that syndicated leader columns were a cheaper option, they let Barrie go.[2] The Scot was just a month younger than Catton and at 5ft 3in was barely five inches taller. Did the pair ever meet during the latter's brief stay in the East Midlands, perhaps drawn together by their close age and diminutive height? It's not impossible. The town had a busy and vibrant newspaper industry that Barrie used as a backdrop for his 1888 novel *When a Man's Single: A Tale of Literary Life*. There were three morning papers, an evening paper and two weekly papers, and journalists from all the titles formed the hard-drinking Kettle Club that convened night and day in a local pub. Barrie was not enamoured of the club's activities and we don't know if Catton was a member, but there would likely have been ample other opportunities for the two young reporters to come into contact. And let's not forget that Catton, like Barrie, had a deep love of cricket. Perhaps the pair whiled away a few summer afternoons in each other's company watching cricket in a sleepy village, reminiscent of Slowcum Podger.

We'll probably never know for sure, but what we can say is that Catton and Barrie represent early manifestations of the different strands that would come to characterise sports writing for the next 100 or so years; the strands Brian Glanville identified in his 1965 *Encounter* article 'Looking for the Idiom'. Barrie's fictional writing represented the sporting literature that would be dominated by the writing classes who played cricket. He was able to write as he pleased

2   Three years later the Journal *was incorporated into the* Nottingham Daily Express, *which would itself merge with the* Nottingham Daily Guardian *in 1953. By 1973 there was just one daily paper left in the city – the* Nottingham Post.

about the game he loved but reached only a small number of readers. By contrast Catton's focus on factual match reports represented the newspaper reportage that would dominate football writing until the late 1980s; able to reach a mass audience but rigidly confined to the highly stylised language of 'sportuguese'. Yet it would be wrong to suggest that during that year in Nottingham, Barrie and Catton were consciously ideologically opposed, that they sowed the seeds of this schism in sports literature. Newspapers didn't just cover football, they covered cricket too, so why was football largely alien to the literary world for so long? Well, the answer can be summed up by that quintessential facet of English culture: class.

• • •

Football literature is almost as old as the game itself. The first book featuring the sport using rules we might recognise today came in 1866 just three years after the formation of the FA. *Beeton's Book of Football* was one in a series of self-help books published on the back of the success of *Beeton's Book of Household Management*. While it's the name of Mrs Beeton that lives on (well, her surname anyway, most would be hard pushed to come up with her first name: Isabella) it was actually her husband Samuel, a publisher, who was the driving force behind the book. When it was first printed there was little doubt who the Beeton in the title referred to and when Mrs Beeton passed away in 1865, at the tragically young age of 28, her husband carried on printing books. They included *Beeton's Book of Needlework*, *Beeton's Book of Poultry* and *Beeton's Book of Jokes and Jests*. As you can see, the title on football fitted in perfectly, giving hints about diet, warning players to steer clear "of foods and habits which are injurious to the wind and general powers of endurance". There was also tactical information, with diagrams showing how to kick the ball, and the book suggested that "a very serviceable dodge and one puzzling to the enemy, is to stop suddenly, and strike the ball backwards between the legs". Perhaps this was from where Johan Cruyff got his turn.

Despite the similarities, it still wasn't quite the sport we know today. We got a step closer in another book, *Football: Our Winter*

Game, written by Charles Alcock and published in 1874. Alcock was a leading early player and also became a leading early administrator and he argued passionately in favour of the "combination game" or what we now call "passing". Alcock outlined a key principle of this new-fangled tactic that was "following closely on a fellow player, to assist him if required, and to take the ball if he be attacked or prevented from continuing his onward course".

Both these titles were relatively dry technical manuals; if you wanted sporting fiction you really had to look to the world of cricket and the likes of our friend Mr Barrie. After being released by the *Nottingham Journal* he headed south to London to begin life as a freelance writer and by 1887 he had formed his own cricket team: the Allahakbarries. Kevin Telfer, who tells the story of the team in his excellent book *Peter Pan's First XI*, writes that "if you were to draw a Venn diagram with each circle representing a well-known writer from the last years of the nineteenth century and the first years of the twentieth, the greatest area of convergence between them all would be the Allahakbarries Cricket Club".

The team's scorecards read like a literary *Who's Who.* Jerome K. Jerome was an early member; Arthur Conan Doyle, who also played first-class cricket for the MCC, became a mainstay, and E.W. Hornung, who created Raffles the gentleman thief, and A.E.W. Mason, who wrote *The Four Feathers,* also played for the team. In its later years younger members included P.G. Wodehouse and A.A. Milne. It's telling that many of these cricketing aficionados are, like the upper-class amateur cricketers of the day, known by their initials instead of their Christian names. Most of them had been to public school and while some, like Conan Doyle,[3] also played football, it is little surprise that cricket should form the backdrop for so much of their writing. Barrie wrote extensively about the sport and his team's escapades and cricket was a regular feature in the pieces that Milne wrote for *Punch* prior to the First World War and which were later brought together in an anthology called *The Day's Play.* Likewise, Wodehouse wrote enough about the sport to enable the publication of *Wodehouse at the Wicket.*

---

3 *It's a misconception that Conan Doyle played in goal for Portsmouth. He actually played in goal for Portsmouth AFC, an amateur team which had folded two years before the city's professional club was formed.*

Often the literary depiction of cricket in this period (and that of football on the odd occasion it occurred) has something to tell us about class. Hornung's creation A.J. Raffles, who first appeared in 1898, was a thief but also an excellent cricketer. A skilful spin bowler, Raffles played for the I Zingari[4] club and England but he was not a member of the aristocracy, he was from the upper-middle class and it was his skill at cricket that enabled him to gain access to the high-society houses which he subsequently robbed. He considered himself an 'amateur cracksman', differentiating himself from the working-class career criminals he dismissively called 'professors', labels which mimic the differentiation between the amateur 'gentlemen' and professional 'players' of cricket. In a similar vein the Sherlock Holmes stories drew a clear distinction between the educated but amateur detective and the professional police force drawn from the lower classes and personified by the bungling Inspector Lestrade. Thus Hornung's stories can be read as an allegory for England's complex class structure, although Raffles was not a class warrior. While the character noted that "the distribution of wealth is very wrong to begin with", it was a justification not motivation for his actions. He stole from the rich to give to himself and would happily have settled into their social circle had he had the means. It was not to be and when his criminal exploits were finally exposed, his easy access to high society ended as, symbolically, did his cricket career.

But these works were light fiction and there was still a schism between those who used sport in their fiction and those who reported on it. In the USA writers came at sport from a different angle. There, Alfred Runyon and Ring Lardner were combining sports reporting with non-sporting literary careers. "In America they didn't believe in a divide between pop culture and high culture," says Simon Kuper, who with Stefan Szymanski, wrote about class and English football in *Why England Lose*. "It wasn't seen that either you write sport or you write high literature but in Europe there was that divide while the Americans were never that fussed." Runyon's work is best known as the basis of the musical *Guys and Dolls*, but he was a baseball

4   The I Zingari club is a real amateur club formed by Old Harovians in 1845 and still playing today. Members have included Alec Douglas-Home, the only British Prime Minister to play first-class cricket.

columnist for the Hearst Newspapers first and continued to write essays about both that sport and boxing. Similarly Lardner began his writing career as a baseball writer before becoming more widely known for his theatrical and satirical work. Lardner influenced a young Ernest Hemingway, who took the pen name Ring Lardner Jr for his school magazine. He was another American literary figure who also wrote seriously about sport, most notably in *Death in the Afternoon*. Printed in 1932 the book charts the history of bullfighting but also explores themes such as heroism, human nature and even the nature of life and death.

It was a far cry from the whimsical writing of the Allahakbarries. For Barrie, village cricket was the true form of the game, due to its countryside setting and, significantly for a man whose most famous creation was a boy with eternal youth, its apparent timelessness. In 1912 he wrote: "A rural cricket match in buttercup time with boys at play, seen and heard through the trees; it is surely the loveliest scene in England and the most disarming sound." In a couple of years this bucolic idyll was shattered by the industrialised slaughter of the 'Great' War, after which the Allahakbarries never played again.

In 1922 both James Joyce's *Ulysses* and T.S. Eliot's *The Waste Land* were published and their *avant-garde* modernist style swept away the work of the Edwardian writers such as Wodehouse and Milne, by then increasingly regarded as parochial and out of date. Among this new vanguard was Samuel Beckett, a keen cricketer and the only Nobel Prize winner to appear in *Wisden*. However, after he moved to Paris in 1937 he stopped playing and he and his contemporaries wrote little about sport. It's the work of these modernists that tends to be regarded as serious literature, studied in English schools and universities. By contrast, the Allahakbarries live on in our literary consciousness thanks to a select few stories about boys who wouldn't grow up, bears with very little brain and consulting detectives. Ironically, despite being widely read they are now, thanks to their screen adaptations, seen as pop culture. The bulk of the work of Barrie, Milne and their teammates – particularly their writing about cricket – tends to be overlooked, something that only served to reinforce the notion that England has no history of sports literature.

● ● ●

The void was filled by footballers themselves and the autobiographies they wrote, or at least pretended to. Eddie Hapgood's *Football Ambassador* was the first football biography and it was written with the help of Roy Peskett of the *Daily Mail*. Hapgood was signed for the Gunners from Kettering Town by the legendary Herbert Chapman. The 19-year-old soon made the Arsenal left-back spot his own, forging a fullback partnership with George Male that rivalled the Lee Dixon–Nigel Winterburn axis of the late 1980s to mid-1990s. Hapgood would go on to play 440 times for Arsenal's dominant team of the 1930s, winning five League titles and two FA Cups in the process. He also played 43 times for England – then a record – captaining his country 34 times, also a record. Like so many of the top players of his generation, he would have achieved significantly more had the Second World War not come along while he was at his peak, but he still managed to play 102 wartime games for Arsenal and 13 for England. In short, he had a story worth telling and his book is insightful for both the similarities and differences it highlights between football now and football in the inter-war years. The fact that Hapgood signed for his first club Kettering because they offered him the best financial deal is a familiar story. That the deal amounted to £4 a week during the season and £3 a week in the close season is less so. The fact that the club also allowed him to continue to work as a milkman is totally alien.

But for the Second World War and the ensuing paper shortage, *Football Ambassador*, or a similar title, would probably have been published earlier. In 1936, the football players' union foiled an attempt by the FA to ban footballers from writing articles for newspapers. The following year the American writer Gertrude Stein released her book *Everybody's Autobiography*, which opened with the line: "Alice B. Toklas did hers and now everyone will do theirs." Stein was referring to *The Autobiography of Alice B. Toklas*, which despite the title she had written herself in 1933 and which detailed her life in Paris with Toklas, who was her lover.[5] Autobiographies had long been the

---

5   *Stein and Toklas' home at 27 rue des Fleurus became a regular haunt of, among others, F. Scott Fitzgerald, Pablo Picasso, Henri Matisse, Ezra Pound, James Joyce, and that famous sports journalist Ernest Hemingway. In* Death in the Afternoon *Hemingway cites Stein's influence as the reason he first watched a bullfight.*

preserve of politicians and writers but what Stein was acknowledging with her unerringly accurate prediction was the beginnings of a trend for entertainers to also release their life stories in book form. That year both Errol Flynn (*Beam Ends*) and Noël Coward (*Present Indicative*) released autobiographies and it was only a matter of time before footballers would follow suit.

Hapgood's book didn't immediately open the floodgates but over the following years the number of footballer biographies grew from a trickle to a steady stream and class was a central theme running through them, albeit one that changed with time. Initially players presented themselves as model professionals, taking on some of the characteristics of the gentlemen amateurs who had played the game before them while also maintaining close links with their working-class roots. However, as more footballers accumulated wealth through their playing and business careers, particularly during the 1960s, so an ideological gap developed between the sentiments they expressed and the working-class backgrounds that the overwhelming majority of them had come from.

With the Second World War not yet over and the Cold War yet to begin, Hopgood the pathfinder nailed his political colours firmly to the mast. I say colours but in reality there was only one: red. The Khaki Election of 1945 saw the returning soldiers reject the paternalistic public-school-educated ruling classes embodied by Winston Churchill and vote in Clement Attlee's socialist Labour Party. Attlee himself was a public-school-educated Oxbridge graduate (*plus ça change*, eh?) but this didn't stop him taking his mandate and running with it, implementing an ambitious programme of social and welfare reform. Hapgood's biography was more than in keeping with this spirit. He told the readers that he had received a letter from a Soviet war hero which he would "treasure to the end of my days". The letter writer was Lieutenant Alexander Divochkin, who gained his heroic status by single-handedly keeping a Nazi unit at bay from his artillery position outside the city of Petrozavodsk in 1941. In the letter written two years after the incident, Divochkin expressed admiration for Hapgood both as a footballer and as a "fellow fighter of fascists" and Hapgood responded in kind saying in his book that "If, as I hope, my ambition to visit Moscow is realised after the war, I hope to shake your hand personally, Comrade Divochkin, and those of your gallant comrades." The pair never did meet as Divochkin died suddenly in 1946 aged just 32.

Stanley Matthews' biography *Feet First*, published in 1948, was not so overtly political but it was also demonstrably rooted in his working-class upbringing, detailing how his father kept him grounded with sage advice. On one occasion he warned Matthews not to write his biography too early in his career but "to wait until you have really lived, and have a story worth telling that may benefit the community. What folk will bother to sit down and read the comings and goings of a lad of twenty-three?" the elder Matthews asked. A lot as it turns out. Even by the late 1940s footballer biographies could shift as many as 30,000 copies and the number published grew progressively until the 1960s.

Following the abolition of the maximum wage in 1961 footballers became increasingly affluent and this was reflected in their biographies, which outlined their cultural and political assimilation into the middle class, in turn reinforcing the fundamental capitalist notion that anyone can improve their social standing through hard work. This was accelerated in the 1970s when Bobby Moore's second autobiography had a chapter entitled 'Bobby Moore – the businessman'. One of his successors as England skipper, Kevin Keegan, wrote in his autobiography that he made twice as much from advertising as he did from football before also pointing out that as his earnings increased "it is noticeable how much the Government is taking". The link between personal wealth and politics was made even more explicit by Alan Ball, another England star, who wrote in 1979: "I have always figured that once you enter a certain earning bracket you are mad to vote Socialist."

A different manifestation of the change in players' social standing was their changing attitude towards club directors. In 1955 Len Shackleton's autobiography *Clown Prince of Soccer* contained a blank page with the heading 'The Average Director's Knowledge of Football'. Yet two decades later Mick Channon declared the idea that directors were "rich ignorant busybodies" to be "old fashioned". The gap between 'them' and 'us' had closed or rather the people footballers classed as 'them' and those they classed as 'us' was changing; a process that

Michael Parkinson identified in his book *George Best: An Intimate Biography*, published in 1975. The biography was written with considerable help from Best, who is quoted at length, but that said it was very much Parkinson's book and he used Best's career to date as an analogy for what he saw as a decline of working-class culture and its replacement by celebrity culture. According to Parkinson: "Once upon a time a professional soccer player was indistinguishable from the fan behind the goal." However, he went on to argue: "Social and economic embourgeoisification has created a rupture between fan and star."

Already football was well down the path that would ultimately lead to one of Hapgood's successors as Arsenal left-back nearly crashing on the North Circular due to his disgust at the offer of a £30,000-a-week pay rise. "I was so incensed. I was trembling with anger," said Ashley Cole in his book *My Defence*. He had just heard from his agent that Arsenal were only offering him £55,000 a week instead of the £60,000 he had wanted. Here was the 'rupture' Parkinson had identified writ large. Cole's book was one of several written by England players following the 2006 World Cup at which Joey Barton took a swipe, saying: "England did nothing in that World Cup, so why were they bringing books out? 'We got beat in the quarter-finals. I played like shit. Here's my book.'" Barton's critique might have been crude but it harked back to the advice Stanley Matthews had received from his father. Because Barton is a volatile and controversial character, many in the press focused instead on the grovelling apologies he'd have to offer when he was chosen for England duty in 2007. Perhaps they should have been asking whether he had, for once, made a valid point.

Whatever their critics might say, there is no denying that the footballer biography is a hugely popular genre. "They take the reader, the fan, closer to their heroes," says David Luxton, a literary agent who focuses on sport. "Or if not their hero then someone they deeply respect and want to find out more about. Also, I think in the last 15 or 20 years the quality of autobiography has shot up as there has been the recognition among publishers of the value of a top-quality ghost writer."

One of the most successful football books of all time is Sir Alex Ferguson's *Managing My Life*, written with Hugh McIlvanney and published after Manchester United's treble-winning season in 1999. The first edition sold more than 500,000 copies and the second edition, printed the following year, sold nearly 300,000. The book's success was in no doubt partly due to McIlvanney's input but also reflected the fact that Sir Alex did have a story to tell; he did have success and wasn't trying to cash in on failure. The book starts with a two-page dedication to Sir Alex's family that finishes with him saying that even as he celebrated the treble it was hard not to think of his early life. Perhaps this also goes some way to explaining the book's success; it is written by a man still grounded by his working-class upbringing.

• • •

Just as the aftermath of the First World War altered many people's worldview and led to the rise in prominence of modernists like Joyce and Eliot, so the aftermath of the Second World War swept away old certainties. This immediate post-war period was notable for the writing of the new Socialists, particularly George Orwell. His post-war books *Animal Farm* and *1984* were a damning indictment of capitalism, and prior to them *The Road to Wigan Pier* gave a voice to the plight of the working class. But this Old Etonian did not speak with a working-class accent and nowhere was this more apparent than in his examination of sport. Orwell touched on football in detail just once, in his essay *The Sporting Spirit* written after a tour of Britain by a Moscow Dynamo XI ended in acrimony in 1945. While he suggested that it is possible to play cricket on the village green for "fun", by contrast Orwell argued that anyone who played even just school football – "a game in which everyone gets hurt" – knows it arouses the "most savage combative instincts". Ultimately his thoughts on football can be reduced to one telling sentence: "There are quite enough real causes of trouble already, and we need not add to them by encouraging young men to kick each other on the shins amid the roars of infuriated spectators." It was not the first time he had demonstrated a far greater appreciation of cricket. A year earlier in his essay 'Raffles and Miss Blandish', Orwell praised Hornung's stories about the eponymous thief. While recognising that cricket was "predominantly upper-class" and not nearly as popular as football,

Orwell saw it as an expression of the moral values he found within the English people as it was "bound up with such concepts as 'good form' [and] 'playing the game'". Furthermore, he argued that "its rules are so ill-defined that their interpretation is partly an ethical business". The contrast between Orwell's dismissive attitude towards the working-class sport of football and his use of the upper-class sport of cricket as an analogy for English moral virtue is telling.

English literature finally gained a genuinely working-class accent in the 1950s in the new genre of so-called 'kitchen sink realism'. Issues such as inter-racial relationships, pregnancy outside marriage, drunkenness and adultery were tackled but class remained a key theme. However, now the perspective was of those at the lower end of the social scale who were disillusioned with their lack of opportunity. John Osborne led the way with his semi-autobiographical *Look Back in Anger*, rejected by several agents before eventually being produced by the English Stage Company. The theatre's enterprising press officer came up with the phrase 'Angry Young Man' to describe Osborne and the term was picked up and used by the media to describe other similar writers emerging at the time like Alan Sillitoe, John Braine and Stan Barstow.[6]

In 1958 they were linked literally and figuratively with their American counterparts, through the anthology *Protest: The Beat Generation and the Angry Young Men*. Here the names of Osborne, Braine and Colin Wilson sat alongside those of Norman Mailer and Jack Kerouac as "rebels without a cause [...] defying society, conventions, the world". Yet, unlike the Beat writers the Angry Young Men were not a movement as such. They had differing political opinions and no unifying ethos; often they criticised each other. Some of them weren't even particularly angry. But they were the first group of working-class writers that had ever existed in England. Also unlike the work of the Beat writers, sport did not form a significant part of their output.

Here again the difference from America was clear. Mailer, for example, covered the world heavyweight title bout between Muhammad Ali and

---

6   *There were female contemporaries to the Angry Young Men who gave another new view of post-war Britain. These included Shelagh Delaney, Lynne Reid Banks and Doris Lessing, who arguably had the most lasting impact of all the writers of that period and who was made a Nobel Laureate in 2007, six years before her death.*

George Foreman in 1974 for *Playboy* and went on to author *The Fight*, an iconic book on the subject.[7] Yet, in *The Angry Years*, which tells the story of the rise and fall of the Angry Young Men from the point of view of one of them, Colin Wilson, sport is not mentioned once. Why? John King, the author of *The Football Factory* who became a friend of Alan Sillitoe's, believes there was a generational aspect. "Alan wasn't really into football, I think he only went to one game," King said. "My dad was the same. People who were a certain age in the war when there wasn't a league weren't really interested in football. It's the only reason I can think of; maybe that hook wasn't there."

The broadcaster and author Melvyn Bragg thinks this difference is because the Americans are more interested in finding heroes than the English are. "They find a lot of their heroes in sport; Ali was a hero in a way that none of our heavyweights were; mind you, none of our heavyweights were as good as him." Bragg played football in his youth (badly, he says), and dreamt of scoring the winning goal for Carlisle United at Wembley. In the late 1980s he was reintroduced to the sport as a fan, watching Arsenal at Highbury with his young son. He believes another reason that football has no literary tradition in England is because supporters prefer to talk about it. "I think it became much more the conversation of the country than the literature of the country. One of the strange things about football is that it's a very simple game if you look at the rules, but the complications seem to be infinite. There's no end to the problems and possibilities in this very, as it were, simple game. I think because football as a game is so universal and so vast, it's so part of our lives that people just find it more rewarding to talk about it and discuss it – which they do end-lessly – than to write it down. And it passes very quickly. The game tends to be about individuals and they have short careers. In a few years they've established themselves and then by the ripe old age of 34 they've gone." Bragg believes that it's this fast pace at which the game is consumed that underpins its popularity on social media like Twitter. "Not everything has to turn into a book to be significant," he said.

7   Sports Illustrated *sent George Plimpton, the founding editor of the literary magazine* The Paris Review, *and along with Mailer he featured prominently in* When We Were Kings, *the Oscar-winning 1996 documentary about the fight. Hunter S. Thompson was also sent to Kinshasa, by* Rolling Stone *magazine, but hours before the fight he gave his tickets away, deciding to lounge about in a swimming pool instead.*

All this isn't to say that the New Wave writers didn't use sport as a backdrop against which to explore what they saw as the relentless monotony of working-class life. *This Sporting Life,* published in 1960, has as its protagonist a northern Rugby League player but its central themes are the death of community and social exclusion. It spoke volumes about the English class system and is as relevant now as it was then. Its realistic portrayal of its subject matter was in no small part due to the fact that it was written by David Storey, himself a working-class former Rugby League player. *The Loneliness of the Long Distance Runner,* one of Alan Sillitoe's best-known works, is a short story about a borstal inmate and cross-country runner called Smith. Again, however, the sport is the backdrop and the story is really about Smith's bitter contempt for the establishment, which he shows by defiantly losing a race he could easily have won while running in the school's team.

The same anthology included another short story with a sporting theme called 'The Match'. In this the protagonist is Lennox, a 40-year-old mechanic whom the reader meets along with his younger neighbour, Fred, at a cold, fog-shrouded Meadow Lane as Notts County lose to Bristol City. Once again the sport is a backdrop for the wider story. Lennox and Fred disagree about the benefits of married life and while Fred happily returns home to his pregnant wife, Lennox returns home and beats his in front of their children. The assault prompts her to take the children and leave him "for the last time". It's a grim, all-too-realistic portrait of working-class life somewhat at odds with the aspirational picture being painted by the footballer biographies that were being written at around the same time. Given that research conducted by Lancaster University in 2013 demonstrated that incidents of domestic abuse rise by as much as 38 per cent when England play and lose a World Cup game and as much as 26 per cent when they win or draw, Sillitoe's portrait appears to be one that is still uncomfortably accurate.

The City Ground on the other side of the Trent provided the backdrop for a work with football at its heart, B.S. Johnson's critically praised but commercially ignored *The Unfortunates,* published in 1969. The public's reluctance to get to grips with the book might have had something to do with the fact there was no book to get to grips with. Instead the 27 chapters, which vary in length from one paragraph to 12 pages, come unbound and, but for the first and last, can be read in any order. Johnson saw *The Unfortunates* as "a physical, tangible metaphor for randomness" and it is in keeping with much of his other work.

Take *Albert Angelo,* for example. Here we have what seems like a fairly standard novel about a man working as a substitute teacher to make ends meet while he pursues his dream of being an architect. I say fairly standard because every so often there are holes cut in the pages allowing the reader to leap forward in the narrative. Then, after 163 pages that narrative stops mid-sentence and Johnson abandons it, exclaiming: "OH, FUCK ALL THIS LYING!" before leading into a section called 'Disintegration' in which he outlines his literary credo (choice phrases: "telling stories is telling lies" and "I have to tell the truth, it's compulsive, yet at the same time agonising"). It was *avant-garde* stuff (and a nightmare for the typesetter) but because of that many critics and academics focus on the structural style of his work at the expense of its substance, which was heavily autobiographical.

In the case of *The Unfortunates* that substance has much to say about the nature of football writing and the work of football writers. When he wasn't cutting holes in the pages of his books, Johnson was a football writer for the *Observer,* and *The Unfortunates* is a novelistic memoir of the passing of his friend, Tony Tillinghast, prompted by an assignment to cover a match between Nottingham Forest and Tottenham. In turns Johnson laments Tillinghast's death from cancer and peels back the thin veneer of glamour that coats football writing, replacing it with cynical disenchantment. In structural terms the 'truth' is demonstrated as Johnson writes and rewrites his copy during the match (the reader is eventually presented with the final report). But the 'truth' is also how the football writer's mind wanders during a game because, as Johnson writes: "I have no interest in who wins, am here to do a job only, competently." He pities the "poor sods" in the crowd who have to pay, and shows the divide between writers for "so-called posh papers" like himself and the "heavy mob" and "bastards" who write for the red tops. Ultimately his disenchantment can be summed up in one phrase: "Bollocks to this stinking match." It's clear Johnson had repeatedly trodden the well-worn path of match reporting; he was someone who had wearily watched a dull 0-0 only too aware they would have to sum it up in 650 words when 100 would suffice. Three years after *The Unfortunates* was published Johnson told his publisher: "I shall be much more famous when I'm dead." The following day, aged just 40, he took his own life by slashing his wrists in the bath while drunk. Sadly, I'm not sure his prophecy has yet come to pass.

The Unfortunates wasn't the first proper novel about football. That accolade goes to another football journalist: Brian Glanville, and his 1963 book *The Rise of Gerry Logan*. Glanville is a prolific writer and *The Rise of Gerry Logan* was his seventh novel, but despite the insight he'd gained as a journalist, Glanville, who was educated at Charterhouse, felt that due to his middle-class upbringing he could never do the working-class characters justice, telling Simon Kuper that: "essentially the football novel should have been a branch of the proletarian novel" and citing *This Sporting Life* as the one sporting novel that had come close to that.

If there is a football equivalent to Storey's novel it's the little-known *From Scenes Like These* written by Gordon Williams. While you might not recognise Williams' name, you will almost certainly recognise some of his work. Brought up on Ferguslie, one of the more deprived areas of Paisley, Williams ended up working as a sports writer on the *Daily Mail*'s colour magazine. He started ghosting articles and books for footballers including Tommy Docherty, Bobby Moore and Terry Venables, with whom he also co-authored a football novel *They Used to Play on Grass* as well as the Hazel detective series. An apocryphal story about their writing partnership suggests that Venables' contribution to one of the Hazel novels can be summed up as follows: "There's a blonde on the bed. Dead. And underneath the bed is a suitcase stuffed with a million nicker. All yours, Gordon."

Either way, Williams also wrote novels on his own including *The Siege of Trencher's Farm,* which became Sam Peckinpah's film *Straw Dogs*. The original novel did not include the highly controversial scene, part of which was banned by the BBFC for more than 30 years, in which the character portrayed by Susan George appears to enjoy being raped, and Williams denounced the film as "neo-Nazi crap". By then Williams had already written *From Scenes Like These,* which was shortlisted for the very first Booker Prize in 1968 alongside Iris Murdoch's *The Nice and the Good* and Muriel Spark's *The Public Image*. It tells the story of Duncan 'Dunky' Logan, a farm labourer in a Scottish town where the outlying farmland is being destroyed by increasing industrialisation. Dunky also plays for the second XI of the local West of Scotland League team and sees football as a potential escape route. Like Johnson, Williams toys with the structure, presenting the football scenes in a dual stream-of-consciousness as if he is both playing and watching. He also uses Scottish dialect to enhance the realism and ask questions about class and nationality, with Dunky musing as to why he was beaten at school for not speaking with a more English accent. Ultimately Dunky is never able to cut the ties that bind him to the community he was brought up in. Picked for a cup final he ends up with a broken arm and two teeth missing, an incident that precipitates his descent into the brutal type of masculinity he had sought to escape.

Like Rugby League in Storey's novel, football is a backdrop, or at least only a character, in the fatalistic picture Williams paints of working-class life. How different would this chapter have been had *From Scenes Like These* – if not about football then still a book with football at its heart – won the first Booker Prize? Of course we'll never know. But it is clear from the fiction of Johnson, Glanville and Williams that gradually the barriers between high and low culture were being broken down. A public school or university education was no longer prerequisite for a serious author. Football writers were writing books. Novelists were reporting on football. The sport was coming out of the literary shadows.

• • •

But only just. Johnson's and Williams' books have all but been forgotten and the same might well have happened to Glanville's football novels – not huge sellers on release – if he weren't still an active, high-profile football journalist well into his 80s. If we remember these writers at all it's as one thing or another: Johnson and Williams as novelists, Glanville as a football journalist. It was still very different in America where Norman Mailer's *The Fight*, his book-length account of the

Ali–Foreman title fight in 1975, and the Pulitzer-prize-winning novel *The Executioner's Song*, which he wrote five years later, are equally well regarded. Yet there are some football books from that period that are deeply woven into the game's cultural fabric.

One is Arthur Hopcraft's *The Football Man,* which took the format of a series of essays on a range of loosely connected subjects like 'The Player', 'The Director' and 'The Fan'. Like the other writers we've just mentioned, Hopcraft tends to get pigeon-holed, in his case as The Man Who Wrote *The Football Man,* which does him a great disservice and overlooks the variety of his output. This included *Born to Hunger,* a study of the problems of the world food supply, and the scripts for the BBC's 1979 adaptation of *Tinker Tailor Soldier Spy* starring Alec Guiness. In fact his TV work was considered to be of a similar quality to that of contemporaries such as Dennis Potter and Alan Bennett but, as I said, it's as a plain old football writer that he's remembered. *The Football Man* was aimed at "an intelligent, wider readership" but it was not a great seller on release. Only 4,000 of an initial print run of 6,000 were sold, a paperback edition fared little better and within a decade the book was out of print. It's only in later years that it came to be recognised for the detailed sociological history it provided. For Hopcraft, football was deeply rooted into our culture and had "more significance in the national character than theatre". So, *The Football Man* wasn't just a book about the sport but also something that was a crucial aspect of working-class life. Its insight came from its objective autobiography, Hopcraft drawing on his own experiences to try "to reach to the heart of what football is". It's perhaps this aspect, the fact that it was "a book by a football fan", as Hopcraft labels it in the final few pages, which explains its enduring appeal. It prefigured by nearly a quarter of a century the style of writing that would supposedly entice the middle classes to the game.

Hopcraft was not the only writer producing serious football writing during that period. In 1972, Hunter Davies managed to get season-long access to the Tottenham dressing room and training sessions – a level of access that would be unheard of today – and the resulting fly-on-the-wall account was *The Glory Game.* However, in a review in *New Society* Ian Taylor criticised Davies for concentrating on providing an "amusing or colourful brand of reportage" that "tells us little about the 'obvious' changes in the structures or culture of professional soccer". The same could not be said of *Only a Game?*, Eamon Dunphy's gritty autobiography of the 1973/74 season told from within the slightly less glamorous dressing room of Second Division Millwall. It shone a particularly harsh light on the internal workings of the football industry and particularly players' relations with the media. It was also around this time that James Walvin produced his seminal history of football *The People's Game* that would lead to a different strand of football writing in a variety of academic disciplines.

However, just as this genre of thoughtful, factual football writing started to develop it was all but stopped in its tracks. England failed to qualify for two consecutive World Cups, the game was marred by hooliganism and tragedy, and people fell out of love with the game. As the sport sank to its late 1980s nadir the idea that it was a working-class ghetto was reinforced. John Gaustad, a New Zealander who moved to England in the mid-1970s and set up the Sportspages bookshop in London about a decade later, remembers: "The perception then was that to follow football you had to be spoiling for a fight and a real thicko and just bad news altogether really. If you were passionate about football it was almost as if you had to hide it. You had to keep quiet about it when you met friends who weren't football followers, or they'd look at you rather aghast."

Let's not forget this was when *The Times* called football a "slum sport watched by slum people". We knew what they meant, but they were wrong. "I was at Oxford from 1988 to 1992," Simon Kuper told me, "and I have a strong memory from that game in 1989 when Liverpool played Arsenal for the title and the common room at my college was packed; I mean, no women but all the men in college, a couple of hundred, were watching the Liverpool–Arsenal game and this was just after Hillsborough, when football was at a very low ebb. No one was saying football was gentrifying. Yet all these people were middle class, they'd all grown up watching football and being football fans."

It was from this time and the interest in football of these types of people that the fanzine culture developed and that, in turn, demonstrated once and for all that there was a sustainable market in football literature. "Fanzines were incredibly important," says

Luxton. "The rise of fanzines, or the rise of the fan's voice, showed publishers that there was an audience that they hadn't really noticed in football terms. It showed them that there were fans out there who were deeply passionate about their clubs, deeply passionate about football and who were also in the market for well-written books about football." Luxton witnessed the explosion in popularity of this market from Sportspages, where he went to work for Gaustad after he finished university, eventually staying for 11 years. "Suddenly as those books took off, more and more publishers became aware that there were lots of people out there who wanted to read good books on football or with football as a theme."

One regular at Sportpages was Nick Hornby and flicking through the fanzines reassured him there was a market for the book he was writing. *Fever Pitch* was a genuine breakout title that sold in the region of 30,000 hardback copies and 246,000 paperback copies within the first three years of publication. Although it's autobiographical (early editions were subtitled *A Fan's Life*) and has a linear narrative starting in 1968 and running through to 1991 (the year before its release) there is, in a sense, no real story. It is instead made up of a series of essays (if Hornby wrote it today, it would probably be a series of blog posts) each using a particular game, not all necessarily featuring his beloved Arsenal, as a starting point. Many focus on the nature of fandom and Hornby's relationship with both the game and the Gunners, but many are just about the game itself.

Gaustad remembers clearly the impact of *Fever Pitch*: "I was talking to my colleagues and somebody asked one of the guys who was a Chelsea fan 'How do you feel about it because it's about Arsenal?' and he said 'No it's not, it's about Chelsea; it's about football.' I think that's the response that it elicited. In its own crazy way it transformed the game and persuaded a whole lot of publishers, who previously hadn't been convinced, that there was a market for an intelligently written book on football. In fact a publisher who I knew had sent me a proof and asked me what I thought of it and I said 'Don't hesitate for a moment; it's brilliant, get the book out there.' And they did and it sold a lot of copies."

Given that class was such a pervasive issue in football literature it's little surprise that Hornby touched on the subject in *Fever Pitch*.

He suggests that there was a temptation in a book about football to apologise for his Cambridge education before arguing that to do so would be wrong as "Arsenal came long before Cambridge, and has stayed with me long after". Furthermore at university he wasn't the only football fan, far from it and in that respect Hornby's comments mirror those of Kuper, who was at university about a decade after him. Yet some people missed the point. The *Observer* claimed that *Fever Pitch* led to the "emergence of a new class of soccer fan – cultured and discerning" and it has long been held up as the book which kick-started football's gentrification by bringing the middle classes flocking through the turnstiles. "I think that's false," says Kuper. "Hornby didn't get the middle classes involved in football, but he allowed them to talk about football in their publications, in their books and in their newspapers. You don't get many people saying 'People shouldn't write literate stuff about football, football's an honest working-class game and all these Johnny come-lately middle-class poseurs should get out', which is what Nick Hornby got a lot of in 1992. That's gone away now." But Hornby wasn't the first writer in this field. "There is the book that everybody forgets; Pete Davies' *All Played Out*," said Gaustad.

Davies got access to the England players during the 1990 World Cup but also spent the tournament travelling around Italy talking to the fans. His book paints a portrait of a nation in decline; a nation whose fans and media were still obsessed with the Second World War. "It was the first time a publisher had produced a book by a fan," said Gaustad. "Davies was like John the Baptist to Nick Hornby's Jesus because then *Fever Pitch* came out a few years later and caught the zeitgeist perfectly and became the book everybody had to read. The reason Davies' book didn't get much publicity, or as much as it should have done – I thought it got underplayed – was that he was so rude about journalists; that's why none of them wanted to give him a helping hand. That was rather intriguing," Gaustad added with a chuckle.

Kuper's book *Football Against the Enemy,* which was published after *Fever Pitch,* had actually been commissioned before Hornby's title hit the shelves and he told me that it was Davies' title that was held up by publishers as "the kind of book I should be writing". He added: "When I was trying to sell *Football Against the Enemy* to publishers in 1991 they all said 'we know books about football will sell, because Pete Davies' book sold well'. Obviously it sold far fewer than *Fever Pitch* but it was a very influential book among people who wanted to write or publish books of that vein."

Both titles followed in the wake of Simon Inglis' *The Football Grounds of England and Wales*, printed in 1983, a book Luxton described as "a classic of sports literature". Although it lacks a narrative structure, has no story and doesn't really tell a biographical history of any individual (apart from perhaps very loosely Scottish stadium designer Archibald Leitch[8]) it's one of the books which led me down the path to me typing this sentence. The book had brief but highly informative sections on: stadia history; the principles of stadia design (it was here I learned what a 'sightline' was); safety; floodlights; and pitches and posts. Then there was the main section on each League club detailing previous grounds and a history and description of the club's current ground. It was thanks to Inglis that when I stood on the Spion Kop at Filbert Street I knew why it was called the Spion Kop.[9] Not only was it meticulously researched and intelligently written, but its publication was tragically fortuitous in its timing. The first edition was published two years before the fire at Valley Parade and the second edition (now including Scottish stadia and retitled *The Football Grounds of Great Britain*) two years before the Hillsborough disaster. The third and final edition came in 1997 in what Inglis described as "the most intense period of ground development since the 1890s" and as Inglis himself acknowledged the book was effectively out of date by the time it hit the shelves. Following an initial print run of 4,000 the first two editions went on to sell in excess of 120,000 copies, undeniably demonstrating that nearly a decade before *Fever Pitch* and more than five years before *All Played Out* there was a popular market for well-written, intelligent factual football writing.

• • •

8   *Inglis went on to produce a full-length biography of Leitch called* Engineering Archie.

9   *The Spion Kop was a hill in South Africa that the British Army tried and failed to capture in a horrifically bloody action during the Boer War in 1900. Afterwards, in tribute, many of the banks on which men stood at football grounds became known as the Spion Kop or just Kop for short. The most famous example is, of course, at Anfield.*

Pete Davies wasn't the only author chronicling the experience of England fans at Italia '90. American Bill Buford was also in Sardinia collecting material for his book *Among the Thugs*, and getting a kicking from the Carabinieri for his trouble. He also got a kicking from *When Saturday Comes*, by proxy any way. The book detailed the eight years Buford spent running with Manchester United's hooligan crew the InterCity Jibbers and on its release in 1991 *When Saturday Comes'* reviewer Ed Horton dismissed Buford's "slumming it" to instead take Martin Amis to task for the contents of his review of the book in the *Independent on Sunday*. Amis' review used a very broad brush to paint anyone who attended football as a violent thug. It was, Horton said, "a poisonous display of ignorance and bigotry aimed at the scum of the earth – you or I, the football fan". In Horton's opinion this was "class snobbery". He adds: "The point remains though that because of the intelligentsia's distaste for ordinary people in numbers, it is possible to find the most offensive attitudes towards football supporters in the most surprising places."

Among the Thugs was one of the first of the sub-genre of football writing that has variously been labelled 'hoolie-lit', 'hoolie-porn' or 'hit-and-tell' books (depending on your feelings towards them). But it wasn't the first. Gaustad relays a story of how he came to publish one of the earliest titles through the Sportspages imprint. "I was sitting in the shop one day and this big guy came in and he put this sheath of papers down and said really aggressively: 'I've wrote a book and they say you can get it published' and I thought 'Fuck me!' So I told him to leave it with me and that I'd get back to him. I took it home that night because I thought I'd better read a bit of it before I said 'no way' but I found it utterly gripping." The big guy was Colin Ward and the sheath of papers became *Steaming In*.

"He had a few O-Levels, he worked as a butcher and followed Chelsea and Leatherhead and he was a hooligan but he felt that hooligans were getting a bad press and he wanted to set the record straight. It was like a burst of truth and honesty and reality, not just the *Daily Mirror* holding up its hands in horror, which struck me as a valuable service to publishing." You can't help but think that because Ward didn't reference William Shakespeare or the likes of Plato and Gustav Le Bon and because he is, as Buford might have said, one of 'them', his arguably more authentic take on football-related violence and the people who perpetrate it was ignored by the likes of Amis. "What that reflects is that the people who were reviewing it were unsophisticated, shall we say, so they were not well enough into the scene to picture what was going on," said Gaustad.

Since Ward's and Buford's books, numerous football hooligan biographies and histories of hooligan firms of varying quality have been written and the sub-genre has been hugely successful. There have also been some notable works of fiction with hooliganism as a backdrop such as John King's *The Football Factory*, an overtly political novel which again has class at its heart, something which King feels loosely links the genre to the New Wave writers of the 1950s. "Alan Sillitoe was someone I read and admired and I actually got to know him in 1999 and he became a friend. It was quite amazing to be sitting in a pub with Alan Sillitoe and thinking 'Blimey, he's my mate,'" said King when we spoke. "The fact that I could pick up one of Alan's books which he'd written in the late 1950s or early 1960s and even though he came from Nottingham I could kind of connect with that book in 1979 shows how good his books were. But also it shows how general these things are and also how little there was that connected with the mass population. It was one of the things I tried to say with *The Football Factory* – you have tribalism in football but really everyone's the same."

In that sense, King went on to explain, *The Football Factory* is not really about hooliganism. "It's much broader than that. It's largely influenced by George Orwell's ideas of the proles fighting among themselves. There are two characters in the book: Tommy Johnson and Bill Farrell. Bill's a war hero and he's probably more important than Tommy in many ways. When I was a kid there was the *World at War* on TV just before *The Big Match*, so as a boy the Second World War was a big thing and the people who'd fought in the war were our heroes really. In the late Sixties up until the early-Eighties a lot of kids who went to football were in a way re-enacting the conflicts of their heroes on a massively smaller scale. In *The Football Factory* it's a disaffected young man who goes to football. He's not particularly party political but he sees himself under attack from every political party. He doesn't see himself as represented. He's powerless basically and going to football makes him feel special, makes him feel strong. When I first went to Chelsea and I used to stand on The Shed I felt part of something and it was good. I just wanted to write something that was a bit more honest than the sensationalism that was in the media." So was King trying to tell a truth through fiction? "They are general truths rather than specific truths," he said. "If you write fiction it gives you a lot more freedom. You can write in different styles, you can try things, but it's something you can't really fake; you're writing from your own experience, your own life in some ways, and it's either right or it's not right."

The issue of authenticity is an important one in books like these. The most infamous passage in *Among the Thugs*, one that, I should stress, is totally unconnected to football, details how a hooligan called Harry knocks a policeman unconscious then sucks out his eyeball. Harry manages to do all of this despite being in a restaurant full of members of the local CID. Having completed the job by biting the eyeball free, Harry gets up and is apparently able to walk out of the restaurant and go home. Is this authentic? Did this really happen? I'm not for one moment suggesting that Buford made this incident up but it's not something he witnessed, it's not even something witnessed by the person who told him about it. Buford is reporting third-hand hearsay and what's more he makes no attempt to verify it. Even when he later meets Harry, Buford doesn't ask him about the incident because, he writes, he's not interested. But if he's not interested why include it in the book? And if he's interested enough to include it in a book that purports to tell the truth, why not first find out if the incident actually happened? Is Buford's book really more authentic than a work of fiction like *The Football Factory*?

Despite the unquestionable success of the genre of hooligan memoirs and related fiction, both King and Dougie Brimson, who has written both factual and fictional books on hooliganism, believes the genre is overlooked. "In literary terms what happened was a massive thing," said Brimson. "Out of nowhere you had a load of people who weren't necessarily even readers let alone writers, suddenly going into print, selling lots of books and dominating the sports charts. That brought a lot of people who just didn't read books back into reading, albeit within this genre, and that was down to people like Colin Ward,

John King, Cass Pennant and me. But that was never acknowledged. It wasn't even acknowledged as a genre in literary circles." Brimson thinks there are several reasons: "It's snobbery and they don't like the perceived concept of people making money out of a violent past associated with football and they don't want to acknowledge that, in essence, as a problem it still exists."

King thinks that the genre is more than just overlooked: "It's ignored, it's dismissed, it's marginalised," he said. They don't want that, they want one of their people to do it. It's like an old pub in an area that gets gentrified: they go in and gut it and turn it into a pizza parlour that's not as good. The power is with those people, the reviews are with those people. It's very hard. I've sold a lot of books, I've got a good publisher but I managed to do that against the odds." It's worth pointing out that *Among the Thugs* didn't want for reviews. *The Economist*, *The New Statesman* and *Time Out* were just some of the many publications willing to devote space to that particular take on hooliganism. But then its Cambridge-educated author was editor of *Granta* at the time; he was one of the intelligentsia. It seems some hoolie-porn is more palatable than others.

• • •

Within a decade of *Fever Pitch*'s release the market for football books was well and truly established and among all the fan confessionals aping Hornby's style a new type of book emerged. "I remember in about 2000 I was with some English friends in a bar in London and Deportivo La Coruna were on TV," said Kuper. "My English friends knew the players and I thought: 'Wow that's really something new.' I think there was a move in British football writing from books about British football to books about international football around that time." Luxton agrees: "At that point we entered a bit of a golden age in terms of publishing, these books about different parts of the game and different parts of the world were coming thick and fast and there was a hungry audience for them." Titles in this sub-genre cover all corners of the globe from Ulrich Hesse-Lichtenberger's *Tor! The Story of German Football* to Simon Freeman's *Baghdad FC*, the at times harrowing story of football in Iraq. But what stimulated this interest in football beyond our shores and what created this increasingly knowledgeable marketplace?

It was a process that began at around the same time as Italia '90 when several England stars went to play in Italy and English clubs began signing increasing numbers of high-profile foreign players. The merger of Sky with BSB presented Channel 4 with the opportunity to pick up the rights to Italian football, which they then started broadcasting in 1992. They were fortuitous in their timing as the newly formed Premier League had just moved to the satellite station. This meant for many who wanted to watch football in the now-familiar Sunday-afternoon slot, Italian football was the only way forward. This was twinned with the Saturday-morning show *Gazzetta Football Italia* hosted by James Richardson, whose witty, laid-back but intelligent demeanour was a revelation.

Football's increasing globalisation was mirrored by an increasing globalisation of youth culture that was in part linked to football. Italian House was all the rage and the summer after the tournament, blissed-out England fans beat a path back to Italy to take in the highs of Rimini's club scene. DJ Terry Farley christened it "Italia '91" in *The Face* magazine. The same year 30,000 Manchester United fans turned up in Rotterdam to see their team beat Barcelona in the Cup Winners' Cup Final and instead of fighting they partied. All of a sudden English football didn't seem quite so parochial.

The first book to look beyond our shores to explore the cultural importance of football was Kuper's *Football Against the Enemy*, published in 1994. Following his success (Kuper won the William Hill Sports Book of the Year), he launched *Perfect Pitch*, a regularly published book-length publication labelled as "The best new football writing". In the first issue Kuper lamented the lack of intelligent football writing over the years before suggesting he hoped to fill the gap with "writing by novelists, poets, journalists and sometimes even footballers", but after four issues released between 1997 and 1999, publication ceased. It was a forerunner to *The Blizzard*, a book-length football quarterly magazine launched in 2011. As I type, the latter publication is still going strong with its 13th edition. Why the difference?

Well, there are adult football fans walking around now who were yet to be conceived when *Fever Pitch* was published. They have grown up in an environment saturated by football media and one in which there is a huge amount of football literature available. It's easy to forget that simply wasn't the case for people in their twenties when *Perfect Pitch* was launched. As we've seen, the interest and the intelligence was already there but the more detailed knowledge and broader horizons that the different forms of media subsequently brought stimulated people's interest further. Channel 4's *Football Italia* has subsequently been followed by the broadcast of football leagues from around the world. You can now watch football pretty much any time of the day, every day, whether that's on TV or live stream on betting websites. The latter have often been forced to hoover up cheaper, so-called 'second-tier' leagues, which have broadened people's horizons further still. And for those of us who can't speak a foreign language (which let's face it is pretty much all English people) there's Google Translate to help you read every European newspaper's website. Plonk a slice of posh cake and an ostentatious hot chocolate on your desk and you can spend the morning pretending to host *Football Italia*.

Then there are computer games. *The Blizzard*'s editor Jonathan Wilson partly attributes the development of the more intelligent football fan, and the subsequent market for intelligent football literature that this has created, to the *Football Manager* computer game. First launched in 1992[10] the game has featured real players since its second edition and now has more than 1,000 researchers and 51 head researchers across the world. The game's player database is so detailed that in 2008 Everton signed a deal with the developers Sports Interactive to allow them to use it for scouting. *Football Manager* has become a form of reportage in itself. An unknown quantity like Ferenc Puskás and his Hungarian teammates couldn't turn up at Wembley or Molineux like aliens from another planet now.

"When Hatem Ben Arfa signed for Newcastle and Alan Shearer said on *Match of the Day* he'd never heard of him, loads of people went on Twitter to say 'he obviously doesn't play *Football Manager*'," says Miles Jacobson, Sports Interactive's studio director. "I think people who play *Football Manager* end up with a far better football knowledge than people who don't because we cover global football

---

10   *The game was originally called* Championship Manager *but following a split from publishers Eidos Interactive in 2004 it was rebranded as* Football Manager.

leagues. They often hear about players from the game that they wouldn't have heard about from real life. We're very proud of the name checks that we get from a lot of journalists and the fact that they enjoy playing it. It's bonkers how this little computer game has influenced so many people. We're obviously very proud of that."

While the increase in football media created a fertile marketplace, it was another new form of media that enabled the producers of *The Blizzard* to tap into that. "*Blizzard* is very good and I admire Jonathan Wilson for doing it," says Kuper, "but I think what helped them in comparison to *Perfect Pitch* was the internet. It just makes it much easier to reach people around the world than when we did it." Wilson agrees: "The huge advantage we have over *Perfect Pitch* is Twitter. We launched with no advertising whatsoever apart from that I'd been on Twitter saying: 'this is what we're doing'. We had 3,000 orders on the first night, which was way beyond what we'd ever dreamed possible. It was a bit like that scene in *The Social Network* where you see the members of Facebook ticking over and ticking over. That was purely through Twitter. People who follow me know what they're getting so when I tweet that advert they know they're going to be interested."

● ● ●

While the market for factual books about football is now a crowded one, novels remain few and far between. There is something about football and fiction that means that they are not passionate bedfellows. Kuper believes that class is still an issue. In *Why England Lose* he points out that although the middle class is growing, English football continues to recruit from the working class – a talent pool which is shrinking. At the same time the anti-intellectual nature of football means it is unwelcoming to middle-class teenagers who drift to rugby and cricket instead. Not only has this limited the pool of talent English football can choose from, it also limits the pool of talent that can write about football from the inside. "From Mike Brearley and Peter Roebuck to Ed Smith you've always had middle-class people who played cricket and could write about it very well," says Kuper. "In English football we've never had that. My favourite writers are the likes of Orwell and Waugh, and none of them wrote about football. Then more recently Julian Barnes, Martin Amis and Salman Rushdie have written a little bit about the sport but not very well. In football you just don't have the middle-class present inside the game at all and so people like me and Nick Hornby are always on the outside looking in."

One contemporary novelist who has used football as an integral part of his writing is David Peace. His most recent book *Red or Dead*, released in 2013, details Bill Shankly's time at Liverpool while *The Damned Utd*, printed six years earlier, focuses on Brian Clough's fateful 44-day reign at Leeds. Does the fact that both novels are fictionalised accounts of real events hint at the reason for the lack of fictional football writing? Luxton thinks so: "The reality of football can be so fantastical. If you wrote some of the situations it throws up as fiction people would just look at it and say: 'well, that's ridiculous. That would never happen.' Take for example, Manchester City winning the League the way they did a couple of years ago – that was very *Roy of the Rovers*. So, I guess there's a worry that even though we witness these things happening on the pitch it doesn't ring true when someone's making up a story." Ultimately Kuper agrees: "Football has all the drama and conflict and personality and it's real. So you want to read about Shankly and Clough. Making it up: who needs that?"

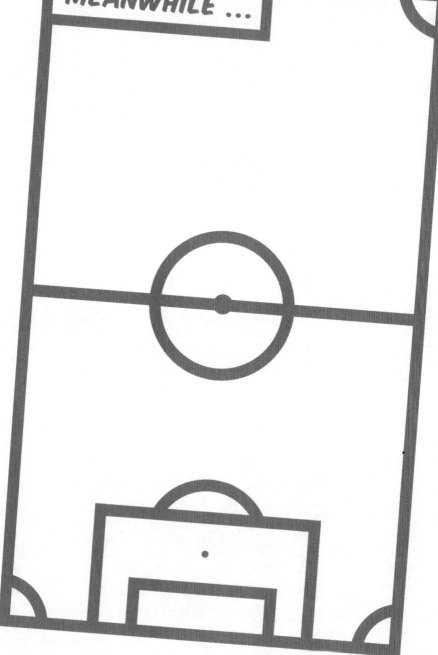

CHAPTER 11

HOLDING OUT FOR A HERO

It's a long path from Beowulf to Roy of the Rovers but it's one that's been taken by the heroic figure in English popular culture. Written somewhere between the sixth and eleventh centuries, *Beowulf* tells the story of a warrior with the strength of 30 men in each arm who travels to Denmark to fight and kill a fearsome monster called Grendel which has been terrorising the kingdom of Hrothgar. Killing Grendel upsets the beast's mother and after she goes on a bloody rampage, Beowulf has to fight and kill her too. After this he returns to Geatland, his home, and eventually becomes king. It's clear that Beowulf, like Roy (and don't worry, we'll get back to him in a bit), never actually existed, although there was a lot of historically accurate detail in the story. The key was that Beowulf, like all heroes, was a role model embodying the values and ideals of his society at the time, while also acting as a unifying force. He represented an archetype, in this case an idealised Anglo-Saxon hero. In an age when every man was known as his father's son,[1] the idea of establishing a valiant reputation to augment that of your ancestors while also creating your own identity was paramount.

The story also highlighted the tensions between the close-knit warrior societies of the day and the threats to their borders. Very little Old English (or Anglo-Saxon) literature survives – around 30,000 lines in four manuscripts – and at 3,182 lines Beowulf is the most complete epic poem, which goes some way to explaining

---

1   *The use of patronyms as surnames (for example, the son or daughter of Olof taking the surname Olofsson or Olofsdotter respectively) was widespread in Scandinavia until the early part of the 20th century when rising populations led to legislation requiring the use of internationally standard family names. Conversely, in Iceland the law enforces the use of patronymic surnames.*

its longevity. That so little of the rest is still around is due to the fact that there wasn't much to start with; Anglo-Saxon culture was essentially oral and not scribal. Back then, when information couldn't be easily reproduced and shared in a hard-copy format, people had to rely on the spoken word to relay stories of greatness. Consequently heroes were larger than life and the stories that surrounded them were exaggerated to make them easy to remember. Early minstrels, called scops, wandered from community to community (and in some cases gained royal patronage) reciting these stories but rarely, if ever, writing them down.

Fast-forward about 500 years and you get to the age of the first printing presses. Oral poetry was increasingly replaced by the written word, which changed what it meant to be a hero. The stories about them no longer had to be easily memorable so their deeds were less fantastic and there could be more of them. This was the age of Robin Hood and his Merry Men. Although the stories from Sherwood Forest are largely fiction, Robin himself was a real person. The stories about him represented something different to that of Beowulf, but something still relevant to the England of his day. Society was becoming more ordered, with the beginnings of a centralised form of governance and taxation. Robin, Little John, Friar Tuck and the rest didn't fight monsters; instead they fought oppression, represented in human form by the Sheriff of Nottingham and King John. The Merry Men were outlaws but in a world ruled by bad people; they didn't fight the establishment, just the corruption of it, and they were ultimately pardoned because of their loyalty to John's brother King Richard I.

You'll have noticed that I haven't mentioned any women yet (apart from Grendel's mother and I'm not sure she counts) and that's because the heroic world is a largely masculine one. In this realm men are active while women tend to be passive and decorative, for example the beautiful princess tied up by a lake waiting to be eaten by a dragon or saved by a hero. If the princess is lucky enough to be rescued she'll more than likely be given to the hero as a prize (no doubt in some cases wishing the dragon had won). If they are active in these stories women are usually evil like King Arthur's half-sister Morgana Le Fay, although that isn't to say there aren't female heroes. Boudica is one but while the broad brushstrokes of her story are well known (led an uprising against the Romans; lost; killed herself) the detail isn't and so she has come to mean different things to different people. All but forgotten during the Middle Ages, the Victorians bestowed heroic status upon her, making her the representation of a strong female leader uniting and protecting her people – conveniently just like their own queen. Ironically Boudica, the great anti-imperialist freedom fighter, had become the embodiment of oppressive Imperialism. A few decades later she again came to represent the struggle for liberty as a suffragette icon. Maid Marian, too, has undergone a transformation. In early Robin Hood stories he had no female companion and Marian existed separately as a figure in May Day celebrations. She was co-opted into the Robin Hood canon in the 1700s when it was thought he needed a dainty, virginal love interest. Following the rise of feminism in the twentieth century she increasingly became his equal.

This continued negotiation of what each hero, and other characters in their story, represents demonstrates the crucial role the media has always played in their creation and our understanding of them. 'Normal' people tend to be separated from their heroes by time, space and perhaps class, so they only learn about them through the stories and images supplied by the media, whether it is spoken, written or visual. During the Age of Empire explorers such as David Livingstone and Henry Morton Stanley, John Hanning Speke and Richard Burton became heroes through the media's portrayal and reportage of their exploits. They were athletic, unpretentious, fair and honest men who embodied the English Corinthian characteristics and amateur values which were being spread across the Empire through the growth of codified sport. The link between sport and empire was made explicit in Sir Henry Newbolt's 1897 poem *Vitaï Lampada* about a soldier who learned his commitment to duty playing cricket as a Clifton College pupil, and which gave us the phrase "Play up! Play up! And play the game!"

Gradually during the twentieth century, the rapid rise in the availability of technology and the increasingly secular and less deferential nature of society diminished the status of figures who had previously been considered heroic. Politicians lost their allure after the brutal dictatorships of the Second World War (even Winston was kicked out of office less than three months after VE Day). Wars have become, we are told, easily won due to our superior technology and we can all act the hero from the comfort of our sofas thanks to *Medal of Honour*. Even travel and exploration is now within almost everyone's grasp. As this happened so sporting achievements were increasingly considered to be key examples of heroism. Sport is an arena in which a person's ability can be visibly tested, quantified and compared to the ability of others and such success has always been celebrated by Western culture.

Ancient Greek athletes were considered semi-divine and became the subjects of fantastical stories. Take Milo of Croton for example. He won numerous wrestling titles at the Olympic Games, the Pythian Games, the Isthmian Games and the Nemean Games and was a five-time winner of the Periodonik (the grand slam of all four titles). This led to the likes of Aristotle and Athenaeus telling exaggerated stories about his appetite and strength. It was reputed that he ate 20lbs of meat and drank 18 pints of wine a day and once carried an adult bull before killing it, roasting it and eating it in one day. Ultimately he got his hands stuck in a tree when he was trying to demonstrate his strength and was killed by a pack of wolves. Still, you can't win them all. On top of all that, sport had the added bonus of conforming to the circular heroic narrative. The heroes (footballers) depart from society (go to a training camp and then on to a tournament), undertake a heroic challenge such as killing a dragon (lose on penalties in a quarter-final) before returning triumphantly to a hero's welcome (wear 'comedy' fake breasts on an open-topped bus parade).

In his 1963 book *The Image,* Daniel J. Boorstin argued that before what he called the Graphic Revolution (mass-market print, radio, TV and although he didn't know it, the internet) 'greatness' and 'fame' were not exactly the same thing, but pretty much bang on. The growing influence of television from the 1950s onwards meant that images could be shared more quickly and as post-war media was constructed around TV so the culture of entertainment became increasingly important. As it did the viewer or reader realised they could, along with the producer or writer, quickly and easily bestow 'fame' and they went a bit crazy, doling out 15 minutes' worth here, there and everywhere. Modern celebrity had been born.

While heroes were rare and their achievements spoke for them, resonating through the decades and beyond, celebrities are mass-produced, highly commercialised and highly commodified. They're cynically used to shift units (of what is immaterial) before being cast aside and, as Naomi Klein argues in *No Logo*, sports stars are ideally positioned to exploit (or to be exploited) in this environment of cross-promotion. Singers can make films, actors can model clothes. Sports stars can do both. But how many singers and actors can play centre forward for England or win Olympic gold? Herein lies the marketing appeal of sport and since the advent of television, football more than any other sport has crossed that divide. Yet it turned off the road marked 'hero' and on to the one marked 'celebrity' long before the small screen entered our lives.

• • •

The rise of the sporting hero was a process that began alongside the development of modern sport. The first great English sporting hero was cricketer Dr W.G. Grace, who came to prominence in the 1860s. Before Test matches began Grace played for the (amateur) Gentlemen against the (professional) Players, helping them overturn a 19-game losing streak and cementing his own place in the history of the sport. The good doctor has come to embody the ideals of the amateur ethos but he was well aware of his worth and ensured he made a significant amount of money from his playing career. Nor was he above the odd spot of gamesmanship. Reputedly on one occasion when given out lbw he declared: "Play on, they've come to see me bat, not you, umpire", demonstrating that from the earliest days sports stars' images were manufactured to appear more heroic than they actually were. K.S. Ranjitsinhji (Ranji for short) was another early sports star who played cricket. The Cambridge-educated Maharaja revolutionised batting while playing for Sussex and England in his trademark silk shirt. An indication of his celebrity came in 1901 when *The Autocar* magazine[2] published a photo-feature of him learning to drive.

2 Now known just as Autocar, the magazine was launched in 1895 "in the interests of the mechanically propelled road carriage". Those interests were quite slim – there were just seven such vehicles in the whole of the UK.

Cricket might have produced the first modern English celebrities but it didn't take long for them to be eclipsed by the stars of football. In October 1892 *The Nineteenth Century* journal published an article by Charles Edwardes called 'The New Football Mania'. Edwardes wrote at length about many aspects of the growing phenomenon and noted that footballers in the North of England had become "objects of adoration" to their fans, who would throng at railway stations to cheer the players off to their next fixture and welcome them in similar style on their return. "They are better known than the local members of Parliament", Edwardes wrote. "Even in their workaday dress they cannot move in their native streets without receiving ovations enough to turn the head of a Prime Minister." It was just seven years after the vote to allow professionalism and five years after the creation of the League, yet most insightfully of all Edwardes labelled the players "marketable goods" and who marketed these goods? Yup, you guessed it. "The football agent numbers his clients and advertises them", noted Edwardes before suggesting there was "a lucrative opening for the smart mediator between players and committees".

From the very earliest days of the sport, footballers were afforded celebrity status and in the growing consumer society, entrepreneurs were quick to recognise the potential benefit of linking their brands or products to the stars of what was quickly becoming the nation's favourite sport. American kids had been collecting and trading baseball cards since the 1860s and it was a chap called John Baines who brought the craze across the Pond. He claimed to be the "sole inventor and originator of the famous packet of football cards" and gained a Royal patent. Soon he was printing millions of cards from his Bradford toyshop and distributing them in his distinctive wagon adorned by the words "Baines the Football Card King" and drawn by a horse with a monkey on its back. The cards were shield-shaped and had colourful representations of players and their teams, some of which, such as Imperial Rovers and Manchester Rangers, have all but vanished from the history books. Very few of Baines' cards still exist as many were damaged in a game called 'skaging'. Players would place piles of cards below a wall, while another player would flick his card at the wall winning the pile on to which the card fell. Furthermore the ultimate aim was not to keep the cards but to exchange them for prizes such as footballs or music boxes.

Baines warned his customers not to be "gulled by feeble imitations" but cigarette companies quickly recognised that they could use football cards' growing popularity to build brand loyalty and the market became swamped. The first known cigarette card to show a footballer was produced in 1892 in a series by Fields Favorites [*sic*] Cigarettes. A year later John Player & Sons produced the first set of cards, which featured Castles and Abbeys. Such sets, which would have between 25 to 50 (and sometimes up to 100) cards on related subjects, quickly became commonplace as they encouraged smokers to stick with the same brand in an attempt to complete them. In 1896 W.D. & H.O. Wills produced the first set with a sporting theme featuring 50 cricketers; however, football wasn't far behind and later the same year Marcus & Company, a small Manchester firm, printed the first set of footballers called "Footballers and Club Colours". The impact of cigarette cards shouldn't be underestimated. By the late 1880s cigarette smoking had become big business, growing by 5 per cent a year,[3] and with moving film in its infancy and photo-journalism all but non-existent cigarette cards provided the most prominent visual representation of the players of the day. Victorian writer Clifford Hough labelled the cards as the "working man's encyclopaedia" because "they brought pictures of famous faces and fascinating places to the attention" coupling them with facts about their subject matter. Where footballers were concerned these often went beyond vital statistics and included Top Trumps-style information on the skills of the player featured.

Between 1892 and 1905, 14 known sets totalling 558 cards featuring recognisable footballers were produced by a range of companies. There may well have been more cards, but where the sets were not numbered there is no way of telling how many haven't survived. Some of these were portraits, others photographs in which the players were occasionally shown in suits rather than their kits. Footballers were

---

3   *It's a common misconception that life expectancy was low in Victorian England. While infant mortality rates were high, if you made it to the age of five you were likely to live as long as, if not longer than, a modern-day contemporary. It was only after the growth in availability of cheap tobacco and alcohol and the introduction into the national diet of processed foodstuffs in the last decade of the nineteenth century that life expectancies began to fall, something which has since been offset by modern medicine.*

also featured in a further 11 general sets such as 'Heroes of Sport'. However not all footballers were featured. In his book *Half Time: Football and the Cigarette Card 1890–1940*, David Thompson identified which footballers appeared on most cards between 1892 and 1905. Top of the list was Aston Villa's England centre forward William (Charlie) Athersmith with 12 appearances. He helped Villa win the League title five times in seven seasons including the Double in 1897. While Athersmith was a professional, the next on the list with 11 cards was the amateur Corinthians player G.O. Smith.[4] Thanks to 132 goals in just 137 games many considered him to be the "first great centre forward" and he also captained England between 1896 and 1901. Two goalkeepers appeared on Thompson's list, both of whom featured on cards six times. One was Ned Doig, who was an ever-present for 14 seasons in Sunderland's Team of All Talents and won four titles between 1892 and 1902.[5] The other was William 'Fatty' Foulke, the 24-stone keeper who won the title and FA Cup with Sheffield United. All 12 of the players Thompson listed were capped by their countries, with eight representing England and four playing for Scotland. Only three of the players didn't win the title in the 13-year period Thompson studied. Smith never had the chance as he was an amateur and another, Everton's Jack Sharp, won the title in 1906. Eight of the players listed were either centre forwards or wingers and at least six were captains of their clubs or countries. So, while you didn't have to be a prolific English centre forward and title winner to feature on a cigarette card it certainly enhanced your chances, and if you'd captained your club and country all the better. Failing that, a penchant for eccentric behaviour between the sticks would do. Already in those early years of football's development the media was defining the hierarchy of stardom within the sport. Roy of the Rovers was never going to be a left-back.

The creation in 1901 of the Imperial Tobacco Company through the merger of 13 British cigarette firms meant that football cards were

4   At the time, amateurs were denoted by placing their initials before their surname, professionals by having their initials after their surname. Thus Gilbert Oswald Smith was known as G.O. Smith. Incidentally, the practice continued until 1962 on cricket scorecards.

5   When Sunderland fanzine A Love Supreme listed the club's top 10 players based on a statistical analysis of their achievements for the club, Doig came out on top.

not merely restricted to local markets, thus ensuring footballers' star status increased dramatically from that point on. The first full-colour set was produced by Ogden's, in 1906 although due to the lack of photographic technology they were paintings and again the focus was on the star players of the big clubs; namely, Aston Villa, Blackburn Rovers, Everton, Middlesbrough, Newcastle United, Sheffield United, Tottenham Hotspur, Wolverhampton Wanderers and Woolwich Arsenal. A year later Taddy & Co produced a set of 595 Prominent Footballers which featured oval black-and-white head-and-shoulder shots. And a lot of impressive handlebar moustaches.

The 1920s and 1930s were the heyday of cigarette card collection. In 1922 Pinnace produced a set of 2,462 cards for Godfrey Phillips. In the year before the Second World War, cards began to use photos regularly and Churchman produced two black-and-white sets of full-length staged action shots in which players replicated action from a game, whether it be dribbling or shooting. Wills and John Player began issuing adhesive-backed cards, and albums to stick them into, making collection easier, although this meant biographical details would be discarded, showing already how little value was placed on the individual behind the face.

Second World War paper rationing brought an abrupt halt to the cigarette card phenomenon yet looking at the cards now it's striking how similar the poses were to those of the players who stare out of Panini stickers, Topps Match Attax cards (of which they were the predecessors) or even the head-and-shoulders shots used in TV team line-ups. In 1934 Wills even produced a Radio Celebrities set that featured our old friends George Allison, Teddy Wakeham and Derek McCulloch among names such as Paul Robeson and Gracie Fields. With their identification of so-called stars and their focus on individual players over teams, the cigarette cards fed into and reinforced the growing celebrity culture within football. Players were often also featured in generic sets alongside military figures and explorers, firmly cementing them in the pantheon of English heroes (even the biographical details on Wakeham and McCulloch's cards cited their military records at length). The cards also reinforced patriarchal gender divisions. As internet 'entrepreneurs' the world over will tell you, if there's one thing that sells better than sport it's sex and the cigarette firms were wise to the fact. When women featured it was, as with the heroic stories of old, almost always in passive roles and because of the way they looked. Imaginatively titled series like *Beauties of Today, Beauties of the World* or *Stage and Cinema Beauties* focused on leading actresses and provocative pictures of pin-up girls.

The focus on 'star' players in the cigarette cards began to be mimicked in newspapers too. By the early twentieth century journalists started to focus on individual players in match coverage, often in special columns distinct from general match reports. The first feature profiles of star players began to emerge and players' names were even used to break up copy in articles. In 1905 the *Daily Mirror* confidently declared that football had replaced cricket as England's national sport and footballers were beginning to be featured not just as players.

The year of the *Daily Mirror*'s declaration saw *Athletic News* publish the first *Hello!*-style feature showing a player relaxing off the pitch. Headlined "A Day in the Life of a Footballer", it centred on Sandy Tait, who captained Spurs and won the FA Cup with them in 1901, and showed him playing golf and billiards as well as doing a bit of training. Similar features followed on other players, some showing wives and children. Footballers became columnists too and the fact was used by papers in their advertising. From this point on, players were central to coverage of the game not just because of what they did but because of *who they were*.

As early as 1883 the production of a play called *Football, Or Life As It Is,* which featured a famous player whose name has been lost to time, demonstrated that music hall and theatre recognised the benefits of aligning itself with the fast-growing sport. From 1890 on, *The Era* printed a seasonal 'Theatrical Football' column detailing which pantomimes' casts were engaged in charity games and by 1911 most touring theatre companies would arrive in a town and play the local football team before their first performance, thus announcing their arrival to the area. Football-theatre hit the big time in 1906 with musical hall impresario Fred Karno's *The Football Match,* which featured several ex-players and told the story of attempts to bribe Stiffy the Goalkeeper, originally played by entertainer Harry Weldon. Stiffy, of course, rebuffed such overtures and the popular play ran for several years, with Weldon being replaced in the role by a young Charlie Chaplin.[6] The play's backdrop was a painted crowd scene with holes through which several star players such as Billy Meredith, who played for both Manchester clubs, would stick their heads to make brief cameos.

Music hall producers like Karno realised that you didn't even need to have the footballers appearing on stage to exploit their celebrity, just their attendance could boost ticket sales, and teams were regularly invited to watch comics, with their presence and recent successes, or failures, referenced by the acts. Many charity matches were played in the inter-war years, with players and ex-players facing actors and entertainers "who could foot the leather". Female entertainers reprised their traditional passive roles, kicking off the games but not taking part, selling programmes, rewarding goal-scorers with kisses and occasionally appearing in revealing football 'kits'. The matches themselves took a variety of formats: sometimes goalkeepers were swapped; sometimes the first half was 'serious', while the second half was 'comic'.

As with the whole sports-star phenomenon, cricket led the way by being the first sport to hold celebrity charity games. Dan Leno, the most popular comedian of the day, created a team called the Dainties that included many of his contemporaries. The games against amateur sides took place in a carnival atmosphere with the entertainers dressed in a variety of costumes – Leno once took to the field dressed as a schoolgirl riding a camel. The fattest player at the game, an entertainer called Buster Mott, was used to roll the pitch. The sporting press was less than impressed but tens of thousands of spectators enjoyed the frolics and carnival atmosphere. Three cricket days were held at the Kennington Oval between 1901 and 1903 and films of the events, now sadly lost, were shown around the country. Leno succumbed to alcoholism and died in 1904 aged just 43 and his fellow artistes soon abandoned cricket for football; a sport which would give them greater exposure.

The FA tolerated footballers' involvement with entertainment. It didn't rival the sport but sat neatly alongside it, acting as an advert enhancing the sport's growing brand. However, they took a different

6   *Stan Laurel was another protégé of Karno's and the pair never forgot the debt they owed him, helping him to get a job in Hollywood after he went bankrupt in 1926.*

view to direct competition. When in 1905 a syndicate proposed an indoor league at London's Olympia to be played on a specially woven £5,000 green carpet, the governing body moved to ban teams and their players taking part. A few did anyway but public disinterest saw the tournament fizzle out. While Soccer Aid had been born, Soccer Sixes would have to wait. Crucially what so-called music hall football did was cement the growing link between the sport and entertainment and footballers' place in the realms of modern celebrity.

As players realised that they weren't just sportsmen but entertainers their perception of themselves changed. Steve Bloomer, the Derby County legend who scored 317 top-flight goals, as well as 28 for England in just 23 appearances, was known for his celebrations, famously turning a cartwheel when he scored a goal. This was no reflexive, spur-of-the-moment gesture. Bloomer commented on the style and deliberate nature of his celebrations in his biography. The cartwheel was borrowed from music hall where it had been intro-duced by Fannie Leslie in 1893.[7] The trend Bloomer introduced to the pitch took off and by 1896 match reports in the *Athletic News* were littered with comments about players turning cartwheels after they scored. Following his return to the Baseball Ground in 1910, after five seasons at Middlesbrough, Bloomer took to kicking the ball high into the air as he entered the field of play. Clearly this entertainer had decided he needed a new trademark.

● ● ●

Despite the growing celebrity status of players among fans there was still a less than sympathetic attitude towards professionalism among the game's hierarchy. Members of this upper-middle-class group clung to the idea that professionalism was morally wrong. As they had the greatest access to the media, they used this to control the image of the football professional by discussing them in negative terms. As late as 1936 the FA tried to stop players writing articles for papers, although the ruling was successfully challenged by the Professional Footballers' Association. However, British society changed fundamentally during

---

7   Bizarre as it may seem now, the cartwheel was a phenomenon and street urchins could earn a penny for turning them in the street, and Leslie was greatly angered by other people stealing her idea.

the Second World War. It was a so-called People's War that saw the total mobilisation of the home front softening class divisions and increasing democratic aspirations in the process.

This change was reflected at the cinema. The upper – and upper-middle-class – gentleman hero of the inter-war years, portrayed by the likes of David Niven and Michael Redgrave, was increasingly replaced by the 'common man', embodied by actors like John Mills and Kenneth More, although this new hero maintained many of the virtues of his predecessor. A similar transition took place in football coverage, where the heroic "gentleman amateur" gave way to a new breed of "model professional". Before the war the embodiment of the gentleman amateur footballer was G.O. Smith the amateur, who featured on a significant number of cigarette cards. Educated at Charterhouse and Keble College, Oxford, he walked onto the pitch with his hands in his pockets – a sign of gentlemanly nonchalance – and he refused to shoulder charge his opponents (at the time still legal) or head the ball, believing both to be unsporting. The post-war "model professional" maintained many of these characteristics, such as a sense of fair play; however, they were overwhelmingly working class.

The paper rations that had killed off cigarette cards during the Second World War were lifted in 1953, allowing for a huge increase in both magazine and book production, two media in which the characteristics of the new breed of model professional could be created and celebrated. These media gave post-war footballers the confidence to control and present the versions of their lives the public saw, enabling them to accelerate the active cultivation of their image that their predecessors had begun. This was the era of players like Stanley Matthews, Tom Finney and Billy Wright. All three wrote biographies (in Wright's case four were published, the first when he was just 23) that focused on their simple lifestyles and humble origins.

Matthews in particular also used his biography to deal with criticism that might undermine the perception of him as meeting the virtues of a model professional. He defended himself against accusations of greed and arrogance when he "declined" to play for Stoke's reserves before his move to Blackpool and also accusations that he was not a team player because he dribbled too much and did not pass the ball often enough. The positive narratives developed around the players were continued in magazine articles. *Picture Post* ran a feature on Finney with a series of photos showing him with his wife and working as a plumber in a boiler suit up a ladder. He was a local player born "almost on Preston's doorstep" who married a local girl, was not "aggressively" ambitious and was instead worried about providing for his family. In short, this model professional was a common man.

He was also a one-club man, just like Wright, who only played for Wolves, while Matthews played for just two – Stoke (twice) and Blackpool. As these men came to define the model professional, so developed the idea that modern players moving from club to club in pursuit of a higher salary was part of a corrupted modern game. However, research conducted by academic and journalist Dr Joyce Woolridge in her unpublished PhD thesis shows that before 1946 the highest percentage of a club's squad players who were local was 50 per cent, and the figure was often much lower than that. In contrast to popular opinion the number of local squad players rose after the war, particularly in the 1980s, although these players were often peripheral.

It wasn't just the images that normalised players by showing them in domestic or professional circumstances that were important. From the start magazines like *Football Monthly* used staged photos on their front covers, which, like those that first appeared on cigarette cards in the run-up to the war, focused almost exclusively on individuals. These images always showed the player perfectly groomed and in pristine kit and were often shot from below to make the player seem bigger, heightening the image of them as graceful and athletic and reflecting the representations of Greek athlete heroes of centuries before.

Perhaps the most striking example adorns the cover of Billy Wright's 1956 biography *The World's My Football Pitch*. The title itself is suggestive for a book about a man captaining a country that had just won a war but was fast losing an empire. The illustration on the front cover mimics a familiar shot of Wright leading the England team onto the Wembley turf. He is in pristine kit, clutching the ball in one hand with a look of steely determination on his face, which has been drawn in a way to make him more classically good looking than he actually was. Because of the perspective he obscures one of the stadium's famous towers and dominates the other, thus reinforcing the iconic nature of the England captain and the national stadium; England's 'twin towers'

as Woolridge labels them. Other titles in the same series featured imperial adventurers and soldiers, thereby rooting Wright's place, and by
association the place of the England football captain, in the nation's
familiar heroic narrative. The model professional might have been an
ordinary man but he was one who could grow (literally in the case of
the illustration) to take on the role of leader of the country from the
politicians and soldiers of the Second World War.

Wright wasn't the first player to captain England (that was Cuth-
bert Ottaway), he wasn't even the first player to captain England in
the post-war era (that was George Hardwick), but he was the first
player to become completely synonymous with the role. He went on
to captain England 90 times between 1948 and 1959 and four years
after his retirement the armband had found its way to that other iconic
England captain: Bobby Moore. The West Ham player's captaincy
reinforced the primacy of the role in English culture thanks to two
key factors. Firstly his captaincy of the 1966 World Cup-winning
team (a success which would also cement Wembley's iconic status) and
secondly the fact that he equalled Wright's 90 games as captain – a
record they continue to share and that looks likely to stand for some
considerable time.

Once again the media's use of imagery, and two photos in particular,
ensured the characteristics of the model professional became synonymous with Moore. Firstly there is the famous shot of him holding
the Jules Rimet trophy aloft while being hoisted on the shoulders
of the other England players. They were a team but one of them
was deemed most important and significantly he was the captain;
not, for example, Sir Geoff Hurst, the player who had scored a hat-
trick. The second photo is from the World Cup of 1970 and shows
Moore embracing Pelé after England's group match against Brazil.
It is arguably one of the most iconic football photos of all time and
it is impossible to tell from the photo that Moore had been on the
losing side. Instead it brought to the fore several key qualities of the
idealised model professional – gallantry in defeat, a sense of fair play
and respect for opponents.[8] Through the media's coverage of Wright

8   The photo is often wrongly shown with Moore on the left and Pelé on the right; however, this
is a reverse image which has been, for whatever reason, 'flipped'. In the background between their
heads a stadium sign which says 'Mexico' can be seen in reverse.

and then Moore the position of England captain was bestowed huge national symbolism, more so than the same role in other sports such as cricket or Rugby Union. Fans, players and journalists cling to this almost mythical status today, much to the bemusement of foreigners.

• • •

One man stands astride the post-war history of English football like a colossus. He has played for England, managed England and more than anyone else defines the nation's football characteristics. That man is Roy Race. Just like Beowulf centuries before, Race came to embodying the values and ideals deemed important to his society while marginalising women and framing what were considered to be threats to that society from outside its borders. He typified the characteristics associated with the archetypal 'model professional' which was being created in the post-war years just as he was pulling on his boots for the first time. Race was a gentleman blessed with talent who always put the team first. He displayed humility and dignity, had an exceptional disciplinary record and he never cheated on his wife. As the player began to dominate the landscape of football literature, so "Roy of the Rovers stuff" became the default phrase for heroic on-field performances, and when a player was labelled the new "Roy of the Rovers", we all knew what that meant.

It's not just in England that cartoon characters are used to reinforce heroic images of nationalism. The French media was packed full of such references during the World Cup the country hosted in the summer of 1998. Ten days after Les Bleus' victory over Brazil in the final the weekly magazine *Télérama,* which at the time had a circulation of 750,000 and a readership of more than a million, ended an editorial about the team's manager with the words: "Aimé Jacquet est notre nouvel Astérix". So well known is the magic potion-guzzling, Roman-bashing Frenchman in his home country and so clear are the characteristics that he represents that the statement needed no explanation.[9] Significantly the comparison was not only invoked because Jacquet's indomitable Gauls had managed to repel

---

9   *To be fair this isn't much of a surprise; the French Army named their first satellite, launched in November 1965,* Astérix.

the invading hordes but also because the coach himself represented an idealised bygone era which stood in contrast to Americanised, consumer-focused, modern France.

In England comics can trace their roots back to 1832 when *The Boys' and Girls' Penny Magazine* was first published. The eight-page magazine ran for just 23 issues but confidently claimed to have had a sale of 835,000 at its peak. The revolution in publishing that occurred in the latter half of the nineteenth century coincided with an improvement in education opportunities. The Elementary Education Act was introduced in 1870 and a decade later school was made compulsory until the age of ten, although many youngsters still attended only irregularly or managed to avoid it completely. While literacy grew among the working classes most were still barely able to read. Furthermore the cost of books made them doubly prohibitive. However there was still a market for cheap, simple, thrilling stories and so the weekly Penny Dreadfuls were born. These new publications focused on violent crime stories and were sprinkled with lurid illustrations but had few strips as we would recognise them today. Sweeney Todd is the most enduring character to come from the genre, having appeared in *The String of Pearls: A Romance,* an 18-part serialisation in *The People's Periodical and Family Library.*

The Boy's Own Paper was launched in 1879 by the Religious Tract Society to provide "first-class stories for boys of all backgrounds" and counter what was considered the corrupting influence of the Penny Dreadfuls. The title ran until 1967 and while the first edition included articles about science and natural history it also presciently included an article entitled 'My First Football Match', although this actually turned out to be a game of rugby. It spawned a new wave of publications that presented an idealised image of masculinity. The main characters were fair-minded, plucky, athletic and had upper lips of the stiff variety.

As literacy increased, the Penny Dreadfuls eventually gave way to titles targeted at a younger audience, which focused on action, adventure and sport. There were superhuman heroes like the Amazing Wilson who featured in *The Wizard.* Wilson, who was born in 1795, played a key role in the Battle of Waterloo, came second in the 1896 Olympic Marathon and won the 1952 Olympic pentathlon before taking 20 wickets as England beat Australia in the Ashes the following year. There were also many football stories but these were either set in schools or were crime stories which featured footballers but used the sport itself as merely a backdrop. However, it wasn't until after the Second World War that publications we might call comics – that is with the stories told through a series of drawings with minimal text – developed. Yet no comic told the story of a modern-day professional footballer, or any sports star for that matter, in a relatively believable way. That all changed in the 1950s when the editor of *Tiger* asked writer Frank S. Pepper to create a realistic football story.

I use the word 'realistic' loosely. Roy Race enjoyed an astonishingly long 44-year playing career during which he won three European Cups, ten League titles, nine FA Cups and eight Cup Winners Cups. He graced the pages of *Tiger* from 1954 to 1976, when he broke out into his own eponymous comic that closed in March 1993. The closure prompted a groundswell of calls for Roy of the Rovers' return. In September 1993 the title returned, but as a monthly focused on Roy's son Rocky and it lasted just over 18 months. Four years later Race found a home as a strip in *Match of the Day* magazine but he has not been seen since that title closed in 2001.

Alan Tomlinson and Christopher Young in their essay on Race argue that the comic's success was built on the excitement generated by what they call "the immortality of the overdog", which mimics the romance of the triumph of the underdog by seeing Roy's team the Melchester Rovers consistently grab victory from the jaws of defeat. In this way the comic replicates the circular heroic narrative of struggle or threat being faced then overcome. In games, Rovers almost always fall behind, only for Roy to save the day with a trademark last-minute, left-foot 'Rocket'. The League title is almost always won on the last day of the season and on the rare occasions the Rovers face relegation this too is avoided at the last gasp, while being almost inevitably accompanied by cup success sustaining the dramatic ebb and flow.

There was something of Billy Wright about the early depictions of Race, with his long shorts, rolled-up sleeves and shock of blonde hair. While his appearance altered over the years as the fashions of the day changed and Roy grew older, he retained his virtuous love of the game. During the 1973/74 season while chasing a unique FA and League Cup double the Melchester chairman offered each player a £7,000-per-goal bonus and the team began to talk of little else. Race was outraged as in his mind the prospect of winning should have been more than enough incentive for the players. His anger led to him making a series of poor tackles and almost getting booked. Only his previously exemplary disciplinary record spared him, meaning that he would retire without a stain on his disciplinary record. Football was moving on however. The 1970s saw the emergence of a very different type of football comic character – Jon Stark "Match Winner for Hire", who graced the pages of *Scoop*. Stark would roam from club to club charging "£1,000 per match plus £250 per goal – no payment for lost game".

We were told Stark was the "footballer of the future", a nightmare prediction of where football was headed but already he was more realistic than Race. Bobby Moore's 1970 autobiography contained a whole chapter on his business activities in which he defended himself against critics who claimed he was "turning his back on football". Could it be that England's World Cup-winning captain, the archetypal player, was more Jon Stark than Roy Race? The echo of the 'gentleman amateur', the idea that the game should be 'played' for love, still resonates through the English game today. In their book *The Italian Job* Gianluca Vialli and Gabrielle Marcotti argue that one of the key differences between Italian and English football is that: "To the Italian footballer, football is a job: to the English footballer it's a game." Expanding the point they explain: "If it's a job, the objective is simply to get the result, which is winning. It doesn't matter how it's achieved. If it's a game, the objective is to compete, to strive, to give 100 per cent effort." Roy Race gave 100 per cent and, for him, winning was a happy accident.

There was a place for women in his world but it was mainly on the periphery. When fans were occasionally shown watching Rovers on TV they were male with women (sisters or mothers) only in the background, either disinterested or providing tea for their menfolk. Similarly players' wives and mothers were mainly on hand simply to fulfil the domestic chores. While sex was never on the agenda of a comic aimed at boys, there was still room for the odd relationship.

Roy's best friend Blackie Gray fell for French film star Suzanne Cerise but her involvement with another man disrupted Rovers' preparations for the 1963 European Cup Final against Nettruno as Blackie turned up late for the Paris final. A goal down at half time, Roy decided his team needed a morale boost and brought Suzanne into the dressing room where she pouted: "Mes heros! You win for me, yes? I have a surprise for you eef you do." The team played like men possessed and Blackie scored the winner (predictably) in the last minute. What was Suzanne's surprise? That she was getting married and wanted Blackie to be best man. Race's opinion was clear: "Phew, now Blackie won't have Suzanne on his mind he can concentrate on football", and back to the edge of his world went the ladies. For a few years at least.

Sir Alex Ferguson once said of David Beckham: "His life changed when he met his wife ... I saw his transition to a different person." He would probably have said the same of Roy when he found love. Race met his future wife – Penny Laine – through her job as secretary to Melchester's chairman. They married at the end of the 1975/76 season; significantly the first in which the Rovers failed to pick up an honour since Roy signed for them. Five years later, with Race and Penny's marriage going through a tough patch, Rovers were relegated for the only time in Race's career and he took up the offer to manage Walford. While there, he was photographed by paparazzi with his secretary at a supporters' club dinner. Race's intentions were both innocent and made explicit to the reader, but once again a woman's influence was causing him trouble. The comic's message was subtle but clear: women have no place in the world of football and when they do enter it, they are a disruptive influence.

English football has always been distrustful of outsiders and *Roy of the Rovers* also tapped into and reinforced a range of xenophobic perceptions. Again the comic's implicit message was clear: abroad is a dangerous place and foreigners, just like women, are not to be trusted. Rovers' success at home led them into Europe on a regular basis and the teams they faced displayed a variety of unflattering characteristics. They were either unfit, tactically naïve, lacking in bottle or sneaky. If they went ahead they didn't try to score more goals, they protected their lead (Kevin Keegan would be disgusted). In short they were everything that fine upstanding *English* Roy was not.

If the Europeans were devious, the South Americans were down-right dangerous. Twice in the 1960s alone the entire Rovers team were kidnapped on the continent, with their plane having been shot down the first time. On the second a couple of 'friendly' rebels gave them some mysterious carioca juice to help them overcome their ordeal and win their game, which they did thanks to Roy (predictably) scoring an overhead kick in the last minute. Were the rebels witch doctors or drug pushers? Either way it was not a flattering portrayal. Rovers continued to face danger on their travels into the 1980s, when it reached its devastating peak. In 1986 the team bus was accidentally hit by a car bomber during a tour of Basran and eight of the team were killed. In the real world the storyline earned the comic a rebuke from the Commission for Racial Equality for its anti-Arab attitude; a line had been crossed.

Race's playing career ended in 1993 when he lost control of his helicopter while on a scouting mission. He survived although his left foot – the one which had launched so many Rockets – was amputated. That the working-class-lad-made-good had his playing career destroyed by the trappings of wealth that very career had brought him seemed a fitting metaphor for English football in the first year of the Premier League. That Race's accident came just a few weeks after the tragic death of another English legend, Bobby Moore himself, made it even more poignant. As Boorstin might have argued, the media and its audience have colluded in creating footballer-celebrities. While it happens at greater speed and to more players now, it's a process which began in the earliest days of the sport. Race still frames the narrative of English football and there is much lamenting the fact that today's celebrity footballers are at odds with the ideal 'model professional' he represented. However, the model professional is itself a media construct. The biggest irony of all of this is that the most heroic of all English footballers – Roy Race – is also the most synthetic; he was the one who never existed at all.

CHAPTER 12

ROY RACE GROWS UP
AND GETS LOADED

Eventually we all grow up (or pretend to at least) and while Roy Race was coming to terms with the loss of his left leg, a whole host of people who had been kids in his heyday were coming to terms with the loss of their youth. As they did it dawned on them that there was no publication that dealt with football in a way that now appealed to them. "I realised there wasn't really a magazine out there that I wanted to buy that was having the sort of conversations I was having with my mates down the pub and at games," said Karen Buchanan, who was launch editor of *FourFourTwo*. "There was only really *Shoot!* and *Match!* and I was getting a bit old to have posters of Ryan Giggs on my wall. I loved *When Saturday Comes* but it didn't really have interviews with players and it was brilliant but quite political back then. I thought there was room for something that could be a bit more fun in some ways."

In the offices of magazine publishers IPC, James Brown, who launched *loaded,* was having similar thoughts: "In the late 80s and early 90s the music industry was full of guys who bonded by talking about football. It had become a big thing but I was just aware that there wasn't a magazine about how our lives really were. The passion people have for football wasn't reflected in the English media that I was subject to. It was dull and I thought football was exciting. If you read *GQ*, if you read *Esquire*, if you read *Arena*, they didn't have any football in and I couldn't understand that." It was 1994 and all this was about to change.

• • •

To chart the history of magazines you have to first define what a magazine is, which is much easier to say than to do. The gravure printing technique that enabled the production of the glossy, full-colour, photo and design-led products we know today wasn't widely available until the late 1930s. Before that there was considerable crossover in terms of design, content and the type of paper stock used by a variety of publications. We can trace the genesis of magazines, in name if nothing else, to the eighteenth century when Edward Cave, under the pen name Sylvanus Urban, launched *Gentlemen's Magazine* in 1731. There had been periodicals before but these tended to be scientific journals or they were written entirely by one person like the German publication *Erbauliche Monaths-Unterredungen* (the catchy English translation is *Edifying Monthly Discussions*), penned by Johann Rist. There were also the numerous pamphlets we discussed way back in Chapter 1. They tended to be one sheet of paper, sometimes printed on both sides, on very rare occasions folded, and they were extremely disposable. What Cave did differently was that he started collecting these pamphlets, grouping together the best ones and printing them on a monthly basis.

Furthermore it was this publication that first used and then popularised 'magazine' to refer to a literary product. At that point a magazine was somewhere to store goods (not necessarily armaments) and Cave decided his publication was also a "storehouse, into which were to be garnered all treasures of Wit, Humor, or Intelligence that could be gleaned from the whole ephemeral press". The term caught on and in 1755 Samuel Johnson included the new meaning in his dictionary, crediting Cave in the process. *Gentlemen's Magazine* was hamstrung by all the problems that beset early newspapers, namely a variety of taxes, print technology that was inefficient and produced a poor quality product, and a distribution network that wasn't really a network and didn't distribute much. Still, Cave's *Gentlemen's Magazine* was a success and was published more or less uninterrupted until 1922.

As taxes on newsprint were repealed, printing technology improved and the railway system developed so the cost of magazines fell, opening them up to the middle classes and children. In 1909, 30 years after the Religious Tract Society launched *The Boy's Own Paper* and with football by then coming to dominate the sports market, Amalgamated

Press launched *The Boys' Realm Football Library*. Was it a magazine? It had many of the characteristics but, although it was aimed at boys, it wasn't a comic because in those early years the stories it contained were written not drawn. The title became so popular it spawned *The Boys' Realm Sports Library* and the *Sports Library*. The stories were in keeping with many from that era, mixing derring-do and adventure more often than not with some plucky schoolboys at the centre of it all. *The Boys' Realm* usually contained two stories: one featuring a lad called Jack Noble (the clue to the type of upstanding young chap he was is in his name) and the other featured the Blue Crusaders, a fictional amateur factory team that over the course of time made it all the way to the first division.

This inclusion of the Football League in a story was a significant acknowledgement of the professionalism of football at a time when it was still frowned upon in some quarters. The sport also increasingly found its way into other non-football titles such as *The Magnet Library* in whose pages Billy Bunter resided. Such was the ubiquity of the sport that Bunter even appeared on the front of one edition of *The Magnet* playing (or at least trying to play) football. Until the First World War these titles co-existed with the early sports newspapers that were also increasingly dominated by football. In 1900 Edward Hulton's weekly *Athletic News* was renamed *Football Chat*. With printing and photographic technology being considerably different to what it is today, the publication can't really be classed as a magazine in the modern sense. It was black and white and printed on paper stock; however, in design terms there were similarities with its modern-day successors. *Football Chat* had minimal writing on its front page, instead being dominated by a large masthead and a large picture usually drawn by Dudley Ward, one of the leading cartoonists of the day.

The First World War created a hiatus in publication. Once peace returned so did the football-related titles but the demarcation between the football newspapers and boys magazines was less clear in the inter-war years. "In the beginning, in the old days, there were newspapers and there was the *Boy's Own*, *Ripping Yarn*-type stories," said Martin Westby who runs the *Soccerbilia* website, which is dedicated to chronicling the history of British football magazines.

"Then somebody very quickly worked out that a few snippets of football news really helped the sales." This merging of sports-news with fictional content brought inter-war publications closer in style to modern-day magazines.

Another modern feature was a good old circulation fight. If you've got kids you'll probably know that any trip to the newsagents is almost guaranteed to lead to plaintive appeals for you to buy them the latest magazine because it has got this or that piece of tat attached to it. This is not a modern phenomenon. Back in the 1920s the big companies DC Thompson and Amalgamated Press slugged it out toe to toe in the football magazine market by offering all manner of prizes and giveaways with their titles. DC's *Topical Times* offered a range of books including *Britain's Best Footballers* and the four- part *Star Team Football Album*. When they launched *Adventure* in September 1921 they hoped to tempt readers with the promise of a free card featuring a footballer each week for the first eight weeks, despite the fact it wasn't an exclusively football title. The first was of "Dimmock the Dazzler" and the others included Charlie Buchan, who would come to have a much greater impact on the football magazine market after the Second World War.

This paled next to Amalgamated's *Football Favourite* that was tempting readers with a "£300 must-be-won contest within" as well as things like a three-part *Football Handbook*. People who bought *Sports Budget* could collect a three-edition *Who's Who of Famous Footballers*. It was during this period that the publishers also started looking towards the men's lifestyle market with serious intent. Pearson launched *Men Only* in 1935 and if you weren't clear from the title who it was aimed at the editorial hammered home the message: "We don't want women readers, we won't have women readers." Despite this, it wasn't until the 1970s, when the title fell into the hands of Paul Raymond, that it would become the pornographic title that it is today. Initially it had articles on a variety of topics, although in a foretaste of what was to come it was the first UK title to print the pin-up pictures drawn by Peruvian artist Alberto Vargas.[1]

1   Vargas' work is now highly regarded, with one piece selling for $71,600 in 2003. In comparison to the current content of Men Only it is incredibly tame; however, in the 1940s the US postal service tried to revoke Esquire magazine's postal permit for printing Vargas' pictures.

In 1939 a real war put paid to DC's and Amalgamated's circulation battle. While the First World War had drawn the adult and children's sections of the football magazine market together, the Second World War separated them again. The immediate post-war years also gave birth to the first publication that can really be considered a football magazine as we would know it today: *Charles Buchan's Football Monthly*. Buchan had played for Sunderland in his heyday, scoring a club-record 224 goals in 413 games before seeing out his career with Herbert Chapman's Arsenal. Some saw Buchan as an awkward character. He had quit Arsenal as an 18-year-old over a row about travelling expenses and he walked out on the first day of his second stint citing a sub-standard kit. But Chapman valued Buchan's independence and intelligence and his faith paid off. During Buchan's time at Highbury the offside law was changed, requiring only two, not three, defenders to be goal-side of a forward player. Many teams struggled to deal with the extra space the rule change created for the attacking side, and Buchan argued that the centre-half should play a deeper-lying, more defensive role as a consequence. Chapman listened and the much-copied WM formation was born. Buchan grabbed 49 goals in 102 games for the Gunners before hanging up his boots in 1928 and becoming a journalist working for the *News Chronicle* and the BBC. In 1947 he co-founded the Football Writers' Association and by the time he launched *Football Monthly* he was a widely respected pundit and commentator.

"*Football Monthly* was important because it was the first to have the whole front in colour," said Westby. "The women's magazines had mastered that technique of full-colour but it still wasn't really happening in sport. Early editions of *Football Monthly* featured a black-and-white photo which someone hand-tinted; that's where you get very evocative 1950s images from. Also, prior to *Football Monthly*, other titles had got stuck on what to do in the summer so they all did boxing or horse racing or cricket. *Football Monthly* was the first one which really took a gamble and tried to fill the summer with football content." As far as Buchan was concerned there was a lack of good football content all year round. Writing in his autobiography *A Lifetime in Football*, Buchan explained his motivation for launching the magazine: "For many years, after the old *Athletic News* closed down, there was no paper or magazine devoted exclusively to the game. It was in a bid to fill this gap that in 1951 I started the *Charles Buchan's Football Monthly*. It has caught on so well that it was obvious something of the kind was desperately needed." Buchan wasn't wrong and the magazine's circulation continued to rise until it hit a peak of 254,000 in the heady days following England's 1966 World Cup triumph.

Buchan himself was not alive to see either, having passed away while on holiday in France in June 1960. He had been contributing to the magazine until the issue before his death and the following edition featured two pages of tributes to the man whose vision had created such a hugely influential title. Although aimed at adults – the cover price of 1s 6d made that clear – it was read by many young boys including a host of future football presenters and commentators such as John Motson, Gary Newbon, Jim Rosenthal and Nick Owen. Of course the magazine is dated in many respects but it is insightful how several of the issues covered are ones that English football is still wrestling with today. Here's Len Shackleton writing in September 1954 after England's defeats to Hungary the previous year: "Now, to be quite fair, it must be remembered that most of our lads had just completed a season, most of them having figured in 40 or 50 League and Cup games. And, from experience I can tell you that by the time a player has operated throughout such a full programme he has had sufficient football for a month or so and is ready for a rest." Shackleton went on to add: "Look at the Hungarians. Their players have the ability to control a ball perfectly. They can 'kill' it stone-dead in an instant or, if the needs be, pass it very accurately first time to a teammate. Every man throughout the team is a master of the ball. Which is more than can be said of any current England team." So, England were trounced by Hungary because they were tired after a long, rigorous season and lacked the skill on the ball their opponents demonstrated? It's good to see those two problems have been put to bed during the six decades since Shackleton pointed them out ...

In 1952 another former Sunderland hero put his name to a weekly publication when *Raich Carter's Soccer Star* was published. Carter had captained Sunderland to the League title in 1937 and the FA Cup the following year, but his link to the *Soccer Star* was relatively short-lived and his name was gone from the title within three years. Unlike *Football Monthly*, *Soccer Star* was printed on news stock and never had colour photos on the inside but it is an important title for two reasons. Firstly, from the 1958/59 season it started printing the attendances, team sheets and half-time and full-time scores for all League matches in England and the Scottish First Division. It was the first time this had been done consistently, making it a goldmine for stats fans then and now. Secondly, its success enabled its owners Echo Publications, to launch a sister title in 1960 – *World Soccer*. Eventually *Soccer Star*, under attack from new weekly titles like *Jimmy Hill's Football Weekly,* a proper glossy magazine, was incorporated into *World Soccer*, although its other sister title, *Speedway Star,* is still going strong. Weekly titles were where the party was at for publishers, who had now worked out there was a market among teenagers and young boys.

In 1968 *Football Monthly*'s owners Longacre Press decided to join the fun and launched *Goal!* It was nothing more than a weekly version of *Football Monthly,* which dropped Buchan's name from the title in 1971. In 1969 IPC launched *Shoot!* and by 1971 the two new titles were each selling 220,000 copies weekly. *Scorcher* was also launched in this period, expanding the *Roy of the Rovers* idea into a full comic focused only on football. However, the bubble quickly burst and *Goal!* was incorporated by *Shoot!* in 1974 (before making a brief reappearance 21 years later) and *Scorcher* also folded. In the process *Football Monthly*'s market was obliterated and it closed in 1974 leaving *World Soccer* as the only football magazine available for adults. "A lot of football titles went under in the 1970s with the three-day week, the power cuts and the strikes in the Winter of Discontent," said Westby. "They could all see that something might work, but the price of paper went crazy and the cost of production and the cost of staff was high as the printers were highly unionised. The margins were so tight that quite a lot of people, like Jimmy Hill, got their fingers burnt."

Gavin Hamilton, who has edited *World Soccer* since 1997, attributes the title's longevity to the fact that it provides a global view of the game and one that can be taken seriously. "The magazine started in 1960 really on the back of what happened with Real Madrid in the European Cup. That opened people's eyes to the wider world of football. In England we're still inward looking. We're an island nation and we don't tend to look abroad for inspiration but with the magazine we've always tried to provide a different perspective and show there is a life outside England and we've always tried to be serious. I wouldn't say we're a trade magazine but we're always trying to produce content that will be useful for people who work in football and who take the game seriously." More recently, the development of a worldwide interest in European football has enabled *World Soccer* to build a global audience that Hamilton suggests is also to the magazine's advantage. "We've grown our readership as English-speaking countries like America, Canada and Australia have become interested in what's going on in Europe and the rest of the world over the last 20 years. That global readership is what's kept us going while other magazines have declined. We're not bracketed by a recession in one country."

• • •

These various amalgamations and the fact that *Football Monthly* could go from a peak circulation of 250,000 to closure in just six years demonstrated the highly volatile nature of the magazine market. In 1962 a Royal Commission said that magazine titles "come and go with a frequency which if it were found in the newspaper press, would indicate alarming instability". By this time the men's sector of the magazine market had all but disappeared. *The Writers' and Artists' Yearbook* of 1963 listed more than fifty titles aimed at women but just seven for men. Of those, four were menswear trade publications and one, *Esquire*, was an American magazine. So, if you were a bloke and you wanted something British to read, your choice was limited to *Man About Town* and *Men Only*. Within a decade the former had shut and the latter had been rebranded by Paul Raymond.

The men's lifestyle magazine market was proving a hard nut to crack. IPC had a go, launching *Club* in June 1970. Pictures of famous women, such as Raquel Welch and Bridget Bardot, displaying maximum amounts of cleavage in minimal amounts of clothing adorned the front (there was even one topless cover shot) while inside pictures of semi-naked women were interspersed with feature articles on a variety of topics. It wouldn't look out of place tucked between the likes of *FHM, loaded* and *Zoo* on the shelves of your newsagent today but it lasted just 21 issues. In a farewell article, editor Terry Hornet claimed that while 500,000 men read *Club* just 80,000 bought a copy, something which made the title financially unsustainable. "The shame is that *Club*'s closing will probably make any other publisher wary of putting out a similar product for young men." How right he was.

During the 1970s the term 'men's magazine' became synonymous with top-shelf titles, the only ones that were prospering as they did not rely on the advertising their mainstream counterparts were losing to TV and the new newspaper supplements. Paul Raymond swept up a series of failed titles such as *Club* and *Razzle* to add to *Men Only* in his growing porn empire. It was perhaps inevitable that someone would try and produce a football magazine that tapped into that market and in April 1982 *Football Kick!* was launched. It labelled itself "The NEW football magazine for adults" and claimed to be "For thinking adults whose minds range further than the Roy of the Rovers coverage currently supplied by the existing publications on the market." An action shot of Kevin Keegan graced the cover along with a picture of a model sporting a strategically placed scarf hinting at what the centre-spread had to offer inside. Content included Malcolm Allison telling readers that "English football is run by fools and television". *Football Kick!* lasted just 11 issues, the final one featuring Sammy Lee as its cover star. Thankfully he was fully clothed.

The women's sector of the magazine market has always been stronger than the men's. While *Men Only* died off in all but name, *Woman* and *Woman's Own,*[2] also launched in the 1930s, are still going strong. The year *Club* went under, *Cosmopolitan* was first published in the UK. These titles didn't just cater for women; as much as 25 per cent of their readership was men starved of their own general interest titles. Titles like *Company, Elle* and *Harpers & Queen* all responded by having sections or supplements dedicated

---

2   *It was in an article in* Woman's Own *that Margaret Thatcher made her (infamous) "there's no such thing as society" comment. The article 'Aids, Education and the Year 2000!' was written by Douglas Keay and Thatcher actually said: "Who is society? There is no such thing!" The furore caused by the comment prompted an extremely rare clarification from Downing Street (but we all knew what she meant).*

to men. *Cosmopolitan* went one further in April 1978 and produced *Cosmopolitan Man*, its front cover featuring Jack Nicholson peering rather ominously over the shoulder of French actress Aurore Clément. It was a one-off. As Dylan Jones, who went on to edit *GQ*, later wrote in the *Independent*, it was "a time when any men's magazine that didn't rely on pornography was considered commercial suicide".

Within a decade that theory had been emphatically disproved and the men's lifestyle magazine was here to stay thanks to the launch of *Arena*. It was dreamt up by Nick Logan, who had previously launched *The Face*, "a visual-orientated youth culture magazine", in 1980. Logan had edited *NME* and *Smash Hits* but *The Face* was the type of magazine he wanted to read. As no one would back him he put up £3,500 of his own money to produce the first issue and sold 56,000 copies (ironically he was helped by a strike that kept *NME* off the news stands when he launched). *The Face* became an iconic title, but as he got older Logan wanted to read a different type of magazine and so the idea for *Arena*, a quarterly, up-market publication, was born in 1986.

Another new magazine hit the shelves in the same year – Robert Maxwell's *Sportweek*. It's easy to forget that at the time the late Cap'n Bob was battling it out with Rupert Murdoch to become the country's least-loved media mogul. *Sportsweek*, a glossy, full-colour weekly, was part of Maxwell's master plan to win that heavyweight bout. One measure of his intent was the fact that he attended the magazine's unveiling to advertisers. Another was the fact that he ploughed £1m into promoting the launch on TV, billboards and the shirts of Derby County, one of the two football teams he owned. "Get inside sport, look inside *Sportsweek*" urged the campaign, which targeted intelligent sports fans. Roger Kelly, the deputy sports editor of the *Mail on Sunday*, was poached to become editor and in what was arguably an even bigger coup Eamonn McCabe, a four-time sports photographer of the year, was lured away from the *Observer* to become picture editor.

The magazine had a cover price of 80p and was aimed at affluent young men (a *Sportsweek* Filofax was one gift designed to tempt them to part with £55 for annual subscription). Early editions sold between 80,000 and 110,000 suggesting that in the long term *Sportsweek* would meet its 75,000 target. It wasn't to be. Despite initial plaudits the magazine offered little different, either in the breadth or style of content, than what was already on offer in the newspapers. Football and cricket were the most covered sports; women were all but ignored. Kelly soon left to join *The Times* as sports editor and Maxwell struggled to find a replacement before losing interest and focusing on the launch of a new newspaper, the *London Daily News*. *Sportsweek*'s sales slumped to 40,000 and in February 1987, less than six months after the first issue, Maxwell announced its closure.

The revenue generated by the cover price is less important for a magazine than the revenue generated by advertising and *Sportsweek*'s failure was in part due to *Arena*'s success. Logan's new title reached sales of 65,000 in its first year and this precipitated the launches of *GQ*, *Esquire* and *For Him* (which quickly became *FHM*). Suddenly the marketplace for magazines aimed at affluent young men, a market that had only recently been considered non-existent, became very crowded. But as James Brown recalled, football, something that was such a key factor in so many men's lives, was anathema to these new titles. "I sold a piece to *Arena* about a new type of football boot called Blades," he said. "While I was writing about that I found out about another boot called Predator, which was developed by Craig Johnston the ex-Liverpool player. That was the first press ever on that boot and it appeared at the back of the magazine as a single column. The people who were working in the lifestyle media didn't seem to have the lifestyle me and my mates had, which was: get drunk; go to football matches; go to night clubs, go on tours, follow bands around."

• • •

This was the cigarette-and-alcohol infused heyday of Britpop and in the wake of the Taylor Report, *Nessun Dorma*, *Fever Pitch* and Sky TV, fans had stopped fighting and started hugging each other in the Haçienda. They were, we were told, no longer a problem that needed to be contained. Yet the magazine market had yet to acknowledge this. "We just happened to launch *FourFourTwo* at the right time I guess," Karen Buchanan, the magazine's launch editor, told me. "Football was becoming cool and people were realising they could come out of the closet and say 'I'm a football fan'. Maybe there was a bit of a backlash after all the shit football had been through in the 1980s. There were intelligent, fun people wanting to have intelligent, fun conversations about football but that had always been there." For Buchanan, the importance of fanzines can't be overstated: "They were absolutely at the crux of *FourFourTwo*," she said. Like Nick Hornby, the author of *Fever Pitch*, Buchanan was a regular at John Gaustad's bookshop Sportspages. "It was just this really gorgeous Mecca for going along and finding really bizarre fanzines from all sorts of different clubs. They'd take people to task and they'd get to the nuts and bolts of their club and they had humour and vibrancy. But the best ones were the ones that could be read by any football fan, and that's what I always wanted *FourFourTwo* to be. What I think unites all football fans is that mostly our teams are all shit. Occasionally something quite good happens and you revel in it. You spend most of your time hoping for that day and there's something quite bonding about that. That was reflected in the best of the fanzines."

At the time Buchanan was working for Haymarket Publishing editing the business magazine *Wine and Spirit International*. When her boss, Simon Canter, took her to lunch and asked her if she had any ideas for a new publication her answer was simple: a football magazine for grown-ups. "We spent a year working on it at evenings and weekends in secret," Buchanan said. "We put together a dummy edition and had some qualitative and quantitative feedback on that which suggested we should go for it and so we launched in August 1994. Newspapers were very narrow in their coverage at the time and I found that very frustrating as a fan and as an avid consumer of magazines. I just felt at the time there weren't really any long interviews with players, or managers, or people involved with the game. I wanted to find out what made people tick, which is the essential thing that all journalists want to find out. We used to create a lot of bizarre random lists. All the fun things you talk about with your mates. The whole idea of *FourFourTwo* was that it would give you the information to either back up your argument in the pub or start another one."

While Buchanan was working on the launch of *FourFourTwo* for Haymarket, over at their rivals IPC James Brown was working on *loaded,* which launched four months earlier. "There's a certain mythology around the idea of *loaded* that I created to help promote it," Brown told me when we met in his London office. "That was that me and my mate were on a trip to see Leeds play Stuttgart in Barcelona and I said: 'We should have a magazine like that.' That's not actually true; I'd been working on it for quite some time in the development rooms of a huge, boring publishing company." That football was at the heart of that mythology demonstrates its importance both to Brown and the magazine. "Football was really important to me because I grew up in an era when Leeds were a genuinely huge club. Between me being six and nine we were in three FA Cup Finals. When I was nine or ten we were in the European Cup final. I can remember Alan Clarke coming back from the World Cup in 1970 and being stood in his kitchen and him unpacking his bag, because he was my neighbour. So football was ingrained in my life and I just wanted to have a magazine that had football and music in it. I'd worked at the *NME* for four or five years. I'd done music so I wanted to have something that had football."

Fanzines had little impact on Brown at the time he was working on *loaded* and while he is a fan of *The End* it was, he said, "just one of a hundred influences". However, he expressed virtually identical sentiments to Buchanan about the newspaper coverage of the time failing to reflect the passion he and other football fans had for the sport. "There was nowhere at all that seemed to write about football properly. The newspapers would very rarely have a footballer in the colour supplements. They'd very rarely have an interesting football story. The sports pages were invariably the same boring questions. A lot of the great writers that I liked were the American new journalists like Tom Wolfe, George Plimpton and Hunter Thompson. A lot of their great pieces were actually sports pieces and I wanted to read stories like that. We wanted sportsmen who were characters. A lot of the sportsmen we interviewed have gone on to be TV presenters: Paul Merson, Steve Claridge, Peter Beagrie. Peter Beagrie rode a motor bike into a hotel on an Isle of Wight pre-season tour. That makes a really great story, a lot more interesting than just 'here's a really boring interview with Gary Lineker'.

"I was just aware as an editor and as a journalist that you'd go and find a good story wherever it was," Brown continued. We would always try and have a big football story in *loaded* or a big sports story, but also at the back end we had the Hedonist's Handbook where we would have single pages on different subjects and we'd have football in there too. So Mike Sheron scores 50 goals for Stoke in the Third Division; I knew that was important. If you were a fan of Wolves, Steve Bull and Andy Mutch were important. Not only were the magazines and the newspapers that came before *loaded* not really doing very interesting big stories, they would never have featured stories from lower League clubs."

Talking to Buchanan and Brown it strikes me that, like Nick Logan with *The Face* and *Arena*, they effectively both created a magazine they wanted to read themselves and that strong sense of identity was the foundation for their success. Buchanan agrees: "I wanted to know lots and lots of things about footballers: their lives, the way they played. I kind of did it for me but I think there were so many people who were un-catered for at the time. I was also a massive fan of *loaded*. I loved their irreverence and humour. It was brilliant. It was just cheeky, funny and it created its own world and its own language and it had that sense of James' humour coming through. You could only do that if you created a magazine for yourself. They say you have to have an ideal reader; well that has to be you. It was definitely apparent in the authenticity of James' magazine and I think with the authenticity of *FourFourTwo* as well."

For Buchanan it was also important for her magazine not just to offer different content but to stand apart visually and stylistically. "We offered a whole new viewpoint and we wanted to show that quite literally," she said. "We wanted to use photography to its maximum and so we had a lot of photo essays, which newspapers weren't really doing. They were just showing the moment a goal was scored or the moment of celebration. We wanted to show a lot of minutiae and a lot of perspectives of games. We had a classic design, we didn't want loads of gimmicks: the content and pictures spoke for themselves. Our first cover was a really grainy four-colour black-and-white of Terry Venables staring down the camera. It's really close, uncomfortably close, and it's really engaging and hopefully it said: 'I've really got something to say and I'm challenging you to pick up this magazine.'" Buchanan thinks this new approach to football had some impact on the mainstream press. "Up until that point a lot of the papers hadn't really done many football features," she said. "At the time pretty much all you got were match reports, stories about people moving on and stories about people shagging. There were some investigations but I like to think we opened the door for newspapers to realise their readers might want a bit more in terms of features."

But how did those inside the game react to this new perspective? "Generally the response was really, really positive," said Buchanan. "We had a few people who said 'oh you don't want to read 2,000 words about me', not quite understanding there was that readership, and we did have to explain to several managers that 4-4-2 was a football formation, which was quite bizarre. It gave players and managers and officials and all the backroom stories – the kit man and the tea ladies – a voice. It gave a bigger voice to the whole match-day experience. Initially people didn't quite know what to make of it but within an issue or two they were like 'oh, this is great' because we could have a proper chat about things."

Again, Brown expressed similar sentiments: "When we were doing *loaded*, footballers realised we weren't like other sports writers. Suddenly they were being interviewed in-depth by fans about the games. We weren't putting them on a pedestal but we weren't just after that quote for the latest bit of news and they hadn't been interviewed like that before. I think the best thing that summed it up was when I interviewed Gary Kelly, Jason McAteer and Phil Babb and asked them if they weren't footballers what jobs would they like and Jason just blurted out: 'Yours of course!' *loaded* was a footballer's magazine. I was at Scribes West in 1996 for some book launch and I got introduced to Terry Venables and I asked him if he knew *loaded* and he said: 'Of course I know *loaded*; I can't get it off the players when I'm trying to do the team talk!' Footballers were the same as any other young lads."

Despite them serving different sections of the magazine market the success of *FourFourTwo* and *loaded* in its heyday before it ceased publication is in part due to a similar ethos. "They were a lifestyle magazine and we were a football magazine," said Buchanan, "and we weren't as cool as *loaded*, but I think there were elements we shared in terms of our personas. We had a shared vision and similar ideas. It was fun and it was an expression of ourselves. There were similar attitudes in the way we wore football. I think we both wore our shirts with the collars up."

• • •

In *loaded*'s case, critics suggest that this attitude was sexist, an accusation Brown denies. "You'd be shocked by how tame it was," he said. "Gary Oldman, Leslie Nielsen and Elle Macpherson were our first three covers. Four was Barry Grant from *Brookside*, five was Prince Naseem Hamed, six was two fashion model girls – not Page 3 girls – wearing football shirts, seven was Frank Skinner winking. In the 36 issues I edited I think we probably had about nine women on the front. That's nearly 30 blokes. We did *50 Women In the Media We Love;* the only flesh in it is a bit of Dani Behr's leg in an evening gown. We didn't use women to sell *loaded*. In my era we just thought women were great and that was it. They were just part of the mix; they weren't the driving sales force by any means. It was an appreciation of women rather than an exploitation of them." When the magazine first launched, between 30,000 and 40,000 women were buying *loaded* each month, accounting for about 10 per cent of the readership, and one of those was Buchanan: "I never thought *loaded* was sexist at all," she told me. "It was by far my favourite magazine of any magazine that's ever existed. The writing was superb, the page furniture was unique. It was inventive and crazy. I think now it has become a pastiche of its former self. I think all the subsequent men's magazines have spectacularly failed to realise how clever *loaded* was."

To compare *loaded* in the years immediately after its launch to what was served up by lads' mags a decade or two later is both wrong and just plain lazy. The market expanded with the launch of *Nuts* and *Zoo* in 2004 and the content also changed significantly. After *FHM* took the market leadership away from *loaded* by regularly using models on its cover, all the other titles followed suit. This led to campaigns for covers of the magazines to be hidden and some shops have stopped stocking them altogether. Yet it's not just the amount and type of images of women that has changed; it's also the narratives that surround them. In 2011 the *British Journal of Psychology* published a study detailing the reaction of readers to a series of statements about women's sexuality made by lads' mags and a series of statements made by rapists. Noting that producers of lads' mags often claim their content is ironic, the researchers wanted to see if the readers interpreted it in the same way. It's dangerous to distil the results of a detailed research paper into a few sentences but the bottom line is unequivocal: the statements were so similar that the subjects of the study couldn't distinguish between them. Perhaps more significantly, the study suggested that if the participants thought a statement was from a lads' mag then they considered it to be acceptable (and vice versa if they thought it from a rapist). In other words, lads' mags have the power to normalise and legitimise very aggressive attitudes towards women. Arguably the most infamous example of this came in 2010 when *Zoo* columnist Danny Dyer responded to a letter from a reader seeking advice after being dumped by his girlfriend. Dyer's answer was emphatic: "You've got nothing to worry about, son. I'd suggest going on a rampage with the boys, getting on the booze and smashing anything that moves. Then, when some bird falls for you, you can turn the tables and break *her* heart. Of course, the other option is to cut your ex's face, then no one will want her ..."

It's hard to know quite what to say to that. To be fair, I should point out that Dyer claimed he didn't write it. Like all the worst columnists he let someone else do the work and then took the credit or said he had been misquoted as appropriate. Either way, the column was dropped, with *Zoo* putting it down to a 'production error' (and if by 'production error' they meant that someone produced those words by actually typing them and it was a error to do so then, yes, I guess it was). But here's the thing: *Zoo* clearly thought their readers viewed Dyer, or more to the point the type of man he represents, as someone whose advice was worth heeding. So, what type of man does Dyer represent? Well, before he took up residence in the Queen Vic, he played the part of Tommy Johnson in the film adaptation of *The Football Factory* and following that he fronted two documentary series on hooligans: *The Real Football Factories* and *The Real Football Factories International*. So, Dyer is a euphemistic 'hard' lad and by using him as a columnist *Zoo* was able to have a regular, tacit link to the increased interest in football hooliganism.

This was sparked by the growth in popularity of hoolie-lit books we've already discussed. For this section of the market 1998 proved to be a pivotal year as it saw two linked events happen in quick succession. Firstly Lenny McLean released his autobiography *The Guv'nor*, which went straight to No. 1 in the book charts and eventually sold more than a million copies worldwide. It was the trailblazer for and remains the premier example of the hard-man non-fiction genre. McLean, dubbed "the hardest man in Britain", was a bare-knuckle fighter,[3] bouncer and East End enforcer who went on to become an actor. Later the same year the film *Lock, Stock and Two Smoking Barrels*, in which McLean had a small but significant role as Barry "The Baptist", was released. Directed by Guy Ritchie, the film launched the acting careers of ex-sportsmen Jason Statham[4] and Vinnie Jones. The part of Big Chris, a debt collector, allowed Jones to reinforce the hard-man credentials he's established on numerous occasions during and after his football career. That career saw him accumulate 12 red cards and famously be photographed getting to grips with Gazza's testicles during a game between Wimbledon and Newcastle. In 1995 Jones bit the nose of *Mirror* journalist Ted Oliver[5] and he has subsequently been convicted of two separate assaults. Jones has clearly lived by the credo he espoused in his infamous 1992 video *Soccer's Hard Men* in which he said that hard men are "not just aggressive on the field, they're aggressive in all walks of life, whether it is an argument with the baker or an argument with the manager". The FA fined him £20,000 for his trouble.

There had been earlier titles in both genres but it was the success of McLean's book and Ritchie's film that really kick-started the loosely linked genres of 'hard-man' non-fiction books and 'gangster-light' films. As both genres expanded, football hooligans were quickly drawn into their orbit. Researchers at the Manchester Metropolitan University's Institute of Popular Culture have catalogued all the

---

3   *'The Guv'nor' is the title given to the leading unlicensed heavyweight boxer, a title McLean won when he beat Roy 'Pretty Boy' Shaw in 1978.*

4   *Statham was a member of the British men's diving squad for 12 years and finished 12th in the 1992 World Championships.*

5   *You have to admire Oliver's professionalism. When a shocked bystander shouted "Get him a doctor", Oliver replied, "No, get me a photographer."*

factual football-hooligan-related books published between 1989 and 2007. Just six were released before 1998 and five were published in that year. Significantly the overwhelming majority – 72 – were published from 1999 onwards, after the release of McLean's book. The same is the case with hooligan-related films such as *The Football Factory* and *Green Street*, the majority hitting the screen after *Lock, Stock*. The lads' mags reviews formed a key part of the marketing for those films. *The Football Factory* got five stars from *Zoo* while *Nuts* claimed that *Green Street* "makes the FOOTBALL FACTORY look like a girly PLAYGROUND SCRAP". Not to be outdone, while Gary Oldman was winning plaudits and an Oscar nomination for his measured portrayal of George Smiley in *Tinker Tailor Soldier Spy*, *FHM* named *The Firm*, Alan Clarke's 1989 film about football hooligans, as Oldman's best role, also claiming a 'killer' head-butt his character delivered was the iconic moment.

• • •

Just as the weekly lads' mags were hitting the shelves for the first time and letting us ogle women in new ways, so a new type of woman was emerging to be ogled at: the WAG. I'm sure I don't need to tell you that a WAG is the name given to a footballer's wife or girlfriend but they are an entirely modern phenomenon and one that Kelly Davitt, who chronicled their exploits as editor of *Kickette.com*, thinks are a media creation. "Footballers – all athletes for that matter – have always had significant others. But in terms of formally introducing them to the general public, "educating" readers on their lifestyle and culture through various glossy spreads and scandalous articles, it was the media who devised and branded these ladies with the WAG tag."

Those glossy spreads arrived in earnest in England in 1988 when Spaniard Eduardo Sánchez Junco created a sister title to *¡Hola!* magazine, which his parents had launched 44 years earlier. Antonio Sánchez Gomez and his wife Mercedes Junco Calderón wanted a weekly illustrated journal that would give Spaniards some light relief in the aftermath of the country's civil war by providing a taste of *"la spuma de la vida"* – the froth of life. The first issue had an illustration on the front and sold 4,000 of the 14,000 copies printed. The second had a photo of Clark Gable on the front and sold out. The celebrity magazine was here to stay. ¡Hola! wasn't a success simply because it covered celebrities, it was a success because of the way it covered celebrities. Gomez and Calderón believed their magazine should consistently show the rich and famous in a positive light; in effect it was a scandal sheet without the scandal and the same editorial policy was subsequently employed in *Hello!* The magazine's launch was greeted with scepticism in media circles. The key selling points of the first edition were an interview with Princess Anne at Buckingham Palace and photos from Burt Reynolds' wedding to Loni Anderson. Anne might have been Princess Royal but Princess Di and Fergie were all the rage at the time and Reynolds' *Smokey and the Bandit* heyday was well and truly behind him. *Hello!* looked, as Princess Anne might have said herself, a bit naff. However it was a sensation.

The magazine subsequently introduced England to the idea of the celebrity wedding feature, devoting 14 "spectacular" pages to the 1989 marriage of ex-Rolling Stone Bill Wyman to his teenage bride Mandy Smith. With Sky's coverage of the Premier League turning footballers into celebrities it was only a matter of time before the wedding of one of them would also fill the pages of *Hello!* When it did it was perhaps inevitable it would be the wedding of the biggest star of the lot: Paul Gascoigne. In July 1996, less than a week after they'd been beaten by Germany in the semi-finals of the European Championships at Wembley, the England squad met up again for their team-mate's nuptials to his long-time fiancée Sheryl Failes. It was a significant moment as, previously, women's magazines had suggested sport was not for women. In June 1994 *Woman's Own* lamented: "Bad news if you hate football. The World Cup starts this week – for a whole month", yet, two years later, here was a footballer gracing the cover of what was a magazine essentially aimed at women. The couple had booked all 95 rooms at Hertfordshire's posh Harbury Manor Hotel as part of a huge security operation to keep out the press and preserve *Hello!*'s exclusive access, for which the magazine had paid £150,000. It was money well spent. The photos of a grinning Gazza, hair cropped and bleached, in his gold knee-length frock coat, and Sheryl in her pink, hand-beaded Isabell Kristensen dress, helped the magazine to a then-record sale of more than 645,000. More than 17 years later, it remains *Hello!*'s sixth-best-selling issue.[6] Brian Reade wrote in the *Daily Mirror* that it was "the nearest the People's Game will ever get to a royal wedding". It would take just three years to prove him wrong.

By then *Hello!* had a rival. *Daily Express* chief Richard Desmond is now unique as the only UK newspaper proprietor to also own a terrestrial TV channel but in 1993 he was best known for being the publisher of slightly less salubrious titles like *Asian Babes* and *Readers' Wives*. He wanted to go mainstream and launching *OK!* as competition to *Hello!* was the first step down the path of respectability. The young pretender was so similar to its older rival in terms of design and content it could most charitably be described as homage but there was no love lost between the pair. Desmond's chief weapon was his cheque book and he scored a stunning coup in 1999 by scooping the rights to the marriage of young Manchester United star David Beckham to Victoria Adams, one of the Spice Girls.

Hello! had been offered the exclusive first but couldn't tie up a deal and when rumours, which subsequently turned out to be untrue, swept the *OK!* office that the *Sun* had bid £1m, Desmond sanctioned his editor Martin Townsend to match the offer and the deal was struck. The *Sun* wasn't to be outdone and scooped *OK!* with a "World Exclusive" picture of the couple sat on their golden thrones. Inside, 'MORE AMAZING WEDDING PHOTOS' were spread across 'Pages 2, 3, 4 & 5'. The *Mirror* also had a snatched photo, but it was a blurred, black-and-white of Sporty Spice. They offered some hints as to how they got the pictures, suggesting that their camera might have been hidden in David Seaman's moustache (which would explain the poor quality). Neither paper managed to dent *OK!*'s momentum. The magazine led with the wedding over three consecutive editions which sold about 3.7 million copies between them. The first issue sold out, shifting about 1.5 million, quadruple the average weekly sale as the public lapped up page after page of the do from fairy-tale Luttrellstown Castle just outside Dublin. Victoria wore Vera Wang. There were thrones for the happy couple, a fanfare, a flag bearing

6   *As of March 2016 the top five were: Princess Diana's funeral, the wedding of the Duke and Duchess of Cambridge, Princess Diana's death, the Christmas 2000 edition and the wedding of the Duke and Duchess of Cornwall.*

their own crest; the Royal jeweller Slim Barret even lent the bride a diamond and gold coronet for the happy occasion. *This* was football's royal wedding and like all good royal weddings it signified the union of two powerful houses: football and pop.

It wasn't just a wedding though; it was also a coronation. Since Gascoigne had married, Glenn Hoddle had dumped him from the England squad. This opened up the need for a new superstar footballer and Becks, by then a regular for England and a treble winner with Manchester United, was on hand to take his place. Tragically, the intervening period had also been marked by the death of Princess Diana. This in turn opened up the need for a new superstar celebrity. In his 2000 book *Posh & Becks*, Andrew Morton claimed the couple moved into "the sentimental terrain once occupied by Diana, Princess of Wales" and that "they are the new Royalty for the common man". Whether the couple formed a similarly strong emotional bond with the British public as the late Princess is debatable but there is no doubt that they occupied the celebrity space her early death created. That summer their wedding was mentioned by TV presenters, politicians, comedians and was the subject of numerous radio phone-ins. Apart from being in *OK!* it featured in a host of other magazines, including *Vanity Fair, Marie Claire, GQ, Time Out, Now, Midweek, Radio Times* and *TV Times*. It totally dwarfed the actual Royal wedding of that year between Prince Edward and Sophie Rhys-Jones. Indeed, the Royals had nothing to match Posh and Becks until 2011 when Diana's eldest son William got hitched to Kate Middleton, the woman he had bumped into during Freshers' Week at St Andrew's University ten years earlier. It goes without saying the Beckhams were on the guest list.

In the first edition of his book *Beckham,* which focuses on the player's celebrity, Ellis Cashmore suggests Victoria was an 'inspiration' for Beckham. In the second edition he acknowledges this was a significant understatement of her role and devotes a whole chapter to her importance in building the Beckham brand, suggesting: "she may have designed a project that, when completed, must have surprised even her". One of the key factors in that project was media management, something at which Victoria had become adept during the Spice Girls' rapid rise to fame (in which time they dumped two managers and started to run their own affairs with considerable success).

Since the launch of *Hello!* the nature of celebrity had changed significantly. Stars were becoming brands that depended on positive coverage. The success of celebrity magazines like *Hello!*, *OK!*, and the rest that followed in their wake depended on access to celebrities. It was a simple *quid pro quo.* "They were the first couple to do things like staging paparazzi shots," says Davitt. "So when they were on vacation, they would call the paps ahead of time, tell them their exact location and time of arrival. There was the sham marriage libel case; there was talk of affairs; but no matter what, Victoria's appearance was very calculated because the long-run was the brand that is Beckham."

The nature of celebrity changed again when a little over a year after the Beckhams got married, the *Big Brother* bandwagon crashed into our living rooms. No one quite knew what to expect of this show where 10 contestants were locked in a house and their every move filmed to help us decide which ones to boot out until only the 'winner' was left. Then 'Nasty' Nick Bateman was discovered to have smuggled a pencil and some paper into the house and, as ludicrous as it may seem, the nation was gripped by this unscripted soap opera. The contestants sang "It's only a game show" and maybe in that first series it was, but not for long. Two years later we got Jade Goody and we laughed at her because she didn't know where 'East Angular' was and because she thought Rio de Janeiro was a person. Perhaps instead we should have been asking how someone could slip through the education system of one of the world's richest countries with such limited knowledge. Still, house prices were on the up, beer was cheap, the World Cup was on. Jade even had a lesbian, disabled mum – the tabloids couldn't have made her up. Then she was evicted and we lionised her. Then a few years later she was racist and we demonised her. Then she died and we canonised her the only way we know how – by buying *OK!*'s memorial edition (issue 666), which helpfully went on sale the week before she passed away, complete with her 'final' words. In the process Jade became a millionaire by virtue of nothing more than the celebrity we bestowed on her, so I guess in the end the joke was on us.

A whole host of 'reality' TV shows followed in *Big Brother*'s wake. These ran from *Popstars*, *Pop Idol* and *The X Factor*, which took the process used to create the Spice Girls and made it public, to *The Only*

Way Is Essex and *Geordie Shore*. The celebrity magazines lapped it all up and the message was clear: you could become famous simply for being famous. This was Daniel Boorstin's concept of synthetic, manufactured celebrity writ large. Then in 2002 ITV broadcast the first series of the soap opera *Footballers' Wives*. The exploits of Tanya Turner and Chardonnay Lane-Pascoe suggested there was an even easier way of becoming famous: by marrying someone who already was, like a footballer. The WAG had been born.

Of course, that's not what we called them back then. The term that would become ubiquitous thanks to the media whirlwind which swept through the unsuspecting German spa town of Baden-Baden in 2006 first saw the light of day four years earlier in, of all places, the *Sunday Telegraph*. The article detailed how in the run-up to the 2002 World Cup the England squad spent five days in Dubai with their "wives and girlfriends (or 'the WAGs', as staff at the Jumeirah Beach Club call them for short)". While there were small hints of what would come in Germany, it was, by comparison, all rather benign. The potentially disruptive presence of the women was questioned by Topaz Amoore, the paper's correspondent on the ground, who suggested that the "extended bonding session by the turquoise waters of the Arabian Gulf was a gamble". However, the squad and their partners kept themselves to themselves and their "privacy was barely breached". Amoore concluded: "The lads and the WAGs, you might think, could have made more of an effort."

Four years later there was no lack of effort as the England squad's partners arrived in Baden-Baden for the World Cup and their every move was helpfully recorded by the English press. The attention was reciprocal and in one instance some of the WAGs, as they were by then emphatically known, asked for a screen erected by their hotel pool to shield them from the paparazzi to be taken down. Davitt thinks this was a pivotal moment: "Up until then it was bubbling under but the WAGs from 2006 were just so blatant about their extra-curricular activities that they are the ones that people still readily know and recognise today even if they are now totally distant from that WAG tag. It was a time when the global economy was good and people didn't have a problem with seeing other people spend a lot of money. Now credit is a little more crunchy people aren't so amused with WAGs who drop $200,000 on a new Bentley. But in 2006, people ate it up and the media ate it up especially as it related to the performance on the pitch."

So great was the impact of the WAGs in Baden-Baden that the media persistently blamed their presence for England's departure from the tournament. The possibility that Sven-Göran Eriksson's striker-lite squad selection was the cause, or that it was the players themselves who were at fault, or even that English football culture had never got to grips with the deficiencies highlighted by Len Shackleton way back in 1954, were rarely considered. Nor did the media consider the possibility that it was the attention they lavished on the women rather than the WAGs' behaviour that was actually the distraction. No, it was all the WAGs' fault and since then the attitude of every subsequent England manager towards their players' partners has been analysed and debated. The WAGs didn't seem to care and nor did countless young women aspiring to be one.

The following year Victoria Beckham lookalike Chanelle Hayes announced to her Big Brother housemates that she wanted to be a WAG.[7] While young boys dreamt of being a footballer, young girls dreamt of marrying one. Being a WAG was now a career. "Think about it," says Davitt, "if you can get £10,000 a week for putting your name on a column that you don't actually write what's the harm in that? In 2006 the WAGs were kind of regular people. Colleen Rooney was just 18, she didn't know any better, then she got a book deal, she got several fragrances. She and Alex Gerrard were the two who said 'to hell with what you think, we're going to be who we are and we're going to make money from that'."

Since then a whole host of WAGs have walked down the aisle to the tune of the celebrity magazine photographers' cameras clicking away. In 2007 four got married in one heady weekend, with Toni Poole kicking off what the *Daily Mail* christened a 'WAGathon' by marrying her childhood sweetheart – some bloke called John Terry. Such is the pull of the football-celebrity aura that in 2010 Posh and Becks were on hand in *Hello!* to invite us to her sister Louise's wedding. We were back where it all started.

---

7   *She eventually got her wish, dating then-Middlesbrough player Matthew Bates in 2009. The pair have a child together.*

"If people are asked to name the wife of a famous athlete, they will still name Victoria," says Davitt. "She was the one who brought the WAG culture that was once behind the scenes to the forefront. People still look to her as the first one and as much as she tried to play that down, she was the first example of what a WAG is, or should be. It was the over-the-top boobs, it was the sky-high stilettos, it was dress to the nines at all times." While it's understandable that people label Victoria Beckham the über-WAG, it's also a little unfair. Like or loathe the Spice Girls, there's no denying they attained global celebrity before Posh met Becks. Conversely, when the pair became an item he was merely a promising young footballer who had just broken into the England senior team. At the time there was little to differentiate Beckham from his Spice Boy contemporaries down the M62 at Anfield. Yes he probably would have continued to play for England. Yes, he probably would have captained his country. But if he hadn't married Posh would he have become the global megastar he now is? It's hard to conjure up a scenario in which he would. No, Posh is more than just a footballer's WAG: if anything, in those early years Becks was a pop star's HAB. That isn't to say that she didn't benefit as well, something not lost on Victoria herself. "I think I wouldn't be as famous if I wasn't with David. And I don't think David would be as famous if he wasn't with me," she said when he picked up his OBE in 2003. Together they achieved celebrity greater than the sum of their parts, in the process helping the media to create a whole new type of celebrity it could feast on. At the same time they provided the template for the way footballers and their partners would be viewed by the modern media, reinforcing the idea that everyone can grab their brief moment of fame.

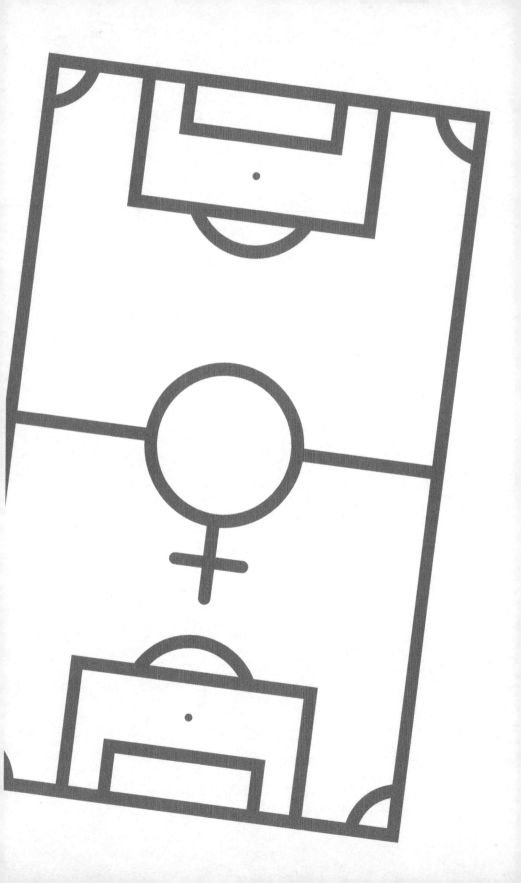

CHAPTER 13

THE MEDIA GIVES WOMEN A RED CARD

In 1978 Derek Jameson, the editor of the *Daily Express*, returned to Manchester to launch the *Daily Star.*[1] Before moving to Fleet Street, Jameson, who passed away in 2012, had made a name for himself in the North West as a consistent circulation builder while northern editor for first the *Sunday Mirror* then the *Daily Mirror*. Now he had just 12 weeks to put together the *Daily Star* from scratch. The paper was aiming for a piece of the tabloid market and when Jameson was asked what type of content it would contain, he supposedly replied: "Tits, bums, QPR and roll your own fags." Jameson strenuously argued that he'd been misquoted and sought to clarify his position in a memo to the *Daily Star*'s new staff. "No newspaper in history lost sales by projecting beautiful birds", he wrote and I suppose he was proved right. The *Star* was the first paper to print colour topless shots (the "Starbirds") and within a year it had reached sales of more than a million. Given the content of the memo and the paper, whether or not Jameson had been misquoted is a rather moot point.

What is clear, however, is that as far as the tabloids were concerned women's involvement in football extended only as far as getting their kit off. For much of the latter part of the twentieth century they were a passive adjunct: the WAG; the 'totty' in the latest footballer-cheats-on-WAG scandal; the Page 3 'stunner' sporting St George's flag knickers and not much else during a major tournament; or the loyal but long-suffering partner of the obsessed fan. Let's not kid ourselves though, the rest of the media could hardly be mistaken for an edition

---

1   *The paper faced an injunction from the* Morning Star *that claimed the new paper had nicked their title. In dismissing the claim the judge, Mr Justice Foster, suggested that only "a moron in a hurry" would confuse the two papers, and having worked for both, I can confirm that's true.*

of *Spare Rib*. In the *Sunday Times* in 1973 Brian Glanville wrote that women's football was "like a dog walking on its hind legs. It's not well done, but it's surprising to see it done at all." That was about as enlightened as it got.

• • •

While Glanville might have been surprised to see women playing football in 1973, the truth is they'd been footing the leather for the best part of 100 years. It seems the first appearance by a women's team purporting to represent England took place on Saturday 7 May 1881, at Edinburgh's Easter Road in a match, rather predictably, against Scotland, who ran out 3-0 winners. Despite the seeming lack of affiliation to any official football body the match was labelled as an 'international' in the *Glasgow Herald*, which set a depressing trend by devoting most of its report to a description of the players' kit. Just over a week later the teams took to the field in Glasgow in front of 5,000 spectators, although it's worth noting that some of the players had swapped sides, suggesting these weren't true internationals; reports on later matches between the teams claimed that all the women were from Scotland.

The Glasgow match was abandoned after a violent pitch invasion in the 55th minute and, according to the *Nottinghamshire Guardian,* the women were "roughly jostled" and chased by a mob as they left the ground in their omnibus. It's impossible to tell whether the violence was a protest against women playing football or simply symptomatic of the rowdiness prevalent in society generally. Either way the players were undeterred and four days later they played another match in front of a crowd of 4,000 at the Hole-i'th'-wall, home to Blackburn Olympic. A month later the teams played on consecutive days in Cheetham in Manchester, with the second match also being abandoned due to a pitch invasion, this time after an hour. The *Manchester Guardian* was scathing in its report of what it labelled a "so-called match" played by teams "attired in a costume which is neither graceful nor very becoming" and which "do not hesitate to gratify vulgar curiosity". The reporter appeared to have little sympathy for the women as they ran for safety although, again, it's not clear if the riot was a protest against women's football.

Two more games in Liverpool followed before the series ended, and that was that. Other than their names, we know nothing of the women who played or what became of any of them, nor do we know who organised the matches. However, the tone which would come to dominate coverage of women's football over the following century and more had been established: barely disguised contempt built on twin narratives, one focused on players' appearance, the other criticising their standard of play. But where did these narratives come from? Well, the short answer is Charles Darwin.

In 1859 Darwin published *On the Origin of Species* which outlined his ground-breaking theory of natural selection as the basis of evolution. Central to this concept is the idea of survival of the fittest – strong species survive, weak species die out. So far, so GCSE biology. What they tend to gloss over at school is the fact that Darwin and many of his contemporaries believed that women were intellectually and biologically inferior to men. According to Darwin, who was amazed "such different beings belong to the same species", men were constantly undergoing a violent process of natural selection – namely war – which strengthened the sex's gene pool by 'pruning' its weaker members. On the other hand, women didn't have to face such a violent selection process and so had no need to develop similar mental and physical capabilities. On this basis some biologists went as far as to classify men and women as different species, *Homo frontalis* and *Homo parietalis* respectively.

As Darwin's theories on gender gained popularity outside the scientific community others used them as 'medical evidence' to underpin the Victorian concept of the family that became an intrinsic part of patriarchal, industrialised society. This was the time when phrases such as 'ladylike' and 'the weaker sex' entered our vocabulary. The man was deemed to be the 'head of the household'. He would go out into the world of work to provide for his wife who 'made the home'; her job being to give birth and raise their children. It was all 'natural' and therefore supposedly free of subjectivity.[2]

2   *The Nazis made similar claims about their ideas of 'racial purity', which were also based on Darwin's theories. Incidentally, in the twentieth century compulsory sterilisation programmes were widespread in the West, with Sweden only bringing theirs to an end in 1976. In America the last forced sterilisation occurred in Oregon as recently as 1981. Whatever we might like to pretend, eugenics wasn't just for the Nazis.*

Sport, considered a quintessentially masculine pursuit, further legiti-
mised that point of view by restricting women to the role of passive
spectator. For public-school-educated middle- and upper-class boys,
sport was linked to muscular Christianity and Britain's Imperialism
(and the handy selection process of war). For the working classes it
became part of the transition to adulthood. For example, football
grounds were, along with pubs, male bastions where boys learned
not only how to play sports but also how to talk about them. By
contrast, strenuous activity for women was considered dangerous
especially during puberty and menstrual periods. It could, it was
claimed, flatten their breasts, drain energy from their vital organs,
diminish their reproductive capabilities and so threaten the very
survival of the human race. If you think that's weird – and you
should – an article printed in the *British Medical Journal* in 1878
argued that "it is an indisputable fact that meat goes bad when
touched by menstruating women". Eventually as women began to
exert their rights their involvement in sport grew; however, it tended
to happen in a way that reinforced the view of them as the weaker
sex. The sports deemed acceptable for women tended to be non-
contact games like croquet, badminton and tennis, which for many
women would essentially keep them in the domestic environment
of their own garden.

Women first played at Wimbledon in 1884 and six years later
the Original English Lady Cricketers' team went on a brief tour of
England. In 1894, possibly inspired by such activities, or perhaps by
the emancipation of women in New Zealand a year earlier, a young
woman called Nettie Honeyball placed some newspaper ads looking
for women to join her football team. There had been sporadic games
during the 14 years since the series of 'internationals' in 1881, but
no regular organised women's football. So it's easy to understand
why most histories of the women's game in England kick off with
Honeyball's British Ladies Football Team (BLFT). In reality it's
merely the starting point for national press attention in the game.
Such is the limited information available to us we can only guess as
to why the BLFT received such attention while the 1881 matches
did not, but in all likelihood it was a combination of reasons. The
fact the team was based in London probably did it no harm and

the fact that it gained the patronage of Lady Florence Dixie[3] almost certainly didn't.

Football itself had become significantly more established and popular. Professionalism was ratified in 1885 and the men's game gained structure through the formation of the League in 1888. The first Saturday football special was printed in 1882 and the amount of coverage of the game had risen dramatically by the time Honeyball was putting her team together. I'm speculating, but I suspect the 1881 women's team was mainly working class, whereas the BLFT was made up mainly of middle-class ladies and in Honeyball had an articulate spokesperson. Lastly, the suffragette movement had begun (although it had yet to acquire that label[4]). Women were becoming increasingly vocal and more and more questions were being asked about their 'rightful' place in society.

As far as the press was concerned, that place was emphatically not on a football pitch and from the start coverage picked up where it had left off 14 years earlier. A cartoon in *The Sketch* in October 1894 gently ridiculed the BLFT players by purporting to show how they would behave during a match. Supposedly they would nag "the poor referee" to distraction and the male spectators would only have eyes for the "attractive goalkeeper". During half time, the flustered and swooning women would have to fan themselves to recover from their exertions before redoing their hair and makeup. A few months later the same paper printed an interview with Honeyball in which she explained that she founded the team with "the fixed resolve of proving to the world that women are not the 'ornamental and useless' creatures men have pictured". In March 1895 after several months of twice-weekly practice under the watchful eye of Tottenham Hotspur centre-half John William Julian, the women took to the field in front of 10,000 spectators at the Nightingale Lane Ground in Crouch End. The match is now frequently referred to as being between the North

3   Lady Dixie is a fascinating character worthy of a book herself. She was a war correspondent during the First Boer War and argued in favour of full emancipation for women and Home Rule for both Ireland and Scotland. Her brother was the Marquis of Queensberry, responsible for both the rules of boxing and the downfall of Oscar Wilde.

4   The term 'suffragette' was first used by Daily Mail writer Charles E. Hinds to describe the Women's Social and Political Union led by Emmeline Pankhurst after they broke away from the more moderate National Union of Women's Suffrage Societies led by Millicent Fawcett. But I digress.

and South of England but Honeyball stated in the *Daily Graphic* that it would be between players from the North and South of London. This is supported by the fact that Honeyball herself, who lived in Crouch End a northern suburb of London, was listed in the 'North' team as printed in the *Lloyd's Weekly Newspaper*.

Despite the large attendance and the fact that the players were cheered off at the final whistle, the press took a dim view. The *Manchester Guardian* correspondent was adamant that "when the novelty has worn off I do not think that ladies' football matches will attract crowds", while also reinforcing gender divisions by focusing on the players' appearances and suggesting that their "'Rational' costume – that is, tunic and knickerbockers – is the only dress in which women will take active exercise in the future." *The Sketch* claimed that "The first few minutes were sufficient to show that football by women, if the British Ladies be taken as a criterion, is totally out of the question." Not for the last time the quality of women's football would be criticised without any context. While the men's game was professional and had structured league and cup competitions, the British Ladies Football Team were amateurs who struggled to find facilities and the time to practise and had no access to regular competition. This fact was not lost on a reporter from the Newcastle-based *The Sporting Man,* who wrote: "I really think the public have taken the wrong view of the lady footballers. [...] If we were to take a similar number of young men at random, who knew nothing about the game, and give them a few days' practice before asking them to perform in public, could we expect any more science than we saw in the North v. South match?"

It was a lone voice and as the team played more than 50 games around the country the press criticism continued; eventually even *The Sporting Man* limited itself to a short report for a match in Jesmond on the outskirts on Newcastle in 1896, which ended: "However, we do not suppose anyone would be any the wiser or the happier if we were to attempt to deal with the proceedings in detail." Interest in the team fizzled out and they appear to have stopped playing after a couple of years. It would be another two decades before the next wave of popularity for women's football.

• • •

As England's men were undergoing another round of natural selection in the First World War, the geniuses left at home in the corridors of power suddenly realised they needed someone to fill traditionally masculine roles. Who was left to work the land and toil in the factories making the weapons to arm the soldiers? You've guessed it. All of a sudden the 'weak' women were sweating away making armaments and loading them onto ships destined for the front. This began to demonstrably undermine the notion that women were inferior to men, something which extended to the football pitch as factory teams such as the Dick, Kerr's Ladies[5] were formed. The team famously played St Helen's Ladies in front of a crowd of about 58,000 at Goodison Park on Christmas Day 1920[6] and also travelled to France and America to play teams of both men and women.

You could be forgiven for thinking they were the best of a very small number of women's teams playing at the time; however, there were similar teams all over the country, all of them able to fill League grounds on a regular basis, and the Dick, Kerr's Ladies weren't the first or necessarily even the best. By the time the Preston outfit took to the pitch for the first time, the Blyth Spartan Ladies had already played 12 matches. By the time Dick, Kerr's Ladies played a French XI in 1920, a team consisting of players from the North East had already represented England three times, with the first match in Belfast on Christmas Day 1917 attracting 38,000.[7] So why are the Dick, Kerr's Ladies and Nettie Honeyball's BLFT the go-to teams in the history of the women's game? Why is it that, as I type, the "Brief History" of women's football (and it is brief) provided on the FA's website states that the first women's football match was the North v South game in 1895 and that the first women's international was the Dick, Kerr's Ladies' game with France in 1920?

---

5 *Their history is traced in a couple of recent books:* The Dick, Kerr's Ladies *by Barbara Jacobs, and* In a League of Their Own! The Dick, Kerr Ladies' 1917–1965 *by Gail Newsham.*

6 *As with most aspects of the history of women's football the facts are not totally clear and quoted attendance figures vary; however, more than 55,000 watched, with several thousand more locked outside.*

7 *The history of women's football in the North East during the First World War is told by Patrick Brennan in his book* The Munitionettes, *and his website:* www.donmouth. co.uk/womens_football, *is an excellent resource.*

The answer begins with the decision by the FA to effectively ban women's football in 1921. The FA and the Football League had initially tolerated the women's game, as the huge amounts of money it helped raise for servicemen's charities (equivalent to millions today) had enabled them to deflect some of the criticism they received for allowing men's League fixtures to continue earlier in the war. However, three years after Armistice Day the FA prohibited affiliate clubs from staging matches with women players, stating that "the game of football is quite unsuitable for females and should not be encouraged". The move was designed to reassert the masculine image of the sport and also ensure that the huge popularity of the women's game did not undermine the men's game as it restarted after the war. While it couldn't – and didn't – stop women playing, the FA's ruling stopped them playing in grounds where large numbers of people could come and watch and, significantly, where gate money could be taken. By removing the possibility of women's football becoming financially independent, the FA at a stroke undermined the possibility of regular league and cup competitions for women.

One of the key consequences of the resulting inchoate competitive structure was that there was effectively nothing for the press to report on. Ad hoc friendlies here and there did not have the appeal of the regular competitive matches around which the men's game was built. Consequently there were no local or national teams upon which to build a history of the women's game. The men's game in England has key moments. These moments may be misstated or overstated (and we've seen examples of this with the White Horse and Matthews Cup Finals) but they provide a structure around which a supposedly definitive history of the men's game is built. There are many ways in which the men's game is memorialised, from club museums to player autobiographies, cigarette cards to newsreels and newspaper match reports. All of them tap into and build upon the supposedly definitive history of the men's game, replaying it, recycling it, becoming part of it and reinforcing its importance. Even the Pools brought a significant number of the adult population into contact with the League and Cup fixtures of men's football on a weekly basis. The nation would stop at 4.45pm every Saturday to listen to the results of those games. Even if they were only trying to find out if their numbers had come up, people would still absorb the names of teams and goal-scorers.

By contrast even now you will struggle to find the fixtures and results of the FA Women's Super League printed in any national newspaper on a regular basis. The Dick, Kerr's Ladies eventually disbanded in 1965 and the Doncaster Belles, perhaps the most famous modern team, were only formed as recently as 1969. So, there are few modern women's clubs with long histories and anyway there would be nowhere to display those histories: no women's team has its own stadium, let alone a museum memorialising its past triumphs. The Dick, Kerr's Ladies and the BLFT gained significantly more contemporaneous media exposure than their counterparts, so there is a temptation, as with the history of the men's game, to overstate their importance and build the limited history of the women's game around them because their achievements are easy to see. However, the real history of women's football is still to be told, it's just hidden in the odd story in local newspaper archives, family photo albums and forgotten boxes in dusty attics.

• • •

The FA's ban was not a knee-jerk decision but one that had been foreshadowed for the best part of a year. During this time, women's football's huge popularity was reflected in a series of comic-book stories based around female players, one of which, believe it or not, was called 'Ray of the Rovers'. Ray Lester appeared in a short story in *The Football and Sports Library*, a regular publication by Amalgamated Press. She moved to Liverpool, readers were told, to work for Rinsford's Drapers with the specific intention of playing for the company's women's football team. However, while working there she immediately came into confrontation with Mark Rinsford, the nephew of the owner, who was trying to gain control of the company from his dying uncle. Ultimately Ray took control of the firm after winning a football match and thus defeated Rinsford. Ray might have beaten the evil Mark Rinsford, but she lost out in the race to be the first female comic-book footballer. That honour goes to Nell Harmer, who appeared a few months before Ray in the eponymous story 'Nell

O' Newcastle', also in *The Football and Sports Library*. "Don't Miss a Line of This Topping Story" the comic implored concerning the tale in which Nell played for the women's football team at the mill of her uncle, John Hood, where she worked. As it transpired the mill actually belonged to Nell, but Hood cheated her out of her inheritance. In the end, thanks in no small part to the team spirit engendered on the football field, Nell and the other women went to work at rival Grey's Mill, leading to the financial downfall of Hood and enabling Nell to reclaim what was rightfully hers.

There were others apart from Ray and Nell. 'Bess O' Blacktown' had a plot remarkably similar to Nell's in which Bessie Booth plays football for the mill team where she worked and defeated the corrupt owner by leading her teammates to another mill, where they then formed a workers' co-operative and put him out of business. The most featured was Meg Foster, who appeared in three separate stories. Meg set up a team independently of the mill where she worked and even got to travel to Australia for a tournament, although unfortunately Meg herself, her teammates and a men's team – the Scardale Corinthians – all got stranded on an island where the natives were cannibals. Other than Topsy Johnson, the goalkeeper in Nell Harmer's team, the islanders were the only black people to appear in any of these stories. It's a damning indictment of Western attitudes at the time, which sadly wasn't unique to these stories. You'll now struggle to find a copy of *Tintin in the Congo* in the children's section of most British bookshops. First serialised in the Belgian newspaper *Le XXe Siècle* over 13 months from May 1930, Hergé's story portrayed the Congolese as infantile and stupid, which led to the Commission for Racial Equality attempting to have the book banned in 2011. They were unsuccessful but their action was enough for bookshops to think about how they sold the title.[8]

Just like contemporary stories about male footballers, the stories about Ray, Nell, Bess and Meg used football as a plot device (remember, it wouldn't be until *Roy of the Rovers* that we'd see a comic that could really be said to be *about* football) but the sport was still

---

8   It also doesn't help that the story is full of numerous incidents of animal cruelty, the most gratuitous seeing Tintin drill a hole in the head of a live rhinoceros, fill it with dynamite and blow the animal to smithereens.

an important enough component for the stories to be considered to be about women footballers. On the surface they appear to fit neatly into the patriarchal narratives of the day that placed women in unchallenging, romantic stories. Unlike some of their teammates, the protagonists were all attractive with hourglass figures, soft skin, lovely hair and dainty hands. Furthermore they were all eventually whisked off their feet by a man of a higher social standing. Or were they? Another reading is that these are strong-willed, independent women who chose the men lucky enough to be with them.

Academic Alethea Melling, who has studied the comics, suggests that if you scratch below the surface what you find – abhorrent casual racism aside – is a series of stories that challenge the dominant narrative of the day; the veneer is merely light camouflage helping them to be published. Here we see working-class – not middle-class – women take centre stage, a rarity at a time, in stories that strongly promote both feminist and socialist ideals. In the aftermath of the First World War as working-class militancy swept across Europe threatening to undermine or even destroy the old ruling classes, the stories were quite radical. Union membership had more than tripled in Britain between 1910 and 1919 and the number of days lost to industrial action rose from six million in 1918 to 36 million the following year. Moderate union leaders were ignored as shop stewards took action and everyone from bakers and cotton spinners to miners and transport workers went on strike. Even 12,000 police marched on Whitehall, with their union leader promising: "the day when the Government can use the police forces as a tool against any other section of the nation is past". Ah well, it was a nice thought.

It was against this political backdrop that the issues of improved workers' rights, co-operatives and the need for unified action to achieve these aims were worked into stories purporting to be about dainty women footballers. Ray organises a mass faint by the shop-floor women at Rinsford's in protest at the poor-quality food they are given; Bessie's success at running the mill is based on profit sharing, and women who betray their teammates are ostracised, just as non-unionists were at the time. Could it be that the storylines were similar for a reason? Could it be that they were hammering home the same metaphor of the poorly run factory (corrupt capitalist society) brought to its knees by the direct action of its employees (the working class) united in their common goal through the football team (union)? I'd like to think so, but we'll probably never know for sure because the authors used pseudonyms and their true identities have been lost to time.

The fact that the main characters were women takes that radicalism and doubles it. While Bessie asks: "Why shouldn't a girl run a factory as well as a man?", Meg asks an almost identical question: "And why shouldn't girls play football, anyway? Coom to that, why shouldn't they play it as well as t' men?" By 1934 the status quo had been restored and in the film *Sing as We Go,* starring Gracie Fields, the factory in which her character works is saved by the intervention of a middle-class man. It's a far cry from the radical football stories a decade earlier in which the resolution was achieved directly because of the actions of the working-class female protagonists. The issue of sexual harassment in the workplace, at the time all but ubiquitous, was also dealt with in those, as Nell, Ray and Bess all successfully fought off assaults. It seems that beyond the socialism the stories held deeper messages specifically aimed at young women. Not only could they redefine the economic and social roles allocated to them in pre-war society, but they could also ignore the social mores of the time and take control of their bodies, whether to rebuff the unwanted sexual advances of the factory foreman or to play football in spite of the FA ban and those telling them it was unhealthy.

• • •

A portent of the future for the women's game came in the story *Captain Meg* that saw Meg Foster's team beat a rival factory team, the Canaries, thus winning ownership of the local football ground. After the game the Canaries boss Dawson shouted: "There'll be no more girls' football at my mill, and before long there'll be no girls' teams in this district!" The implications were clear: "There was sudden silence in the stand." The story continued: "Practically everyone present was a keen supporter of football for girls, and with old Dawson, who had great wealth and influence, and up to now had been a great supporter of the movement, suddenly abandoning them, the outlook was bleak." Another metaphor? Either way, from the point that the FA – the real-world Dawson – withdrew its support until the 1970s the women's game in England existed in more or less underground fashion.

With the FA's ban in place (and reinforced in 1946), the Second World War did not act as a catalyst in the way the previous conflict had. Teams played on an ad hoc basis, or in ephemeral local tournaments on a variety of grounds from municipal parks to school and company sports grounds. However, the limited media attention means the inter-war and immediate post-war years are relatively unchartered in terms of the history of the women's game. What little coverage there was (or we know about) tended to focus on the fact that the players were doing something considered to be masculine and therefore 'unladylike'. When 16-year-old Jean Seymour made her debut for the Dick, Kerr's Ladies in June 1946, the *Daily Dispatch* said she scorned "dolls and girlish toys" and had "always been a tomboy whose idea of a good time has been to play football with boys". The report made no mention of her football ability.

This continuing gender differentiation around football also manifested itself in the television coverage of the sport (and sport in general) that began in earnest during this period. Ideas about how best to structure commentary for the benefit of viewers were being taken from radio and developed for the new medium, and it was recognised that the audience was not homogeneous. Those watching at home would incorporate both people with expert knowledge of the relevant sport and those with very limited, or no knowledge of the sport and both groups needed to be accommodated. One feature of the resulting guidelines was the assumption, derived from those Darwinian notions of female inferiority and the idea that sport was a uniquely masculine environment, that the experts in the audience would be men. By contrast it was assumed women would be observing the sporting culture from the outside and so, as cricket commentator Brian Johnston wrote in 1952, liked "to be told little tit-bits about the players. They like to be told how old so-and-so is [...]"

Despite this attitude, many women and young girls were avid viewers of sport on TV; one of them was Julie Welch. Her love of football began while she watched *Grandstand* with her father and in 1973 she became the first woman to write a football report for a national newspaper. Named the *Daily Telegraph Magazine* Young Writer of the Year in her final year at university, Welch joined the *Observer* sports department as a secretary. "Back then it was a way in for women," she recalls. "It was such fun on the sports desk and I liked sport so much I decided I wanted to try writing about sport." Welch found herself in the company of some of the greats like Hugh McIlvanney, whom she described as "quite possibly the greatest sports writer who's ever lived", and Arthur Hopcraft: "an extremely gifted writer". "As it happened, in 1973 Arthur decided he didn't want to write football anymore, he wanted to go away and write plays, so I said casually to the sports editor: 'Why don't you send me to write a football match?' And he did."[9]

On the opening day of the 1973/74 season Welch was in the press box of Highfield Road to report on Coventry's 1-0 win over Tottenham (which came courtesy of a rare Mick Coop goal). The following Monday the paper was inundated with calls asking if Julie was a man's name. "I knew people would take a bit of notice that there was a female byline but rather naïvely I had no idea that it would be such a big deal." There was also a negative reaction from some within the press box. "The attention I got caused some of the hostility. There was one reporter who was so unfriendly and so hostile; he was very, very anti-women in the press box yet when I talked to him away from football he was perfectly nice and pleasant. I think there is a problem that sport and football is the place that men used to go to get away from women, so the idea of a woman being there was quite difficult for some of them. It was something I put up with really because it was such a fantastic world to be in and such a fantastic job to be paid to watch football. It became easier for them when they realised I wasn't some sort of airhead or a snob who wouldn't like to hear swearing. I think I was kind of an honorary bloke and that got me by."

Welch moved on from match reporting to focus on writing books in the 1990s when football began to change and access to players became more restricted. "Mind you, I used to think I could get these

---

9   *The editor was Ronald Atkin, whom Welch later married.*

interviews because I was so talented and brilliant at interpreting football. It never, ever occurred to me that they just thought they could shag me. I think there was a great fear of female reporters; that they were a bit like groupies and I really had to steer clear of anything like that. I was terribly straight-laced all the time because this was my job and I wanted to be taken seriously. But I did get sent on certain stories and interviews because I was female."

Many of the sentiments that Welch expressed about her early experiences as a football writer were echoed by Jacqui Oatley, who 34 years later became the first woman to commentate on *Match of the Day*. Like Welch, Oatley was drawn to football by television, but in her case it was coverage of the women's game on Channel 4. She went on to play at university and then for Chiswick Ladies FC while she worked in intellectual property. However, after she dislocated her kneecap and ruptured some ligaments during a match in 2000 and was told she would not be able to play again she decided to retrain as a journalist. Stints on local radio led to commentary on Five Live where she became the first woman to commentate on British network radio in 2005. But none of this prepared her for the reaction when she was chosen to do the television commentary on Fulham's match with Blackburn at Craven Cottage in 2007.[10]

"It was extraordinary. It was just eight and a half minutes of high-lights at ten to midnight on a Saturday night in April but the reaction was incredible," Oatley said. "I wasn't naïve; I realised there could have been a bit of a fuss about it, but I didn't realise there would be so much in advance of the day. The problem was it was a Saturday and it was in the *Daily Mail* on the Tuesday morning and that gave it a lot of time to grow legs. So by Wednesday there was a full-page spread in the *Mail* of the pros and cons, with some people saying: 'It's not a problem' and others like Dave Bassett saying: 'it's a disgrace! Football's against it.' He asked how someone who'd never kicked a ball in their life could commentate on football, which made me laugh because he didn't know anything about me. He didn't know I'd played football for years. He didn't know I was a qualified coach. He just made assumptions purely based on my gender and that's what

10   *The game ended in a 1-1 draw, with Vincenzo Montella opening the scoring for the home side in the ninth minute and Benni McCarthy equalising with half an hour to play.*

really caused the storm, not that I was doing it but that someone said I shouldn't do it. That made it a 'sexism storm' so it became a much bigger story. I had so much support from other commentators. I had a phone call from John Motson, Jonathan Pearce – all the regulars. When I did my second *Match of the Day* commentary at Anfield my FiveLive colleague came up to me and said: 'I can't believe all the stick you got: I've never kicked a ball in my life and people assume I have, and you've played and people assume you haven't.' If you're female you have to prove yourself but if you're male it's assumed you know what you're talking about – that sums it up, you're fighting against prejudice."

Despite the support, Oatley told me that initially she found it hard. "It was difficult because every time you opened your mouth you were under scrutiny, which was really quite unpleasant. It's not a nice way to go about your job and I didn't really enjoy that. I was used to being the only female in the press box and I was used to being the only female with a microphone in the press box, but to have people looking at you and knowing people are judging you every time you say anything became really hard and not very enjoyable at all even though I'm quite a strong character. I've had to be strong throughout this, otherwise I would have gone and done something else altogether by now. Knowing people are talking about you and knowing people are being unpleasant about you is not very nice. So I've had to grow layers of skin; I had to make the best of it and just get on with it. But now I really enjoy it, I really enjoy my life."

There's a clear line from the early thoughts on TV football commentary expressed by the likes of Brian Johnston and negative reactions to Welch and Oatley to the infamous off-air conversation between the ultimate press-box 'lads': then-Sky presenters Andy Gray and Richard Keys in January 2011. The pair expressed disbelief that Sian Massey was to run the line in a Premier League match between Wolves and Liverpool at Molineux because, in Gray's words, "women don't know the offside rule". "The game's gone mad," Keys agreed, his Darwinian worldview crumbling in front of his eyes.[11] Whatever Gray and Keys might have thought, women clearly *did* know the

---

11   *Gray and Keys were sacked by Sky for a series of sexist comments before quickly resurfacing at talkSPORT.*

offside rule. Massey made a crucial, but correct call in the build-up to Fernando Torres' goal during the game and has gone on to receive widespread praise for her performances since.

What's more, women had been officiating in men's games since 1981 when Elizabeth Forsdick ran the line in an FA Cup tie. Eight years later Kim George refereed an FA Cup preliminary-round match and when interviewed by *The Times* she felt compelled to reassure the readers she was "not a strident feminist carrying the banner for women in sport". The idea that women didn't watch football (or didn't watch it 'properly') can also be found in subtle ways elsewhere. Of the 1,000 fans interviewed for the Popplewell Inquiry following the fire at Bradford's Valley Parade in 1985, not one was female. This was despite the fact that 11 of the 56 victims were female and that women made up about 15 per cent of football crowds at the time.

• • •

The television coverage of the men's game in the 1960s which inspired Welch also kick-started the slow journey towards genuine recognition for women's football in England, as women like Sue Lopez were also captivated. "The World Cup was the catalyst for a renaissance," she told me. "Women's football had been booming in England in the Twenties and it was the FA's ban that crushed it. Even though some teams like Manchester Corinthians and Fodens had continued playing charity matches it never captured the enormity of how successful the game was in terms of participation in the Twenties. So there was a big gap until the World Cup when lots of women said: 'hang on, this looks good'."

Lopez, who was on the verge of representing Hampshire at hockey before England's World Cup win made her a football convert, helped launch the Women's Football Association in 1969 and became a driving force in ensuring that the upsurge of interest in the women's game would be sustained. A few months after Bobby Moore lifted the Jules Rimet trophy, Lopez joined the Royal Assurance Exchange works team in Southampton (despite not working for the firm) and a couple of seasons later she began to play for the city's newly formed representative team. In November 1969 she was part of an England

XI (made up of players from the Chiltern Valley and Southampton clubs) that played in a four-nation tournament in Italy. Her goal-scoring exploits would lead, two years later, to her becoming the first female English player to play abroad, spending just under a season with Roma where she scored 11 goals in 14 games as they lifted the Coppa Italia and finished League runners-up behind Piacenza.

It was during this period that the FA finally lifted its 50-year ban on women's football at League grounds and started working more closely with their female counterparts in the recently formed WFA. Their hand was forced following the second unofficial women's World Cup in Mexico in 1971. While some aspects of the tournament were dubious to say the least – the goals were pink and the players were encouraged to wear hot pants and blouses – it was also a huge success and a crowd of 108,000 watched the opening game. If there's one thing guaranteed to make a football governing body take notice it is money, so UEFA leapt into action and requested all national associations take responsibility for the women's game in their country. However it wasn't until 1993 that the English FA took on the administration of the women's game and it did not lend its name to a women's League until 2011 when the Women's Super League (FAWSL) was launched.

It's little wonder it took so long given the prejudice the women's game continued to face in the national media. In 1969 as the FA was considering lifting its ban, John Morgan, then sports editor of the *Daily Express*, wrote: "There was some formal tut-tutting over the possible problems like ... What do we do about referees? (well, they couldn't be women, could they?). What do we do about disciplinary measures? (well, can you imagine the disciplinary commission having to adjudicate on 'Who pinched Ethel's bra?')." In 1972 Lopez was approached by a reporter from *Titbits* magazine, whose main focus appeared to be whether she had problems working with a male manager. Despite Lopez dismissing the idea, the resulting article suggested players and coaches had more on their minds than football, and it was printed with a picture of a man surrounded by women in provocative positions in a changing room. The focus on trivial (or in fact non-existent) off-field issues continued to be married to a disparaging attitude towards the players themselves, exemplified by Brian Glanville's *Sunday Times* report of England's 8-0 defeat of Scotland at Nuneaton in June 1973. It was the report in which he compared the women's game to a dog walking on its hind legs (a line he was still using in radio discussions several decades later). Under the headline "Goals and Gals Don't Mix", Glanville added that he doubted anyone who paid to watch the game would be willing to pay again, before giving a broad critique of feminism: "One's chief doubt about women's football is the same one has about Women's Lib itself; the most insidious triumph of the male-dominated society is that it has lured women into pursuing masculine goals."

Lopez had met Glanville in Italy where he had worked early in his career and he appeared to be a fan of the women's game, while also suggesting he thought it would struggle to gain acceptance in England because of the macho attitude of the establishment and media. However, according to Lopez, on his return home: "He followed the rest of them in England and just pooh-poohed it." That attitude was in stark contrast to the coverage Lopez experienced in Italy, which was, she said, "from another planet" and consistently better than anything to be found in England even now. "You had the *Corriere dello Sport* – a national publication – always featuring league tables as well as match reports and previews – and that was when I was there in 1971; apparently it had been going on before that." The paper had a reporter, Gianni Bezzi, dedicated to coverage of the Roma women's team and also gave full coverage to the women's national team as well as general features and articles about the politics and economics of the women's game. Lopez's move to Italy was also covered by the Milan-based news magazine *L'Europea,* which interviewed her and printed three full-page colour action shots of her playing. By contrast the English press exaggerated the financial aspects of the deal and that led to threats from the WFA that Lopez would be banned from playing for the then-amateur England team. So she returned home to ensure she remained eligible for national selection and went on to win 22 caps.

That isn't to say there was no positive media coverage in the English press. While most of it tended to come in the local press where players could send in their own reports and cultivate relationships with journalists, there was also some in the national press. In November

1974 England beat France 2-0 at Wimbledon's Plough Lane ground and Lopez says the quantity and quality of coverage was remarkable. In particular the team was flattered by Jimmy Hill's positive comparison with the men's team in the *News of the World*. Under the headline "Take a tip Revie – it's time to follow the girls" Hill praised the team's short passing game and their organised 4-3-3 system. Several years later in February 1977, following England's 1-0 victory over Italy also at Plough Lane, John Morgan of the *Daily Express*, who had been so dismissive of women's football eight years earlier, was moved to begin his match report with some self-reproach:

> Ladies, I apologise unreservedly and wholeheartedly. I went to Wimbledon to watch England play Italy expecting to snigger. I went with all the usual male prejudices about soccer being 'unfeminine'; that the girls would break down and cry if someone kicked them or if the referee was a bit nasty and did not allow a goal. I saw instead the best game of football I have seen since the famous Wolves managed by Stan Cullis terrorised Europe in the 1950s.

Lopez is convinced that the media have a role to play in the development of women's football. "It's like anything: if it's not in the media then it's not going on; it's kept a secret. But it needs more than just reports in papers, it needs reporting that is interesting and exciting." She cited the example of Lawrie McMenemy, then manager of Southampton's men's team, being photographed with the five of the club's women players picked to play for the national team against Belgium at The Dell in 1978.[12] "His public gesture of endorsing the fact that we were playing for England helped convey the message that women's football was acceptable and gave us a huge crowd," she said. England won 3-0 in front of 5,471.

However, the amount of coverage wasn't consistent and the women's game found it hard to gather momentum. In 1984 the England women's team reached the two-legged final of the inaugural UEFA European Championships, ultimately losing on penalties to Sweden. The first

---

12 *The five were: Sue Buckett, Pat Chapman, Linda Coffin, Maggie Pearce and Lopez herself.*

leg in Stockholm was broadcast live in the host country, which also sent a camera crew and 36 journalists to cover the second leg in Luton. The English media barely mentioned the final. The following year England won the Mundialito tournament – a forerunner to the Women's World Cup – beating hosts Italy 3-2 in the final thanks to two goals from then-19-year-old Marieanne Spacey. As with the UEFA final the year before, it should have become one of those key moments around which the history of the game is built but, as Spacey told me, it also went all but unnoticed by the media. "It was one of the first trophies an England team had won for some time, but when we flew back you wouldn't have known. It was really only our teammates and our friends and family that recognised our achievement. There was very, very, limited coverage. I think there might have been a couple of lines in one of the papers but that was it."

As a consequence of her brace in the final, Spacey, who went on to score 28 times in 91 games for England, was offered a contract by Italian club Lazio but it was a short-lived spell abroad and, as with Lopez's move to Italy 14 years earlier, the press were determined to put their own spin on things. "I came home after four days because the club couldn't guarantee that they'd always release me for England training unless it was for a UEFA- or FIFA-recognised game. All I wanted to do was play for England but the press picked up on the story and made out I was homesick and that I missed my boyfriend. It had nothing to do with that, I came home for football reasons, but I guess it made a better story to say I came home for other reasons."

• • •

Despite this, positive coverage of the women's game was steadily increasing. In 1987 BBC2 broadcast a documentary called *Home and Away* focused on the talent drain away from England, featuring some of Spacey's contemporaries such as England striker Kerry Davis and national captain Debbie Bampton, who both joined Italian side Despar Trani 80. The national team won the Mundialito again in 1988 and were surprise, but deserving, recipients of the *Sunday Times* Team of the Year award. The following year Channel 4 commissioned Trans

World International to produce a series of one-hour highlight and magazine shows presented by Hazel Irvine. They also covered some women's matches live and three million people tuned in to watch Leasowe Pacific (now Everton Ladies) beat Friends of Fulham 3-2 at Old Trafford[13] in the 1989 WFA Cup Final. If there was a watershed moment for the media coverage of the modern game, Channel 4's programming was it.

"When we got back from the match," said Spacey, who was on the losing side, "we went into the local McDonald's. There were a couple of people in there who'd just watched the match and they were staring at us saying: 'we've just seen you on telly'. We'd never been recognised before and it was quite a moment of realisation at how powerful television could be in getting the game out to a wider audience who don't attend the matches. Channel 4 did a great job, they even filmed me at work – a leisure centre in Brixton. It suddenly hit us that the game was out there and it changed our mentality – we started taking a more professional approach but it was also from there the game grew; that was the start of when it became something people knew was out there happening."

The scheduling of WFA games on Sunday afternoons (this, remember, was in the days when the men's Premier League didn't exist and kick-off times weren't being shifted all over the place to suit Sky) allowed for continuity of coverage and the shows regularly pulled in excess of 2.5 million viewers, often more than the channel's coverage of the NFL. It began to look as if the women's game could build a regular TV audience. There had been some limited coverage before, for example the BBC had shown highlights of Southampton beating QPR in the 1976 WFA Cup Final, but following Channel 4's sustained coverage the WFA received hundreds of letters asking how players could join or set up a women's team. This was reinforced by the channel's drama *The Manageress*, also broadcast in 1989, which was written by Stan Hey and starred Cherie Lunghi as Gabriella Benson, the manager of a fictional Second Division men's team. "The fun was having a look at the game from a female perspective," said Hey. "It came at a time when the game was especially brutal, with the European ban,

13 *The next women's game to be played at the stadium would be the match between the USA and North Korea during the 2012 Olympic Games.*

hooliganism and the unintended brutality of stadium tragedies. It just felt like that male culture of football was coming to an end."

While the series provides a snap-shot of the woeful state of the men's game in the late 1980s, if you take away the amusingly obsolete technology and the terrible 1980s fashion it is way ahead of its time. It deals with a host of issues ranging from racism and sexism to England's insularity from the rest of the football world. Benson changes the team's tactics and the menu in the canteen (both decisions are greeted with consternation) and – even worse – she orders the players not to tackle in training but to instead win the ball through anticipation. Tackling, she argues, is a last resort (remember, this was seven years before some bloke called Arsene Wenger strolled into Highbury and introduced novel concepts like grilled broccoli, much to Ian Wright's disgust, and started moaning when his players had their legs broken). Hey continued: "She's not just an outsider but she's also a fan. That's why we had the scene at the beginning where she's watching Real Madrid beat Eintract 7-3 as a girl. It was saying: 'women like football too', that was the agenda – with a small 'a'."

After Channel 4 pulled its WFA coverage ahead of the 1992/93 season, Sky picked up the baton but with satellite TV still in its infancy the potential audience was considerably smaller, a problem compounded by the programme being parked on a women's lifestyle channel – *UK Living* – instead of a sports channel. The women's game is only now receiving comparable exposure, with the BBC's Director of Sport Barbara Slater committing to significant coverage of women's international football tournaments across TV, radio and the internet, plus programmes on the Super League complemented by coverage on BT Sport. Channel 4's coverage didn't stop some journalists making derogatory comments; football commentator Archie Macpherson, for example, wrote in the *Sunday Times* in 1990: "I'm not saying a woman's place is purely in the home – though some skivvying does not do them any harm. If Channel 4 wants to show us how entertaining football can be outside the senior game then let them put the cameras at other places. Like any school playground." Despite the visible evidence to the contrary, the double stereotype that football wasn't feminine and that, anyway, women weren't any good at it persisted.

A couple of years before Macpherson's article Spacey was interviewed by researchers at the Sir Norman Chester Centre for Football
Research and told them that she felt that in the eyes of many men
(and women) female footballers were "just a bunch of dykes running
about a football field; women trying to be men". Spacey laughed
when I reminded her of the comment. "How naïve was I then?" she
said. "We hadn't had any media training so when people asked a question you were honest and gave an answer you might not give today
but it probably was how I felt at the time. It was frustrating because
that was the perception. Back then the media always wanted to put
you in ball gowns and do your hair and makeup. As long as it was a
positive piece, we saw it as a way of promoting women's football and
we really enjoyed it because we had a girls' day out which was fodder
for us in the dressing room but the media took it as 'this is what they
could look like if only they tried'."

This attitude is the more insidious manifestation of the idea that
women who play football are tomboys, and several studies of the
women footballers at college or club level have since shown that the
perception of a link between lesbianism and women's football was
both the strongest theme to develop within the research and the most
important issue for the interviewees.[14] There is a flipside of course.
While female footballers are damagingly masculinised, so male
footballers who do not conform to the euphemistic English 'big lad'
stereotype – those players who don't go in for the equally euphemistic
'hard tackle' – are damagingly feminised, or as Spacey put it: "the
men are moisturising and the women are shaving".

The most recent example of this was the anti-snood backlash in the
2010/11 season. The *Mail on Sunday* kept a close eye on the "epidemic"
of "top-flight softies" wearing the winter neck-warmers and (heaven
forbid) gloves while also helpfully pointing out how many of the players
were foreign. Their campaign was backed by a chorus of disapproval
from the likes of Sir Alex Ferguson, who said snoods were for "powder
puffs" and that "real men don't wear things like that". His former player
Paul Ince, then manager of Notts County, said snoods "weren't right'
and that players "will be wearing skirts next". Even Karren Brady was

---

14   *If you're interested, check out the work of John Harris and Jayne Caudwell.*

moved to say that if she saw a West Ham player wearing a snood she'd "rip it off with her own bare hands". The *Observer*'s Paul Wilson also made his feelings clear in a piece following Everton's win at Manchester City that season: "Not only did they [Everton] sport short sleeves at Eastlands on one of the coldest nights of the year, there were 11 bare necks, which makes them even more deserving of some kind of award from the campaign for real football. Or perhaps real men."

Let's not kid ourselves, the debate was not really about an innocuous item of clothing. It was about what it took to be a man in the world of English football. It would be laughable, but when such loaded and aggressive terminology is used it is little wonder there are no openly gay players in the Premier League. Also underpinning coverage of men's football is the related sexual objectification of women. This ranges from the *Sun* offering video goal alerts of one of their "stunning Page 3 girls celebrating in her own classic Page 3 style" (that's topless, in case you hadn't guessed) during the 2014 men's World Cup to the *Daily Mail* detailing how "English football's finest other halves line up ahead of the 2015–16 season". It probably goes without saying that the article was accompanied by pictures of said other halves without many clothes on. Whether it is the patriotic Page 3 girl or the supportive WAG, the focus on their femininity and physical features demonstrates that Derek Jameson's "tits and bums" perception of women lives on, further reinforcing what is expected from them in the world of English football media.

• • •

While the tabloids might be stuck in the past, social media offers women footballers the opportunity to challenge these perceptions and take control of their own image. "It would be crazy of us not to utilise the power of things like Twitter to raise the players' profiles and the game's profile," said Spacey, who was appointed assistant manager of the England team in 2014. "It's a lot easier to do it than even five years ago, but when I was playing social media didn't exist. We just relied on the pen and paper of the journalists who might come out and support us. Now the players can put out lots of positive and vibrant messages for people who follow them."

Steph Houghton, who captained the Lionesses to the semi-finals of the 2015 World Cup, agrees. "I think young girls who are wanting to be footballers now aren't really going to pick up a newspaper or read a magazine; they're more likely going to find something on YouTube or Twitter or Facebook," she told me. "Social media can be really quite powerful. Players can show a different side to themselves and we can push the game to young girls and boys and their parents." It's one of the many changes Houghton has seen in the coverage of women's football since she made her first-team debut for Sunderland in 2002. "When I started playing in the first team at the age of 14 I don't think you could find the fixtures on any website or in the papers and there were no women's football games on television. Even a few years ago you might find that just the quarter-final of a tournament was on TV. But after our games in the London Olympics were broadcast I think we've seen massive strides. There's one league game shown every week and at the World Cup in Canada every single group game was broadcast and we were doing interviews leading up to the games. There's a chance now for players to be part of adverts and appear in magazines and in big newspaper articles. Social media's been a massive part of it and something we want to embrace as we want to be seen in a positive light."

Success on the pitch is one thing almost certain to generate positive coverage and Houghton and her teammates achieved that in the 2015 World Cup, winning a knockout game for the first time and beating the hosts Canada in the quarter-finals before losing in the semi-finals to holders Japan thanks to a last-minute own goal from Laura Bassett. They then went on to beat Germany in the third-place play-off but the manner in which the Lionesses took to social media and the positive response they got only seemed to increase the feel-good factor. "We had so many good luck messages through Twitter, Facebook and Instagram it was unbelievable," said Houghton "and the feedback after the games was nice; when you're playing well you like to read that. There's been a massive difference between the World Cup in 2011 and 2015 when we received a lot more messages. It was great that we were able to post selfies after the games and I think that the way the girls handled themselves in terms of social media in the World Cup was fantastic. There was a lot of letting the fans know where we were travelling to and what we were up to. We were still focused on the games but after them maybe we relaxed a little bit and showed a little bit of our personalities. I think it was great we were able to show that side and the fans responded to it very well."

Jacqui Oatley, who fronted the BBC's coverage of the World Cup, believes the tournament was a turning point for the women's game: "It's made a huge difference. I've covered women's football for the BBC for well over a decade and the perception used to be very, very negative even among some colleagues I'm ashamed to say. But I think they were just reflecting wider perceptions in the country – not the world – about whether or not women could play football to a high standard and what standard of men's player could beat the women. It was just negative and frustrating but since the Women's World Cup I've had people stopping me coming out of Premier League matches and wanting to talk about the women – not about the men that they've just seen – and saying they've got really into it."

For Oatley, even though the tournament ended in heartbreak, the manner of the semi-final defeat helped as it created an interesting story. "Being in the semi-final of the World Cup for the first time was absolutely huge and the nation really got behind the team. But what happened after that only served to increase the recognition of the women's game. Even though it was a devastating way to end the semi-final, Laura Bassett's own goal actually raised awareness a huge amount."

Despite the game kicking off at midnight in the UK, some 1.7m viewers were watching when Bassett put through her own net against Japan, while England's victory over the Canadians to set up the semi-final tie dominated the back pages and even made the front page of Derek Jameson's baby the *Daily Star* with a picture of Jill Scott and Jodie Taylor celebrating the latter's winner headlined "Goalden Girls" (although for anyone concerned the paper had suddenly become a bastion of feminism, the same front page reminded readers that the paper was still the "HOME OF THE PAGE 3 BABE").

Houghton and her England teammates also made history when they were one of 12 women's national teams to be included in EA Sports' *FIFA 16* game for the first time. "It's a bit surreal to be honest, to be part of the game and have your cousins and your friends playing as you," Houghton told me about seeing herself digitally rendered on screen. "In fact at the last England camp we all played on it as each other, which was quite funny." However she recognises that the team's inclusion in the game, which was the second-highest entertainment product of 2015, only behind Adele's album *25*, is a huge stride forward. "When we first heard we were going to be part of it we were a bit shocked but it shows how far the women's game's progressed. Now young girls and boys playing that at the age of six or seven will just see us as the norm."

It's a point on which Oatley agrees: "It's all part of the bigger picture of making women's football mainstream, which of course it should be. It should be on a par with men's football in terms of acceptability and recognition. Football is a global game for everybody. If the women are in *FIFA 16* it normalises it, not just for girls but boys too. If they grow up playing games like *FIFA* it means when their sister asks if they can play football they'll say: 'Of course, why not?' The better the women's players do and the more women that work in the media, the more people will recognise that football is for everybody and it's not just a man's game. Girls that play football shouldn't be called 'tomboys' – they're just girls who like football."

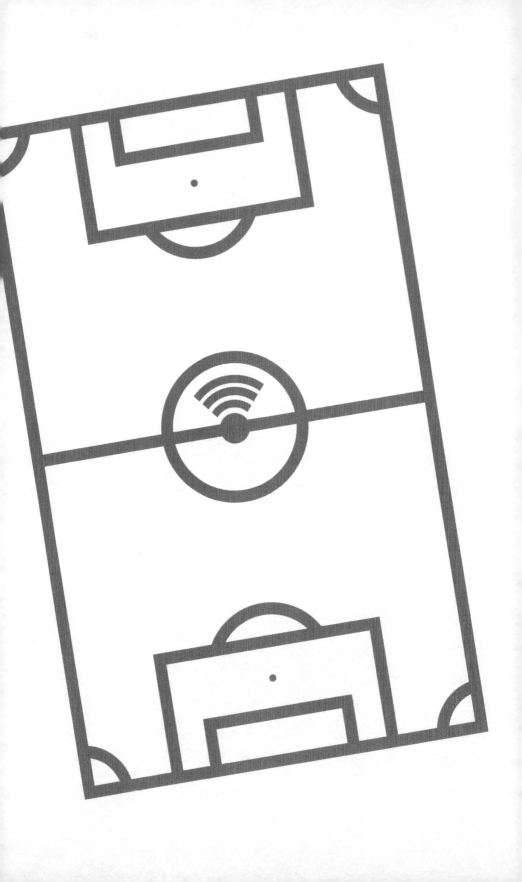

CHAPTER 14

BACK OF THE NET

Sir Alex Ferguson retires #thankyousiralex". With that Tweet at 9.17am on Wednesday 8 May 2013, Manchester United confirmed the news many of us had already guessed: Twitter is the dominant media for discussing football. We may watch it on TV and read about it in newspapers, books and magazines (or watch and read about it on our tablets or smartphones) but when it comes to actually talking about the beautiful game, Twitter's where it's at. The 2012/13 season saw Chelsea use Twitter to announce Roberto Di Matteo's sacking and the appointment of first Rafael Benítez and then José Mourinho. QPR tweeted the firing of Mark Hughes and the hiring of Harry Redknapp and Everton broke the news of Roberto Martinez's appointment via Twitter. The fact that the Old Trafford media team decided to eschew the tried and tested methods of the press conference or press release and instead used Twitter to confirm that Sir Alex was stepping down speaks volumes.

Within eight minutes the club's self-styled hashtag '#Thank YouSirAlex' was the top trend worldwide. Within an hour there had been 1.4 million mentions of the story on Twitter, 400,000 more than the announcement of Margaret Thatcher's death received a month earlier, over the same period. The following year Germany's 7-1 rout of Brazil became the most tweeted about event ever, with a staggering total of 35.6 million tweets or retweets. That number peaked when Sami Khedira netted Die Mannschaft's fifth, generating a record 580,000 tweets per minute (breaking the previous set when Miley Cyrus twerked her way to controversy with the help of Robin Thicke at MTV's 2013 VMAs). "We know that sport is a very, very rich conversation area on Twitter and two-thirds of our users talk about football," said Alex Trickett, the company's UK Head of Sport. "It's one of the most powerful, unifying real-time conversations. The only thing that occasionally rivals it is an important moment around a huge pop star. Sport has that traction, but football has that traction first and foremost."

• • •

Twitter was developed by a guy called Jack Dorsey while he was working for American podcasting firm Odeo. Dorsey envisaged Twitter (originally called Twttr) as an SMS-based platform for friends to keep in touch with each other via their status updates and it was he who sent the first tweet in March 2006. It said simply: "just setting up my twttr". From that point Twitter's growth was exponential and this led to regular system crashes signified by Yiying Lu's illustration of a whale being lifted out of the water by eight birds; the 'fail whale'. As Twitter went from being an SMS-based platform to a web-based platform so the need to constrain tweets to 140 characters disappeared but Dorsey and his colleagues decided to keep it; it was a smart move as the need to be brief enhances Twitter's speed – one of its strengths. That constraint aside, the Twitter team followed the paths beaten by their users. Retweets, hashtags and the "@" sign to denote a user's name were all user-generated innovations that became part of Twitter's functionality. So, why is Twitter the perfect medium for discussing football (and other stuff like *The X Factor*)? Well, there are two reasons. Firstly it is immediate, in terms both of the speed with which you can communicate and with whom, and secondly it complements live television.

Twitter taps into something that has come to be known as 'internet time', the concept being that technology has increased the pace at which events happen and they happen at the fastest pace on the internet. This in turn is affecting the pace of change in society more generally (internet time is different to 'Fergie time' in which time expands by six minutes ...). In the past we had a much broader, less accurate concept of time. There was the light bit: day, and the dark bit: night. The length of the day was determined by whether it was spring, summer, autumn or winter and the position of the sun in the sky would indicate roughly what time it was. In pre-industrial societies man-made clocks – dials around which the sun would cast shadows or hourglasses through which sand flowed – only served to reinforce the fact that nature dictated the pace at which events happened. This began to change with the invention of mechanical clocks and the introduction of clock towers with bells in the Middle Ages. These bells would be rung at certain times to signify important events (such as the start or end of work, the opening or closing of markets and so on). Time was becoming more regulated; the pace of life had sped up a little. That said, there was still a disparity in the time across the country – as much as 20 minutes between some towns – until in 1840 the Great Western Railway introduced 'railway time'; the standardisation of local times to Greenwich Mean Time.

This was driven by the need to eradicate timetable confusion. Once again time was becoming more regulated; the pace of life sped up a little more. Well, I say 'sped up'; it actually took 40 years before the whole of Britain was brought into one time zone following the passing of the 1880 Statutes (Definition of Time) Act. Around then, Frederick Winslow Taylor, chief engineer at the Midvale Steel Company in Philadelphia, started timing how long it took his workers to complete each part of their job, in a bid to increase productivity. The time-and-motion study had been born. Capitalists the world over rubbed their hands and the pace of life sped up further still. Now we have wristwatches with more memory than an Apollo rocket and we can measure time to a fractional level of 10^{18}. To put it another way, the world's most accurate clock loses only one 'tick' in 10^{18} 'tocks'.[1] I'll be honest and admit I have absolutely no concept of how big that number is, but I do know that along with these increased levels of accuracy have come more time constraints and less patience.

Alongside this, the development of media technology effectively decreased the time it took to communicate information. Initially you had to rely on heralds like Pheidippides who ran from Marathon to Athens.[2] They were replaced by men on horseback who could courier

1   This ridiculously accurate clock was unveiled by boffins at the National Institute of Standards and Technology in May 2013. Of course you can make all sorts of claims about the accuracy of one clock so, just to be sure, they built two.

2   It goes without saying that Pheidippides' heroic but fatal feat inspired the modern marathon and it would be nice to think the modern distance is based on the distance he ran, but no. That was the case up until 1908 when the British added 2.2 miles for the benefit of the Royal family. So the distance of the modern marathon – 26.2 miles – is equivalent to the distance between Windsor Castle and the Royal Family's box at London's White City Stadium – the route of the 1908 Olympic marathon.

your message more quickly. The postal service brought structure, the railways and the telegraph speed, and radio and television greater intimacy and immediacy. Now you can browse the internet, get the latest stats and talk to your mates almost wherever and whenever you like (without the hassle of actually having to meet them). Just months after becoming President in 2008, Barack Obama lamented a political "attention span that has only grown shorter with the 24-hour news cycle". Similarly, Britain's former Prime Minister Tony Blair argued in his evidence to the Leveson Inquiry that the impact of rolling news channels meant the Government has to respond to the demands of the media more quickly then ever before. Recalling Roy Jenkins telling him that in the past some Cabinet meetings lasted two days, Blair suggested this would have been impossible when he became Prime Minister or "there would have been total crisis mode for the whole of the Government".

This impatience has also found its way into sport. Basketball players used to be able to take as much time as they wanted to get the ball down court and have a shot; alternatively they could 'freeze' the ball if they had a slim lead near the end of a game. In 1954, just after the advent of television, this was no longer deemed acceptable, so in an attempt to speed up the game, the shot clock was introduced limiting offensive teams to just 24 seconds in which to attempt to score. Tie-breaks were introduced into tennis 11 years later for the same reason.[3] In his 1986 book *Sports Spectators*, historian Allen Guttmann wrote of cricket that "the length of Victorian and later matches symbolised the pace of life in a rural society not yet dominated by an industrial sense of time". By 1937, we'd seen the last timeless Test after a match between England and South Africa in Durban ended drawn after 11 days because the visitors had to catch their boat home. *The Times* argued that: "A match without the discipline imposed by time is null and void of all the elements which go to make cricket the enchanting game it naturally is." From then on Test matches were restricted to five days – the equivalent of a nicely controlled, industrialised working week. Within 30 years the one-day game had been introduced and

---

3   As the tie-break doesn't always apply to the final set, tennis can still throw up the odd anomaly like the eleven-hour-five-minute Wimbledon epic between John Isner and Nicolas Mahut in 2010 in which Isner eventually took the fifth set 70-68.

in 2003 T20 was born. It is cricket for the Twitter generation – short and quick. No one even bothers to use its full name.

The increased speed and immediacy created by social media was initially seen as a challenge to the traditional model of broadcasting. The introduction of any new form of media leads to uncertainty among those who use existing technology and football broadcasters were concerned that audiences would be lost to them as they began to talk among themselves. However, sociologists Brett Hutchins and David Rowe argue that internet access and social media have combined with television to create "a transmedia sport experience irreducible to its constituent parts". They go on to suggest that sports fans are able to personalise their viewing experience through a combination of TV, internet and social media and so "the key to the future of media sport is the *relationship* between screens". The concept of the second screen has been born. It allows people to call up stats, bet on matches or snipe at poor punditry literally seconds after it has left the co-commentator's mouth. While not a noted sociologist, will.i.am, a judge on the BBC's *The Voice*, the main rival to *The X Factor*, appears to think the same thing. In the second series of the programme the former Black Eyed Pea took to tweeting during the live shows even when contestants were singing and the other judges were talking. He dismissed suggestions he was being rude by saying (predictably in a tweet): "I told the bbc: 'It may seem odd me tweeting … but trust me … this will be the norm one day & people are going to copy it' … #thevoiceuk." As it transpires, he was right.

As television technology has changed so watching it has become an increasingly personal experience. Those 'cord-cutters' we met back in Chapter 9, who are leaving Sky for digital streaming companies, can now watch what they want, when the want, where they want. The likes of Netflix and Amazon are making their own shows, like *House of Cards* and *The Man in the High Castle*, and releasing all the episodes in one go. Watch them on the train on your tablet or at home on your TV; ration them out over several weeks or have a weekend box-set marathon: the choice is yours. Just as social media has arrived on the scene with its power to build communities around TV shows, viewing habits are fracturing and becoming more individualistic. Except, that is, with 'live' broadcasts such as breaking news and shows like

The Voice, Strictly Come Dancing or *The X Factor* and, of course, live, televised sport. Here the whole thrill is watching the drama unfold in real time, and millions, sometimes billions, do so. Let's be honest, very few people will regularly record a football match and watch it on a delay – so-called 'timeshifting'. Twitter's Alex Trickett told me, the company has a lot of evidence to prove that there's a symbiotic and complementary relationship between TV and Twitter, particularly during live sports broadcasts. "We know that sport is possibly the one thing that people won't timeshift," Trickett said. "If you think of that *Likely Lads* episode where they try to avoid seeing the England score – people have given up doing that now. They know they need to watch in the moment or the moment will pass."

Incidentally, given that a welcome message to David Moyes was accidentally posted on Manchester United's Facebook page before he'd been confirmed as Sir Alex's successor, you might think Mark Zuckerberg and his chums would disagree about Twitter's dominance. While it's true Facebook has considerably more users (about 1.59bn compared to about 305 million for Twitter) there are some key differences between the two social networks. Facebook is like a house party: you invite in who you want, it remains a fairly select group, and while they might not all know each other, you know all of them. Twitter is like a pub: anyone can be listening in to your conversation. They might interject with something of value and you'll happily chat again the next time you're both in for a pint, eventually becoming friends, or they might interject with a drunken, racist slur and you'll have to notify the police. "You could be sat at home with your nan watching a particular match or incident unfold," said Trickett. "The beauty of Twitter is that you can then extend beyond your own four walls and say: 'I'm actually watching this with an ex-player, with rival fans, with referees, with pundits all at the same time.'" So, as far as talking about football is concerned, Twitter bests Facebook because while the former is relatively enclosed, the latter allows for the quick formation of ad hoc communities of interest. The proof of the pudding is in the tweeting – in a bid not to get left behind, Facebook has introduced hashtags.

• • •

Before the world went digital it was analogue and any football fan over the age of 30 will know that the analogue version of the internet was teletext. As with a fair few technological innovations, teletext came about by accident when BBC technicians trying to create subtitles for the hard-of-hearing realised that they could transmit whole pages of text using "spare lines" transmitted via the analogue signal. In September 1974 the Beeb took this technology and created Ceefax, a news and information service which gave the viewer access to the latest information more or less as soon as it came into the newsroom (in other words, to "see facts"). Veteran journalist Colin McIntyre was appointed to oversee the service's 24 pages, which contained the latest news headlines, sports scores, weather updates and TV listings. Initially they were only updated during weekday office hours but soon there was a team of eight working on Ceefax and at its peak it ran to 2,000 pages. ITV launched a rival service called ORACLE, which wasn't named after a Greek priest imparting wisdom from the Gods but was an acronym for Optional Reception of Announcements by Coded Line Electronics (it's almost like they thought of the name first and made up the meaningless techno jargon second). Subsequently in 1993 ORACLE was replaced after being outbid for the franchise by Teletext Ltd.[4]

In the early days McIntyre and his colleagues would monitor copy from the wire agencies then type their story into a terminal. This would create a punched tape about a metre long. The tape would then be taken from Ceefax's sixth-floor office down two flights of stairs to the Central Apparatus Room and fed into a metal box that would transmit the pages. It was only when the writer was back in the office that they would see if they had made a mistake, and if they had, well, the whole process had to be started again. While this laborious content management system sounds like it came from the mind of Heath Robinson, the service itself was very fast because the low-level technology meant Ceefax had no video, audio or pictures embedded into it. The rudimentary technology also necessitated that the writers be brief. Ceefax had a maximum of 24 lines per page and

4   It had been ORACLE's idea to create the franchise in the first place and they were a little bitter to have missed out. On 31 December 1992 – their last day – they refused to list TV programmes which came after midnight, instead displaying: "00.00 The End of Oracle, Now the Nightmare Begins".

a maximum of 40 characters per line. Some of the lines were lost to headlines so most Ceefax stories consisted of about 80 words. The combination meant that Ceefax provided fast, bite-sized chunks of news, things which are now the norm.

While it wasn't pretty to look at – a black background, with white, green and yellow words seemingly made from large pixels – football fans lapped it up. Anyone born before the 1990s will have certain page numbers seared into their memory: 312 for the 'football news in brief'; 324 for the tables; 337 for the 'rolling vidiprinter'; 338 for the day's tabloid transfer rumours; and in the summer months 341 for the all-important cricket news. If you were really posh you might have had a remote with red, green, blue and yellow buttons that could be used to jump about within Ceefax's colour-coded index. There was also a 'hold' button for the slow readers but this was about as much control as you had. As the technology developed there was even an 'in vision' facility so you could keep track of the scores via a little bar at the bottom of the screen while you actually watched the TV. Ceefax page 303 came into its own on Saturdays with the scores from the First Division (this was back before the Premier League, when you still had as many as 12 games kicking off at 3pm). At the start of the afternoon the games were sub-divided into three pages that would scroll round at a set pace. However, as the goals and associated facts like goal-scorers and sending-offs started coming in, so the number of pages needed grew, which meant you had to wait longer for the page with *your* team on to scroll round. The viewer could employ certain tactics like re-keying the number of the page they were on in the hope they would get the updated version of the sub-page they wanted more quickly. More often than not, Ceefax just skipped past it to spite you for trying to beat the system.

Initially very few televisions could get Ceefax but as its popularity grew in the 1980s it drove the sale of sets with the capacity to receive it. The service reached the peak of its popularity in the mid-1990s, just after the launch of the National Lottery, when around 20 million people were checking the service every week. In 1994 Wolves' fans inundated Molineux to complain about manager Graham Taylor changing the club's famous orange kit to all-white. He wasn't – it was an April Fools' story on Ceefax – but it underlined how pervasive the service was at the time.[5] However, in 1995, just as Ceefax reached its peak, Microsoft founder Bill Gates sent a confidential memo to his executive staff (on paper) titled 'The Internet Tidal Wave'. The internet was, he said, "the most important single development to come along since the IBM PC was introduced in 1981" and one to which he assigned the "highest level of importance". The company launched the Windows 95 operating system, including something called 'Internet Explorer 2.0', and in the following few years access to what was quaintly called "cyberspace" became increasingly widespread.

In the long run Ceefax didn't stand a chance but, despite the fact its death sentence had been signed, the service held its own against websites for a good few years. In the days when you had to dial up a connection to the internet, if you wanted the latest football news Ceefax was still the place to go. Switch on the TV, hit the 'Text' button, key in the number 302 and you had all the day's headlines. In the same time, your PC was probably still deciding whether it was going to let you type in your password. Famously in 1997 Bruce Rioch learned he'd been sacked as assistant manager of QPR via Ceefax. "I am bitterly disappointed they didn't have the courtesy to phone me before I read it on television," said the Scot. On 11 September 2001, when confronted with one of the biggest breaking news stories of all time, the internet, in its youth, was simply unable to cope with the demand and froze. Ceefax, however, like a hardened hack kept churning out the stories for all to see. While they might seem incredibly archaic from today's perspective, Ceefax and its ITV rivals were precursors to the internet, live blogs, Twitter and 24-hour rolling news channels. They showed there was a demand for instant, constantly accessible news and sports coverage and in a sense also created that demand by changing the way we viewed information. No longer were we prepared to wait until *Final Score* for the football scores or the tail-end of the one o'clock, six o'clock or nine o'clock news bulletins for the latest football headlines; we wanted information literally at our finger tips.

Ceefax has gone now but its younger relative – digital text – lives on. You probably know it as 'the red button' which gives all sorts of

---

5   According to the story, Taylor, still traumatised by England's non-qualification for that summer's World Cup at the hands of Holland, declared: "I do not like orange."

extra functionality, like choosing which game you watch, or which commentary you listen to. The BBC started offering their TV viewers the option of listening to Radio Five Live commentary while watching matches via the red button and in Euro 2012 even let the CBBC presenters have a crack at commentating during the final. It was designed to appeal to younger viewers but for some strange reason the analysis of Hacker T Dog proved a hit with older fans too. The commentary team, in a surreal world of their own, managed not to notice it was half time and were oblivious to Spain's third goal, but who cares? At one stage 'CBBC' was trending higher than 'Spain' or 'Italy' on Twitter. A few months after the tournament, in November 2012, the last analogue transmitter was shut down.

• • •

By the time the final few TV owners stumbled blinking into the digital era the internet was ubiquitous. It has become such a huge part of our lives that, like electricity, we only realise how much we rely on it when it stops working. It was all very different when Gates sent his memo in 1995. Back then there were fewer than 40,000 domestic internet connections in the UK[6] and one of them happened to belong to Greg Hadfield and his 12-year-old son, Tom. Hadfield, at the time an investigative reporter for the *Daily Mail*, was prompted to get the connection as Tom began spending more and more time using the internet at his friend's house. "Tom would call us at 9pm to say his friend had gone to bed," Hadfield told me from his office in Brighton. "Then his friend's parents would call at 11pm saying they were going to bed and asking us to pick Tom up. That obviously wasn't the way to go, so we were one of the first people to get the internet."

These were the days before unlimited broadband and Tom was soon running up massive monthly telephone bills. However, as he did so he found a large number of ex-pats desperate for the latest football scores from England. They'd been used to having to wait for the latest papers to be shipped over to wherever they were living, so for them the internet, which could transmit information across the

6   *To put this into perspective, by 2015 86 per cent of all UK households (around 22.5m) had an internet connection, up from 57 per cent in 2006.*

world instantaneously, was a godsend. So was Tom. "He recognised the importance of live football scores," Hadfield continued, "and sometime between his birthday in October 1994 and the end of the season in 1995 he rented some space on a server in Chicago – I still don't even know how he did that – and started putting up live football scores on a very basic web page that he created called *Mystic Meg's Premier League Service*. Every Saturday he was posting the football scores from teletext as they came in and it was getting huge traffic apparently. I learnt all this in retrospect."

It was during the close season that Tom told his dad what he'd been doing and how he thought it could be improved. "In June 1995 I was having a bath and he came in and told me his vision for what became *Soccernet*. I got it straight away. I got out of the bath, dried, got dressed and wrote a three-page business plan for the site. Being at the *Daily Mail* I thought I must go and see the editor Paul Dacre, not least because in June 1995 Sir David English – the famous journalist, who in old print journalism is a god – had appeared at a conference with a young politician called Tony Blair and basically said this: 'I don't know what the internet is but I do know there will be little people with big ideas and organisations such as ours should support them'. I thought: 'This is fantastic; my son's just told me this idea about the internet which nobody knows anything about and here's my super-boss saying: 'We should support little people with big ideas.'" Hadfield's business plan persuaded his superiors at Associated Newspapers[7] that there might be something in Tom's idea and a deal was struck whereby the pair were allowed to use football reports from the *Daily Mail* and its sister Sunday title to complement their live scores.

With the help of a designer the site was spruced up and officially launched on Saturday 19 August 1995 for the start of the new season. "I took apart my computer and we drove up to the *Daily Mail* newsroom where there was only one actual computer and that was the IT department's, and we took down the match reports, copied them across and supplemented them with live scores. At about 7pm when we'd put up all the reports we chased back to our home in Brighton with our computer on the back seat of my Ford Mondeo to put it back

---

7   To demonstrate they'd finally gone digital, Associated Newspapers ditched the analogue name in early 2013, becoming DMG Media, complete with one of those modern, lower-case logos.

together in our house so we could log on to the internet just to change the date on the front page of *Soccernet*." It was the day Aston Villa beat Manchester United 3-1 and Alan Hansen confidently declared that you couldn't win anything with kids. By the end of the season it wasn't just Fergie's Fledglings that had proved if you were good enough you were old enough and Tom's idea took off.

As Hadfield remembers: "Things got crazy in 1995" and by the turn of the year Associated Press was including the *Soccernet* web address in their TV advertising – a first for the English press. "We were the only website in the world doing live scores – that was the secret," said Hadfield. "It became the most popular website in Europe; there was no server in Europe that could handle the traffic that the site was receiving. Initially, however, few of Hadfield's colleagues understood the implications of what he and his son were doing: "There were people I met in Africa on my travels as a journalist who'd heard of *Soccernet* at a time when people sitting next to me in the *Daily Mail* newsroom hadn't. People I know told me at the time: 'Oh, it's a fad, it's like CB Radio. No one will ever want to get their football scores off a computer when they've got Ceefax.'"

Another redesign came in late 1997 in time for the draw for France '98. *Soccernet* covered it live and the demand crashed their servers – by that time based in Fort Lauderdale, Florida. "The Americans couldn't believe it," said Hadfield. "It was France '98 when people around me started to get it. There were hundreds of journalists in France covering the World Cup and I was sitting at my kitchen table in Brighton running a website, hosted in Florida, and we led the world. We were probably one of the busiest websites in the world at the time. We took $5m in advertising and sponsorship. We had five million page impressions a day, 300,000 unique users a day. I made the claim that France '98 would do for the internet what the Vietnam War did for television news, which I still believe." In 1999, less than five years after *Soccernet*'s launch, Associated cashed in by selling 60 per cent of their stake in the website for £15m to Disney's interactive division. The site was rebranded *ESPN:Soccernet* before becoming its current incarnation: *ESPN FC*. That deal with Disney was an early indication of the huge online value of football.

• • •

I wasn't blessed with Tom Hadfield's technical knowledge or his business acumen and so I took a fairly conventional path from school to university. After graduation I briefly worked part time in the Press Association (PA) as one of the team receiving phone updates from football match-reporters, and then uploading them to the database that fed, among other things, *Grandstand*'s vidiprinter. There I saw an advert to be a reporter on *Sportinglife.com*, a newly launched venture between Mirror Group and the PA. Somehow I got the job. At the time, as far as the internet was concerned, the PA was leading the way among news organisations. In 1994 it launched one of the first genuinely dynamic websites that updated a range of news and sport headlines as well as financial and weather information automatically from the company's databases. In his history of the PA, *Living on a Deadline*, Chris Moncrieff argues that one of the reasons the PA took the lead in the internet was that, unlike other media organisations which had regular but specific deadlines, "for the Press Association every second of every day was, and is, a deadline". In effect they were already working in internet time. Furthermore, staff were encouraged to give voice to their ideas and told that often the best ones were the ones that sounded bizarre to begin with, an ethos that was notable by its absence in successive newspaper offices I worked in.

I was only the second full-time member of editorial staff at *Sportinglife*, and to be honest in those early days in 1997 it felt like there weren't that many more people actually looking at the site. However, the office just outside Leeds City centre quickly filled up with a (sometimes combustible) mix of techies and journalists, and slowly people in the outside world began to take notice. The number of page views increased from a few thousand one month (mostly us looking at our own handiwork) to more than 10,000 the next and so on until the 1998 World Cup when things went through the roof. By the end of the tournament we were getting significantly more than one million hits a day and this despite demand crashing the site on a not irregular basis. As its name suggests, the site had, and still has, a strong focus on betting, offering previews, analysis and statistical information.

Yet the whole point of the internet was its immediacy so it was decided that we should offer some form of live coverage of football matches broadcast live on TV. "We were the first ones that ever did it, despite what other people might say," said Graham Shaw, who was editor of the site at the time. "We did it because we recognised the benefit for our users and the internet allowed us to do it. If you're not restricted to one publication deadline you can change the copy as many times as you want in the 90 minutes; that's the beauty of the internet. And, if you're a user and you're not able to access live TV or radio coverage, it's a useful tool." We called these early versions 'in-running' match reports. We had no template to go by as no one else was doing anything similar, so effectively we were making it up as we went along. The reports we wrote followed the process that a newspaper might employ on a breaking news story, with one person writing a constantly changing version of the story as new information came in. While newspapers were working towards a final version just before the print deadline, we were publishing, then overwriting and republishing on a regular basis. As we wrote the reports we constantly changed the introductory paragraphs to reflect what was happening; less important bits were added at the bottom; even less important bits were discarded. It was like writing several different match reports for the same game within the 90 minutes and then a final report at the end. It was hard work. So, as we were not constrained by time and space in the same way a newspaper match report is, we decided to abandon their way of working too.

Shaw continues: "I remember you and me sitting with one of our colleagues and discussing how we should do it and the first game we did minute-by-minute, which everybody's copied subsequently, was Italy v England in Rome in 1997. It was much easier to do editorially because you weren't constantly changing it and it's a much better way of displaying it for the readers. It's much easier to publish the key moments faster." It still tickles me that just over an hour before kick-off in the 1998 World Cup Final I was probably the first person in the world to write the words "Ronaldo has been dropped from Brazil's starting line-up" for general consumption. Of course, about 30 minutes later I was probably also the first person in the world to write the words "Ronaldo has been reinstated to Brazil's starting line-up".

When Ceefax and Teletext started copying us we knew we were onto something, although their space constraints meant that for them it was a brief experiment. The internet had unlimited space and could use pictures but Ceefax, which ran on the analogue network, was faster to access from a standing start and didn't break when 'too many' people tried to use it. But the technology was inevitably going to improve so *Sportinglife*'s problems were never going to be anything other than short term. Ceefax and Teletext were always fighting a losing battle. But fight they did in a bid to demonstrate they were still relevant. With speed their strongest area, how could they do that? By being the first with the news, and one way of doing that was by preparing a different version of a story for each possible outcome. So it was that just after Carlos Roa saved David Batty's penalty in the second-round shootout against Argentina at France '98, Teletext declared: "England through after dramatic penalty win". The headline was very quickly changed to "England out of World Cup after penalty miss" but not quickly enough to stop the person responsible from being demoted. The pressure to be first with the news had told, just as it did all the way back in 1913 when the *London Star* printed the wrong result from the Boat Race.

That pressure didn't just come from *Sportinglife*. This was the period of the dotcom boom and no doubt enticed, at least in part, by the £15m Associated pocketed for its 60 per cent of *Soccernet*, a whole host of sports and football websites were springing up. *Carling.net* was the first and others quickly followed including *Football365*, which was launched in 1997 by internet entrepreneur David Tabizel and journalist Danny Kelly and at its peak was valued at £500m. The following year Rob Hersov, a South African entrepreneur, who had worked as Rupert Murdoch's private secretary, launched *Sportal*. Hersov had financial backing from a range of blue-chip firms like Morgan Stanley and his old boss at News Corporation and he appeared to know the customer base.

In an interview in *Marketing Magazine* in July 2000 he talked about the fact that sports fans were increasingly using the internet while they watched sport on TV, for example to check facts. Here he had identified the rise of the 'second-screen', way before the term became common currency. The company ran websites for some of the world's leading football clubs such as Real Madrid, Juventus, Inter Milan and Bayern Munich as well as the official website for Euro 2000. *Sportal* even became an official UEFA partner during the tournament and the firm's name was broadcast around the world, sat snugly on billboards between the likes of more well-known sponsors such as McDonald's and MasterCard. They even signed up England manager Kevin Keegan to appear in adverts and write an online column.

However, critics questioned the cost-effectiveness of the Euro 2000 sponsorship deal and pointed to the fact that *Sportal* produced little in the way of financial return. The month before the tournament, Vivendi Universal had pulled out of a deal to buy *Sportal* for a whopping £270m. The French media giant was wary that the online sports market was overcrowded and of the predicted dotcom crash. A year later *Sportal* needed to find £8m to stay afloat and after it did Hersov stepped down from running the company on a day-to-day basis. Eventually, in November 2001, *Sportal* was sold to *UKBetting.com* for just £1. The online bookmaker also paid £191,000 for *Sportal*'s technology and in a separate deal bought *Sportinglife.com* for just £2, merging and relaunching them under the name of the latter. Shaw, who would became editor-in-chief of the new company, told me: "*UKBetting* were quite savvy, they realised that the best way to build a betting brand was to align with content and obviously it was around the time a lot of websites were struggling financially because I think they hadn't worked out how they were going to make money. Lots of people say: 'there's death and taxes'; well I would probably add betting to that list as well. It's the most constant revenue stream, if you can get it right."

Sportal's demise was symptomatic of the dotcom crash that many were quick to file under "I Told You So"; however, it really should have been led under "History Repeating Itself". The dotcom crash followed a pattern that can be seen over and over again from the Dutch Tulip mania of the 1630s to the heady early days of the railway industry in the 1840s. Let's not forget the railway was a new invention that was set to revolutionise our way of life. Numerous entrepreneurs saw their chance to make money, as did numerous investors. The price of shares in railway firms rose dramatically as more and more money was pumped in by speculators. A peak was reached in 1846 when 272 companies were established. However it soon became clear that many were simply unviable and the market as a whole had become overvalued on the basis of speculation and, in some cases, fraud. Many companies collapsed and the share price plummeted.

The car industry went through a similar process as did the UK satellite TV market. Although there were only two firms, Sky and BSB nearly spent themselves to destruction in their battle for supremacy, losing hundreds of millions of their investors' money before eventually merging. In all the cases, huge amounts of speculative investment were coupled with huge amounts of technical experimentation. A lot of the experiments failed and a lot of the money was lost, leading to a negative correction in the value of the market, the collapse of a significant number of firms and consolidation among the rest.

In short, the dotcom crash was entirely predictable. Yet all those lost dollars did pay off in some way. According to venture capitalist Fred Wilson, who has invested in companies such as Twitter and Tumblr, the period of massive expansion before the market's consolidation was vitally important. Wilson argues that it is only such periods of 'irrational exuberance'[8] that persuade investors to fund the technological experiments that lay the foundation for the ultimate success of the relevant industry. During Railway Mania thousands of miles of track were laid, creating the UK's early transport network; during the dotcom bubble thousands of miles of fibre optic cable were laid, creating the country's digital telecommunications network. And remember, while *UKBetting.com* bought the *Sportal* name for just £1 they paid £191,000 for the company's technology. If there was a difference between Railway Mania and the dotcom bubble it was that the latter was expanding an already existing market – communications. Therefore there were already established players able to step in once the dust had settled. Firms like the BBC, BT and Sky have ultimately led the way in the digital revolution and football was there from the start to help them do so.

The BBC might have a fairly conservative image – it's not called Auntie for nothing – but it has always been at the forefront of technological innovation. It led the way with radio and television and was instrumental in the pan-European broadcasts of the 1954 World Cup, the introduction of colour TV and the first satellite broadcasts

8 Wilson was citing a friend, who in turn had borrowed the phrase from Alan Greenspan, who slipped it into a speech in 1996 to warn that the dotcom market might be overvalued. When his warning proved prophetic, bumper stickers saying "I want to be irrationally exuberant again" sprang up around California's Silicon Valley.

during the 1966 World Cup. Before launching its own website in 1997, the BBC collaborated with the PA on experimental live coverage of both the Budget and the Olympics. Football content drove traffic to the site and the 2002 World Cup meant June of that year saw the site record what was at the time its highest number of hits. During the same tournament the *Guardian*'s website recorded record traffic, with 10 days seeing in excess of 2.8 million views, this compared to 2.4 million on the day of the 9/11 attacks and 2.7 million on the day after.

Football was also a driving force in BT's plans, announced in 2002, to sign up five million broadband customers by 2006. High-quality content was crucial to get people to switch away from dial-up and so, in a precursor to their current battle with Sky, the company turned to football, offering streaming coverage and highlights from the UK, Brazil and Argentina as well as delayed 'as live' coverage of Serie A matches. By 2007 they had signed up 10 million broadband customers. Sky sought to strengthen its online portfolio in 2007 by shelling out £95m on 365 Media Group (a rebranded *UKBetting*) which had added several other football-related online businesses to their portfolio, including TeamTalk which developed from the football news phone-line service of the same name. It was a significant consolidation of the market. While the BBC, as a public service broadcaster, has not commercialised its online service, BT continues to see football as a way of driving sales of other products. Similarly, News International paid around £20m for rights to show Premier League highlights on the websites of the *Sun, The Times* and the *Sunday Times,* content which was central to the company's brief attempt to drive customers behind the *Sun*'s £2-a-month paywall. Even companies like YouTube are snapping up sports rights. They have broadcast matches from the Copa America and cricket's Indian Premier League but in 2012 the company's global head of sports content, Claude Ribal, said a $2bn swoop for the Premier League was beyond them. Instead they have settled for supplementing the coverage from other broadcasters and they do this by hosting a series of channels for major clubs like Barcelona and Manchester City and brands like Nike Football.

• • •

Although Ceefax altered the way people wanted to receive information (at their convenience) it didn't change how the information they received was chosen. People like you (the readers) were still at the mercy of people like me (the so-called journalist) deciding what was 'news'. By the time the full force of Gates' internet tidal wave had swept through the media the decades-old relationship between 'producer' and 'consumer' had been washed away and an irrevocably changed landscape been left in its wake, and it was one fanzine writers liked the look of. However, the wave's initial ripples didn't change much. As Dr Peter Millward, who has researched online football fan culture, put it to me: "initially it was still one-way media, it was just online". Millward, a Reader in sociology at Liverpool John Moores University, suggests that while the launch of Windows 95 and the widespread availability of web access laid the foundation for the take-up of internet use by fanzine producers, it wasn't immediate. "Without that technology it just wouldn't have been possible but it was a few years after that that things began to take off. You also needed the people who write the online fanzines and the people who read them."

A key event was the launch of *Rivals.net* in 2001. Along with other web-hosting companies such as *Footymad.net* and *FansFC.com* it enabled fanzine producers to create websites supported by centrally sourced advertising for a variety of football-related products such as betting or club merchandise. Significantly this enabled fanzine producers to reduce their overheads. The websites were a medium through which the hard-copy fanzines could be advertised for free and eventually, for some fanzines at least, it was a way of continuing to produce content but without having to undertake the printing costs and the time-consuming process of design. "The Rivals network was really popular and lasted for a good few years," said Millward. "Each club had its own website and it was quite vibrant in the early years. However, many of them created their own websites when the parent company [365Media Group] was bought by Sky. Lots of the people who were connected left the network out of protest."

It's easy to assume that the launch of these websites led to the decline in fanzine sales, and that may well be the case; Millward has seen no hard evidence either way but their importance in one area is clear. "It was with the launch of the websites' message boards that fans began to talk with each other online rather than just reading fanzine-like or magazine-like products," he said. "To me these message boards where you could converse with people seemed to instantly chime with the ethos of the fanzines. They're a bit tongue-in-cheek and they're the places where fan resistance is talked about and grows. Sky have an area for each club and the things that get discussed there are really very different. I wouldn't see them as a form of fanzine culture, they're just a form of interactive media that Sky host."

In a sense the difference that Millward is describing is the same as the difference between the types of fan conversations that happened in the letters pages of fanzines and those found in the letters pages of the mainstream press. But according to Millward the new technology has dramatically increased the speed of communication on both fanzine websites and those of mainstream media organisations. "On the high-traffic message boards you'd get someone posting a point of view or starting off a conversation and they'd get responses within seconds and you'd have a whole debate that would have started off before you finished your cup of tea. Conversely there were only very few paper fanzines that would be sold at every home game. Most were once a month or once every other month, so the pace of the conversation was much slower and also there are fewer people contributing to those conversations in the paper fanzines." However, every silver lining has a cloud and Millward recognises this brings a downside as the tone of the conversations has also changed. "I think the contributions to the paper fanzines were better thought out than those that open up on the message boards, not least because it only takes a second to post a very poorly communicated message. Anyone can say anything in the heat of the moment."

It's a characteristic that Anthony Vickers, the *Middlesbrough Evening Gazette*'s chief sports writer, also acknowledges. "Message boards are completely disposable and they also become the platform for a small number of vocal people. The majority might read it but very rarely will they get their voice heard, because if you're not part of the clique you'll get shot down very quickly." Vickers himself writes the Untypical Boro blog, which is regularly one of the three most popular in the regional press, but this popularity comes in part from Vickers' active but counter-intuitive approach to encouraging debate. "It's built a community around an articulate expression of what's happening at the club. I edit and moderate all the comments before they get published for legal and diplomatic reasons. So, you don't get the antagonism between posters and anything that's a bit naughty gets removed. That creates the impression that it's quite a reasoned and articulate forum and that encourages people to write at a little bit more length. It's totally divergent to the logic of the internet, which is more immediate, written in shorter text-speak and contains a lot of insults."

• • •

While message boards might have encouraged quicker, less thoughtful conversations between fans, another online development soon created an environment for longer, more considered writing which is perceived by many to pose a direct challenge to the mainstream media, in particular the press. And that was blogging. The first recognised blog was a personal homepage created by American student Justin Hall in 1994. Three years later the term 'weblog' was coined and this was shortened to 'blog' in 1999 when a guy called Jesse James Garrett decided to compile a list of other sites similar to his. It ran to just 23 (you read that right, I haven't left off any zeros). It was, however, a key year for blogging, as the platform that would become known as Blogger was launched, eventually making it a simple process for anyone to start a blog and lighting the fuse for the explosion in their popularity. By 2006 there were 50 million around the world and by July 2013 an average of 38,853 blogs were being started each day on Blogger's rival WordPress alone. By the end of 2010 football blogging in England appeared to have taken off as sites such as *Zonal Marking, The Equaliser* and *In Bed With Maradona* were in full stride and *The Swiss Ramble*, which had launched the previous year, had started focusing exclusively on football.

Some of these bloggers specifically articulated their reasons for blogging as a reaction to the narratives disseminated in the traditional media. Michael Cox, the author of *Zonal Marking,* said the blog was "inspired by *Inverting the Pyramid* and the standard of punditry on British television, in very different ways". The creators of *IBWM* described themselves as "revolutionaries" and appealed for new writers by saying: "You can stay on the outside if you like, but … join the revolution." OK, they were having a bit of a laugh but as Shakespeare never actually wrote, many a true word is spoken in jest and the sentiments expressed by the bloggers suggested they believed there was something they need to "fight" against and the internet had given them the weapons to do so. You no longer need a huge printing press to produce content for people to read; you no longer needed an expensive camera and a massive satellite dish to broadcast video across the world to millions. You can do it all from your phone.

Although the technology has changed, the reactionary sentiments are the same as those expressed by the producers of *Foul!* – the self-styled "alternative football magazine" – or *WSC*, which claimed to be an antidote to "clichéd, hackneyed, lazy journalism". While football blogging might not be directly linked to the football fanzine movement, it certainly shares the same do-it-yourself ethos and presents a similar challenge to the mainstream media. Perhaps inevitably this has created tensions between mainstream journalists and bloggers. "It's a great shame but you can sort of understand why it happens," says Jonathan Wilson, the author of *Inverting the Pyramid*. "Journalists feel threatened by people who write for websites. They see their jobs being challenged and so they're often very negative. There's still this perception among certain journalists, and I think there is a generational thing there, that people who write for websites are not as serious, not as worthy as people who write for newspapers. This is possibly more the case in cricket than football and yet the readership figures you get on *CricInfo* for instance are way higher than those you get on British papers on cricket so purely in those terms you have to take those people seriously."

While in many ways Anthony Vickers of the *Middlesbrough Evening Gazette* agrees, he also thinks some mainstream writers open themselves up to criticism: "It's a very complex cultural cocktail going on here. Some journalists have always lived in a little ivory tower; they tend to write for themselves and their immediate coterie and this can come through in the way they write. But so much of football writing is formulaic and maybe journalists are frustrated by the fact that the nature of the timetable and the restrictions of the size of the page mean they don't get to express themselves creatively in that way.

"The other thing is journalists feel threatened because in the past what they wrote was sacrosanct. They might have got a letter but it might not arrive for five days. Now, that's immediate; if you write about something you're going to get comments underneath it straight away and journalists take that personally. There's also a fear that if there are people out there writing well they might be a threat to your job. I don't think they are because I think it's a different mentality and I don't think a lot of bloggers would want to be journalists or necessarily have the other parts of the skills sets."

Yet, clearly some do and, further emphasising the similarities with the fanzines, they have made the same journey into the mainstream. Wilson considers this to be a positive development: "What's happened over the last 10 years or so is that the process of becoming a football writer's become democratised. Take Michael Cox [writer of *Zonal Marking*] for example. Three years ago he was sitting in his bedroom writing a blog but because it was something people wanted to read about and because he did it really well he's gone mainstream. So the route from the outside to the inside has opened up. Anyone who writes a good blog, who has a good idea and who executes it well has the opportunity to get into the mainstream media."

Henry Winter, *The Times*' chief football writer, is another who sees benefits from social media. He describes Twitter as "undeniably a force for good", suggesting it has enhanced relationships between journalists and both fans and players. "Twitter is incredibly useful for giving a feel of specific things," Winter told me. "No one knows what's going on at a club – in terms of mood, in terms of things they can see like the match-day experience or how they were treated by stewards – better than the actual fans who go. So social media is brilliant for someone like me; it's like having 20 advisers at every club. Just as I walk up to the ground I can go on my phone and check out 10 or 20 fans which I follow from each club and I get an immediate feel from that."

Winter also outlined how Twitter can help after he's written a piece: "If I wrote something about Chelsea and Chelsea fans don't like it, they can have a go at me, we can communicate. I see Twitter in terms of how it can help me understand their club more." For this, Winter feels the antagonism between fans and journalists is a price worth paying: "The only thing I would worry about on Twitter is apathy – if fans weren't defending their club – and part of that is having a go at journalists who criticise their club. As a journalist you're incredibly lucky, you get paid to go around the world. If someone wants to have a go at me on Twitter, I'm not going to lose any sleep over it. That said, one of the groups of people I feel sorry for – and one of the reasons I won't complain about any of the abuse I get on Twitter – is the female presenters at Sky. Some of the stuff they get is absolutely disgusting."

Winter went on to describe how Twitter has also broken down barriers between journalists and players, bringing them closer together than they've been for some time. "Here's a classic example," said Winter. "Joleon Lescott split from his management company and there were two or three people out there purporting to be his advisers or to be his spokesperson. It was quite a sensitive time for him because he couldn't get in the Manchester City team and he wanted to be playing regularly because he wanted to go to the World Cup. I then get a Direct Message from him – because I follow him and he follows me – saying: 'I need to talk to you, can you DM me your mobile number'. We swap a few texts then two or three days later I go up to Manchester City and we meet and have a coffee and I do a piece with him. No agents, no advisers, no PR people, just pure old-school player-to-reporter, reporter-to-player. As a courtesy I let Manchester City know the day before it went in. In a way, that's how it should be and a lot of the players are using that more. There's contact there that can shape your views on something. Wayne Rooney sent me a Direct Message once because I got something wrong and I was able to address that. There wasn't that contact two or three years ago when press–player relations were in a real dip. I think it's actually picked up and I think social media's helped."

Alex Trickett, of Twitter, highlights how the social media has completed the triangle by also bringing players and fans closer together. "The best example is Germany at the 2014 World Cup," he said. "As much as they were the best team on the pitch, and they showed that when they won, they were also the best team on Twitter and they showed that from the very moment they left Germany; they took their fans on the journey. They were answering tweets in the airport; they took selfies on the flight. There's no need for downtime now; there's Wi-Fi on the plane and symbolically as a fan you're there with them. That works both ways: the fans were delighted that they were being responded to and acknowledged from afar and the players felt supported and loved and cared about. That bond grew tighter as the tournament went on. So it meant that when they won the World Cup the first thing that Lukas Podolski thought to do – and this was the first bit of media from the team – within seconds of the final whistle was to tweet from the middle of the pitch a selfie with him and Bastian Schweinsteiger just saying: "AHA!" That moment was a moment of unity between the players and the fans – 'we did this together; we shared this experience and we shared it through Twitter' and I think that's where we're moving to and I think Germany were ahead of the game in 2014. I think all teams understand now; the same was true with the England Women's World Cup team in 2015. They knew they were in the thoughts of people back home and they really carried that with pride to each venue."

• • •

So, where next? Who knows; perhaps in a few years you'll be able to watch live coverage of games on the inside of your eyelids and download match reports direct to your brain without even having to bother reading them. Or perhaps I'm talking rubbish and the really smart ideas are being dreamt up by a bunch of 12-year-olds as I type. While us Luddites wait, let's go back to that day in May 2013 when Twitter nearly melted over the news that Sir Alex had decided to retire. United's cross-city rivals Manchester City released their own news which, although it passed most people by, will likely have a far greater impact on the game in the long term. They revealed they were going to install high-density Wi-Fi at the Etihad Stadium, creating one of the most "immersive, video rich experiences in sports". What does that actually mean? Well, apart from the fact everyone in the stadium will be able to text, tweet or access the web at the same time without any problems, it will effectively turn every smartphone in the ground into a live video scoreboard. By opening up the City MatchDay app, fans can receive live commentary and watch a feed of match highlights from several cameras (a live feed is not allowed due to Premier League restrictions) or a 'tactical camera' view of the whole pitch from high up in the stadium. They can also take part in 'be the ref' quick polls about in-game incidents, vote for their Man of the Match and access live in-game statistics, and the hope is that soon they will be able to order food from their seats.[9] The club has also launched an app for the Android smartwatches – a world first. The club say that at the moment this is an experiment, but the upshot is that the second-screen experience is moving out of your living room and into the stadium, whether that's on your phone or on your wrist. In short, even watching a game live will become a mediated experience.

But if fans can get all this straight to their smartphones while they're at the ground watching a match, where does this leave older forms of media? Cheaper hardware and quicker, easier ways to disseminate content hasn't just democratised the means of production, it has also changed the nature of consumption. Previously, primary consumption was buying the newspaper and secondary consumption was borrowing a copy from a friend, picking up a discarded copy on the train or in a pub, or maybe looking at a back issue in a library archive. But this rudimentary social network was limited by the number of people you knew or the distance you were able to travel. New and social media have made it much easier to cross the boundaries of time and space, meaning your social network is much larger. A blog post, video or a tweet can be liked or retweeted by just one reader and it's instantly in the possession of all their Twitter/Facebook/Snapchat/NextBigThing followers.

There is no escaping the fact that fans are no longer just consumers, they're producers too. "The power of that fan-created, community-sourced content is only going to grow and that's going to be a

---

9   *Of course our friends in America have led the way. In early 2013 the Brooklyn Nets baseball team introduced the technology into their stadium, the Barclay Centre. No fan who watched Super Bowl 50 at the San Francisco 49ers' Levi Stadium in February 2016 was more than three metres away from a Wi-Fi access point.*

significant focus for us now," said Trickett. In particular, he sees Twitter becoming a more visual medium. "When Twitter started, the immediacy was still there – that was the founding block – but it was about text. Today Twitter is about the rich media you put into it, by which I mean video specifically but also pictures and emojis. With sports probably more than anything else people want a visual frame of reference because they want to be placed at the scene; they want to see it with their own eyes. For us video means video that's natively placed in a tweet, so it plays the moment you open that Tweet. It means Vine, the six-second video loops that highlight a particularly outstanding moment that you just want to see again and again, and of course it also now means Periscope real-time live broadcast. The key thing with Periscope is that beyond being broadcast live, it's effected in real time by the people watching it. So if I'm watching a live broadcast from ITV or Sky or the BBC, that's brilliant, but I don't have a direct interface to change it or affect it in any way. With Periscope the comments that flow through the screen as people are broadcasting take it to a new level because not only can they respond in real time to questions but they can also change the nature of what they're filming in response."

Some media are better equipped to deal with this than others. TV and radio are immediate and intimate and are less restricted by time and space. Just as TV has already gone digital, so radio will have made the switch by 2019. It's significant that the BBC and Sky are just as strong now as they were before the dotcom bubble burst in other people's faces, but what about the Grand Old Man of the media? What about newspapers? In 2011 the *Daily Mirror*'s chief football writer Oliver Holt told an interesting anecdote on Sky's *Sunday Supplement* about the incident in which Manchester City substitute Carlos Tevez refused to come on during the club's Champions League match with Bayern Munich. Holt had been covering the game but said that because of the position of the press box at the Allianz Arena he didn't see Tevez's confrontation with manager Roberto Mancini. The first he knew about it was when he started receiving texts and Tweets from people watching the game on TV. OK, the stadium's layout played a part but the fundamental point remains: here was a journalist who was writing a report for a newspaper which wouldn't hit the shops until the following morning, finding out about the game's top line from people watching the match live on TV via a social networking site accessible to all. But Trickett thinks that far from undermining traditional forms of media, social media can enhance what they do by changing the way that journalists go about their job. "Your point about Oliver Holt is a good one," Trickett said. "He was blind-sided by that particular incident because he couldn't see what was going on. But he was able to rely on his huge number of followers on Twitter to help him put the full story together. It's really just a case of traditional media responding to the digital age in general, not just Twitter, and working out how that fits with what they do."

Football journalism is thriving; we're probably reading more about football than ever before – but newspapers as a delivery mechanism for that journalism? Well, that's a different issue altogether. Really their days have been numbered since 1936 when BBC Radio's Richard Dimbleby scooped them all from a phone box with his live report on the Crystal Palace fire. Newspapers as we know them were born in the age of railway time. They might have been at the cutting-edge of media technology when the *Sheffield Evening Telegraph* took less than 10 minutes to get the result of a match nearly 80 miles away into the paper and onto the streets, but that was in 1889. The fact is that in the age of the multi-screen 'transmedia sport experience', of smart stadia and of internet time, newspapers just can't keep pace. To stave off the inevitability of death, newspaper companies have been forced to evolve. The internet is increasingly central to their plans and many have made great strides to adopt other new and social media techniques to drive traffic to their websites. Also central to their plans is football – the most popular sport on the planet. Which just goes to show: the more things change the more they stay the same.

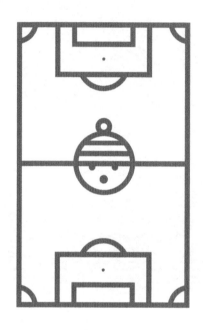

ACKNOWLEDGEMENTS

First of all I'd like to thank Keith and David Hartrick for having faith in both me and the project and for their unerring support throughout. I'd like to thank all those people who gave up their time to answer my questions; the insight and information they have given me has been invaluable.

I'd also like to thank the numerous other people who have taken the time to help me. In no particular order they are: Helen Cooper from the University of Central Lancashire, Christine Stevens and Lucy Keating at Newcastle University Library, Paul Brown, Huw Davies of *FourFourTwo* magazine, Paul Walker of BBC Radio Sheffield, Natalie Cullington at the BBC, Ian Nannestad of *Football History* magazine, Dr Anne Beggs-Sunter at the University of Ballarat, Dr Stephanie Fremeux and Mick Stockton at the University of Teesside, Professor Ann Moyal, Andrew Glover, Philippe Auclair, Carrie Cunliffe, Katherine Knight at the FA, Greg Leadham at the *Morning Star*, Jodie Thind and Larry Colcy at Lyceum Media, Lizzie Lea at Manor House Stables, Chantelle Fraser at Chase More Farm, Anna Redman at Yellow Jersey Press, Natasha Little at the Royal Society, Fiona Hillary, Jane Legrice at BBC Radio Norfolk, Sophie Arnold, Rebecca Mundy at Hodder & Stoughton, Daniel McLaren, Katie Wagner Lyons at Activate Management, Stanley Jackson at Performing Artistes, Jeff Livingstone at *In Bed With Maradona*, Anna Pallai at Faber, Ciaran Brennen at Sports Interactive, Roger Williams at *Hello!* magazine, Tom Hocking at *When Saturday Comes*, James Hodgkinson at John Blake Publishing, Lesley Caton at Directors Cut Productions, Emma Steele and Ros Slobodan. If I've missed anyone off this list it's down to nothing more than an oversight on my part.

Finally, I'd like to thank Kes for giving me two beautiful daughters and her incredible support and patience while I've been writing this. She may be my ex-wife but she's still a great friend.

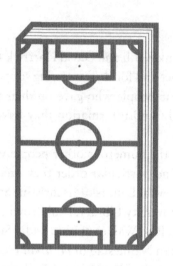

Abramson, A. (1987): *The History of Television, 1880 to 1941.*
McFarland & Co. Inc.

Abramson, A. (2003): *The History of Television, 1942 to 2000.*
McFarland & Co. Inc.

Amoore, T. (2002): 'Footballers' Wives' in the *Sunday Telegraph*,
19 May.

Belfield, R. Hird, C. & Kelly, S. (1994): *Murdoch: The Great
Escape.* Warner Books.

Bergman, J. (2011): *The Dark Side of Charles Darwin: A Critical
Analysis of an Icon of Science.* New Leaf Publishing.

Best, G. (2001): *Blessed: The Autobiography.* Ebury Press.

Birley, D. (1993): *Sport and the Making of the British.*
Manchester University Press.

Birley, D. (1995): *Land of Sport and Glory: Sport and British
Society 1887–1910.* Manchester University Press.

Boyle, R. (2006): *Sports Journalism: Context and Issues.* Sage.

Boyle, R. & Haynes, R. (2004): *Football in the New Media Age.*
Routledge.

Boyle, R. & Haynes, R. (2009): *Power Play: Sport, The Media and
Popular Culture*, 2nd Edition. Edinburgh University Press.

Bragg, M. (2009): 'Melvyn Bragg on Becoming an
Arsenal Fan' in the *Observer*, 17 May.

Brailsford, D. (1992): *British Sport: A Social History.*
The Lutterworth Press.

Brennan, P. (2007): *The Munitionettes: A History of Women's
Football in North East England During the Great War.*
Donmouth Publishing.

Brennan, P. (2008): 'An Unseemly Exhibition: Women Footballers
of 1881' in *Soccer History,* Issue 20.

Brewster, B. (1993): 'When Saturday Comes and Other football Fanzines' in *The Sports Historian*, Volume 13, Issue 1, pp. 14–21.

Brimson, D. (2000): *Barmy Army: The Changing Face of Football Violence*. Headline.

Brimson, D. (2006): *Kicking Off: Why Hooliganism and Racism are Killing Football*. Headline.

Brookes, R. (1999): 'Newspapers and National Identity: The BSE/ CJD Crisis and the British Press' in *Media Culture and Society*, Volume 21, Issue 2, pp. 247–63.

Brown, A. (2005): 'Past Imperfect' in *When Saturday Comes*, Issue 226.

Brown, J. (ed.) (2012): *The End: Every Issue of the Groundbreaking Fanzine*. Sabotage Times.

Brown, L. (1985): *Victorian News and Newspapers*. Clarendon Press.

Brown, P. (2011): 'Baines Football Cards: The Victorian Panini' in *In Bed With Maradona*, 5 April.

Brown, P. (2011): 'Got, Got, Got, Need' in *FourFourTwo*. September 2011.

Burrell, I. (2013): 'Thanks a Billion ... Body Blow for Sky as BT Lands Champions League' in the *Independent on Sunday*, 10 November.

Buscombe, E. (2000): *British Television: A Reader*. Clarendon Press.

Carruthers, B. & Christie, D. (2009): *The Bonzo Dog Doo-Dah Band – Jolity Farm*. Angry Penguin Ltd.

Cassy, J. (2001): 'Sportal Wins £8m Reprieve' in the *Guardian*, 25 August.

Caudwell, J. (2004): 'Out on the Field: Women's Experiences of Gender and Sexuality in Football' in Wagg, S. (ed.): *British Football and Social Exclusion*. Routledge.

Cavallini, R. (2005): *The Wanderers: Five Times FA Cup Winners*. Surrey, Dog and Duck Publications.

Chenoweth, N. (2001): *Virtual Murdoch: Reality Wars on the Information Highway*. Vintage.

Chippindale, P. & Franks, S. (1992): *Dished: The Rise and Fall of British Satellite Broadcasting*. Simon & Schuster.

Chippindale, P. & Horrie, C. (1999): *Stick It Up You Punter! The Uncut Story of The Sun Newspaper*. Pocket Books.

Clapson, M. (1992): *A Bit of a Flutter: Popular Gambling and English Society, c. 1823–1961*. Manchester University Press.

Clavane, A. (2013): *Does Your Rabbi Know You're Here?* Quercus.

Clayton, P. & Rowbotham, J. (2009): 'How the Mid-Victorians Worked, Ate and Died' in *International Journal of Environmental Research and Public Health*, Volume 6, Issue 3, pp. 1235–53.

Cocozza, P. (2007): 'Move Over Motty!' in the *Guardian*, 19 April.

Cohen, S. (2011): *Folk Devils and Moral Panics: The Creation of the Mods and Rockers*. Routledge.

Collins, M. (2008): *Roy of the Rovers: The Unauthorised Biography*. Aurum.

Collins, P. (2008): 'In a Different League' in *British Journalism Review*, Volume 19, No. 2, pp. 25–31.

Collins, T. & Vamplew, W. (2002): *Mud, Sweat, and Beers: A Cultural History of Sport and Alcohol*. Berg.

Conboy, M. (2002): *The Press and Popular Culture*. Sage.

Conboy, M. (2004): *Journalism: A Critical History*. Sage.

Conboy, M. (2006): *Tabloid Britain: Constructing a Community through Language*. Routledge.

Conboy, M. (2010): 'From "We" to "Me"' in *Journalism Studies*, Volume 11, Issue 4, pp. 500–10.

Conboy, M. (2011): *Journalism in Britain: A Historical Introduction*. Sage.

Conlan, T. (2015): 'Men Behaving Better: How the Lads' Mags Gave Way to Digital' in the *Guardian*, 22 November.

Conn, D. (1997): *The Football Business: Fair Game in the '90s?* Mainstream Publishing.

Conn, D. (2013): 'Premier League Finances: Accounts Reveal £1.6bn Spent on Wages' in the *Guardian*, 18 April.

Crolley, L., Hand, D. and Jeutter, R. (2000): 'Playing the Identity
    Card: Stereotypes in European Football' in *Soccer and
    Society*, Volume 1, Issue 2, pp. 107–28.
Curry, G. (2001): 'Football: A Study in Diffusion'. Unpublished
    PhD thesis.
Curry, G. (2003): 'Forgotten Man: The Contribution of John
    Dyer Cartwright to the Football Rules Debate' in *Soccer and
    Society,* Volume 4, Issue 1.

Daily Mail (2007): 'John Terry Kicks-off Wedding WAGathon',
    16 June.
Dart, J. (2009): 'Review Essay: Tackling a Nation's Football
    History' in *The International Journal of the History of Sport*,
    Volume 26, No. 11, pp. 1748–57.
Davies, C. (2012): 'John Moynihan 1932–2012' in
    www.footballwriters.co.uk
Davies, H. (2007): 'A Chat With Gazza' in *The New Statesman*.
    12 March.
Davies, N. (2008): *Flat Earth News*. Chatto & Windus.
Dunning, E. & Sheard, K. (1979): *Barbarians,
    Gentlemen and Players*. Martin Robertson & Co.
Dunning, E, Murphy, P. & Williams, J. (1989): *The Roots of
    Football Hooliganism: An Historical and Sociological Study*.
    Routledge.
Dyke, G. (2005): *Inside Story*. Harper Perennial.

Engel, M. (2011): 'Can We Have Our Ball Back?' in
    Financial Times, 18 February.

Ferguson, A. (2000): *Managing My Life: My Autobiography*.
    Cornet.
Fishwick, N. (1989): *English Football and Society, 1910–1950*.
    Manchester University Press.
Fletcher, R. (2000): 'Hersov Seeks Media Buyer for Sportal'
    in the *Independent*, 15 October.
Foot, J. (2006): *Calcio: A History of Italian Football*.
    Fourth Estate.

Forrest, D. (1999): 'The Past and Future of the British Football Pools' in *Journal of Gambling Studies,* Volume 15, Issue 2, pp. 161–76.

Forsdick, C., Grove, L. & McQuillan, L. (eds) (2005): *The Francophone Bande Dessinee.* Editions Rodopi B.V.

Fox, N. (1998): 'X Marks Millionaire's Spot' in the *Independent,* 16 August.

Franklin, B. (ed.) (2008): *Pulling Newspapers Apart: Analysing Print Journalism.* Routledge.

Fynn, A. & Guest, L. (1991): *Heroes and Villains: The Inside Story of the 1990/91 Season at Arsenal and Tottenham Hotspur.* Penguin Books.

Fynn, A. & Guest, L. (1994): *Out of Time,* 2nd edn. Pocket Books.

Gallagher, B. (2006): *Sporting Supermen: The True Stories of Our Childhood Comic Heroes.* Aurum Press Ltd.

Gelder, K. (ed.) (2005): *The Subcultures Reader* (2nd edn). Routledge.

Gibson, O. (2002): 'Sportinglife.com to Relaunch' in the *Guardian,* 16 January.

Gibson, O. (2013): 'BT Sport Wins £900m Champions League TV Rights from Sky and ITV' in the *Guardian,* 9 November.

Gilmore, P. (1993): 'Local Radio Sport from the Producer's Point of View' in *The Sports Historian,* Volume 13, Issue 1, pp. 26–30.

Glanville, G. (1963): *The Rise of Gerry Logan.* Secker & Warburg.

Greaves, J. (2003): *Greavsie: The Autobiography.* Time Warner Paperbacks.

Greenslade, R. (2004): *Press Gang: How Newspapers Make Profit from Propaganda.* Pan.

Griffiths, G. (1992): *The Encyclopedia of the British Press 1422–1992.* St Martin's Press.

Halliday, J. (2013): 'ITN to Produce Sun and Times Highlight Packages' in the *Guardian,* 24 June.

Hanson, C. (2008): 'The Instant Replay: Time and Time Again' in *The Spectator,* Volume 28, Issue 2, pp. 51–60.

Hargreaves, J. (1994): *Sporting Females: Critical Issues in the History and Sociology of Women's Sport.* Routledge.

Hargreaves, J. (2002): 'The Victorian Cult of the Family and the Early Years of Female Sport' in Scraton, S. & Flintoff, A. (eds), *Gender and Sport: A Reader.* Routledge.

Harris, J. (2004): 'Still a Man's Game? Women Footballers, Personal Experience and Tabloid Myth' in Wagg, S. (ed.): *British Football and Social Exclusion.* Routledge.

Harris, M. & Lee, A. (1986): *The Press in English Society: From the Seventeenth Century to the Nineteenth Century.* Fairleigh Dickinson University Press.

Harris, N. (2012): 'YouTube Sports Chief Rules Out Any Bid For Premier League Rights' in *sportingintelligence.com*, 20 March.

Harris, R. (1983): *Gotcha! The Media, the Government and the Falklands Crisis.* Faber & Faber.

Hastings, M. (2003): *Editor: An Inside Story of Newspapers.* Pan Macmillan.

Haynes, R. (1995): *The Football Imagination: The Rise of Football Fanzine Culture.* Ashgate Publishing.

Haynes, R. (1998): 'A Pageant of Sound and Vision: Football's Relationship with Television, 1936–60' in *The International Journal of the History of Sport*, Volume 15, Issue 1, pp. 211–26.

Haynes, R. (1999): '"There's Many a Slip 'Twixt the Eye and The Lip": An Exploratory History of Football Broadcasts and Running Commentaries on BBC Radio, 1927–1939' in *International Review for the Sociology of Sport*, Volume 34, Issue 2, pp. 143–56.

Herd, H. (1952): *The March of Journalism: The Story of the British Press from 1622 to the Present Day.* George Allen and Unwin Ltd.

Hey, S. (2008): 'Our National Love Affair: The History of the Betting Shop' in the *Independent*, 5 April.

Hill, J. (2002): Sport, *Leisure and Culture in the Twentieth Century*. Palgrave Macmillan.

Hill, J. (2006): *Sport and the Literary Imagination: Essays in History, Literature and Sport*. Peter Lang.

Holt, R. (1989): *Sport and the British*. Clarendon Press.

Holt, R. & Mason, T. (2000): *Sport in Britain 1945–2000*. Blackwell.

Home Office (1989): *The Hillsborough Stadium Disaster*, Interim Report.

Hornby, N. (1992): *Fever Pitch: A Fan's Life*. Gollancz.

Horne, J. (1992): 'General Sports Magazines and "Cap'n Bob": The Rise and Fall of Sportsweek' in *Sociology of Sport Journal*, Volume 9, Issue 2, pp. 179–91.

Horrall, A. (2001): *Popular Culture in London c. 1890–1918: The Transformation of Entertainment*. Manchester University Press.

Horrie, C. (1992): *Sick as a Parrot: The Inside Story of the Spurs Fiasco*. Virgin Books.

Horrie, C. (2002): *Premiership: Lifting the Lid on a National Obsession*. Pocket Books.

Horrie, C. (2003): *Tabloid Nation: From the Birth of the Daily Mirror to the Death of the Tabloid*. André Deutsch.

Horrie, C. & Clarke, S. (1994): *Fuzzy Monsters: Fear and Loathing at the BBC*. Heinmann.

Horrie, C. & Nathan, A. (1999): *Live TV: Tellybrats and Topless Darts: The Uncut Story of Tabloid Television*. Pocket Books.

Horsman, M. (1998): *Sky High: The Amazing Story of BSkyB – and the Egos, Deals and Ambitions That Revolutionised TV Broadcasting*. Orion Business Books.

Horton, E. (1991): 'Something Slightly Amis' in *When Saturday Comes*, Issue 59.

Huggins, M. (2000): 'The First Generation of Street Bookmakers in Victorian England: Demonic Fiends or "Decent Fellers"' in *Northern History*, Volume 36, Issue 1, pp. 129–45.

Huggins, M. (2005): 'Researching the Game's Past: Football on the Newsreels' in *Soccer History*, Issue 12.

Huggins, M. (2007): '"And Now, Something for the Ladies": Representations of Women's Sport in Cinema Newsreels 1918–1939' in *Women's History Review*, Volume 16, Issue 5, pp. 681–700.

Huggins, M. (2007): 'BBC Radio and Sport 1922–1939' in *Contemporary British History*, Volume 21, Issue 4, pp. 491–515.

Huggins, M. (2007): 'Betting, Sport and the British 1918–1939' in *Journal of Social History*, Volume 41, Issue 2, pp. 283–306.

Huggins, M. (2007): 'Projecting the Visual: British Newsreels, Soccer and Popular Culture 1918–39' in *History of Sport*, Volume 24, Issue 1, pp. 80–102.

Huggins, M. & Williams, J. (2006): *Sport and the English 1918–1932*. Routledge.

Hughson, J. (2011): 'Not Just Any Wintry Afternoon in England: The Curious Contribution of C.R.W. Nevinson to Football Art' in *The International Journal of the History of Sport*, Volume 28, Issue 18, pp. 2670–87.

Humble, L. & Cooper, C. (1987): *The World's Greatest Blackjack Book* (Revised edition). Doubleday.

Hutchby, I. (1996): *Confrontation Talk: Arguments, Asymmetries and Power on Talk Radio*. Lawrence Erlbaum.

Hutchins, B. & Rowe, D. (2012): *Sport Beyond Television: The Internet, Digital Media and the Rise of Networked Media Sport*. Routledge.

Hutton, R. (2001): *The Stations of the Sun: A History of the Ritual Year in Britain*. Oxford Paperbacks.

Inglis, S. (2010): *The Best of Charles Buchan's Football Monthly*. Malavan Media.

Jacobs, B. (2004): *The Dick Kerr's Ladies*. Robinson Publishing.

Jarvis, M. (2005): *Conservative Governments, Morality and Social Change in Affluent Britain 1957–64*. Manchester University Press.

Johnes, M. & Mellor, G. (2006): 'The 1953 FA Cup Final: Modernity and Tradition in British Culture' in *Contemporary British History*, Volume 20, Issue 2, pp. 263–80.

Johnson, B.S. (2004): *Omnibus: Albert Angelo, House Mother Normal & Trawl*. Picador.

Johnson, B.S. (2009): *The Unfortunates*. New Directions Publishing Corporation.

Jones, D. & Watkins, T. (2000): *A Necessary Fantasy: The Heroic Figure in Children's Popular Culture*. Garland Publishing.

Kelner, M. (2012): *Sit Down and Cheer: A History of Sport on TV*. Wisden Sports Writing.

Kibble-White, J. & Williams, S. (2008): *The Encyclopaedia of Classic Saturday Night Telly*. Allison & Busby Ltd.

Klein, N. (2001): *No Logo*. Flamingo.

Kuper, S. & Szymanski, S. (2012): *Why England Lose & Other Curious Football Phenomena Explained*. HarperSport.

Kynaston, D. (2007): *Austerity Britain, 1945–1951 (Tales of a New Jerusalem)*. Bloomsbury Publishing Plc.

Lamb, L. (1989): *Sunrise: The Remarkable Rise and Rise of the Best-Selling Soaraway Sun*. Papermac.

Ledbrooke, A. & Turner, E. (1955): *Soccer From the Press Box*. The Sportsmans Book Club.

Leith, A. (1998): *Over the Moon, Brian: The Language of Football*. Boxtree Ltd.

Levine, C. (2006): 'Propaganda for Democracy: The Curious Case of Love on the Dole' in *Journal of British Studies*, Volume 45, Issue 4, pp. 846–74.

Linfoot, M. (2011): 'A History of BBC Local Radio in England c. 1960–1980'. Unpublished PhD thesis.

Lopez, S. (1996): *Women on the Ball: A Guide to Women's Football*. Scarlett Press.

Lord, B. (1964): *My Fight For Football*. S. Paul.

Lovejoy, J. (1992): 'Gascoigne's Norwegian Blue Note' in the *Independent*, 12 October 1992.

Lowndes, W. (1952): *The Story of Football*. Thorsons Publishers Ltd.

Lunt, D.J. (2009): 'The Heroic Athlete in Ancient Greece' in *Journal of Sport History*, Volume 36, Issue 3, pp. 375–92.

Macintosh, I., Millar, K. & White, N. (2012): *20 Years of Beautiful Obsession: Football Manager Stole My Life*. BackPagePress.

Mance, H. & Blitz, R. (2015): 'Premier League Broadcast Rights Smash Forecasts' in the *Financial Times*, 24 June.

Mangan, J.A. (2012): *Athleticism in the Victorian and Edwardian Public School: The Emergence and Consolidation of an Educational Ideology*. Routledge.

Marcin, T. (2015): 'NFL "Thursday Night Football" Live Stream Simulcast Could Set Precedent For Online Future of Digitally Broadcasting Sports', *in International Business Times*, 17 December.

Marketing Magazine (2000): "Profile: Contact Sport – Rob Hersov, Chief Executive Officer", *Sportal*, 20 July.

Marr, A. (2004): *My Trade: A Short History of British Journalism*. MacMillan.

Mason, T. (1980): *Association Football & English Society 1863–1915*. Branch Line.

Mason, T. (1988): *Sport in Britain*. Faber & Faber Ltd.

Mason, T. (1993): 'All the Winners and the Half Times ...' in *The Sports Historian*, Volume 13, Issue 1, pp. 3–13.

McKibbin, R. (1979): 'Working-class Gambling in Britain 1880–1939' in *Past and Present*, No. 82, pp. 147–78.

Meisl, W. (1956): *Soccer Revolution*. The Sportsmans Book Club.

Melling, A. (2007): '"Ray of the Rovers": The Working-class Heroine in Popular Football Fiction, 1915–25' in *The International Journal of the History of Sport*, Volume 15, Issue 1, pp. 97–122.

Millward, P. (2008): 'The Rebirth of the Football Fanzine: Using E-zines as Data Source' in *Journal of Sport and Social Issues*, Volume 32, Issue 3, pp. 299–310.

Moncrieff, C. (2001): *Living on a Deadline: A History of the Press Association*. Virgin Books.

Moorfoot, R. (1982): *Television in the Eighties: The Total Equation*. BBC Books.

Morley, D. (2000): *Home Territories: Media, Mobility and Identity*. Routledge.

Moyal, A. (1984): *Clear Across Australia: A History of Telecommunications*. Nelson.

Mullock, S. (2015): 'Premier League Set for TV Revolution With EVERY GAME Available for Streaming Under £4billion New Deal' in the *Daily Mirror*, 10 January.

Munting, R. (1993): 'Social Opposition to Gambling in Britain: An Historical Overview' in *The International Journal of the History of Sport*, Volume 10, Issue 3, pp. 295–312.

Munting, R. (1996): *An Economic and Social History of Gambling in Britain and the USA*. Manchester University Press.

Nannestad, I. (2008): 'Glory Nights: How Wolves Restored Pride in English Football' in *Soccer History*, Issue 20.

Nannestad, I. (2009): 'Experimental Vision: Closed Circuit TV Matches of the 1960s' in *Soccer History*, Issue 24.

Nannestad, I. (2013): 'An Account of an Early Televised Game: Barnet vs Wealdstone, October 1946' in *Soccer History*, Issue 30.

Neubauer, H.J. (1999): *The Rumour: A Cultural History*. Free Association Books.

Newsham, G. (1994): *In a League of Their Own! The Dick, Kerr Ladies Football Club*. Pride of Place UK Ltd.

Nickolds, A. & Hey, S. (eds) (1976): *The Foul Book of Football No 1*. Imprint unknown.

O'Sullivan, T. (2014): 'Sky Faces Fiercest Battle Yet for Premiership TV Rights' in the *Financial Times*, 1 December.

Orwell, G. (1963): *The Road to Wigan Pier*. Penguin.

Orwell, G. (1965): *The Decline of the English Murder and Other Essays*. Penguin.

Orwell, G. (1968): *The Collected Essays, Journalism and Letters of George Orwell*. Penguin.

Osborne, J. (1987): '"To keep the life of the Nation on the old lines": The Athletic News and the First World War' in *Journal of Sports History*, Volume 14, Issue 2, pp. 137–50.

Owen, W. (2005): *Kicking Against Tradition*. The History Press Ltd.

Pegg, M. (1983): *Broadcasting and Society 1918–1939*. Croom Helm.

Pfister, G, Fasting, K, Scraton, S. & Vázquez, B. (eds) (2002): 'Women and Football – a Contradiction? The Beginnings of Women's Football in Four European Countries' in Scraton, S. & Flintoff, A. (eds), *Gender and Sport: A Reader*. Routledge.

Pollard, L. (1999): 'The Secret of My Success: Julie Welch' in the *Sunday Independent*.

Pollard, S. (2009): *Ten Days that Changed the Nation: The Making of Modern Britain*. Simon & Schuster.

Qureshi, H. (2012): 'Jacqui Oatley: "I've had to grow extra layers of skin"' in the *Guardian*, 24 October.

Reade, B. (1996): '... And Yes, Gazza Cried' in the *Daily Mirror*, 2 July.

Redhead, S. (1986): *Sing When You're Winning: The Last Football Book*. Pluto Press.

Redhead, S. (1991): *Football With Attitude*. Ashgate Publishing.

Richards, J. (1984): *The Age of the Dream Palace: Cinema and Society in Britain 1930–1939*. Routledge & Kegan Paul.

Richards, J. & Aldgate, A. (1985): *Best of British: Cinema & Society 1930–1970*. Wiley-Blackwell.

Riches, A., Parker, T. & Frankland, R. (2009): *Football Comic Book Heroes: The Ultimate Fantasy Footballers*. Mainstream Publishing.

Ridley, I. (2011): *There's a Golden Sky: How Twenty Years of the Premier League Has Changed Football Forever*. Bloomsbury.

Roberts, R. (1988): *The Classic Slum: Salford Life in the First Quarter of the Century*. Penguin.

Ronay, B. (2010): *The Manager: The Absurd Ascent of the Most Important Man in Football*. Sphere.

Sanders, R. (2009): *Beastly Fury: The Strange Birth of British Football*. Bantam Books.

Scannell, P. & Cardiff, D. (1991): *A Social History of British Broadcasting: Volume One 1922–1939: Serving the Nation*. John Wiley & Sons.

Scholar, I. (1992): *Behind Closed Doors*. André Deutsch.

Scraton, P., Jemphrey, A. & Coleman, S. (1991): *The Hillsborough Project First Report*. Liverpool City Council.

Scraton, P., Jemphrey, A. & Coleman, S. (1995): *No Last Rights: The Denial of Justice and the Promotion of Myth in the Aftermath of the Hillsborough Disaster*. Liverpool City Council.

Scraton, P. (1999): *Hillsborough: The Truth*. Mainstream Publishing.

Sharpe, G. (1997): *Gambling on Goals: A Century of Football Betting*. Mainstream Publishing.

Shawcross, W. (1997): *Murdoch: The Making of a Media Empire*. Simon & Schuster.

Sillitoe, A. (2007): *The Loneliness of the Long Distance Runner*. Harper Perennial.

Slater, C. (2009): 'Behind the Mike: The Evolution of Football Reporting on Local Radio' in *Soccer History*, Issue 23.

Smart, B. (2005): *The Sport Star: Modern Sport and the Cultural Economy of Sporting Celebrity*. Sage.

Southwell, T. (1998): *Getting Away With It: The Inside Story of Loaded*. Ebury Press.

Steen, R. (2008): *Sports Journalism: A Multimedia Primer*. Routledge.

Stelling, J. (2013): 'Goodbye Squarials, Hello Success' in *TwentyFour7 Football*, November.

Sterling, C. (2003): *The Encyclopaedia of Radio*. Taylor and Francis.

Stott, R. (2002): *Dogs and Lamposts*. Metro Books.

Tate, S. (2005): 'James Catton, "Tityrus" of the Athletic News (1860 to 1936): A Biographical Study' in *Sport in History*, Volume 25, Issue 1, pp. 98–115.

Tate, S. (2007): 'The Professionalisation of Sports Journalism, c. 1850 to 1939, with Particular Reference to the Career of James Catton'. Unpublished PhD thesis.

Taylor, D.J. (1997): 'Rally Round You Havens!' in Kuper, S. (ed.) *Perfect Pitch: Home Ground*. Headline.

Taylor, F. (1995): *The Day a Team Died*. Souvenir Press Ltd.

Telfer, K. (2011): *Peter Pan's First XI: The Story of J.M.Barrie's Cricket Team*. Sceptre.

Tennenbaum, P. & Noah, J. (1971): 'Sportuguese: A Study of Sports Page Communication' in *Sport, Culture and Society: A Reader on the Sociology of Sport*. The MacMillan Company.

Thornton, P. (2003): *Casuals: Football, Fighting and Fashion: The Story of a Terrace Cult*. Milo Books.

Tongue, S. (2009): 'Graham Taylor: If People Spit At You the Turnip Joke's Not Funny' in the *Independent on Sunday*, 29 March.

Tossell, D. (2012): *In Sunshine or in Shadow: A Journey Through the Life of Derek Dougan*. Pitch Publishing.

Toulmin, V., Popple, S. & Russell, P. (2004): *The Lost World of Mitchell and Kenyon: Edwardian Britain on Film*. British Film Institute.

Toulson, A. (2006): *Media Talk: Spoken Discourse on TV and Radio*. Edinburgh University Press.

Vialli, G. & Marcotti, G. (2006): *The Italian Job: A Journey to the Heart of Two Great Footballing Cultures*. Bantam Press.

Walker, A. (2006): 'Reporting Play: The Local Newspaper and Sports Journalism, c. 1870 to 1914' in *Journalism Studies*, Volume 7, Issue 3, pp. 452–62.

Walsh, J. (2008): 'Hello! Magazine Celebrates its 20th Anniversary' in the *Independent*, 9 May.

Walton, J. & Walvin, J. (1983): *Leisure in Britain, 1780–1939.* Manchester University Press.

Walvin, J. (1978): *Leisure and Society 1830–1950.* Longman.

Walvin, J. (2000): *The People's Game: The History of Football Revisited.* Mainstream Sport.

Warner, S. (2013): *Text and Drugs and Rock 'n' Roll: The Beats and Rock Culture.* Bloomsbury.

Watterhouse, R. (2004): *The Other Fleet Street: How Manchester Made Newspapers National.* First Edition Ltd.

Wenner, L.A. (ed.) (1998): *Media Sport.* Routledge.

Whannel, G. (1992): *Fields in Vision: Television Sport and Cultural Transformation.* Routledge.

Whannel, G. (2002): *Media Sport Stars: Masculinities and Moralities.* Routledge.

Whannel, G. (2006): 'The Unholy Alliance: Notes on Television and the Remaking of British Sport 1965–85' in *Leisure Studies,* Volume 5, Issue 2, pp. 129–45.

White, J. (2013): 'Graham Taylor: I Will Take England's Failure to Reach 1994 World Cup Finals to My Grave' in the *Daily Telegraph,* 7 October.

Williams, J. (2003): *A Game for Rough Girls? A History of Women's Football in Britain.* Routledge.

Williams, J. & Woodhouse, J. (1991): 'Can Play, Will Play? Women and Football in Britain' in Williams, J. & Wagg, S. (eds), *British Football and Social Change: Getting into Europe.* Continuum International Publishing.

Williams, J.M. (1994): 'The Local and the Global in English Soccer and the Rise of Satellite Television' in *Sociology of Sport,* Volume 11, Issue 4, pp. 376–97.

Williams, K. (2009): *Read All About It! A History of the British Newspaper.* Routledge.

Williams, R. (2011): *The Long Revolution.* Parthian Books.

Williamson, D.J. (1991): *Belles of the Ball: Early History of Women's Football.* R&D Associates.

Wilson, C. (2007): *The Angry Years: The Rise and Fall of the Angry Young Men.* Robson Books Ltd.

Wilson, J. (2011): *The Anatomy of England: A History in Ten Matches*. London, Orion.

Winner, D. (2006): *Those Feet: An Intimate History of English Football*. Bloomsbury Publishing.

Winner, D. (2012): 'Beautiful Mind, Beautiful Game' in *The ESPN Magazine*, 16 May.

Wood, G. (2001): 'Tote to Accept Single Football Bets' in the *Independent*, 25 September.

Zengerle, P. (1998): "A Little Story About Joe Gaetjens", Reuters, 28 April.

WEBSITES

bainesfootballcards.co.uk

bairdtelevision.com

bbc.co.uk/historyofthebbc

bbc.co.uk/news

boxscorenews.com

charlesbuchansfootballmonthly.com

donmouth.co.uk/womens_football

digital-football.com

eadweardmuybridge.co.uk

earlycinema.com

europeancuphistory.com

hillsborough.independent.gov.uk/

homepage.ntlworld.com/carousel/ITV

hopeforhillsboroughjustice.wordpress.com

ibcstudio.co.uk

magforum.com

mds975.co.uk

mybrightonandhove.org.uk

offthetelly.co.uk

soccerbilia.co.uk

sportsjournalists.co.uk

televisionheaven.co.uk/history.htm

testpressing.org

thebioscope.net

thefa.com

theverge.com

vichist.blogspot.co.uk

victorianlondon.org

TV PROGRAMMES

F Troop, Treatment and the Half-way Line
BBC1, 14 November 1977.

Hillsborough: How They Buried the Truth
BBC1, 24 May 2013.

The Night Football Changed Forever
Peter Williams Television, unbroadcast.

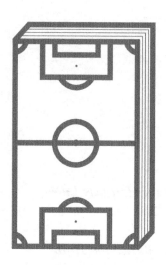